MENTAL HEALTH IN EDUCATION

MENTAL HEALTH IN

MERL E. BONNEY

Professor of Psychology, North Texas State College

ALLYN and BACON, Inc.

EDUCATION

PRINTED IN THE UNITED STATES OF AMERICA.
LIBRARY OF CONGRESS CATALOG CARD NUMBER: 60-10651

FIRST PRINTING .... APRIL, 1960

SECOND PRINTING .... AUGUST, 1961

FOREWORD . . .

From the earliest days of the modern mental hygiene movement, schools and the means of education have been recognized as being of the utmost importance for achieving and maintaining good mental health. It was the teachers themselves, in the early days of mental hygiene activities in New England, who demanded the kind of help that resulted in the foundation of *Understanding the Child,* a professional journal devoted for many years to the cause of mental health and education. When the Commonwealth Fund in 1938 completed its investigation of mental health through education, it concluded from its nation-wide field study that mental hygiene principles had definitely taken hold in at least two significant educational fields — the nursery school and parent education — and that there were significant developments on all levels and in all types of educational activities.

Through the years certain mental health needs have been met while others have not. There has been a special need for practical suggestions as to ways in which the schools and other educational institutions can work for mental health. Professor Bonney's book goes far toward meeting this need. It is particularly helpful in making clear what good mental health really is, and what can be done about it in the everyday work of the schools — not only where community mental health services and agencies are available, but also (and especially) in the hundreds of communities where such facilities are deficient or wholly lacking. The problems and cases will be especially good as a basis for group discussion in the class — whether this be in a course on the college or university campus or in off-campus courses for teachers, administrators, and others in service. Here are actual, down-to-earth situations in home, school, and community; the book is rich in the kind of human material that will help administrators and other school workers to understand that "behavior is caused," and to deal with children, youth, and adults accordingly. In short, this book has the best material I have seen anywhere on what school people can actually do to further mental health.

W. Carson Ryan

Kenan Professor of Education Emeritus
University of North Carolina

School Mental Health Consultant
National Association for Mental Health

PREFACE . . .

THE PRIMARY PURPOSE of this book is to present to teachers, prospective teachers, and other school personnel, a body of materials that bear on the total development of children and that, although related, are not closely involved in the teaching of academic skills and content. The subject matter of mental hygiene is focused on the development of children and youth who are mentally healthy in the broadest sense of this term, but this does not mean that the pursuit of mental hygiene objectives is in any way contrary to the successful execution of instructional duties. In fact, as Redl and Wattenburg say: "A teacher who is ineffectual in helping children to learn is harming their mental health, no matter how wisely he can talk about psychology."*

A teacher's principal task is that of stimulating maximum growth of pupils through instructional activities. This means that a teacher is a *teacher* and not a clinician, a substitute parent, a group psychotherapist, a counselor, a test specialist, or a psychologist. It follows, then, that what teachers do to promote mental health among pupils must be those kind of things which are intimately involved in their usual roles as teachers. Since these "usual roles" are nearly always in group situations, the major emphasis in this book is on how teachers can promote mental health objectives *in and through groups.* Usually all teachers, from the time they go on duty until the time they go off duty, are in charge of some kind of group. This constant involvement in groups makes inescapable a social-psychological basis for teaching. Unless a teacher can help achieve mental health goals through socialization procedures, classroom management, sociodrama, class discussions, physical education activities, clubs, programs, and pupil contributions to all kinds of group endeavors — then all that is left is the stimulation of intellectual growth through assignments which are prepared

* Fitz Redl and William W. Wattenberg, *Mental Hygiene in Teaching*, New York: Harcourt, Brace and Company, 1951, p. 193.

and "handed in" on an individual basis. Although this is important, and should always be provided for, it falls far short of the potentialities of the school for helping to prepare our young people for the diversities of life and for the fuller satisfactions of living of which they are capable.

Some readers may be surprised at the lack of organization of the materials of this book according to chronological age-levels, especially since the book is designed to be used on both elementary and secondary levels. This kind of organization was not adopted because of the belief that all, or nearly all, of the concepts, procedures, and principles that are considered in this book apply over a wide age-range from kindergarten through the high school, with differences only in emphasis and in application. An attempt has been made in every chapter to bring in some representative materials on elementary and secondary levels, and also to point out how the content developed in each chapter can be applied over a wide age-range.

A preview of this book may be had by stating the main contributions of the six parts into which this volume is divided.

Part 1 gives the basic concepts that have determined the psychological frame of reference of this book, and also presents the chief sources of mental hygiene problems in schools. These problems are seen to arise from certain aspects of the home environment, from personality adjustments, and from the social aspects of physical and mental traits.

Part 2 describes and evaluates the major goals or behavioral objectives for mental health education in our schools. The purpose here is to orientate the reader to the kind of total individual who is regarded, from the standpoint of this volume, as possessing a high degree of positive mental health.

Part 3 is devoted to a description and evaluation of some instruments and procedures for obtaining information about the personality traits and interpersonal adjustments of pupils. This material is included because of the conviction that mental health education needs not only concepts and ideals as guides, but also test data that are relevant to its objectives.

Part 4 deals directly and specifically with the teacher as a director of those classroom activities which are most related to developing children into socially competent individuals.

The main purpose of Part 5 is to stimulate teachers to see their classes as *groups* and not simply as aggregations of individuals, and to see themselves as group leaders and not simply as instructors. This section brings in some materials from social psychology and educational sociology which this writer believes should be given major consideration in mental health education.

The aim of Part 6 is to stimulate teachers to try to make the most of *themselves* through their teaching, and to see this kind of objective not only as a major source of satisfaction to themselves, but also as a primary source of superior teaching.

ACKNOWLEDGEMENTS

The writer wishes to express his appreciation to the following publishing companies for permission to quote from their books:

To Harper and Brothers for permission to quote from Maslow's *Motivation and Personality* in Chapter 1, and from Combs and Snygg's *Individual Behavior* in Chapter 7.

To Houghton Mifflin Company for permission to quote from Roger's *Mental Hygiene and Elementary Education* in Chapter 1.

To Rinehart and Company for permission to quote from Fromm's *Sane Society* in Chapter 1.

To W. W. Norton and Company for permission to quote from Horney's *Our Inner Conflicts* in Chapter 1.

To Prentice Hall, Inc., for permission to quote from Rotter's *Social Learning and Clinical Psychology,* in Chapters 3 and 10.

To the Bureau of Publications of Teachers College, Columbia University, for permission to quote from Jersild's *When Teachers Face Themselves* in Chapter 17.

Appreciation is also hereby expressed to the editorial staff of Allyn and Bacon for many valuable suggestions in regard to the content and organization of this book.

Finally, the writer wishes to express his appreciation to the members of his family: to Myrle, his wife, and to Lewis and Carol, for the many inconveniences which they cheerfully endured during the years this manuscript has been under preparation.

CONTENTS . . .

PART ONE — THE PROBLEMS: THEIR NATURE AND SOURCES

PART TWO — OBJECTIVES AND GOALS

PART THREE — MEASUREMENT

PART SIX — TEACHER ADJUSTMENTS

THE PROBLEMS: THEIR NATURE AND SOURCES

1

1

THE OBJECTIVES AND

WHY SHOULD TEACHERS study mental hygiene? To answer this question let us turn first to some brief descriptions of typical behavior problems found in school groups, together with some comments and questions which will direct the reader's attention to the mental hygiene implications of these and similar problems.

Martin caused his first-grade teacher a lot of trouble with his aggressive and attention-demanding behavior. He tripped other pupils, hit them without provocation, shot them with rubber bands, and sometimes messed or destroyed their materials. The

THE BASIC CONCEPTS

teacher tried to control him by isolating him from the other pupils "until he could act like a big first-grader." This only intensified his hostility and aggressiveness. Finally the teacher did some investigating into the boy's home life and found that his parents were divorced and that his mother, with whom he lived, had abused him and threatened to drown him in the bathtub. He was taken from her by court order and sent to live with his father, who had remarried. In this new home he was punished severely for behavior ordinarily considered normal for children of his age. From these experiences Martin had apparently learned that he could not trust anybody, and consequently had developed feelings of hostility toward everyone around him.

Possessing this knowledge of his home-background, the teacher had a much better understanding of Martin's needs in her classroom. Instead of punishing and isolating him, she showed him in numerous ways that she accepted him, believed in him, and wanted to be his friend and confidant; also she appointed him to take care of some classroom duties, such as cleaning up the work tables. Although Martin never became a "model" child, the severity of his aggressiveness markedly decreased and he eventually became a contributing member of his class.

What principles of mental hygiene did this teacher use? Was Martin's ego-involvement in classroom responsibilities the main thing that helped him? Or did the chief source of aid lie in the teacher's emotional support of Martin through her personal relationships with him?

Henry just sits in his fifth-grade class. He has the ability to learn but he says there is no use or sense in it for him. He is an adopted child and there are two younger children in the home, both of whom were born after Henry was adopted. These foster parents say they love Henry, have given him equal advantages with the younger children, and have not shown discrimination among the three children. However, Henry does not see his home situation as his foster parents describe it. Instead he thinks his parents do not really want him. He daydreams frequently about running away from his home and trying to find his real mother. He thinks if he could do this all his difficulties would be solved.

Henry's case points up an important aspect of mental hygiene in education, namely, the need of considering *why* children learn and not simply *how* they learn. Because of the way Henry has sized up and reacted to his social environment, he is practically devoid of human satisfactions. He thinks nobody cares about him. Lacking interpersonal satisfactions, and lacking an ego-ideal in an adult, he is left in a motivational vacuum. Not having a rewarding social anchorage in the present, nor an upward pull toward a conception of himself in the future, he may well ask, "*Why* should I learn?"

Henry's case calls attention to another mental hygiene principle, i.e., the importance of finding out how a child views himself and perceives his social world. Mental health, or the lack of it, is always much more related to inner psychological states than to external circumstances.

Finally, the question may be raised as to what Henry's teacher should have tried to do. Should he have worked harder than he did with the parents? Should he have tried to be a substitute parent?

Should he have seen to it that Henry was included in many group activities? Or should he have concentrated his efforts on trying to help Henry develop just one mutual friendship?

George is a buxom, effeminate type of boy in the sixth grade. He will not voluntarily play outdoor group games with his own age-group, but he frequently plays tag and other simple games with some first- and second-grade boys. When forced to play baseball in a physical education class he tries to act cute, does a lot of clowning, and makes an "out" every time. The other boys make fun of him but he shrugs it all off and pretends not to care. He never fights, never gets angry, never argues a point, and never attacks others. His only interest in girls is to annoy them, apparently on an attention-demanding basis.

Although George has normal intelligence he makes extremely poor use of it. His level of functioning is far below his tested I.Q. He is retarded in all of his school subjects and especially in reading. Efforts to aid him through remedial reading have been largely futile because he will not put forth consistent efforts, is restless and easily distracted, is overly encouraged by small successes, and cries when scolded or criticized. Even though George is already overweight he frequently eats a mid-morning meal in addition to a large lunch at noon. Eating for George is a substitute pleasure.

From this brief description it is clear that George is in a condition of bad mental health. He is rejected by his classmates, is emotionally immature, and is failing in his school tasks. What responsibility does a classroom teacher have toward such a child? Will involving him more in group work and other socializing activities help him or only make matters worse for him? Should he be punished more and be put under more rigid controls? On the other hand, is it possible that a child like George cannot be effectively helped with the usual public school facilities? If not, then a teacher needs to learn how to utilize public and private agencies that offer psychological and psychiatric aid for children and for parents.

Sally is a seventh-grade girl who has been a fringer in her school group for several years. She has tried a wide range of behavior adjustments in her efforts to win a place for herself in one or more of the dominant cliques in her class, but without success. Her latest effort of this nature is to hang around on the periphery of a small group of girls, listen in on their conversation, move when the group moves, and occasionally smile and make a remark to one of the girls. She will repeat this behavior pattern even though she is ignored by the group she caters to.

Why doesn't Sally stop this kind of behavior when it obviously does not succeed? Could class discussions on personal-social problems help children and adolescents to understand how such behavior is self-defeating? Could a teacher utilize classroom groupings to help a girl like Sally achieve some interpersonal group status? Or, on the other hand, is a child like Sally apt to be so maladjusted that only extensive counseling would offer much promise of long-range benefits?

Paul is a very intelligent high school sophomore who transferred to a large city school from a selective private school. He has strong academic motivations, has read extensively, is very much of a home-boy, has not participated in athletics, and has never had close friends except for a few very much like himself. Shortly after he transferred to the city high school he went with his father to a football game. The next day at the beginning of his first class the teacher and students were discussing the game. In the course of this discussion Paul made the following remark: "I feared our opponents would launch an aerial attack and I was apprehensive lest our boys should not be able to cope with it."

As might be expected this remark aroused laughter from most of the class, together with a variety of humorously derisive voice tones and gestures. Paul was embarrassed and hurt. During the next three months many other incidents occurred which caused this verbalizing, highly sensitive boy to realize his lack of understanding of and integration into the adolescent culture around him. Finally, in desperation he ran off from home, using part of his weekly allowance to buy a bus ticket to another city. He was found and returned home in a few days. He was resistant, sometimes talked incoherently, and couldn't sleep without sedation. The parents took immediate steps to obtain psychiatric aid for their son and conferred with school officials and counselors in regard to what was best for Paul. At this writing the effects of these efforts are uncertain.

How could Paul's difficulties have been avoided? What responsibility does a school have for trying to make sure that very bright pupils have a good total development and not simply intellectual stimulation? How can a classroom teacher be helped to see that a good mind depends on the quality of functioning of the whole person and not merely on the quality of brains?

MEANING OF MENTAL HYGIENE

The above case reports give some indication of the content teachers may expect to find in a course dealing with "mental hygiene in education." A more comprehensive definition of this content runs as follows: *A study of mental hygiene in education is concerned with the facts, conditions, techniques, and policies necessary for the promotion of mental health in children and youth.* If the question be asked, "What is mental health?" the best answer would be: *Mental health is a state of being conducive to harmonious and effective living.* It will be evident, however, from the case reports above, that mental health is a very broad term which includes physical, mental, emotional, and social aspects of adjustment. A teacher with a mental health point of view is concerned with the total development of children, and he sees all phases of a child's growth as contributing to the over-all goal of an integrated personality. He believes that if a child is properly developed he will be able to live in such a manner that all of his capacities and needs support and enhance each other — thus creating an integrated whole.

More specifically, the study of mental hygiene in education is a branch of knowledge which places major emphasis on (1) understanding and preventing emotional and behavior disorders in children and youth and on (2) describing the conditions for the attainment of harmonious and effective living.

MENTAL HEALTH A POSITIVE ACHIEVEMENT

At first those who identified themselves with the mental hygiene movement confined their efforts almost entirely to the prevention and treatment of mental illness. During the last thirty years, however, there has been a rapid extension of the hygiene point of view into most areas of modern living, including all types of institutions, government bodies, industrial settings, and religious organizations. With this extension has come a much greater emphasis on the preventive and positive aspects of mental and emotional health for all people, as contrasted with the earlier concentration on mental diseases. With this emphasis, as Chisholm (7) has pointed out, has also come a clear recognition that health, whether physical or mental, is a positive achievement and is not simply the absence of disease or infirmity. This means that a constructive program based on clearly understood principles and definite procedures must be established if mental hygiene objectives are to be realized.

CONTENT AND CONTRIBUTIONS OF MENTAL HYGIENE COURSES

It is important to make clear at the outset that courses dealing with mental hygiene in education do not present a distinctive or unique kind of subject matter. Rather, such courses present materials that constitute applications of concepts and of factual data developed in the subject-matter areas of abnormal psychology, social psychology, educational sociology, and psychology of personality. In stating these applications the chief purpose is to promote a mental hygiene point of view toward all aspects of a school's program. As mentioned above, this point of view has come in recent years to lay great emphasis on the attainment of personal-social effectiveness, satisfying human relationships, wholesome emotional states, and the *prevention* of behavior difficulties in *all* children and youth, as opposed to simply treatment of those who are most maladjusted.

One thing which all textbooks dealing with mental hygiene in education have in common is a focus on the social or interpersonal aspects of education and on group learnings. Although mental hygienists recognize the first-rate importance of developing individuals *as individuals,* they also believe that these same persons would be better individuals if their education were also weighted with mental health objectives. In other words, they see no necessary conflict between individualism and socialization, but they do believe that either of these two major approaches may be pushed so far as to interfere seriously with the other. Furthermore, it seems certain that teachers who are prepared to integrate these two approaches in the classroom possess a major asset in coping with all aspects of teaching. Fritz Redl has said: "We should stop trying to sell teachers on the idea that their problems will disappear to the degree to which they know more about the individual. We should start giving them more help on their group psychological problems." (23 — p. 87.) The viewpoint of this volume is that effective teaching requires a constant integration of individual and group approaches, and that each one supplements the other.

The chief purpose of courses on mental hygiene in education is to develop one point of view in regard to all aspects of a teacher's work. This conception is well expressed by Herbert Carroll[1] when he says that "mental hygiene is now considered by some educators as being primarily an attitude which influences the teacher's behavior at all times — in his personal relationships with pupils, in his practices in marking, promoting, and counseling boys and girls, and in other major and minor incidents of his entire school day."

SOURCES OF MENTAL HYGIENE PRINCIPLES

The psychological and educational principles and concepts that are utilized throughout this book have been drawn from numerous sources. However, only those sources will be acknowledged at this point which are most helpful in orienting the reader to the kind of ideas basic to the descriptions and evaluations of behavior presented here.

Freud and unconscious motivations

Probably anyone who writes a book on mental hygiene today would acknowledge a debt to the psychology of Sigmund Freud (11). This is true of the present writer even though this book is not orientated around or heavily weighted with Freudian concepts. Probably the most definitive thread of Freudian psychology in this volume is found in the references to unconscious influences in determining attitudes and overt behavior. Freud is generally credited with being the first to perceive the significance of unconscious processes in such behavior

[1] Chairman of the Committee of Mental Health in Modern Education for the Fifty-fourth Yearbook of the National Society for the Study of Education (Chicago: The Universiy of Chicago Press, 1955), p. 2.

as expressions of hostility feelings, guilt reactions, psychosexual problems, inferiority and self-devaluative attitudes, and a wide range of other kinds of personality adjustments. These processes are not conceived to be entities which are located in a place or area known as a subconscious mind, but rather as psychic contents (presumably with a neurological basis) which are activated by appropriate stimuli, even though the individual is not aware of the specific nature of the stimuli or of the deeper significance of his responses. How do unconscious processes get started and why do they persist? Although many of them have their origin in infancy and early childhood before conscious memory is functioning, those that have the most dynamic significance for personality are due to repression.

Freud has explained repression as a process whereby an individual is able to deny to those ideas which are threatening to his standards, or to some important conception of himself, admission into consciousness. These repressive efforts, however, are not entirely successful, since the affect or feeling content associated with the repressed ideas frequently breaks through the defenses and influences attitudes and overt behavior. These kinds of influences are seldom perceived for what they are, since they are unconsciously motivated (11).

All repression is seen as being due to anxiety over some kind of threat to one's status, security, or self-respect. In order to protect himself from these kinds of threats, a person can deny to any threatening ideas or impulses, entrance into clear consciousness. Apparently he does this primarily by not allowing the threatening psychic content to become verbalized, i.e., he does not translate this content into language, which is a necessary aspect of thinking. Since he cannot think about his feelings, impulses, and vaguely formed ideas, he cannot understand his problems; consequently his problems persist and continue to influence his attitudes and behavior in ways that he cannot comprehend. Furthermore, he is frequently impelled to say things to people and to engage in overt actions which are irrational from an objective point of view, but which can be understood from the standpoint of his need to obtain some form of temporary relief from the inner tensions created by his problems. Even though the achievement of these partial and temporary satisfactions often brings the individual some kind of punishment or disapproval from others, he generally continues his maladaptive type of behavior since, lacking understanding of his motivations, he cannot learn or profit from his mistakes. Experience is not a good teacher when self-insight and self-understanding are seriously deficient. It does not necessarily follow, however, that if these assets exist a person can forthwith resolve his difficulties. Some children, as well as adults, need not only insight and psychotherapy but also considerable guidance to learn more rewarding kinds of adjustments.

From the standpoint of our schools, one of the most effective means of reducing the need for repression is to do everything possible to promote ego-strengthening among children. This is done by helping them to make progress in assuming social obligations, in learning academic content, in developing self-confidence, and in acquiring numerous abilities whereby satisfactions can be wrested from their physical and social environments. As these satisfactions are increased, greater frustration-tolerance is developed, so that a child is better able to cope with unpleasant realities and control his impulses, and is also able to acquire positive and aggressive attitudes toward his limitations and failures. Thus, he is able to keep going in spite of difficulties; he does not engage in constant complaining, surrender easily, or live simply for immediate pleasures.

As these objectives are attained, he is able to develop more rational controls over his conduct. As a child's ego is strengthened, he has more effective contact with realities around him and can, therefore, think more objectively. He is more free from the distracting influences and from subjective needs, and is also less likely to be dominated by a hypersensitive conscience; he is, therefore, less threatened and thus has less need to repress certain psychic contents.

References to unconsciously motivated behavior, together with examples, will be found at numerous points throughout this volume, but particularly in Chapters 3, 4, and 17, dealing with inferiority feelings, hostile behavior, and the mental health of teachers.

Adler, Fromm, and Horney

Much more significant for the present volume than the works of Freud are the writings of a group of neo-Freudians, i.e., those writers who have followed many of the basic concepts of Freud but who, at the same time, have broken away from some of his teachings and established some of their own. Reference is made particularly to the writings of Alfred Adler (1-2), Erich Fromm (12), and Karen Horney (14-15). The basic ideas emphasized by these psychologists which have greatest pertinence to this volume are those which stress the importance of social interests, the predominance of social needs over biological drives, the uniqueness of each total personality, the persistent striving for self-completion, and the importance of satisfying interpersonal relationships on a psychologically mature, as opposed to a neurotic, basis.

One of the strongest themes running throughout the writings of Adler, Horney, and Fromm is the emphasis on the significance for mental health of satisfying interpersonal experiences through friendship and love. A large part of personality successes and failures is seen as being due to greater or lesser amounts of satisfactions obtained from affiliative bonds with other human beings.

Adler (1) goes so far as to say that "everything we call a mistake" in reference to our dealings with other persons, "in work and in love originates in lack of social feeling," and that "our present-day burdens are the result of the lack of a thorough social education" (pp. 284-285). Although Adler (2) does not hold that social feeling as such is inborn, he does believe that it is an innate potentiality which will readily respond to the proper stimulations (pp. 75-76).

Horney stresses the importance of personal and social adequacy to mental health largely by describing the characteristics of people who seriously fail in these areas. In one discussion she describes how individuals who have developed neurotic conflicts in their interpersonal relationships may be classified as moving *toward* people, moving *against* people, or moving *away* from people (14). Those in the first category are too compliant and eager to please, those in the second are too aggressive and hostile, while those in the third are too detached and alone. These maladjusted conditions are true, however, only of people who have neurotic conflicts in these areas. Horney (14) makes it clear that all normal people need all three of the kinds of interpersonal adjustments listed above, since each one has positive values. She says:

> In moving toward people the person tries to create for himself friendly relations to his world. In moving against people he equips himself for survival in a competitive society. In moving away from people he hopes to attain a certain integrity and serenity. As a matter of fact, all three attitudes are not only desirable but necessary in our development as human beings. It is only when they appear and operate in a neurotic framework that they become compulsive, rigid, indiscriminate and mutually exclusive. (14 — p. 89.)

Fromm holds to the thesis that man has emerged above the level of animals into *self-awareness* and has, therefore, lost the direct supports and protective controls of instincts and of hereditarily given mechanisms (12). This means that men must find other supports and other means of control and direction. Fromm sees as the only solution the development of much greater interdependence and mutual support among human beings wherever they are. He writes:

> Man's evolution is based on the fact that he has lost his original home, nature — and that he can never return to it, can never become an animal again. There is only one way he can take: to emerge fully from his natural home, to find a new home — one which he creates by making the world a human one and by becoming truly human himself. (p. 25.)

Additional sources

The significance of interpersonal relationships to mental health and to personality formation has also been stressed by Sullivan (27), a psychiatrist, by Symonds (28), speaking from a psychoanalytical orientation, by Tagiuri (29), writing from a social-psychological frame of reference, and by Rotter (26), a clinical psychologist.

J. L. Moreno (22), too, the founder and chief promoter of sociometry in this country, has added greatly to our knowledge of interpersonal relationships from the standpoint of both theoretical formulations and practical applications. Furthermore, his discussions of sociodrama and of the many uses of sociometric data in the management of groups have provided us with much detailed knowledge on how to create social conditions which facilitate the forming of interpersonal bonds.

Emphasis on the importance of friendships, of interpersonal satisfactions, of self-realization, and of affiliative bonds with others is a recurrent theme in this volume, but especially so in Chapters 2, 3, 5, 10, 11, and 12, dealing with home factors, inferiority feelings, social aspects of physical and intellectual traits, group-centered behavior, interpersonal measurements, and classroom grouping.

Another major theme in the writings of the neo-Freudians, as indicated above, is the stress on various aspects of positive self-adjustments such as the need for self-completion, achievement of individuality, and maintenance of personal integrity. This is a basic theme in all mental hygiene literature, and it is one which has been pursued with unusual diligence by many psychologists during the past twenty years in their discussions of positive and negative self concepts. The deep-seated and persistent conceptions that any individual holds toward himself have been shown in writings by Lecky (18) and by Combs and Snygg (9) to be among the most important factors that explain behavior. The mental hygiene implications of these ideas for pupils and for teachers are developed in Chapters 7 and 17.

Maslow and Allport

A psychological theme which has a close bearing on the one just presented above is a conception of personality maturity which stresses continuing self-enlargement from lower levels of growth or of satisfaction. Maslow has developed such a theme in his description of a hierarchy of needs. This hierarchy consists of five levels. The first level consists of such basic physiological needs as hunger and sex. The second level consists of needs for safety from external dangers. The third level includes all kinds of needs for love and affection from other people. The fourth level consists of needs for self-esteem and also for the respect and esteem of others. On the fifth level is the need for self-realization through achievement.

Maslow presents these needs as being in a hierarchy since he views the satisfaction of the higher-level needs as being based on adequate satisfactions of lower-level needs, although he does admit there are some exceptions to this thesis, as in those people in whom creative desires are stronger than any counterdeterminants (19). However, in discussing martyrs who give up everything for the sake of an ideal, Maslow maintains that in many such cases his thesis of a hierarchy of needs is upheld. He bases his contention on his hypothesis that the satisfaction of lower-level needs results in greater capacity to withstand frustration or denial of these lower-level needs in later life. As he puts it:

> People who have been satisfied in their basic needs throughout their lives, particularly in their earlier years, seem to develop exceptional power to withstand present or future thwarting of these needs simply because they have strong, healthy character structure as a result of basic satisfaction. They are the strong people who can easily weather disagreement or opposition, who can swim against the stream of public opinion, and who can stand up for the truth at great personal cost. It is just the ones who have loved and been well-loved, and who have had many deep friendships, who can hold out against hatred, rejection, or persecution. pp. 99-100.)

Most of a child's needs that are on levels one and two of Maslow's hierarchy are met with varying degrees of adequacy in the home during preschool years. All the other need-levels are also greatly affected by home influences, but the school begins to enter the picture in a very definite manner with the third-, fourth-, and fifth-level needs, as each child tries to establish affiliative relationships with his classmates, tries to win their respect, and tries to actualize his potential through achievements. According to Maslow's thesis, if a child's home life has provided him with adequate satisfaction of his basic needs, and the school helps him to gain additional satisfactions from the affectional responses and the respect of his classmates and his teacher, then he is free to use a maximum amount of his energy for higher-level realizations — and especially for constructive achievements. If, on the other hand, a child's more basic personal, social, and emotional needs are not well met at home or at school, then he is forced to use a considerable amount of his energy in trying to satisfy these needs, and is thus prevented from making maximum utilization of his higher-level ego resources. Some of this dissipated energy may go into various forms of compulsive-type efforts which serve to crowd lower-level needs out of conscious awareness.

These conceptions of Maslow, as well as those of Allport (3), subsequently presented, are criticized by some psychologists as lacking in objectivity of definitions and of supporting evidence. However, many psychological formulations which are of greatest significance for mental health cannot at the present time be validated with precise scientific data. These conceptions are presented here because they have influenced the writer's thinking in regard to the importance of providing maximum stimulation for the mental and personality development of all individuals.

In 1959 Maslow pointed out that his concept of self-actualization should not be thought of as simply an end-result in a mature adult life, but rather as a process which is going on all the time and is, therefore, contributing to behavior motivations and personal satisfactions at all stages of life (20).

This view is strongly supported by Gordon Allport in his book *Becoming* (3). His chief contention is that one of the most distinguishing characteristics of a psychologically mature person is that he seeks to *become* something more than he is, and that the quality or level of this striving is the most important single clue to an individual's personality. It is Allport's view that if early childhood is normal, the impulses, adjustments, and behavior patterns of this stage of one's life are not simply extended into adulthood, but rather one's adulthood is *built on* childhood, and is an ever-increasing realization of higher-level potentialities for self-structure, achievement, and character. It is only when childhood is seriously distorted from its normal course that this period of life is projected directly into adult levels. The psychologically mature person, according to Allport, is not simply a grown-up child; he is indeed an adult with a unique organization of personal and intellectual capacities which cannot be explained simply as direct extensions of infantile fixations or childhood adjustment patterns. Furthermore, he is always much more interested in where he is going than where he has been, i.e., he is always much more concerned about his future than about his past.

The mental hygiene implications arising out of the emphasis on higher-level satisfactions and aspirations growing out of lower-level satisfactions and achievements are most directly stated in this book in Part Two, which deals with the positive goals of mental hygiene and how our schools can contribute to their attainment.

Dewey's educational theory

Finally there are numerous indications throughout this book that the writer has been influenced by the kind of educational theory developed from the thought of John Dewey (10). From his writings have come these concepts: that a child should actively participate in the educative process; that what the school has to offer should be integrated as closely as possible with the varying abilities and interests of pupils; that emphasis should be placed on stimulating thinking and problem-solving abilities, as opposed to simply habit-formation and memorization; that our schools should be committed to the maximum development of total individuals and not simply to teaching skills and information; and that our children and youth should be helped to understand and to cope with the problems of living in a dynamic society as opposed to being prepared simply to understand the past.

Although it is true that all these concepts have been distorted, pushed too far, and applied in superficial or perverted ways in some situations, these abuses should not blind teachers or prospective teachers to the essential validity (from the standpoint of education in a democracy) of these basic ideas. Further elaboration and applications of these concepts are found in most of the chapters of this book, but particularly in Part Two dealing with the major objectives of mental health education, Part Four dealing with classroom management, and Part Five dealing with various aspects of the class as a group.

SERIOUSNESS OF THE PROBLEMS

Elaborate data need not be presented to convince teachers that large numbers of pupils in our schools suffer from a wide range of personal limitations, emotional difficulties, and social conflicts. All teachers have observed these kinds of problems; and they have also observed that these kinds of maladjustments are by no means confined to children from poor home backgrounds, but, instead, are found in varying degrees among pupils from all socio-economic levels.

Adults in the general population, as well as teachers, are well aware that there are large numbers of people who are suffering from a wide range of emotional and social problems. This is evident from observation, from reading magazines and newspapers, and from research reports. These research reports, as summarized by Coleman (8) and by Kaplan (16), show clearly that there are in the United States today approximately one million psychotics, between 8 and 10 million psychoneurotics, over two-thirds of a million chronic alcoholics, fifty thousand drug addicts, seven million people with criminal records, and 250,000 first admissions to mental hospitals every year.

All of these people were at one time pupils in our schools. Furthermore, the people who will compose statistics similar to those above within the next twenty or thirty years are now in our schools. Numerous studies on the percentage of maladjusted pupils in our schools, particularly those by Benson (5), Rogers (25), and Ullman (30), and others summarized by Kaplan (16), show that at least 25 per cent of our public school pupils are characterized by personality handicaps to the extent that there is serious interference with objective achievement and personal happiness. These data also show that at least 10 or 12 per cent of our school pupils (included in the 25 per cent above) have maladjustments of a sufficiently serious nature to lead eventually to mental illness or crime. In discussing this topic Dorothy Rogers makes the following summary statement:

> In any random sampling of 100 typical children, 1 or 2 will commit major crimes and serve time in jail; 8 to 10 of them will become seriously ill mentally and will have to be admitted for treatment; 3 or 4 will be too retarded to become self-supporting unless they receive specialized training; 30 to 50 of them will be sufficiently maladjusted to add to the statistics of petty crime, vocational failure, chronic unemployment, emotional instability, marital unhappiness or divorce, and to other expressions of failure.[2] (p. 10.)

When all the higher of the alternative figures given in this quotation are added the sum is 66 per cent. This leaves only 34 per cent, on the basis of this summary, who are relatively free from serious personal and social problems. This is, indeed, a relative matter since it is probable that most people in the 34 per cent category also have some

---

[2] Dorothy Rogers, *Mental Hygiene in Elementary Education* (Boston: Houghton Mifflin Co., 1957), p. 10.

personality difficulties. In fact it may well be asked, "Who hasn't?" This leads to the point that the major objective of mental hygiene is not to develop people who have no personality problems, but rather people who have sufficient ego-strength and inner resources to cope with their problems, their reverses, and their traumatic experiences; not only this, but also the capacity to utilize life's tragedies as well as its triumphs in order to build a firmer foundation in character and to rise to higher levels of significant living.

The seriousness of mental health problems requires that all of our social agencies and institutions, not just the school, assume some responsibility for changing the conditions that produce these problems. As far as the school is concerned, it seems certain that one of its major contributions lies in trying to develop children and young people who will be strong and competent as individuals, who at the same time will be able to work *with* and *for* others, and who also will be able to enjoy companionship and intimate responses with at least a few other persons.

Is the school equal to this kind of task? There are varied answers to this question, and none can be said to have scientific validity; but the writer agrees with a statement bearing on this question by Karl A. Menninger, psychiatrist, and one of the directors of the Menninger Foundation of Topeka, Kansas:

> Ultimately, education is more important than therapy, not only because it can be applied to more people, but because in effect it is prophylactic. The time will come when the study of the child and of the threats of his development will be recognized, not as a pretty little hobby for a few earnest missionaries and weary pedants but as a task equal in importance to the directing of a railroad or the compounding of new poisonous gases.[3]

One of the major assumptions of the mental hygiene point of view in education is that our schools have far greater resources and potentialities for human development than are now being utilized.

---

[3] Karl A. Menninger, "Present Trends in Psychoanalytic Theory and Practice," *Bulletin of the Menninger Clinic,* 8: 14-17, 1944.

REFERENCES

1. Adler, A., *What Life Should Mean to You.* Boston: Little, Brown and Co., 1931.
2. ———, *Social Interest.* New York: G. P. Putnam's Sons, 1939.
3. Allport, G., *Becoming.* New Haven: Yale University Press, 1955.
4. Andriola, Joseph, "The Development of the Concept of Mental Hygiene," *Mental Hygiene,* 36, 1955, 657-664.
5. Benson, G. P., "An Evaluation of Teacher Identification of Maladjusted Children," Ph.D. dissertation, University of Colorado, 1956.
6. Bernard, H. W., *Mental Hygiene for Classroom Teachers,* Ch's XII-XVI. New York: McGraw-Hill Book Co., 1952.
7. Chisholm, B., "Mental Health in Our New Kind of World," *Mental Hygiene,* 36, 1955, 529-532.
8. Coleman, J. C., *Abnormal Psychology and Modern Life,* Ch. I. New York: Scott, Foresman and Co., 1956.
9. Combs, A. W. and D. Snygg, *Individual Behavior* (2nd Edition). New York: Harper and Brothers, 1959.
10. Dewey, J., *Experience and Education.* New York: The Macmillan Company, 1938.
11. Freud, S., *A General Introduction to Psychoanalysis.* Garden City, New York: Garden City Publishing Company, 1943.
12. Fromm, E., *The Sane Society.* New York: Rinehart and Company, Inc., 1955.
13. Harriman, P. L., "In Defense of the Introvert," a lecture in print, The Hogg Foundation of the University of Texas, 1944.
14. Horney, Karen, *Our Inner Conflicts.* New York: W. W. Norton and Company, Inc., 1945.
15. ———, *The Neurotic Personality of Our Time,* Ch's VI, VII, VIII, IX. New York: W. W. Norton and Company, Inc., 1937.
16. Kaplan, L., *Mental Health and Human Relations in Education,* Ch's. II and III. New York: Harper and Brothers, 1959.
17. Lindgren, H. C., *Mental Health in Education.* New York: Henry Holt and Co., Inc., 1954.
18. Lecky, P., *Self-consistency.* New York: Island Press, 1945.
19. Maslow, A. H., *Motivation and Personality,* Ch. V. New York: Harper and Brothers, 1954.
20. ———, "Cognition of Being in the Peak Experiences," *Journal of Genetic Psychology,* 94, 1959, 43-46.
21. Menninger, K. A., "Present Trends in Psychoanalytic Theory and Practice," *Bulletin of The Menninger Clinic,* 8, 1944, 14-17.
22. Moreno, J. L., *Who Shall Survive?* New York: Beacon House, Inc., 1953.
23. Redl, F., "Group Psychological Elements in Discipline Problems," *American Journal of Orthopsychiatry,* 13, 1943, 77-81.

24. ——— and W. Wattenburg, *Mental Hygience in Teaching.* New York: Harcourt, Brace & Co., 1951.

25. Rogers, C. R., "Mental Health Findings in Three Elementary Schools," *Educational Research Bulletin,* 21, 1942, 86-91.

26. Rotter, J. B., *Social Learning and Clinical Psychology.* Englewood Cliffs, N.J.: Prentice Hall, Inc., 1954, p. 414.

27. Sullivan, H. S., *The Interpersonal Theory of Psychiatry.* New York: W. W. Norton and Company, Inc., 1953.

28. Symonds, P. M., *Dynamic Psychology.* New York: Appleton-Century-Crofts, Inc., 1949, p. 394.

29. Tagiuri, R., "Relational Analysis: An Extension of Sociometric Method with Emphasis upon Social Perception," *Small Groups,* edited by P. A. Hare, Edgar F. Borgatta, and Robert F. Bales. New York: Alfred A. Knopf, Inc., 1955, pp. 246-251.

30. Ullman, C. A., "Identification of Maladjusted School Children," Federal Security Agency, Public Health Service, Public Health Monograph, No. 7, 1952.

QUESTIONS AND EXERCISES

1. Present to the class examples of maladjusted children, such as those given at the beginning of this chapter, and discuss some of the possible causes and corrective measures.

2. Give some examples or applications of what you consider to be the "mental hygiene point of view in education."

3. If in satisfying interpersonal relationships, friendship and love are as important and basic to human happiness as they are said to be by Adler, Horney, and Fromm, why is so little done in the way of formal or organized programs to promote these objectives?

4. What kinds of educational practice are contrary to the psychological conceptions presented in this chapter from Maslow and Allport? What kinds are in accord with these conceptions?

5. What is the chief difference between people of good mental health who have problems, and people with similar problems who are in a condition of poor mental health?

6. Discuss various implications of what is meant by "a normal personality."

7. Bring to class magazine articles and newspaper stories that bear on the data given in this chapter on the seriousness of mental health problems in this country.

SELECTED FILMS

Emotional Maturity. 20 minutes. Emphasizes consequences of lack of mental health principles in life of an adolescent.

Unconscious Motivation. 38 minutes. Experimental demonstration of the operation of repression and of unconscious influences upon overt behavior.

Mental Health: Keeping Mentally Fit. 30 minutes. Stresses the need of emotional balance for both individual health and social stability.

What Is on Your Mind? 11 minutes. Presents some of the fallacious ways in which people try to solve their problems and points out the value of more scientific approaches.

The films listed at the end of each chapter throughout this book can be obtained on a rental basis from numerous sources, such as state universities and colleges and state departments of health. Some of the centers and agencies which have exceptionally large collections are:

The Audio-Visual Center of Indiana University
Bloomington, Indiana

Audio-Visual Aids Library of Pennsylvania State Univ.
State College, Pennsylvania

Young America Films, Inc.
18 East 41st St.
New York City

Coronet Films
69 East South Water St.
Chicago, Illinois

McGraw Hill Book Co.
330 W. 42nd St.
New York City

United States Office of Education
Visual Services
Washington, D. C.

Mental Health Materials Center
Room 713
1790 Broadway
New York City

2

HOME INFLUENCES ON

NO CONSIDERATION of the sources of mental hygiene problems in schools would be complete without a strong emphasis on home factors. Various references have been made to these factors in the preceding chapter. Attention will now be directed more systematically to the psychological impact of the parent-child relationships on a child's status and social adjustments in his school groups. Some attention will also be given to several other home conditions, namely, family size, broken homes, and country-versus-town pupils in consolidated schools in various social settings.

SCHOOL ADJUSTMENTS

Most teachers have always been aware that nearly everything a child does in school is affected directly or indirectly by a wide range of home conditions. So fundamental and pervasive are the influences of a child's family upon him that he carries the stamp of his home with him wherever he goes, and to a large extent throughout his life. This does not mean, however, that early home-influences are so all-powerful that they dominate an individual throughout his life — so that a man can be said to be simply a grown-up child. Rather, the home should be viewed as the place where foundations in personality and character are laid. If these foundations are well laid, in terms of our cultural expectations, an individual can continue to *build on* his childhood in ever-increasing areas of both intellectual competence and personality growth. He can, indeed, become a man, activated by adult rather than childish motivations. On the other hand, if early family-influences are especially frustrating to a child's developmental needs, then a poor foundation is laid, resulting in some seriously distorting influences being carried into adult life. In these people whose lives are built not on solid rock but on shifting sands, the demands of childhood may be so insistent that a mature personality structure can never be formed. However, except in the extreme cases, some help toward personality maturity can be given these individuals in our schools, especially by helping them acquire abilities and by providing them with interpersonal satisfactions with their classmates.

Although schools should always try to develop ego-strength and security feelings in those pupils who have some kind of negative home-stamp upon them, teachers should not do this to the neglect of developing a school program that promotes continued growth in those pupils who have a solid foundation in mental health assets from their homes. Generally, too, the parents in such homes are eager to cooperate in any way which will enrich the lives of their children.

GOOD PARENT-CHILD RELATIONSHIPS

What are good parent-child relationships? How can a teacher tell if a child comes from a very favorable psychological home environment? The principal answer to all these questions is: The main thing to look for is the quality of the interpersonal relationships between parents and children. By quality is meant the degree to which one or both parents show a genuine concern for the maximum total development of their child and the degree to which they respond to him with warmth and intimacy and objectively oriented love. Opposite qualities are attitudes of indifference or of rejection, and efforts on the part of parents to thwart the maximum development of their child because to do so would bring them some kind of material or psychological gain. The latter is generally unrecognized for what it is; instead the action involved is rationalized as being done "for the good of the child."

The importance of the quality of interpersonal relationships as the chief factor that teachers should look for in trying to assess a child's home background is supported in two studies conducted by Grace Langdon and Irving Stout (17). These authors report two studies — one in Milwaukee and the other in New York City — both of which were concerned with finding out what factors or conditions were most characteristic of homes of "well-adjusted children." In the two studies there were 261 children who were selected by school principals and teachers on the basis of eight criteria of good adjustment, such as playing well with others, possessing a happy disposition, being dependable, and being liked and respected by peers.

When the parents of these children were interviewed it was discovered that the only common thread running through all these families was a persistent and a genuine concern for the best development of the child. There was not much uniformity among all the parents in regard to disciplinary methods, the giving of allowances, the presence of religious influences, use of specific rules, control of the child's earnings, payment of the child for doing chores, the child's working outside of home, and the extent of control over comic-book reading. While most of the families frequently engaged as a unit in some kind of fun or recreation, a few didn't. In other words, there was wide variation in the kinds of overt things which were done in these families of well-adjusted children, but there was great uniformity in the kinds of attitudes and feeling responses behind these overt behaviors. These two studies emphasize to teachers the importance of being neither favorably nor unfavorably impressed with any particular aspect of a child's home background until they know more about the feeling content involved in the relationship between the child and his parents. What appears on the surface to be a very desirable practice may not result in the kind of child behavior expected because the "good act" is not supported by the right kind of feelings.

This point is confirmed in a study reported by Baldwin on democratic practices in the homes of preschool children (2). His data show that even though some homes were rated as using democratic types of control, the children in these particular homes did not show the kind of responsive, outgoing, active approach to the world which was characteristic of most children reared in democratically managed homes. Further observation revealed that these homes had the form but not the spirit of genuine democratic relationships. There was much permissiveness, but the control exercised by the parents was much more laissez-faire (let alone) than democratic, since there was not much discussion or interchange of ideas or information between parents and children. Apparently an unresponsive environment in which there is not much meaningful communication on either a verbal or a feeling level lacks the emotional tone necessary to promote a maximum degree of confidence and spontaneity, even if there are many outward signs of democratic management.

The conclusion of most value to this discussion, from the three studies just reviewed, is that teachers who wish to understand home environments as a source of behavior problems in schools should not make quick judgments in regard to the significance of any kind of overt behavior on the part of the parents, but should instead try to grasp the quality of interpersonal relationships between parents and their children. This means for one thing that teachers should not be overly impressed with the financial standing of a family or with the high educational status of the parents, since some of the children suffering most from distorted parent-child relationships come from homes with these external characteristics.

LOVE IN PARENT-CHILD RELATIONSHIPS

It seems certain that when teachers try to assess the quality of interpersonal relationships between parents and children, the main focus of attention should be on the extent to which the children are loved on a mature as contrasted with a selfish or immature basis, and on the extent to which love may be entirely absent.

Characteristics of mature love

How can mature love of a child by his parents be described? Primarily it is a strong and persistent affectional attachment to the child simply because he is their child and is a distinct human being. Mature love is not based primarily on what the child can do, how important he is likely to become, or how he may be used to enhance the parents' prestige. Love of a child is not something that is based on value received or on rewards to come. It is not a kind of trade or bargain. Parents who love their child do not talk a lot about how smart he is or about how much they expect of him in school. Neither do they frequently compare him with other children, regardless of whether he is considered superior or inferior to others of his age-level. They do, however, have a sincere and objectively oriented desire to help their child realize his maximum potentialities.

Love is a deep appreciation for a child as a person — a feeling response that brings reciprocal satisfactions to both the loved and the lover. This means that a child who is loved on a mature basis is a source of profound satisfaction to the parents. In fact, a parent who is so self-sufficient that he does not sense a need for others to help him fulfill his life cannot love his own child. Symonds and others have taken the position that love grows out of a feeling of insufficiency within one's self, a sense of incompleteness, and a deep-seated need to find personal self-realization through close emotional rapport with another individual (23).

Fallacy of buying or earning love

The hard-driving, authoritarian parent who is too busy to talk to school teachers and feels too important to take time out to play with his child is incapable of love no matter how many "good things" he may do for his family, and such a parent may do many "good things," especially in the way of giving his children money and gifts. In fact a teacher may suspect that a pupil who has an unusual amount of things, and who makes a great deal of them, is suffering from lack of love. When this is the case it is not surprising that such a child tries to buy the friendship of other children by offering them money, candy, or other material favors. He has learned from his parents that this is the way people show love.

The kind of parents under consideration frequently expect their child to make very high grades, to win contests, or to be especially well behaved — and with the implication that if these things are not done, parental "love" will be withdrawn. Such parents do not know that there is no *product* in love but only *process,* that there is no record of achievement but only spontaneous expression. Love cannot be bought, nor can it be earned by strenuous efforts, by outstanding successes, or by virtuous living. Yet these false conceptions are what many children learn from their parents. These learnings the children reveal in their compulsive striving to be first, in their attitude that because they are "so nice" other pupils ought to like them, and (particularly in adolescence) by their occasional expressions of disillusionment through such expressions as "Life is a mixed-up affair,"

"How do you know what to do," "Sometimes I think I'll just quit trying," or in a more bitter vein, "People are no damn good."

Fallacy of love as ownership

Some parents who avoid any implications that they can buy their child's love, or that he should earn their affection, assume another position that is equally damaging to the child; namely, that they *own* him and therefore are free to manipulate him in any way they wish. This means that they dominate and overprotect their child by making all major decisions affecting him, even into his adolescence; they choose his clothes, his friends, his subjects in school, and the vocation that they are sure he should follow. They shape his personality to fit their preconceived model for him.

How can a teacher recognize a child from this kind of home, especially a home in which the parents have succeeded quite well in their unconsciously motivated objectives? The major symptoms consist of various indications that the child does not *own* himself, such as difficulty in making decisions about anything, always wanting to be told what to do and how to do it, inability to evaluate his own work, feelings of inferiority about himself even when he is doing very well in his school work, resistance to being placed in a situation in which he is "on the spot" and must produce something which will be critically evaluated by others, and a feeling that other children do not like him even though they show no outward signs of hostility.

When the kind of family pattern described above is confined to mother-son relationships, the typical effeminate boy is produced. Such a boy is said to have a *mother fixation.* This kind of adjustment is typical of all personality fixations, in the sense that there is a stopping of a developmental process on a particular level, due to the fact that an inordinate amount of satisfaction is gained on this level and the person feels inadequate or threatened in regard to trying to move to a higher level of adjustment.

Some mother-fixated boys are quite responsible and do very well in school, although they seldom have any close friends among their classmates. In other cases in which such boys are strongly pampered and indulged by their mothers as "the reward" for their submission to the demands and needs of the mother, they are highly irresponsible, do poor schoolwork, and are frequently rejected by many of their classmates. In these boys there is so little "ownership of self" that there is a marked lack of inner controls, resulting in much restless and aimless behavior, like a ship without a captain or a plane without a pilot.

The overly indulged child, whether boy or girl, comes to school expecting the same kind of favored treatment that he or she has received at home. When such treatment is not forthcoming this kind of child may engage in a wide range of behavior adjustments, but the most typical ones are pouting and attention-demanding behavior, or some type of regressive response such as thumb-sucking, crying, withdrawal, or daydreaming. It is interesting to note, however, that occasionally a pampered child is found who becomes strongly attached to a teacher who deals with him forcibly and insists that he live up to the school's demands. He seems to sense that this treatment is exactly what he needs, and he admires and identifies with a teacher who is understanding and who is also strong enough to stimulate him to try to make something out of himself. This kind of teacher is aware of the first positive goal of mental hygiene, as developed in Chapter 7.

It is important to point out that the overly indulged child is not overly loved; rather, he is loved on an immature basis. His parents have used him as they would use a material possession, to satisfy their own neurotic needs.

Confusing love with sympathy and duty

Sometimes parents confuse love with sympathy or with a sense of duty or obligation. This is most likely to happen in the case of an unwanted child or in the case of a child with some kind of limitation or defect that is embarrassing to the parents. Many parents of such children regard them with mature affection, but others, although claiming love, are primarily motivated by sympathy or duty. How is this latter adjustment shown? Primarily by excessive talk about how much they love their child, by unwarranted overprotection lest the child be hurt, by compulsive striving to "make the child learn" or "get well" irrespective of the child's reactions or of established facts about his limitations, and by talking a lot about how much they have sacrificed for their "dear child."

A child with this kind of parental background comes to school with some distorted perceptions of the social world around him. He is likely to expect the teacher and other pupils to help him out, not because they like him, but because they ought to, and because they feel sorry for him. However, this "poor little me" attitude seldom produces the kinds of response expected because it does not arouse respect. Consequently the child from the home in which sympathy and duty have masqueraded as love comes eventually to feel that he is picked on, abused, and not understood or appreciated.

Distortion of love with hatred

A particularly subtle way in which love is distorted is when it is integrated with hatred. This is called ambivalence, since two contrary feelings toward the same object or person are involved. When one or both parents hold ambivalent attitudes toward a child he never knows where he stands, nor is he sure of his own worth since he cannot introject consistent values about himself from his parents. At times he is treated with kindness and consideration, including some expressions of love; but there is always a drastic change. For reasons which the child cannot understand or predict, his parents (frequently only one of them) turn against him; now he is severely criticized, punished, and deprived of any expression of affection. These changes on the part of the parents are due partly to their own mixed-up emotional development, partly to confusions and conflicts in their own present life-situation, and partly to the existence within themselves of both positive and negative feelings toward their child because of the kind of child he is; i.e., he is of the "wrong sex," or is "not smart," or is not "good-looking."

How does a teacher recognize a child who has been the victim of considerable ambivalence? Primarily by the fact that he is very hesitant about trusting anyone very far. He prefers to keep his relationships with others on a superficial basis so that he won't get hurt by being rejected. Occasionally, however, when his defenses are down, he may overrespond to another child or to the teacher — thus revealing his desperate need for affection — but he will soon sense the danger of getting too involved and will withdraw behind his defenses, or he may strike back with hostile aggressiveness against the person who has aroused his affectional needs. Thus he repeats through unconscious motivations the behavior patterns learned in his home.

Neglect and rejection

A few parents have a minimum degree of affection for their children, or none at all. These attitudes are shown by persistent neglect or by outright rejection. When neglect is the predominant pattern, the parents do not adequately look after the child's needs, and they seldom talk to him about anything, do not take him to places of interest to children, do not invite playmates into the home, do not guide him in acquiring any particular skills or personal adjustments, and frequently do not know where he is for several hours at a time even when he is under school age.

There is no one set of symptoms shown by a schoolchild which inevitably indicates that he is seriously neglected at home; however, there are some common symptoms which a teacher can be sensitive to. Very often the neglected child comes to school in an unkempt condition with hair uncombed, clothes in need of repair, or clothes that do not fit or are out of style, even when the family is in good economic circumstances. His psychological state will vary considerably according to the extent to which compensating factors have entered into his life; if these factors are favorable he may make a fringe-level adjustment; on the other hand, he may be hostile and even cruel to other children since he has little feeling-rapport with them. Frequently, however, his adjustment is best described as a condition of passivity in regard to others and also in regard to expectations of the school. Not having been loved by his parents he lacks the normal capacity to relate himself to others, nor has he learned to introject the values of adult society. Consequently he is left in a state of indifference toward the world.

Finally, parents may openly reject their child by frankly admitting that they wish he hadn't been born, by subjecting him to sarcasm and ridicule, and by punishing him severely either by physical blows or by deprivations of food, comforts, privileges, or freedom of movement. The highly rejected child is well aware that he is not wanted and not loved.

When this type of child comes to school he is likely to show one of two extreme types of adjustment depending upon his temperament and out-of-the-home circumstances. Either he is likely to be very submissive and cowed with strong feelings of defeat and unworthiness, or he is likely to be hyperaggressive and full of hostility which he compulsively releases on the school situation. When this kind of child is severely punished in school, as he frequently is, this treatment only confirms his conception of the world as a hostile place, and reinforces his need to fight back all the harder. Generally, this kind of child cannot be effectively controlled or helped within the resources of the ordinary school. He needs psychotherapy such as that provided in some of the very large school systems, as in New York City; or he needs special treatment in a center or camp devoted to the rehabilitation of severly maladjusted children and youth.

The well-loved child

How can a teacher judge if a child is loved on a mature basis in his home? Although there are not traits that are universally indicative of well-loved children, there are some broad behavior categories which characterize such children in varying degrees. In the first place, they give an over-all impression of *owning* themselves as revealed by a sense of serenity, a deep-seated feeling of self-assurance, and a capacity to act on their own initiative rather than watch or copy others. They hold trusting attitudes toward other pupils and toward the teachers, and they give every indication that they expect to be liked and respected by others. They are generally in a buoyant mood, frequently give spontaneous expressions to their feelings, and usually develop close friendships with at least a few other pupils. If the school situation is normally attractive and stimulating, the well-loved child is generally eager to participate in some responsible way. Since his own self is securely anchored in affection, he is free to use his energies to explore and attempt to master the external environment.

FAMILY SIZE

Some teachers and other adults believe that family size is in itself a source of certain kinds of mental health problems. This belief stems from the assumption that large families make for better socialization of children, that small families do less well, and that *only* children are very likely to be egocentric, dominating, and undersocialized.[1] Many teachers have accepted these assumptions and frequently passed judgments on the basis of family size as to why particular pupils are having social difficulties.

It seems certain from our present evidence, however, that family size, as such, has very little explanatory value in regard to the personal-social adjustments of pupils in our elementary and secondary schools. This statement is supported in studies conducted by Bonney (6), by Damrin (11), by Hardy (15), and by Young and Cooper (28). In several of these studies small advantages were found for children from family units of two or three children, over those from family units of six or more children. However, even these small advantages should not be credited simply to differences in family size. Particularly at the time the above studies were conducted, large family units in our culture were characterized by low economic levels together with a multitude of personal and social handicaps.

Surveys of our evidence in regard to *only* children, such as the one presented by Norma Cutts and Nicholas Mosley (10), show that some *only* children are as maladjusted as traditional assumptions call for, particularly in regard to overindulgence, but that, on the whole, these children hold their own very well with children from larger family units in all desirable characteristics.

Sociometric studies in school populations reported by Bonney (6), by Damrin (11), by Feinberg (12), and by Loomis, Baker, and Proctor (19), have all shown *only* children to be quite evenly distributed from the top to the bottom of their respective sociometric hierarchies, thus leading to the conclusion that there is no special or inherent handicap in being an *only* child.

It seems certain, then, that the number of brothers and sisters with whom a child grows up carries in itself no special psychological significance for this child. It does not tell us anything about his level of socialization, since in itself it does not tell us anything about the *kind* or *quality* of interpersonal relationships that have existed between him and his parents, or between him and his brothers and sisters, if any.

[1] See reference by Appel and Smith (1) at end of this chapter.

As far as the *only* child is concerned, it is possible that the danger of his being reared in relative isolation has greatly decreased during this generation due to our improved means of transportation, the greater number of playschools and nursery schools, and more contacts between homes because of the much greater use of automobiles. However, it is also probable that most *only* children never have been as bad off as they have often been pictured. Furthermore, the point should not be overlooked that an *only* child may have considerable advantage in his total development because he receives more adult attention and stimulation than can be given to two, three, or more children. Alhough this can be a social handicap if carried to excess, it may also be a definite contribution if well balanced with other needs.

Teachers, then, should not expect to find any particular kinds of personality assets or liabiilties associated with children who come from large, medium, or small family units. Furthermore, each *only* child should be judged in terms of his particular merits rather than with preconceived notions.

BROKEN VS. UNBROKEN HOMES

Probably all teachers have known pupils from broken homes who are seriously maladjusted and unhappy. Probably, too, all teachers have read accounts of how children from broken homes are frequently involved in delinquency and other other types of problems. Although a broken home may create a condition of extreme seriousness in the personality development of particular children, this factor is often overplayed because of centering attention entirely on children from broken homes who have failed in some conspicuous way.

Many studies dealing with children from broken homes have not included any information on the personal-social adjustments of these children in their school populations. Those that do include this type of information show a wide range of results depending largely upon the kind of personality assessments used and the criterion groups with whom the broken-home pupils have been compared.

Investigations conducted by Bartlett and Horrocks (3), by Rouman (22), and by Torrance (24), in which self-ratings or adult ratings were used, have shown some reliable disadvantages for broken-home children, but other studies using similar methods, such as one conducted by Washburne (26), have shown the broken-home condition to be indiscriminating or to possess both negative and positive values.

In three sociometric studies utilizing friendship criteria, reported by Cooke (9), by Hardy (15), and by Young and Cooper (28), elementary school pupils from broken homes could not be reliably distinguished from equivalent groups of pupils from unbroken homes in number of positive choices received or in number of mutual friendships. In Cooke's study, even when those pupils who came from homes broken by divorce or separation (45 cases) were singled out for analysis, there was only one point difference between their average sociometric score and the average of a group of pupils from the same classrooms from unbroken homes, with whom they had been matched for sex, intelligence, and neighborhood rating.

Considering all the findings reported above, it seems best to think of the broken-home situation in the same light as that of family size, namely, to regard it as an external condition from which we cannot safely deduce anything in reference to the personality adjustments of any particular child. The presence or absence of one or both parents in the home is a purely objective fact, and as such tells us nothing about the *quality* of the interpersonal relaionships which are carried on in the home. Teachers and counselors would be on safer ground not to assume anything in respect to either good adjustment or maladjustment from the sheer background fact of a child's home being either broken or unbroken.

This conclusion is supported by the findings of a comprehensive investigation reported by Wallenstein (25), utilizing measures of personality and character which yielded scores on honesty, ascendency, extroversion, neurotic tendency, and reputation. The subjects were in grades 5 to 8 in public schools in the New York City area, and included 1600 who were from unbroken homes and 400 from broken homes. Group differences were determined between these two types of homes as well as differences between matched pairs taken from these two categories.

From a wide range of statistical analysis, Wallenstein states that "for the grand total of comparisons, 68 per cent of the instances are found where the direction of the mean differences is in favor of the normal home children." (p. 82.) However, Wallenstein goes on to say that even though his evidence on the whole shows the broken-home situation to be associated with inferiority in certain aspects of character and personality, this inferiority, as compared with unbroken homes, is not very marked and may not be very significant. Writing on this point Wallenstein says: "Yet possibly because of compensatory factors in life, the differences in disfavor of the broken-home children are rather small for the most of the tests and comparisons, so that broken- and normal-home children cannot be looked upon psychologically as two distinctly different groups in school. In fact, it seems more proper that the term 'broken home' be viewed as primarily a sociological but not necessarily a psychological concept, since there is no evidence that the impairment of a home biosociologically inevitably in every case entails also a psychological break." (p. 83.)

In so far as the broken-home condition is concerned, teachers can best promote the objectives of mental health by making sure that they are not overly sensitive to the behavior problems of a child simply because they know he is from a broken home. However, they should provide all of the personal and emotional supports possible to those children who are from broken homes and are obviously experiencing unusual difficulties.

ADJUSTMENT OF TRANSPORTED PUPILS

A home condition that affects the school lives of many thousands of pupils in this country is that of living in the country and being transported via bus to a centralized rural school or to a town school. What problems in social adjustment arise from these consolidation programs? From our present evidence the answer to this question depends primarily upon (1) whether country pupils are brought into a consolidated rural school as opposed to a predominantly town school, (2) whether or not the country pupils are on approximately the same socio-economic level as the town students, and (3) whether or not any special efforts are made to aid the social integration of bus and town students.

These statements are supported by evidence presented in reports by Becker and Loomis (4), Blanchard (5), Hays (16), and Ovzack (21). Of these studies, the data most significant for this book are those which reveal the inferior social status of rural students who are brought into a predominantly town high school that makes no effort to aid the social integration of the country students. This problem is best illustrated in Hays' study of a senior high school in a North Texas community in which a little over a third of the students were brought in buses from the open country to a town high school. Utilizing a comprehensive friendship questionnaire, which was completed by all of the 160 students in the high school, Hays' findings showed statistically reliable differences in favor of the town students on all three grade-levels (10th, 11th, and 12th) and in regard to both intrasex and intersex choosing.

The lowest-ranking subgroups were the three grade-level groupings of rural girls. No group in the high school showed a preference for the rural girls, including the rural boys; and worst of all, they even (as a group) rejected themselves. By contrast, both the town girls and the town boys showed strong in-group preferences since they choose other town students to a much greater extent than they chose country students.

In an effort to explain the generally inferior acceptance of the rural students in this town high school, Hays investigated the extent to which participation in group activities at school was related to the friendship acceptance scores. For this purpose a questionnaire was administered which obtained data on frequency of participation in school clubs, parties, dances, and sports. The results showed that there was not much difference between town and country students in their extent of participation in group functions held during the school-day, but that there was a marked difference in regard to those held after school and at night. The rural groups on all three grade-levels showed less participation than town groups in after-school events, and the difference was greatest for the rural girls. It seems reasonable to assume that this lack of participation of rural girls in group functions held after school hours was an important factor accounting for their relatively low acceptability in the student-body.

Teachers and school administrators in a consolidated town-school who wish to establish a satisfying mental health climate for bus students should: (1) make special provision for bringing country students to after-school events; (2) have a large number of activities such as auditorium programs, intramural sports, and parties during the regular school hours; (3) see to it that at least some homerooms and classes have commitee and small-group work and that country and town students are mixed in these assignments according to the principles for grouping given in Chapter 12; (4) avoid any practices that would tend to separate country and town students into identifiable units, such as frequent references to "the bus students," or pitting country and town students against each other in competitive events in classrooms or on the playground. In one school, known to the writer, in which boxing matches were held, a country boy was always matched against a town boy. The country and town students sat on different sides of the arena as they cheered their respective representatives and razzed the boy on the other side. It is no wonder that the principal reported considerable "bad blood" between the bus and town students in this school.

REFERENCES

1. Appel, K. E. and L. H. Smith, "Approach to College Mental Hygiene," *Mental Hygiene*, 15, 1931, 52-71.
2. Baldwin, A. L., "Socialization and the Parent-Child Relationship," *Child Development*, 19, 1948, 127-136.
3. Bartlett, C. J. and J. E. Horrocks, "A Study of the Needs Status of Adolescents from Broken Homes," *Journal of Genetic Psychology*, 93, 1958, 153-159.
4. Becker, M. G. and C. P. Loomis, "Measuring Rural Urban and Farm and Non-Farm Cleavages in a Rural Consolidated School," *Sociometry*, 11, 1948, 246-260.
5. Blanchard, B. E., "A Social Acceptance Study of Transported and Non-Transported Pupils in a Rural Secondary School," *Journal of Experimental Education*, 15, 1946-47, 291-303.
6. Bonney, Merl E., "Relationships Between Social Success, Family Size, Socio-Economic Background, and Intelligence among School Children in Grades III to V," *Sociometry*, 7, 1944, 77-87.
7. ———, "Parents as the Makers of Social Deviates," *Social Forces*, 20, 1941, 77-87.

8. ——— "A Sociometric Study of the Peer Acceptance of Rural Students in Three Consolidated High Schools," *Education, Administration, and Supervision*, 1951, 234-240.
9. Cooke, Eunyce A., "A Study To Determine the Difference in Scholastic Achievement and Sociometric Standing Between Children from Broken and Unbroken Homes," Unpublished M.S. thesis, North Texas State College, 1951.
10. Cutts, N. E. and N. Moseley, *The Only Child.* New York: G. P. Putnam's Sons, 1954, p. 245.
11. Damrin, D. E., "Family Size and Sibling Age, Sex and Position as Related to Certain Aspects of Adjustment," *Journal of Social Psychology*, 29, 1949, 93-102.
12. Feinberg, M. R., "Relation of Background Experience to Social Acceptance," *Journal of Abnormal and Social Psychology*, 48, 1953, 206-214.
13. Fromm, Erich, *The Art of Loving.* New York: Harper and Brothers, 1956.
14. Gallagher, James G., "Rejecting Parents?," *Exceptional Children*, 22, 1956, 273-276.
15. Hardy, M. C., "Social Recognition at the Elementary School Age," *Journal of Social Psychology*, 8, 1937, 365-384.
16. Hays, W. L., "A Study of the Peer Acceptance of a Rural Group in a Town High School," Unpublished M.A. thesis, North Texas State College, 1949.
17. Langdon, G. and J. W. Stout, *These Well Adjusted Children."* New York: The John Day Co., 1951.
18. Langdon, G. and J. W. Stout, *The Discipline of Well-adjusted Children.* New York: The John Day Co., 1952.
19. Loomis, C. P., W. B. Baker, and C. Proctor, "The Size of the Family as Related to Social Success of Children," *Sociometry*, 12, 1949, 313-320.
20. Menninger, Karl, *Love Against Hate.* New York: Harcourt, Brace and Co., 1942.
21. Ovzack, Louis H., "Preference and Prejudice among Rural and Urban Schoolmates," *Rural Sociology*, 21, 1956, 29-33.
22. Rouman, J., "School Children's Problems As Related to Parental Factors," *Journal of Educational Research*, 50, 1956, 105-112.
23. Symonds, P. M., *The Dynamics of Parent-Child Relationships.* New York: Bureau of Publications, Teachers College, Columbia University, 1949.
24. Torrance, P., "The Influence of the Broken Home on Adolescent Adjustment," *Journal of Educational Sociology*, 18, 1944-45, 359-364.
25. Wallenstein, Nehemiah, *Character and Personality of Children From Broken Homes.* Columbia University Contributions to Education, Teachers College Series, 1937.

26. Washburne, John N., "Factors Related to the Social Adjustment of College Girls," *Journal of Social Psychology*, 13, 1941, 281-289.
27. Welberg, Lewis R. "The Character Structure of the Rejected Child," *The Nervous Child*, 3, 1944, 74-88.
28. Young, L. L. and D. H. Cooper, "Some Factors Associated with Popularity," *Journal of Educational Psychology*, 35, 1944, 513-535.

QUESTIONS AND EXERCISES

1. Give an example from your experience of children who are seriously maladjusted even though they have come from homes that, on the basis of external criteria, are "very good homes." From your knowledge of the home situations, what qualities are lacking?
2. What relationships do you see between the kind of parents who were found to be "the best parents" in the Langdon and Stout studies and the kind of teachers who are the "best teachers"?
3. Point out ways in which teachers are often misled in regard to the kind of home influence upon a child?
4. Try to arrange for a parent-teacher meeting in which the subject of nature and immature love of children is presented in some manner, as by a speech, a panel discussion, or role playing.
5. To what extent do you think a teacher should be a substitute mother to primary-grade children who lack love at home?
6. Try to visit an institution, a camp, or a clinic where rejected and other maladjusted children are treated.
7. What psychological fallacy is involved when judgments are made concerning a child's family size being an important explanation of his behavior adjustments?
8. Under what conditions will a child from a broken home be least likely to suffer seriously from this fact?
9. Visit a consolidated school and try to obtain some evidence with sociometric or other types of data on how well the bus students are being integrated into the total school.

SELECTED FILMS

A Criminal Is Born. Illustrates how lack of parental interest, love, and supervision can lead to personal disaster in lives of children.

Discipline During Adolescence. 16 minutes. Very good in showing weakness of both too much and too little discipline in adolescent years.

Family Circle. 31 minutes. Very useful in showing relationships between home experiences and school life.

Who Is Sylvia? 27 minutes. Illustrates very well the problems of a sensitive girl in early adolescent years when parents do not understand her.

Guidance Problem for School and Home. 17 minutes. Illustrates how the parent-child relationship affects the adjustment of an elementary school child.

3

INFERIORITY FEELINGS AND

PROBABLY ALL TEACHERS, even those of limited experience, have observed some pupils who have appeared to be suffering from inferiority feelings. As a matter of fact, such feelings are quite common even among people who are generally very competent. The issue before us, then, is not the sheer presence or absence of inferiority feelings, but rather the extent to which these feelings exercise a crippling effect upon an individual's total personality. When these feelings of self-evaluation are persistent and strong they constitute a serious problem in the mental health of an individual. They are psy-

DEFENSIVE ADJUSTMENTS

chic sores which are frequently aggravated by interpersonal contacts and which cause numerous perceptual distortions of his experiences. Furthermore, if these sores are not healed, their influence frequently extends throughout life even in spite of numerous successes and achievements which should presumably appease the inferiority feelings. But appeasement as a psychological policy is as much of a failure in meeting inner emotional needs as it is in satisfying the unreasonable demands of national dictators. There are always demands for more and more payments. It is from this standpoint that the phrase "childhood is a blackmailer" takes its meaning. In other words, unless the real problem producing serious inferiority feelings is met in some satisfying way, the motivations involved in this problem persist into adult life and continue to force a person to do many things that are attempts to heal his psychic sores, but that fail to do so, because the "payments" are inappropriate to the nature of his affliction. Thus the wounds remain unhealed.

Many of these inappropriate attempts to appease wounded self-feelings are referred to as ego-defensive mechanisms. This term refers to those behavior adjustments that are adopted by individuals as a means of defending themselves against the realization of failures and of personal inadequacies which are threatening to their conception of themselves. The motivations to such behavior are largely unconscious, i.e., the individuals involved do not recognize or understand why they act the way they do. Their behavior adjustments are dictated by emotional and self-defensive needs and are therefore not very rational. Obviously, the more a child or young person adopts this kind of behavior the more he is developing mentally unhealthy ways of responding to himself and to others.

CAUSATIVE FACTORS IN INFERIORITY

The most frequently recognized causative factors in inferiority feelings have been described and evaluated in numerous writings such as those by Coleman (3), Shaffer and Shoben (15), and Vaughan (17). These causative factors will not be reviewed in detail at this point since those which are most directly involved in school situations are described in connection with appropriate topics throughout this volume. A simple listing at this point of the more important social and psychological conditions that produce inferiority reactions will, however, serve to call attention to the wide range of motivating factors that are known to be involved in these feelings.

In regard to home background conditions, a child suffering from serious inferiority feelings has most likely been subjected to one or more of the distorted kinds of parent-child relationships described in Chapter 20. He is especially likely to have been pampered so that he lacks ability to depend on himself. On the other hand, he may have been rejected so that he feels unworthy; or he may have been subjected to excessive criticism or unreasonable demands so that he has learned that no matter how well he does, it is not good enough. In addition, he may have some negative self-feelings because of the very poor house his family lives in, or because of the bad reputation of his parents.

Aside from home background factors a child may suffer from

inferiority feelings due to (1) some kind of obvious physical defect or limitation, (2) lack of proficiency in the kind of skills emphasized in a particular situation, (3) arbitrary discriminations against him due to his race, nationality, or religion, (4) inappropriate sex role, such as effeminacy in a boy, (5) failure for numerous reasons to succeed on a personal basis with opposite-sex members, and (6) rejection of his or her normal sex role. This latter condition is most likely to be found in girls, and can be found in a few girls who are relatively free from all the other sources of inferiority listed above.

In considering these causative conditions it is important to emphasize that all of these influences have a reciprocal effect upon each other within a child's total personality. For example, a child who is, or who believes he is, unloved by his parents may come to devaluate his appearance and thus believe that others think he is not "good-looking" when, as a matter of fact, he may be rated above average. Likewise, an adolescent who is ashamed of some aspect of his home situation may let this factor unduly influence him to the point of believing that no one of the opposite sex would want to be seen with him and thus adds to himself another source of inferiority feelings. Furthermore, in the examples just cited, it is quite likely (but not necessarily so) that both the child and the adolescent would underrate their abilities as compared with others and thus add a third source of inferiority attitudes. This process can continue indefinitely until, in a few individuals, it produces a generalized attitude of inferiority toward themselves and all aspects of their world, and especially so in reference to their dealings with other people.

This analysis points up the fact that serious inferiority feelings may or may not be closely related to actual conditions in a person's life situation. In some instances definitely unfavorable conditions may exist, but in others the problem is almost, if not entirely, one of unwarranted self-devaluating attitudes. On the other side of the ledger is the equally important fact that the existence of definitely unfavorable conditions may not be productive of serious inferiority feelings. These two statements add up to saying that inferiority feelings in many people are much more closely related to their perceptions of themselves than to actual conditions as assessed from an external frame of reference. In other words, rejecting and devaluating self-attitudes, as opposed to factual conditions, can be the chief motivating factors in serious inferiority feelings. Also, individuals who set for themselves very high aspiration levels may suffer from such feelings even though, as compared with others, their contributions and achievements may be quite superior.

From these statements it is obvious that a teacher cannot accurately judge the extent to which a child is or is not suffering from inferiority feelings by observing certain objective or external facts about him in regard to the grades he is making, his playground skills, his competence in art, his home background, etc. Instead, a teacher must try to gain this kind of insight into a child from conferences with him, or from use of some of the measuring instruments described in Chapter 11, or from noting the presence of certain kinds of overt behavior patterns which have been shown in numerous studies and clinical reports to be strongly indicative of inferiority feelings.

The next division of this chapter is devoted to a description of these behavior patterns, together with some suggestions for aiding pupils who show these behavior characteristics. It is important to point out, however, that these suggestions must not be viewed as entirely adequate for dealing with the problem behaviors listed. Instead they should be regarded as the suggestions considered most specific for a particular problem. Every maladjustment that a person possesses is affected to some extent by all the other liabilities and assets that he has in his total personality. From this fact it would naturally follow that all kinds of corrective efforts are interrelated and reciprocal in their effects. Therefore, teachers should look upon all the suggestions for child and youth development offered in this book as having direct and indirect values for reducing the severity of inferiority feelings.

OVERT BEHAVIOR AND INFERIORITY

1. Inferiority feelings may be shown by various kinds of submissive and withdrawal behavior, such as shyness, undue sensitivity, fantasy, avoidance of competition, and marked inability to be aggressive or self-assertive against others.

Shy pupils can generally be identified by such behavior as standing on the sidelines in social situations, being alone a large portion of the time in school, and lacking initiative to start conversations or any other kind of activity involving participation with others. However, these kinds of behavior must not be taken as conclusive evidence of inferiority feelings, since at least a few children who are shy and withdrawing nevertheless feel quite adequate. Most of these latter children are introverts, as originally described in 1923 by C. G. Jung, a Swiss psychiatrist, in his *Psychological Types.*

Jung's views are well summarized by Harriman (4) when he points out that the introvert as originally defined by Jung is not one who is to be regarded as neurotic, or as necessarily maladjusted and therefore in need of some form of correction. Instead he should be regarded as a person who has a strong subjective orientation, a high degree of emotional sensitivity, a tendency toward self-analysis, and a rich inner life of fantasy and imagination.

Some children who possess these qualities suffer from inferiority attitudes but others do not. Instead they are quiet, serene individuals who have a large capacity for enjoying themselves and who do not, as persons, feel inferior to anyone. It is important, then, that teachers be cautioned against assuming that every child who is not a so-called extrovert and who is neither popular nor a leader is suffering from feelings of inferiority.

One of the more certain clues that a shy child does feel inadequate is the presence of undue sensitivity to criticisms, slights, and minor failures. Such a child cries with little provocation, his feelings are easily hurt, he frequently imagines that other pupils are discriminating against him, and he cannot stand up well under the normal expectancy of give-and-take in classroom social groups. He interprets kidding remarks and mild rebukes more seriously than the facts warrant, and he sees slights where none were intended. Although such a child is likely to be low in both prestige and personal preference in his class, he frequently imagines that he is more isolated or rejected than he actually is. Also this kind of child is likely to be very sensitive to teacher criticisms, may cry when corrected, and may believe that the teacher doesn't like him and is picking on him.

---

[1] C. G. Jung, *Psychological Types* (New York: Harcourt, Brace and Co., 1924).

Sometimes the hypersensitive child, in an effort to try to insulate himself against both classmates and teachers, will develop a feeling of emotional detachment or aloofness which, on the surface, creates the impression of self-sufficiency. This armor of indifference and coldness, which is put on as a defense against psychological wounds, may bring him some superficial and temporary "feelings of triumph" over others, but in the long run such protective adjustments are likely to increase his deeper feelings of bitterness and despair over himself as a person.

Obviously a child with these kinds of problems needs the aid of a psychological counselor or a child guidance clinic. However, when such facilities are lacking, a sensitive teacher may help such a child by showing genuine interest in him, not only in reference to his school work, but also in regard to his personal needs. This can be done through short conferences outside of regular class periods, through showing concern over his feelings, and through numerous small indications of friendliness, such as cheerful greetings, smiles, and an occasional pat on the back.

That these kinds of interpersonal relationships between a teacher and pupil are likely to have some beneficial results is indicated in a study by Thompson (16) among nursery school pupils. His evidence showed that nursery school pupils whose teachers manifested toward them a large amount of warm, friendly, and helpful relationships made much more progress in various aspects of personal-social behavior than did a similar group of nursery school pupils whose teachers were considerate but who were somewhat detached and who gave help only when it was specifically requested.

There are some child specialists who hold that a teacher should avoid building up a close rapport with any pupil since this bond must be broken when the child passes on to the next grades. Rotter (14), a clinical psychologist, considers this point of view and takes a stand against it when he says:

> The assumption is that the child becomes so dependent upon this type of satisfaction that he will be traumatized when it is withdrawn. However, many children in the course of growing up become attached to adults other than their parents and are

> liked in return by such adults. They are not traumatized by such experiences because they do not last forever; they are negatively affected only when they perceive the separation or the ending of the relationship as an indication of their own inadequacy or failure. Such supportive interest can be helpful to the child who has no other source of love, affection, or interest, providing he understands the termination of such relationships as necessary and not reflecting upon his own adequacy as a person. (pp. 421-422.)

The ultimate aim of the kind of teacher-concern described above and of the kind favored by Rotter is to help a hypersensitive, emotionally insulated child to establish some intimate rapport with one or more of his age-mates. It seems likely, however, that in school situations the teacher will need to be the one to "break the ice," since he has presumably an objective or professional interest in a maladjusted child, whereas such a motivation cannot be expected of age-mates.

A characteristic frequently found in pupils who feel submissive and inferior is an unwillingness or hesitancy in regard to entering into competitive situations, particularly those in which individual performances can be readily observed, such as in games like baseball or checkers, or in contests involving public speaking or musical abilities.

It is not difficult to see why children or adolescents who feel inferior should try to avoid exposing themselves, since their own attitudes cause them to underrate themselves. Furthermore, they lack the ego-strength to tolerate possible failure or unfavorable comparisons with others. Rather than risk these psychological hazards, the inferior-feeling pupil plays safe by avoiding all competitive situations, and particularly those in which some weakness of his might be exposed in front of others. He might, however, be willing to enter competitive events such as those involving writing essays, solving puzzles, etc., in which only the identity of the winners is revealed.

It must not be assumed, however, that any person who does not like or enjoy competitive situations is afflicted with inferiority feelings. There are people whose temperaments and social outlooks orient them toward the more quiet pursuits of life, such as those found in nature study, hobbies, reading, music, and companionship, and who place no value on trying to be superior to others in anything.

Those, however, who are afraid of any overt comparison with others are obviously revealing feelings of inadequacy. This withdrawal from competitive effort is frequently only an aspect of a larger personality adjustment, namely, a marked inability to be aggressive or assertive against others. This kind of individual lets dominating people "run over him"; he often takes insults without retaliation; he finds it very difficult, if not impossible, to "tell anyone off" or even to demand his legitimate rights. These inadequacies further deepen his inferiority feelings which are often complicated and abetted by deep-seated guilt feelings about himself as a person. Thus a vicious circle is perpetuated — a person with a weak self expects to act in a weak manner when confronted by aggression from others; his overt behavior in turn reinforces his expectancy for another submissive type of response. Even when he occasionally manages to be assertive this may not be sufficient to make a permanent dent in his fundamental conception of himself as a submissive or cowardly person. This point is well expressed in the following quotation by John Reed, as he writes of his boyhood experiences:

> Outside of a few friends, I wasn't a success with the boys. I hadn't strength or fight enough to be good at athletics, except swimming, which I have always loved; and I was a good deal of a physical coward. I would sneak out over the back fence to avoid boys who were "laying" for me, or who I thought were "laying" for me. Sometimes I fought, when I couldn't help myself, and sometimes even won; but I preferred to be called a coward than fight. I hated pain. My imagination conjured up horrible things that would happen to me, and I simply ran away. One time, when I was on the editorial board of the school paper, a boy I was afraid of warned me not to publish a joking paragraph I had written about him — and I didn't. My way to school was through a sort of slum district, called Goose Hollow, peopled with brutal Irish boys, many of whom grew up to be prizefighters and baseball stars. I was literally frightened out of my senses when I went through Goose Hollow. Once a Goose Hollowite made me promise to give him a nickel if he didn't hit me, and walked up to my house with me

> while I got it for him. . . . The strange thing was that when I was cornered, and fought, even a licking wasn't a hundredth as bad as I thought it would be; but I never learned anything from that — the next time I ran away just the same, and suffered the most ghastly pangs of fear.[2]

It is important to note, however, that the kind of submissive person under consideration has difficulty in asserting himself only against *other people.* This same person may be very aggressive in pursuing work-type objectives such as making high grades or achieving unusual skill in music, art, or public speaking. In extreme cases such efforts are regarded as overcompensations for personal weaknesses.

The pupil who is overly submissive and afraid to assert himself against others (regardless of ability-assets) needs to be encouraged to stand up for his rights and to be self-assertive, by being helped to respond to others with kidding remarks, being induced to express his opinions openly, and being shown how to resist efforts on the part of others to dominate him. With children through the primary grades, teachers can often take a direct hand in coaching a child to be more self-assertive, to fight back, and to resist efforts to push him out of line, to take his materials, or to force him into a particular kind of behavior.

Evidence from a number of experimental investigations among preschool children by Jack (5), Mummery (10), and Page (11) shows that at this age-level those pupils who are selected as being too submissive can be definitely helped through special training sessions to become more aggressive, self-confident and ascendant. It is probable, however, that none of the children included in these studies was seriously maladjusted.

Aside from individual coaching of highly submissive pupils by remarks as, "Don't let him take your book," "It's all right to fight back," or "Go ahead — tell her how you feel about it," a teacher can sometimes help such a child by arranging for him to acquire some kind of skill that most of the other pupils do not possess and in which the teacher can coach him. This gives him a chance to take the initiative and assume the role of the leader. Possibilities in this area include

---

[2] John Reed, "Almost Thirty Years," *The New Republic,* 1936, 269-270.

new games either for classroom or playground use, and new techniques or processes for doing something such as mounting butterflies, using a chemistry set, carving soap, or preparing a particular kind of food. With pupils who are very unassertive it will probably be best to let them start their leadership efforts, not with the whole class, but with a subgroup containing from four to eight other classmates. All such efforts will be more effective if the child's parents can be induced to help him acquire whatever new skill he is trying to utilize at school.

Finally, the overly inhibited child can sometimes be helped by stimulating him to be more spontaneous in expressing himself in any media appropriate to him, such as play activities, soap carving, music, art, dance, or dramatization. When a highly rigid, inhibited child becomes more spontaneous in a constructive endeavor, he does not simply "find himself"; he creates some important aspects of himself which were not there before.

2. *Inferiority feelings may be shown by dominating, attacking, and other forms of hyperaggressive behavior directed against others.*

Overcompensation for a feeling of inferiority is a well-known form of psychological defense. One of the most frequently adopted behavior patterns for this purpose is domination and hyperaggressiveness, as evidenced in such behavior as attacking and blaming others in an irrational manner, striking and pushing behavior among young children, efforts to make others submit completely to one's will, bullying younger or weaker individuals, and showing off knowledge or skill simply to embarrass others or to gain a sense of power over them.

Many children and adolescents who manifest overcompensatory behavior are characterized by strained relations with others, since they are always ready to embarrass or attack with a sharp wisecrack, a derogatory statement, or an invidious comparison. These individuals can seldom carry on a normal conversation since a relationship is soon disrupted by their assuming the role of a lecturer, or by their launching into a boastful description of some of their own exploits or areas of knowledge.

It is not unusual for the hypercritical person to hide behind the virtue of frankness as a rationalization for his persistent attacks on others. He may say: "I believe in being frank." Regardless of the reasons a person gives for persistent, irrational attacks on others, it is essential to see how such behavior enhances his feelings of power. This kind of reaction to inferiority brings an individual more "personality gains" than does withdrawing or fantasy-type adjustments. He experiences a good many feelings of adequacy, and occasionally on a fairly legitimate basis since aggressiveness against others is in some situations a socially appropriate response. In fact, it seems quite certain that those who respond to any kind of frustration with aggressive behavior are less likely to develop neurotic symptoms than are those who respond by some form of retreat or submission.[3]

We must not, however, lose sight of the fact that the individual who achieves feelings of adequacy from attacking others is building on sand rather than solid rock. Furthermore, these ego-enhancing victories increase his alienation from others and thus intensify his needs for security, affection, and belongingness, which are also essential to the reduction of inferiority feelings.

What objectives and procedures should a teacher pursue and utilize in trying to help a child who is characterized by overcompensatory aggressiveness against others? In the first place, more approved avenues for expression of aggressive behavior and self-assertion may be opened up within the group, such as competitive games, organization of committees for some kind of action project (making a map, arranging a science fair), or providing for much more verbal expression through class or small group discussions. This latter suggestion when well carried-out (as described in Chapter 13) affords many opportunities for training in thinking *with* others rather than against them.

A teacher, however, must recognize that the dominating child who is overcompensating for inferiority feelings wants not just more chances for power or recognition, but also he wants someone to like him. He needs security as well as adequacy. Accepting this fact the teacher could (a) confer with the overly assertive child and try to get him to understand how his overt behavior keeps him from achieving what he really wants, (b) coach him in specific acts of helpfulness and consideration for others, and (c) induce his parents to invite a

[3] Percival Symonds, *Dynamic Psychology* (New York: Appleton-Century-Crofts, Inc., 1949), p. 59.

few selected children into the home for the purpose of promoting some friendship affiliations.

It is important that a teacher make sure that hyperaggressive behavior directed against others is not rewarded. This means that the dominating child must not be allowed to "get away with it" in the sense that he takes another child's turn, grabs and retains another child's materials, etc. Instead, such behavior must be corrected when it occurs, by forceful means if necessary.

In addition to forceful restraints, a teacher may also combine these restraining efforts (particularly with primary-level pupils) with various kinds of positive appeals such as "If you do not strike other children near you this morning you may lead the class into lunchroom" or "carry the news report to the principal" or "direct your group's dramatization of our reading story." Obviously such positive appeals would need to be adapted to each child and each situation.

The theory upon which such positive appeals are based is that antisocial behavior is more likely to be inhibited if some kind of desirable behavior is held up as a reward. Numerous learning experiments have shown that positive reinforcements or rewards are much more likely to induce behavior changes than are punishments. Apparently there is much more incentive to *work for* something than there is to simply avoid a form of behavior that is punished. Furthermore, the assumption is that as a child successfully performs approved roles in the school setting he will develop more ego-strength and thus reduce his feelings of inadequacy.

It is important that the kind of positive appeals listed above be in accord with the abilities and wishes of a particular child and that the reward-behavior be clearly defined and available (especially with small children) within a few hours or less.

These kinds of short-term positive incentives will be superficial and ineffective with those children whose hyperaggressive behavior springs from deep-seated maladjustments within the personality. Such children seldom profit from retraining in short-term socialization procedures. Instead, these more seriously disturbed pupils need psychotherapy, and it is safe to assume that their parents do also.

In concluding this section it is well to emphasize that some children who are hyperaggressive, and who are dominating and bossy at times, are not suffering from inferiority feelings. Instead they may be strong, self-confident individuals with an abundance of energy; and they may be well accepted by their classmates. Observation of such pupils, however, will reveal that they possess numerous kinds of personality assets which counterbalance their dominating behavior.

3. Inferiority feelings may be shown by the adoption of some form of attention-attracting behavior.

It seems likely that one of the behavior-responses to inferiority feelings which is most frequently observed by teachers is some form of attention-attracting behavior, such as "showing off," use of peculiar language, adoption of bizarre mannerisms, or the voicing of unusual beliefs. Similar motivations are frequently involved in the wearing of unconventional clothing and gaudy jewelry. It is not difficult to see how any kind of attention-attracting behavior may be adopted by a person suffering from inferiority feelings, since such behavior does temporarily and superficially serve his ego-needs. It does force some people to notice him in a favorable or an unfavorable manner, and in some instances involving protest behavior (such as voicing antimoral or antireligious beliefs) the individual gains some feelings of power over others by rejecting some of their most cherished values.

4. Inferiority feelings may be shown by concentration of perfectionism in a narrow field of endeavor.

In some pupils, inferiority feelings are manifested in perfectionist behavior in one or more areas of personal or social endeavors. The primary objective of such behavior is to be "absolutely right" in regard to some form of moral, ethical, or religious standard, or in regard to some kind of productive effort. Among school children this kind of behavior is most likely to be evidenced in unusual fussiness about personal appearance, or in extreme conscientiousness in regard to promptness, getting answers completely right, doing an assignment just exactly "like the teacher said," and striving to be one hundred per cent obedient to all rules and regulations. This supergood child is often too anxious about being right and proper to be creative, spontaneous, or interesting, or to establish a good rapport with even one other child.

What should a teacher try to accomplish with this kind of child? Unfortunately a good many teachers would not see anything wrong with all this compulsive goodness, but would instead say (in the case of a girl) "I wish I had a roomful like her."

A more insightful teacher, on the other hand, would do all he could to try to get a child with a perfectionist defense to relax his standards. He would need to do this, not by a direct attack on the child's supergoodness, but by seizing opportunities to praise the child for non-perfectionist behavior, by not giving positive reinforcements to the already exaggerated behavior, and by trying to establish some genuinely friendly relationships with the child in the hope that these kinds of personal satisfactions will come to displace the unbalanced valuations accorded to "doing the right thing." Furthermore it would be hoped that, as satisfactions were gained from greater personal rapport with the teacher, the child would be able to make some transfer of these kinds of relationships to at least a few other children. Obviously these efforts are more likely to bear some fruit if the teacher or school counselor is able to confer with the parents in regard to relaxing their expectations and demands in reference to the child, and is able to help them to see the need of developing in their child the feeling that he is accepted for what he is rather than for what he "ought to be."

These remarks, however, should not leave the impression that there is no value in a child's wanting to do some things exactly right. Obviously this is a highly desirable characteristic, even from a personality point of view, provided it is not primarily motivated by the need to conceal personal weakness.

As a matter of fact, a teacher can often begin working with a perfectionist-type child by having him do some things that really need to be done exactly right, such as checking the roll, counting the "milk money," lettering a poster, or writing a detailed report for a class or a school paper. By capitalizing upon the child's present tendencies the teacher may more easily get him to move away from the neurotic aspects of these tendencies, since on the basis of this approach a large change is not expected. He can utilize techniques and values he already possesses; and it would be hoped that the personal-social rewards coming from successful performance of his duties would encourage more normal behavior patterns. Of course, more flexible-type tasks would need to be introduced soon after some evidences of security arising from social approval became apparent.

5. *Inferiority feelings may be shown by concentration on body satisfactions.*

Probably every experienced teacher has known a few pupils who have engaged in an extreme amount of such behaviors as eating (especially sweets), gum chewing, getting a drink, and sucking on things. In many instances the teacher would discover that this same child engages in all these behaviors to a marked degree at home.

It seems reasonable to assume that serious deficiencies in feelings of self-adequacy are a major factor in all children in whom body pleasures bring an inordinate amount of satisfaction. Having failed to achieve higher-level satisfactions, these children concentrate on lower-level pleasures that bring them some relief from tensions, provide immediate gratifications, and serve also to divert their minds from their worries. Such children are frequently characterized by an unusual amount of passivity and dependence; and, according to several studies (2-9), are likely to be ignored or rejected by their classmates, presumably because they are regarded as being immature for their age. A teacher who endeavors to assist a child who falls in this category will need to help to him to develop at least a few close friendships, to acquire proficiency in some skills that the members of his group admire, and to grow up in every way possible to higher-level ego satisfactions.

6. *Inferiority feelings may be shown by wit, humor, and clowning.*

Putting on a good front to help keep up courage or hide wounds is in many circumstances an admirable kind of behavior, but not so when an individual persistently adopts some form of wit, humor, or clowning as a compensation against inferiority feelings. Evidences of irrational nature of his behavior are that it is exaggerated beyond normal expectations, that it is often inappropriate to specific situations, and that it is highly persistent in spite of frequent failures to "score successes." In other words, these evidences show that the efforts to be clever or amusing are determined primarily by inner need rather than by spontaneous interactions with the nature of situations.

How should a teacher deal with this kind of pupil? Certainly not by purely negative methods such as by making fun of him, suppressing him, or by otherwise trying to "knock the foolishness out of him." Although some suppression is probably desirable, such efforts should also be accompanied by numerous positive-type appeals such as letting him play the part of a humorous character in a play, letting him present humorous anecdotes and cartoons (usually obtained from magazines) to the class on appropriate occasions, encouraging him to produce some form of original humor (stories, poems, drawings) for regular classwork, and letting him be the "class expert" on the latest humor. The theory back of such efforts is that there is nothing wrong with his goal of wanting to please or impress others; rather, the only thing wrong is his method of trying to meet these social needs. By helping him to use his talents for constructive and socially approved ends, the hope is that he will gain enough real satisfaction and confidence to build up his ego-strength to the point that his inferiority feelings will be reduced.

ADDITIONAL DEFENSIVE ADJUSTMENTS

In the preceding divisions of this chapter a considerable number of defensive types of adjustments are mentioned or described in conjunction with the discussion of different reactions to inferiority feelings. These types include irrational aggression, abnormal withdrawal into fantasy or submissive adjustments, retreat behind the barriers of perfectionism, attention-attracting behavior, and efforts to hide behind a humorous exterior. In addition to these, there are other defensive-type adjustments which teachers will sometimes observe in their pupils. A wide range of behaviors may be used by different people to defend themselves against the threat of failure, criticism, or humiliation (as indicated by the discussion above), but the remainder of this chapter will be centered only on those defense adjustments known as regression, projection, and rationalization.

Regression

The term *regression* refers to a kind of adjustment which is a return to lower-level behavior, or some form of retreat to more infantile ways of meeting situations. The chief motivation in regressive behavior is a strong feeling of inadequacy in regard to meeting the demands of a present life-situation. The dominant need is to return to a less complex level where previous satisfactions were experienced. A child who regresses is obviously indicating that he cannot solve his developmental tasks, and that higher-level values are ineffective as motivating factors in his life. Instead of his growth process moving forward in what Allport describes as *becoming*,* it moves backward into less differentiation, less realism, and less responsible participation.

In school populations, the following kinds of regressive behavior are most likely to be observed:

> An upper-grade child who regularly plays (outside of scheduled play periods) with first- and second-grade children.
>
> A pupil who frequently dwells on pleasant experiences which happened to him several years ago, but are not happening now.
>
> A child who brings to school and plays with toys that are much more appropriate for a younger age-level.
>
> All pupils who give up trying hard tasks in arithmetic, music, etc., and adopt patterns of passivity and helplessness so that the teacher will have to assist more, coax and cajole them, or possibly even scold them like their mothers used to do.
>
> Children who substitute fantasy and daydreaming for reality achievements, falling back into the imaginary-type satisfactions so common in early childhood.
>
> Pupils at any age who resort to tears as a means of arousing sympathy or of trying to force concessions from others.

In dealing with all types of regressive behavior it is obvious that any kind of stimulation that helps move children toward greater maturity should be consistently maintained in classrooms. It is particularly necessary that those pupils who show regressive behavior be given praise, or some other form of approval, when they behave in

---

*See Chapter 1.

mature ways. For example, a child who has frequently cried when frustrated should be praised privately when he meets a problem without crying. Undoubtedly in the most severe cases of regressive behavior, the individual is suffering from strong feelings of insecurity, arising from lack of love at home, or from overprotection from the normal hazards of growing up. Such cases require more assistance than a classroom teacher is able to give.

Projection

The term *projection* refers to a psychological process whereby an individual perceives in others impulses, feelings, and attitudes which are actually within himself. This process generally operates in regard to thoughts and feelings which a particular individual has come to regard as bad or dangerous for him.

The projection of such impulses and feelings onto others is clearly a defensive type of adjustment. It is a way of protecting one's self against threat. Unconsciously the individual who does this is building up barriers against recognizing his own inner problems and conflicts. He lacks the ego-strength to face his own real feelings of unworthiness, guilt, or hostility, so he protects himself by perceiving in others the traits that he is trying to hide from his own awareness. This subjective motivation causes him to be unduly sensitive to the kinds of behavior in others against which he himself is struggling. He makes mountains out of molehills. He is constantly responding to "a world that isn't there." His cognitive structures, in reference to many behaviors that he observes, are basically wrong; and no one can have good mental health and be wrong about important aspects of his social environment.

Among children and adolescents in our schools the most frequently observed manifestations of projections are found in various forms of exaggerated or unwarranted suspiciousness, such as a pupil who complains to the teacher about other pupils criticizing him, cheating him, or talking against him. Of course, in some instances, there may be considerable justification for these complaints, but the child who has adopted the mechanism of projection as a form of ego-defense is responding primarily to problems or weaknesses within himself. In other words, when such a child makes the complaint,

"Others are criticizing me," the more basic truth is that he holds very critical and self-devaluating attitudes toward himself, but is not willing to face this fact since this would be a threat to his self-esteem. Therefore, "I criticize me" becomes through projection, "They criticize me." Likewise, the child who makes unwarranted accusations about other pupils rejecting him or not liking him is really trying to defend himself against his own self-rejecting attitudes. Furthermore, the child who is hypersensitive to dishonesty in others is unconsciously motivated to build up his defenses against his own dishonesty impulses.

Among younger children teachers can often find evidences of projection by listening to their comments about each other. For example, such remarks as "Paul is a sissy," "Mary is a fraidy-cat," "Ruth is a cry-baby," are frequently motivated by self-defensive needs. The children who shout these comments the loudest are likely to be the very ones who are, underneath their bravado, suffering the most from ill-defined feelings of immaturity and inadequacy.

Teachers who consult with mothers of problem-children can sometimes find evidence of projection. For example, a mother who asks, "Is my child driving you crazy?" may be revealing primarily her own rejecting attitudes toward her child. On an unconscious level she may be saying, "My child is driving me crazy." Also a mother who says, "My child wants to succeed so much," may be projecting her own wishes onto her child, so that her statement might better be paraphrased as, "*I* want my child to succeed so much."

It is evident, then, that a person who projects is seriously lacking in objectivity, and therefore cannot profit by his mistakes or build up more rational controls over his conduct. Until his self-insight and his interpersonal perceptions improve, he must fall short of his maximum potentialities.

What kinds of development offer the best guarantee against the more extreme forms of projection? Obviously every child should be helped to develop sufficient ego-strength to enable him to accept the fact that he has some weaknesses and faults, and sufficient self-regard that he can tolerate some unworthy impulses within himself. Everything that a school can do to lay a solid foundation in skills and knowledge whereby a child can win recognition, admiration, and self-respect, is helping to build the kind of person who can perceive himself and others objectively and, therefore, is in less need of the mechanism of projection. Adequacy, however, must be supplemented with security in interpersonal relationships if projection is to be greatly reduced. The competent person who is nevertheless insecure will be motivated in numerous ways to defend himself against his weaknesses by seeing in others what is primarily within himself. This means that the school must also provide for the promotion of ego-strength through the development of the kinds of personal qualities necessary to cope with the realities of the interpersonal environment.

One special way by which teachers can help reduce projection tendencies is maintaining kindly and permissive relationships with pupils, so that they feel free to admit mistakes and faults instead of being constantly on guard lest a weakness be discovered and punished.

Rationalization

The term *rationalization* refers to a process whereby an individual is unconsciously motivated to think of good reasons for certain aspects of his behavior in order to make it appear that this behavior is being motivated entirely by rational considerations. The purpose of this ego-defense mechanism is to help one's self-concept in regard to his good judgment, moral principles, and feelings of adequacy.

Teachers who are perceptive of pupils' motivations have frequently observed the rationalization process. A pupil, for example, may say that he could make high grades, but, after all, only "grinds" get high grades, and grades don't mean anything anyway. Although this may be an accurate statement for certain pupils, such a remark can usually be taken as a face-saving type of reasoning used to defend one's self against recognition of academic inadequacies. This particular kind of rationalization is called a "sour grapes" type of adjustment, since the supporting attitude is that what cannot be had is not worth having.

An opposite kind of adjustment is found in those pupils who present "good reasons" for being contented with some kind of condition that is below their possibilities. A child who in all probability could achieve some leadership roles or win an award in some kind of competitive event may nevertheless refrain from trying anything in these areas and may "explain" his refusal by saying that those who "get to be important become snobs and act superior, and then nobody likes them." Or he may say that if he won some kind of honor this would keep someone else from winning it, and that he would rather be unselfish than important. Again, although there are some pupils for whom these statements are sincere and accurate reflections of their attitudes, it is much more likely that such statements are cover-ups for unreasonable fears of failure. The kind of rationalization exemplified in the above statements is usually referred to as "sweet lemon," since the supporting attitude involved is one of trying to make something appear pleasant which is ordinarily considered to be unfortunate, limiting, or painful. This adjustment must be clearly distinguished from the mature attitude of making the best of an unavoidably bad situation.

Children and adolescents reveal a wide range of "good reasons" to explain why they don't play certain games, are not interested in particular subjects, don't like their teachers, are not popular with the opposite sex, have to have an expensive car to drive to school, don't belong to certain clubs, have to quit school, etc.

As stated above, it is important for teachers to try to distinguish between genuine and irrational motivations. This can be done only by being sensitive to the possibilities of unconsciously motivated ego-defensive reasoning, and by endeavoring to assess each behavior incident on its merits. If the latter is not done, it is quite possible for a teacher to become unduly sensitive to irrational motivations and to be constantly looking for hidden motives to the point of seeing things that are not there. In extreme cases this attitude leads to cynicism.

How can a teacher detect ego-defensive reasoning? There are three kinds of behavior clues which are generally given by psychologists as evidence of rationalization. These are (1) hunting for and elaborating upon reasons for one's behavior, even when not questioned, (2) considerable annoyance and even anger when reasons are questioned, and (3) inability to recognize inconsistencies and even contradictions between different reasons given and between these reasons and certain obvious factual conditions.

Clearly, these kinds of mental processes limit a child's ability to profit from his experiences and to direct his behavior primarily on a rational basis.

How can a teacher reduce the need for rationalization on the part of his pupils? In the first place, he can establish a permissive type of relationship with them in order to minimize their need to justify all of their deviate behavior by trying to discover "good reasons" for what they have done through impulse, emotional need, and unconsciously motivated drives. Furthermore, a teacher will often gain more insight into a child's behavior by refraining from a lot of direct questioning on "Why did you do it?" or "How could you do such a thing?" Instead of excessive questioning, a teacher should learn to depend more upon letting a child talk about an incident in his own way. However, it will frequently be appropriate for a teacher to help a child to realize that he is not facing the real reasons for his behavior, by stimulating him to consider motivations of which he apparently is not aware. Sometimes, too, such topics as "fallacious reasoning" or "crooked thinking" can be made a topic for the kinds of discussion described in Chapter 13.

The most basic way, however, to reduce the rationalization mechanism is to help all pupils to greater ego-strength and personal security, so that they are more able to accept faults and weaknesses within themselves and are not constantly threatened by all kinds of minor psychological blows.

REFERENCES

1. Beller, E. K., "Dependency and Autonomous Achievement Striving Related to Orality and Anality in Early Childhood," *Child Development*, 28, 1957, 287-315.
2. Blum, G. S. and D. R. Miller, "Exploring the Psychoanalytic Theory of the 'Oral Character'," *Journal of Personality*, 20, March 1952, 287-304.
3. Coleman, J. C., *Abnormal Behavior and Modern Life*, Ch's III and IV. New York: Scott, Foresman and Co., 1956.
4. Harriman, P. L., "In Defense of the Introvert," A Lecture in Print, The Hogg Foundation of the University of Texas, 1944.
5. Jack, L. M., "An Experimental Study of Ascendant Behavior in Preschool Children," in L. M. Jack, E. M. Maxwell, I. G. Mengert, *et al., Behavior of the Preschool Child*, University of Iowa Studies in Child Welfare, No. 9, 3, 1934, 7-65.

6. Kanner, L., "The Role of the School in the Treatment of Rejected Children," *The Nervous Child,* 3, 1944, 236-248.
7. Lowenstein, P. and M. Svendsen, "Experimental Modification of the Behavior of a Selected Group of Shy and Withdrawn Children," *American Journal of Ortho-psychiatry,* 8, 1938, 639-653.
8. Mase, D. J., "Emotionally Insecure and Disturbed Children," *Childhood Education,* 32, 1956, 218-220.
9. Miller, D. R. and M. E. Stine, "The Prediction of Social Acceptance by Means of Psychoanalytic Concepts," *Journal of Personality,* 20, 1951-1952, 162-174.
10. Mummery, D. V., "An Analytical Study of Ascendant Behavior of Preschool Children," *Child Development,* 18, 1947, 40, 81.
11. Page, M. L., "The Modification of Ascendant Behavior in Preschool Children," University of Iowa Studies in Child Welfare, 12, No. 3, 1936.
12. Preston, R. C., "Alternatives for the Persecuted Child," *Mental Hygiene,* 28, 1944, 273-278.
13. Ray, Marie B., *The Importance of Feeling Inferior.* New York: Harper and Bros., 1957.
14. Rotter, J. B., *Social Learning and Clinical Psychology.* Englewood Cliffs, N.J.: Prentice Hall, Inc., 1954.
15. Shaffer, L. F. and E. J. Shoben, *The Psychology of Adjustment* (2nd Ed.), Ch. VI. Boston: Houghton Mifflin Co., 1956.
16. Thompson, G. G., "The Social Emotional Development of Preschool Children Under Two Separate Types of Educational Program," *Psychological Monograph,* No. 5, 56, 1944.
17. Vaughan, W. F., *Personal and Social Adjustment, Foundations of Mental Health.* New York: Odyssey Press, 1952.

QUESTIONS AND EXERCISES

1. Make an oral report to the class on someone you know who is suffering from inferiority feelings but who is quite capable and adequate in numerous ways. Ask the class to discuss how this person may have developed his self-devaluating attitudes.
2. Why do some individuals develop generalized feelings of inferiority whereas others feel inferior only under certain conditions?
3. Distinguish between a child who is shy and one who is shy and also feels inferior.
4. What kind of help does a person need who continues to feel inferior and submissive in spite of many experiences which presumably should strengthen his self-confidence?

5. Why is it that a person who overcompensates for inferiority by aggressive attacks on others nevertheless continues to have his basic problem of inferiority?
6. Cite examples in class of some bad things and some good things you have seen teachers do in reference to pupils characterized by serious inferiority feelings.
7. Give original examples in class of the mechanisms of regression, projection, and rationalization.
8. Why is it so difficult to help people overcome the kind of behavior included in the above mechanisms?

SELECTED FILMS

Facing Reality. 12 minutes. Presents a clear discussion of defense mechanisms and how these interfere with good adjustments; illustrates how a teacher can help.

Shy Guy. 10 minutes. Focuses on the chief characteristics of shyness and offers constructive suggestions.

Shyness. 22 minutes. Describes various forms and degrees of shyness in elementary-age children, and points out some ways of helping such children.

4

HOSTILE AND AGGRESSIVE

PROBABLY IF TEACHERS were polled to determine the kind of child who gives them the most trouble, the winner by a wide margin would be the child characterized by hyperactivity, by excessive aggressiveness, and by acts of hostility against other pupils. As a matter of fact, several investigations such as those by Hunter (12), by Stouffer and Owens (24), and by Wickman (26) have shown that most teachers do regard the type of child described above as being the source of their most serious problems. Although teachers have been justly criticized on the basis of these studies for

BEHAVIOR PATTERNS

overrating the long-range seriousness of aggressive-type behavior and of underrating the long-range seriousness of withdrawing-type behavior, it is easy to understand why most teachers regard the overly aggressive child as the chief source of their problems. They must deal with this kind of child every day, and a large part of their success in classroom management depends on how well they cope with this task. The hyperaggressive child must be curbed.

Of course, there is a wide range within which aggressive and self-assertive behavior is normal and desirable. If the question be asked, "What kind does not come within this range?" a good answer is given by Sager. He points out that pathologically aggressive behavior is that which "is not called for by the objective situation . . . and is essentially antisocial in nature" and therefore "is not a healthy reaction, but rather an evidence of some damage to the psychological organization of the individual." Such behavior is self-defeating.

The material in this chapter bears on a wide range of hyperactive, aggressive, self-assertive, and hostile behavior — some of which is pathologically motivated, as defined above, and some of which is only the normal aggressiveness a teacher must hold within limits in the interest of classroom control.

CAUSATIVE FACTORS

What are the most likely causes of hyperaggressiveness in school situations?

1. In the first place, the hyperaggressive child may be struggling to gain ego-strength due to inferiority feelings arising from academic deficiencies, lack of love at home, denial of legitimate attention-needs at school, or membership in a minority group that is "looked down on." This kind of behavior has been discussed in the preceding chapter and will not be further developed here.

2. In some instances of hyperaggressiveness, the child is trying to assert his independence of adults (particularly his parents) in a kind of compulsive effort to "grow up" and to gain status with his peers. This latter motivation may also be found in those pupils who have been "over-praised" by a teacher for some kind of good conduct, and who feel compelled to perpetrate some antisocial acts in order to regain the respect of their classmates.

3. In other cases, the aggressively hostile child is suffering from guilt feelings that are due to sex habits or sex thoughts, to feelings that he has disappointed his parents, or to overly strict religious teachings which he has introjected but cannot live up to. The factors motivating a guilt-ridden child to hostile acts appear to be a compulsive effort to gain some ego-strength to compensate for the ravages of guilt, and to induce others to punish him for his bad behavior in order to reduce his guilt feelings through suffering or by "paying the penalty." In some instances a child in this category delights in proving to himself and to others how much punishment he can stand.

4. Some pupils are motivated to aggressive behavior against others primarily because of displaced aggression. This means that they hold hostile feelings toward certain persons but are unable to release their hostility against these persons, and consequently they "take out" these feelings against innocent individuals who happen to

be available. Thus a boy who is angry with his father may strike or verbally attack other children near him without any provocation from them. Or this same boy may hold hostile attitudes toward the teacher, and do numerous things to annoy him, because he is unconsciously motivated to perceive the teacher as a displaced hate object. This is possible since the teacher is an authority-figure similar to that of the boy's father. In other instances of irrational hostility, a child may be suffering from anxiety states, undifferentiated fear, and vague worries. Apparently such a child gets some release from muscular tensions and psychic pains by attacking innocent persons around him, since he cannot identify the "real enemies" who are bedeviling him. A teacher's responsibility in such cases is primarily that of recognizing the nature of the problem and trying to get counseling or psychiatric services for the pupils involved.

5. In most classrooms there are probably a few pupils who annoy other children around them and who irritate teachers with various types of obnoxious aggressiveness, primarily because the work-situation is too easy for them. Not being challenged by the school tasks, such pupils resort to mischief-making, partly as a source of self-assertive satisfactions and partly as a means of striking back at a situation which is frustrating to their ego needs. Obviously such a child needs to be given higher-level reading materials and more problem solving and creative work, or he may profit most from more leadership roles in the class, such as those provided through group work and realistic projects. In some instances he may need to be promoted to a higher grade.

6. In rare instances, hyperactivity with consequent aggressiveness is due primarily to a pathological physical condition within the individual, such as glandular imbalance, brain injury, or postencephalitis. When cases of very persistent and especially irrational types of hyperactivity are encountered, a teacher should take immediate steps to have such pupils referred to appropriate specialists.

CONTROLLING AND REDIRECTING

Assuming that some aggressive and hostile behavior is necessary for effective personality growth, what are some principles or general considerations of which a teacher should be aware in his efforts to control these kinds of behavior when they become excessive or inappropriate to particular situations?

Tension-reducing activities

Tension-reducing activities and program flexibility are particularly important. Especially in the kindergarten and primary grades, hyperaggressiveness that springs from disturbed emotional states may be partially controlled and directed by providing some ready means for constructive release of muscular tensions. Some teachers do this by setting up an easel (such as 3′ by 2′) with large pieces of paper for freehand paintings and drawings. Although all pupils in the class will have times to paint, the tense and restless child is encouraged to go and "paint out his feelings" whenever it appears to the teacher that this would be appropriate. Also, such a child may be allowed to go of his own accord as long as he does not abuse this privilege. This permissiveness is much more feasible when more than one easel is provided.

In addition to painting, constructive releases for hyperactive children can be made available by providing modeling clay at a special table or in the pupils' desks. Some schools go further and provide a workbench with a few tools in a side room adjoining a classroom. Also, when tensions appear to be mounting, a short active game can be introduced to give overt release for taut muscles and aggressive impulses. These are things in which an entire class can engage profitably, but they will be most beneficial to those who have accumulated tensions.

All of the above suggestions definitely lead to the conclusion that good classroom management, particularly from the standpoint of handling the problem of excess aggressiveness, is one which is characterized by considerable flexibility in schedule and procedure as opposed to highly routinized procedures and a rigid program. However, this point must be immediately counterbalanced by emphasizing that aggressively hostile children also profit by strong controls over their behavior. They need to learn that there are limits beyond which they cannot go. When these controls are exercised by a respected teacher the hostile child is given "outside support" to help him control his impulses and to bolster his weak ego. These psychological values, however, are not likely to be obtained unless the teacher is seen by the erring child as having a genuine concern for him.

In those classrooms in which "the limits" are narrow and are rigidly enforced, some pupils with strong hostile feelings may adopt the mechanism of repression described in Chapter 1, and thereafter be characterized by meekness. Such pupils generally turn their hostility inward upon themselves and develop feelings of inferiority because of their inability to assert themselves, or they may develop psychosomatic symptoms such as tics, skin eruptions, and headaches.

Utilizing aggressive, hostile behavior

An important principle in responding to aggressive and hostile acts is to try to turn such acts into social assets. What is meant here is that a teacher can sometimes utilize a hostile act to serve a group purpose and to help integrate an offender into group processes. This is often possible when pupils bring things to school (such as toads, snakes, noise-making gadgets, and peculiar decorative items) with the obvious intention of annoying other pupils and frustrating the teacher.

Instead of simply taking these things away from the offending pupils, or punishing them in some other way, a teacher can frequently ask the child to bring his possession in front of the class and tell how he caught it (in cases of live possessions) or how his particular gadget works. The animal may be utilized as an object for drawing in an art class, or become a subject for further study in science work. Inanimate objects (depending upon their peculiar qualities) may be made the center of a story, put in a class collection, or written up in a class newspaper. All this must be done in a sincere spirit of trying to turn a hostile act into a social asset. If the teacher is largely dominated with a spirit of revenge, a desire to humiliate an offender, or a desire to be clever, no good effects are likely to be forthcoming.

Other kinds of aggressive behavior which may be turned into social assets include derogatory drawings of the teacher and mimicking of other pupils or of the teacher. Those teachers who are psychologically mature and have a sense of humor can quickly devise suggestions whereby the kinds of talents mentioned above can be integrated into classroom activities. The child who makes drawings of the teacher can be asked to make additional cartoons of the teacher and of the other pupils in the class, and his drawings can be exhibited. The mimicking child can be asked to mimick, not only certain behaviors of the teacher but also some behaviors of T.V. performers and movie actors. Again these things must be done with a cheerful attitude, with poise, and with a sincere interest in trying to turn hostile acts into group contributions.

This principle may also be utilized in dealing with the problem of surreptitious reading of comic books during school study periods by having pupils produce oral or written appraisals of the personality and character make-up of their favorite comic book heroes. This may also be done through a panel discussion dealing with the merits and limitations of particular comic strips. One teacher who used these procedures in an eighth-grade class has reported that she was delighted at the insight and good sense shown by the pupils, and that, as if by common consent, the reading of comic books was thereafter confined to free-time periods.[1]

Democratic management

Aggressively hostile behavior will be less in a democratically managed classroom in which emphasis is placed on individual development and cooperative activities as opposed to authoritarian control and competition. Numerous investigations involving both children and adults have produced data in support of this statement. In a series of studies dealing with the effects of experimentally created "social climates" in boys' groups, Lewin, Lippitt, and White (13) have shown that acts of hostility may be as much as thirty times as frequent in autocratically managed as in democratically managed groups. Other studies by Haythorn (11) and by Deutsch (6) using adult subjects, have shown that in competitive as contrasted with cooperative work-situations there is significantly greater frequency of unfriendly acts and of evidences of group disharmony.

These findings are not surprising, since a severe type of authoritarian control arouses hostilities among the members of a group, and then these hostile feelings are released against each other because the

[1] Dorothy Rogers, *Mental Hygiene in Elementary Education* (Boston: Houghton Mifflin Co., 1957), pp. 99-100.

autocratic leader cannot be directly attacked. Frequently scapegoats emerge and become the innocent victims of group hostility feelings, as was the case in the boys' groups studied by Lewin, Lippitt, and White (13). Also, competitive activities, especially when greatly stressed, tend to arouse bitter feelings, jealousies, and counteraggressions to "get even."

However, it should not be assumed that competition is inherently bad. As a matter of fact, competition should be considered bad only to the extent that winning over others becomes an end in itself and the primary satisfaction obtained is one of feeling superior to those who are beaten. In such instances there is an obvious lack of genuine interest in what is being learned or accomplished.

The more emphasis is placed on some kind of badge of superiority (such as a star, a pennant, or an A grade) the less we would expect to find evidences of intrinsic motivations. Also, in a school situation in which striving for external rewards is the paramount objective, some children become so anxious that they cannot admit real failures; they cover up and defend their inadequacies and thus are unable to profit from their experiences. Furthermore, some pupils who are very capable in winning these external rewards nevertheless develop anxiety lest their successes result in psychological barriers between themselves and their classmates. Other pupils may engage in dishonest acts since they are motivated to win at any cost. Still other pupils who are never among the winners, particularly for academic honors, become discouraged and lower their aspiration levels — sometimes below their actual abilities.

The need of developing cooperative skills and attitudes in schools is greater now than a generation ago, since our adult society has become more highly organized and operates more through committees and other kinds of groups and subgroups. This trend has been variously referred to by numerous writers as the "new individualism."[2] In other words, more and more individuals are finding that in our highly interdependent society they must find expression for their initiative, aggressiveness, and creative abilities through various kinds of groups and corporate bodies rather than simply through individual

[2] *Fortune,* February 1959, 6, 113. Also see references at end of chapter by Callahan (3) and Counts (4).

endeavors. This does not mean, however, that the individual no longer counts; it only means that cooperative skills and attitudes are more essential for the effective expression of individual contributions. This condition of affairs, together with a caution against its dangers, is well stated by Lindeman (14), a sociologist, when he says:

> Healthy-mindedness resides in the art of operating through groups without becoming groupized, collectivized. The "plot" of most modern societies has become a group affair. All important activities sooner or later tend to become organized. There is no way of avoiding group experience, except in eccentric individualism. In fact, it is probably more correct to assume that healthy-mindedness can only be attained through the proper participation in group experience. But it still remains true that an individual who subordinates himself completely to collective control thereby sacrifices an element of health.

Value of competitive effort

There are positive values of various kinds in competitive efforts. In spite of the above criticisms there are, nevertheless, some real advantages in competitive efforts, both for general personality development and for the constructive direction of aggressive and hostile behavior. These advantages are most likely to be found when competitive endeavors are used moderately and therefore are not the regular "order of the day," when those who are superior are not constantly played up (such as having those who make a 100 on a test hold up their hands or stand up), and instead, when competition is viewed as a source of self-actualization. A child (or an adult) who tries his skill or his knowledge against others learns more definitely his strengths and weaknesses, he learns if he is as good as he thought he was, and he becomes more differentiated as a total person.

An additional positive consideration in regard to competition is that it is one way through which frustration tolerance can be developed. Through numerous trials of his knowledge and skills against the knowledge and skills of others, a child discovers not only his strengths but also his weaknesses, and he experiences some failures.

Provided that these discoveries and failure-experiences are not too severe or overwhelming, they can and should be an important source of learning to tolerate the fact of limitations and to tolerate the feelings of frustration arising from these learnings. Many psychologists and psychiatrists have emphasized the importance of *high frustration tolerance* as a bulwark against the anxieties created by our modern complex society. Although it is undoubtedly true that high frustration tolerance is due largely to positive self-regarding attitudes and to self-confidence based on real successes, it seems equally apparent that a real contribution is also obtained from being able to "stand up to" a realization of inadequacies and failures in particular areas. A child who is reared in a social climate that "leans over backwards" to avoid competitive situations may be overprotected from frustrations and thus be deprived of some important psychological bricks necessary to build a strong personality. Lacking these supports he may engage in various forms of excessive aggressiveness in a blind struggle for ego-strength.

Teachers, therefore, should not take an absolute or arbitrary stand against competition, but rather they should encourage their pupils to look upon competition primarily as a means of self-improvement and as a source of enjoyment both on an individual and a group basis. They should try to counteract the use of competitive successes primarily as sources of feelings of power over others. These attitudes can be promoted through class discussions on the uses and abuses of competition, through role-playing situations that portray good and bad attitudes toward competition, through classroom and playground practices that avoid excessive attention to winners, and, as emphasized above, by promoting cooperative activities in which each one is expected to make his contribution to a committee, class, or school endeavor.

Furthermore, pupils can be encouraged to compete against their own previous records or performances regardless of how good or poor these may have been, and without reference to what other pupils are doing. Some kinds of recognition can be given to those who improve the most or who improve their records by a certain number of points. Competition between groups or between teams also helps to reduce the emphasis on individual superiority over others and brings about a better distribution of success-feelings, since all the members of a group or team can share in such satisfactions.

However, the main emphasis of teachers in evaluating pupils' efforts, whether in group or individual work, should be to stimulate the pupils to evaluate their own efforts and those of others, not on the basis of whose is the best, but rather on the basis of strong and weak points and on ways of improving. This kind of evaluative emphasis applies particularly to oral reports, art products, musical renditions, role-playing skits, and dramatizations.

CONSTRUCTIVE USE OF PUNISHMENTS

Probably all teachers make use of some form of punishment — if punishment is defined as including all those actions taken against another person for the obvious or expressed purpose of restraining or controlling some of his present or latent patterns of response. Probably, too, all educators would agree that some punishments are necessary for successful classroom management — at least under typical public school conditions. The issue before us, then, is not whether "to punish or not to punish" but rather what kinds of punishment are most likely to promote mental hygiene objectives. What principles and procedures should a teacher keep in mind who wishes to utilize punishments as aids in the personality development of children? Some of these have been described in the preceding section dealing with general considerations. In this section attention is centered on more specific suggestions bearing on the uses and abuses of punishments.

Identification with teacher

In the first place, it should be understood that the effect of any kind of punishment, correction, or disciplinary control imposed on a child will be greatly affected by the extent to which this child likes or admires the teacher. The more positive feelings a child holds toward a teacher, and the more he regards the teacher as a kind of ego-ideal, the more the teacher's corrective efforts will tend to be incorporated into the child's behavior. Conversely, the more social distance there is between a child and his teacher, the more the teacher's corrective efforts will be rejected, although there may be some outward conformity for the sake of avoiding consequences. There would seldom be, however, a one-to-one correspondence between the degree of positive and negative feelings which a child holds toward a teacher and the effectiveness of this teacher's punishments, since there would nearly always be other influences affecting the child's responses, such as the expectations of classmates or of parents.

The theory involved in this point is that when a child has some feelings of affiliation with the teacher, he wants to hold the teacher's approval and he fears that this approval may be lost if the teacher is disappointed in him. Thus, a child's introjection of a teacher's behavior standards depends upon both affection and fear. If positive feelings exist for the teacher but the child has no fear of him, due to the fact that the teacher does not disapprove or punish no matter what the child does, then the introjection of the teacher's standards will be weakened or completely negated. This happens because the teacher does not help the child to discriminate between good and bad conduct; in fact, it may appear to the child that the teacher has no standards for him to introject since "anything goes." This emphasizes the need of some forms of punishments for promoting personality growth.

Mild vs. severe punishments

Another principle that should be followed in classroom discipline is that punishments administered to children should be mild rather than severe. This is a general principle and cannot always be followed, especially in cases of persistent offenders who have already been subjected to severe punishments at home and school. In such instances some drastic measure such as temporary suspension from school may be necessary.

The theory in support of mild punishments is that such punishments are less damaging to a child's self-feelings and are therefore less likely to lead to extreme kinds of defensive reactions. Mild punishments include such measures as verbal corrections in regard to specific things to be done or not done, temporary deprivation of privileges, making up time wasted, change of position in the classroom group, repairing of damage done, loss of some kind of leadership role (such as a part in a play or chairmanship of a group), and the taking away of distracting objects.

An additional point to stress in regard to mild punishments is that severe punishments sometimes result in repression, i.e., a child may be so frightened by severe treatment or the threat of it, that he unconsciously forces certain impulses or thoughts out of his conscious mind. For example, a sensitive child who needs to be more assertive may completely repress all aggressive impulses after being severely reprimanded for a minor infraction of rules. Other sensitive pupils who only witness severe punishments may be so frightened that they repress normal desires to speak out in class, to be spontaneous, or even to stand up for their rights against attackers.

Leeway for deviate behavior

The above remarks in regard to nearly all punishments being mild rather than severe should not create the impression that every deviation from conduct codes should be punished — either mildly or otherwise. Competent teachers realize that a smoothly functioning classroom control is facilitated by allowing some leeway for the appearance of minor types of deviate behavior. The maxim "do not let an exception occur" is too rigid and arbitrary since it does not take into consideration the drive, which is present in most children, to be at least mildly aggressive in order to satisfy their needs for ego-assertion. To such children (especially boys) a very strict adherence to rules and social definitions is very frustrating and often leads to daring and explosive outbursts "against the regime." The point is that the social stability of a group is more solidly based when some flexibility is allowed in the group structure. A teacher must learn to react to a good many minor deviations by ignoring them or by responding to them with a sense of humor. Just how much flexibility should be allowed cannot be stated in exact terms, since the amount safely permitted would vary greatly with different classes and teachers. This is an area in which successful teaching is indeed an art and not a science.

Clear and immediate punishments

In working with children it seems to be highly desirable that punishments be clearly defined and administered rather quickly after an offense, as opposed to being vaguely defined and postponed until the next day or next week. The basis for this statement is that punishments which are clearly understood and quickly administered are much less likely to produce anxiety states than are those which are postponed. This is true because, in the first instance, the offensive act is dealt with "on the spot" and the incident is closed, whereas, in the second instance, the child is left to brood over his behavior and to become anxious over what is going to happen to him. Some sensitive children have become so upset over vague threats of punishments to be given the next day, that they have been unable to eat supper, cannot sleep, and in a few instances have refused to go back to school until one of the parents has seen the teacher and obtained an agreement on just what the punishment is to be and made arrangements to get it over with. Such anxiety states create barriers between a child and a teacher and thus greatly reduce the effectiveness of the teacher's constructive efforts for the child.

Knowledge of pupils' motivations

One of the requirements for successful handling of disciplinary situations is to be able to adapt corrective measures to particular children as a consequence of knowledge of their motivations. An example of what is meant here is found in an incident that occurred in the second grade. The class was engaged in a project in which various materials were utilized, including a bucket of water. During the course of this activity the teacher spoke firmly to a particular girl and asked her to stop making a distracting noise. The girl flared up and said, "What would you do if I threw this bucket of water on you?" Here was a situation calling for some kind of disciplinary action. What should the teacher do?

In this instance the teacher's quick insight into the motivations of this girl led to an easy resolution of the flare-up. She was sure that she was liked and admired by this girl and she was equally sure that this child was rejected by her mother. Consequently, when the girl made her threat the teacher sensed immediately that this was an impulsive act motivated by the desire to test the teacher's affection. Although not well verbalized by the girl, it seemed highly probable that she had frequently wondered if the teacher's interest in her was genuine or "Will she let me down, like my mother has?" The teacher's scolding was a sufficient stimulus to trigger off the girl's anxious and hostile feelings. What did the teacher do? She looked at the girl intently and then said in a quiet but firm voice: "But, you wouldn't do it." The girl responded with the flicker of a smile and turned to her assigned duties. The incident was closed.

In the case of another child who had had a different kind of relationship with the teacher, and whose motivations were differently assessed, the teacher's response toward a very similar incident would be considerably different. Also it does not follow that this same teacher would make a similar response to another disciplinary incident involving the same child.

It is sometimes said that teachers, as well as parents, should be consistent in their handling of a child, especially in regard to punishments. This should not, however, be interpreted to mean that exactly the same responses must be made to the same kinds of disciplinary incidents, since circumstances and motivations constantly vary. The only legitimate basis for consistency in punishment is always to have in mind the best, long-range interests of the child, as opposed to mere expediency, revenge, or release of anger.

Importance of pupils' discussion

One practice of general value in attaining better direction of aggressive behavior in school settings is to have pupils discuss the implications of disciplinary incidents. When any such incident is approached a teacher should not be dominated by an attitude of "Who is to blame here?" but rather by an attitude of "Let us see if we can find out what led up to this trouble." There should be a *we* approach with the purpose of determining causes rather than simply to fix blame. Furthermore, the pupils involved should be encouraged to discuss how a similar incident could be avoided in the future. Sometimes an entire class can participate in this "how to avoid" type of discussion. Through such procedures students can be helped to think about their conduct and thus to make progress in establishing rational controls. Furthermore, when pupils have a responsible part in setting up rules for regulating their group affairs they are much more likely to become ego-involved with these controls and therefore to want to abide by them and to help see to it that others in the group do likewise.

When a disciplinary incident is handled simply with punishments and is not analyzed in regard to causes or discussed in terms of broader implications, the whole experience is left on a purely specific level and nothing may be learned either by the offenders or other group members. However, not all disciplinary incidents should be dealt with on this broader basis. Some are too minor, and in other instances the problems are highly personal, such as those involving stealing or sex offenses. Open discussion of these kinds of conduct problems can be very embarrassing to the offenders and thus create additional burdens for them.

In many schools, particularly on the secondary level, some type of student jury or student court is established and given considerable responsibility in dealing with certain kinds of disciplinary problems and making recommendations to administrative officials in regard to both corrective and punitive actions. It would seem that in these student groups special emphasis should be placed on investigating why a particular disciplinary incident arose and how similar ones could be avoided in the future, rather than placing major attention on fixing blame and finding someone to punish. When the latter emphasis is paramount the students are trained to believe that the only way to deal with a problem is to find a so-called culprit and then devise ways to make him suffer.

The value of discussing the implications of a disciplinary incident, and of considering future alternative actions, is emphasized when it is realized that there is no guarantee that children will learn anything from punishments *as such* except what not to do in specific circumstances. There is no assurance that they will learn what *to do* in a positive way to avoid future punishments. The old admonition "Behave yourself," assumes that the child always knows exactly what he *should* do, but this is not always true. There are many children, for example, who have learned from numerous punishments what they should not do to attract attention to themselves, but they have not learned what they can or should do to gain some favorable attention. This requires guidance and instruction beyond anything punishments can do. As a matter of fact, in complex situations we cannot assume that a child learns from punishments even what he should not do, since circumstances are constantly varying and many children have poor insight into the consequences of their behavior.

Undesirability of "name-calling"

A particularly vicious disciplinary practice is that of calling a child bad names such as idiot, simpleton, delinquent, barbarian, blockhead, dumbbell, liar, etc. Such terms are generally highly inaccurate and unfair in reference to what a child has actually done, and they also arouse hostility responses and create barriers between the child and the teacher — both of which work against the utilization of a disciplinary incident for personality development. Name-calling has particularly bad psychological effects since the implication is very clear (even if not actually intended) that the total child fits the bad name rather than simply a particular act, thus constituting an attack on a child's conception of himself. As stated previously, however, this kind of name-callng will have little effect on a child who rejects the teacher.

Undesirability of group punishments

Another bad disciplinary practice is that of punishing a whole class for the offenses of a few individuals. This is done generally because the teacher cannot identify the particular offenders or because he hopes that by punishing the whole class the "well-behaving" pupils will be stimulated to help induce the "misbehaving" pupils to change their ways and "get in line." Punishments in this category usually include keeping a whole class after school or depriving them of their play period because "some pupils talked too much," or making a whole class write an extra theme because some students misbehaved while the teacher was out of the room. Since such practices are manifestly unfair to those who have "done no wrong," they create additional psychological barriers between the pupils and the teacher.

Undesirability of sarcasm and ridicule

The use of sarcasm and ridicule by teachers as a method of punishment or control has been universally condemned from a mental hygiene point of view, yet a visit to almost any school will reveal that these psychological whips are still being used.

In one second-grade room visited by the writer, the teacher made six sarcastic and belittling remarks within less than an hour. For example, she said to a girl who forgot to bring her pencil to a reading group: "If you can't remember your pencil you are not big enough to do second-grade work. There is a second-grade class in here every year. I'll save a seat for you for next year."

The teacher of a sixth-grade class in a small town felt a strong obligation to squelch all "boy-girl relationships." Whenever she discovered a boy and girl engaging in what she considered to be a flirtation, she endeavored to humiliate them by requiring them to come before the class and smile, wink, and "make eyes" at each other for ten or fifteen minutes.

Since sarcasm, ridicule, and other types of humiliation are ego-devaluating, they are among the worst forms of punishments, especially with small children; in many instances they are undoubtedly more damaging to a child's personality development than are physical blows. Here again, the seriousness of these psychological blows to a child's ego structure will depend to a large extent upon the degree of respect and affiliation which the child feels toward the teacher. It will also be affected by the extent to which this child believes the teacher is respected by other class members.

Undesirability of nagging

Teachers should occasionally check on themselves to make sure they are not doing a lot of nagging, either of particular pupils or of a whole class. Constant nagging is a persistent reminder to pupils of their "falling short of expectations," while at the same time no effective action is taken to remove the sources of the teacher's complaints. The result is constant ego-devaluation of the pupils together with loss of respect for the teacher.

Fallacy of punishments that "work"

Quite frequently teachers are heard to say that a certain form of punishment is good because "it works." Although there may be considerable validity in such statements there is no assurance that any educational or mental hygiene objective has been promoted when there is not a clear statement of what is meant by "it works." If all that is intended in this phrase is that somehow a child is made to submit to external authority, it is obvious that developmental objectives are not being fostered. Instead, only teacher-control objectives are promoted. The phrase "it works" must also be evaluated in reference to a particular set of values.

Sometimes disciplinary practices that are initiated and voted on by classmates may also "work" in the sense of bringing about submission of a particular child to group pressure, but without regard to mental hygiene principles. For example, a writer of a journal article (18) reports the case of an aggressive, quarrelsome boy in a fourth grade who was punished by his classmates by being forced into social isolation. He was made to sit in a corner by himself, was not spoken to by anyone, had to eat alone, was avoided in the halls, received no help from anyone, and was barred from participation in class games, trips, and projects. After fifteen days of this kind of treatment, the boy submitted to the group pressure, asked to be taken out of isolation, said he was sorry for his previous misconduct (although he still did not know why he acted that way), and is said by the writer of the article to have "caused no more trouble."

Although there is no way of knowing from this journal article how such extreme social isolation affected this problem boy, it is probable that from a mental hygiene point of view his last condition was worse than the first, since apparently he simply repressed his hostile impulses and adopted a superficial conformity in order to avoid group ostracism.

Certainly any teacher who is genuinely interested in children will want to examine any disciplinary practice, whether imposed by an adult or by a peer-group, from the standpoint of its personality effects upon the individuals punished, and not simply from the standpoint of whether "it works" because "we had no more trouble from him."

REFERENCES

1. Baumgardner, C. H., "Some Elementary Principles of Discipline," *The School Review,* 63, 1955, 347-348.
2. Bond, Jesse A., "Analysis of Observed Traits of Teachers Who Were Rated Superior in School Discipline," *Journal of Educational Research,* 45, 1952, 507-516.
3. Callahan, R. C., *Introduction to Education in American Society.* New York: Alfred A. Knopf, Inc., pp. 158-164.
4. Counts, G. S., *Education and American Civilization,* Ch. IX. New York: Bureau of Publications, Teachers College, Columbia University, 1952.
5. Cunningham, R., "Group Discipline," *National Education Association Journal,* 38, 1949, 34-35.
6. Deutsch, M., "The Effects of Cooperation and Competition upon Group Process," *Human Relations,* 2, 1949, 129-152 and 199-231.
7. ———, "The Effects of Cooperation and Competition upon Group Process," *Group Dynamics,* Ch. XXIII, ed. Dorwin Cartwright and Alvin Zander. Evanston, Illinois: Row-Peterson and Co., 1953, p. 642.
8. Du Bois, F. S., "The Security of Discipline," *Mental Hygiene,* 36, 1952, 353-372.
9. Hartley, R. E., "Some Safety Valves in Play," *Child Study,* 34, 1957, 12-14.
10. Havighurst, R. J., "What to Do About the Tough Hostile Boy," *Phi Delta Kappan,* 30, 1958, 136-138.
11. Haythorn, W., "The Influence of Individual Members on the Characteristics of Small Groups," *Journal of Abnormal and Social Psychology,* 48, 1953, 276-284.
12. Hunter, E. C., "Changes in Teachers' Attitudes Toward Children's Behavior over the Last Thirty Years," *Mental Hygiene,* 41, 1957, 3-10.
13. Lewin, K., R. Lippitt, and R. K. White, "Patterns of Aggressive Behavior in Experimentally Created 'Social Climates,'" *Journal of Social Psychology,* 10, 1939, 271-299.
14. Lindeman, E. C., *Mental Hygiene and the Moral Crisis of Our Time.* Austin, Texas: The Hogg Foundation for Mental Hygiene, The University of Texas, 1952.
15. Mummery, D. V., "An Analytical Study of Ascendant Behavior of Preschool Children," *Child Development,* 18, 1947, 40-81.
16. Newman, R. G., "The Acting Out Boy," *Exceptional Children,* 22, 1956, 186-190.
17. Page, M. L., "The Modification of Ascendant Behavior on Preschool Children," *University of Iowa Study of Child Welfare,* No. 3, 12, 1936.

18. Reynolds, Mary S., "Who Should Discipline?" *Educational Forum,* 20, 1955-56, 457-465.

19. Riccie, A. C. and H. J. Peters, "Needed: Cooperation and Competition in the School Program," *Phi Delta Kappan,* 30, 1958, 97-99.

20. Rockwell, J. C., "Pupil Responsibility for Behavior," *Elementary School Journal,* 51, 1950-51, 266-270.

21. Sager, C. J., "The Concept of Aggression in Modern Psychiatry," *Mental Hygiene,* 36, 1952, 210-219.

22. Siegel, Alberta Engvall, "Film-mediated Fantasy Aggression and Strength of Aggressive Drive," *Child Development,* 27, 1956, 365-378.

23. Small, S. M., "Psychiatric Evaluation of the Educator's Role in Mental Health," *Mental Hygiene,* 41, 1957, 61-65.

24. Stouffer, G. A. and Jennie Owens, "Behavior Problems of Children as Identified by Today's Teachers and Compared with Those Reported by E. K. Wickman," *Journal of Educational Research,* 48, 1955, 321-331.

25. Thompson, G. G., "The Social and Emotional Development of Preschool Children under Two Types of Educational Program," *Psychological Monographs,* No. 5, 56, 1944.

26. Wickman, E. K., "Children's Behavior and Teacher's Attitudes." New York: *The Commonwealth Fund,* 1928.

QUESTIONS AND EXERCISES

1. Locate a hyperaggressive, hostile type of child in your neighborhood or in one of your local schools and find out all you can about him in an effort to understand the basis for his behavior.
2. In what sense is hostility behavior an outgrowth of weakness or of failure?
3. What psychological gains does a hostile child obtain even though he is frequently punished?
4. What criteria can you have for distinguishing between a compulsively hostile child and an aggressive child who is just "full of energy"?
5. Find out what clinics or other specialized resources are available in or near your community where a child could be referred for counseling or other types of treatment.
6. Describe the kind of classroom management under which there would likely be the least amount of irrational aggressiveness and hostility.

7. Stimulate a class discussion on how a school can maintain a desirable balance between competitive and cooperative activities.
8. Give examples from your own school experience of teachers who used very poor methods of punishment and also of teachers who used psychologically sound punishments.
9. Point out the fallacy that may be involved in saying that a method of punishment is good because "it works."

SELECTED FILMS

Angry Boy. 32 minutes. Portrays a case of stealing at school and shows relationship of this conduct to emotional problems.

Balloons: Aggression and Destructive Games. 18 minutes. Presents an experimental-type situation to illustrate differences in aggressive trends in young children.

The Feeling of Hostility. 16 minutes. Dramatizes one case to show causes and effects of hostility in personal relationships.

Maintaining Classroom Discipline. 14 minutes. Shows good and poor methods of controlling a class.

5

SOCIAL ASPECTS OF MENTAL

A FREQUENT SOURCE of inner stress and of interpersonal difficulties among school children is some kind of obvious deviation from group norms in physical characteristics and mental abilities. These deviations may constitute problems within themselves, but their seriousness is frequently intensified by unfavorable social valuations placed on them within a particular peer-group culture. In a society such as ours in which much emphasis is placed on competitive striving, and in which large rewards frequently await those who win, it is easy to see that a child's status in

AND PHYSICAL ABILITIES

those physical and mental characteristics which enable him to share in these rewards is of first-rate importance to his feelings of personal worth and to his social adequacy. How well he rates or compares with others in any physical property or area of intellectual competence has numerous mental health implications.

Since those children who fall within the normal range of their school groups in physical and mental characteristics do not experience problems from these sources, except when extreme demands are made upon them, attention in this chapter will be centered primarily on those pupils who deviate from group norms in some physical or mental traits to the extent that they are noticeably different.

In the first place, it is evident that upward deviations from a group norm have obvious personal and social advantages, especially when these deviations enable a person to cope more effectively with his environment or when these deviations carry prestige value in his particular group. From the standpoint of social consequences, the individual who is superior in one or more physical skills or mental abilities has an essential asset for arousing admiration and inspiring identification. Others endow him with prestige status, are suggestible in reference to his ideas and behavior, and are proud to be associated with him, provided he is not ineffective or obnoxious as a person. Furthermore, the child who is superior in one or more important skills and abilities has an essential ingredient for building the ego-strength required to complete his developmental tasks, and for achieving self-realization. Although a very high degree of competence is sometimes found in individuals who are emotionally and socially immature, the mental-health point of view stresses both the possibility and the desirability of outstanding contributions to society arising from people who are strong in personality assets, rather than assuming that such contributions can be had only at the expense of serious personal maladjustment.

PHYSICAL CHARACTERISTICS

Since many physical characteristics such as height, weight, features, body-proportions, etc., can be readily observed, they are certain to be involved in numerous social evaluations. This is especially true in a society such as ours where many forms of communication, including national advertising, clearly stress which kinds of physical qualities are desirable and which are undesirable.

Competence in physical skills

Probably all elementary school teachers have observed that those pupils, especially boys, who are most successful on the playground are frequently the ones who have high social prestige in their respective groups, and are quite generally admired as persons. These observations are supported by Hardy's study of 215 pupils in Joliet, Illinois, in which it was shown that seventy per cent of the best-liked children scored above the means of their respective groups in a wide variety of physical achievement tests (11).

For boys, social prestige continues through our secondary schools to be strongly associated with superiority in physical skills. This point is clearly shown in a study of over 400 junior high school boys in Austin, Texas, in which degrees of physical skill were determined by performance on designated tests, ratings on all-around athletic ability, and extent of experience in one or more sports (22). On each of these criteria, those boys who were superior were found, as a group, to show statistically reliable differences over all other boys in the population studied in measurements of personal desirability. Especially marked were the differences between the best-liked and the least-liked boys. For example, one-half of the former were outstanding in one or more of the criteria of physical skills listed above, whereas three-fourths of the latter received no nominations as all-around athletes, and very few had had experience in a school sport.

These findings emphasize that one of the ways to promote the social adjustment of a boy is to help him to participate effectively in one or more physical skills. Outside of school activities this goal is being achieved for many boys through sports programs promoted by community recreational agencies after school hours and on week ends. Members of school staffs often take leadership roles in these programs.

Although physical activities are obviously important for the development of health and vigor among girls, and although some elementary school girls are proud of how fast they can run or how far they can throw a ball, competence in physical skills is never so essential to the personal or social adequacy of girls as it is to that of boys. Lest this point be overstressed, attention should be called to the fact that there are some boys who attain a high degree of both personal adequacy and social prestige who are not outstanding in any form of physical skill.

Over-age and under-age children

One of the physical characteristics in which some children deviate from the normal range of their school groupings is that of being over-age or under-age.

Problems arising from being over-age are confined almost entirely to the elementary school. On this level, some authorities believe that a child who is more than one year older than the median for his grade is very likely to be in a condition of psychological stress and social difficulty.[1] The greater the age-differential the greater the likelihood that the over-age child will be involved in both internal and external conflicts. In Bedoian's study of over-age pupils in twenty-two sixth grades these children were found to be, as a group, less acceptable as persons and more rejected than either average-age or under-age pupils (2).

It seems evident that the problems of the over-age child are due primarily to his feelings of inferiority over his academic failures, his resentment at being kept back with younger pupils, and the additional fact that he is seldom succeeding in his studies any better than when he was first exposed to them. Although there are instances of children who have apparently profited by repeating a grade, the best educational policy in regard to very slow learners seems to be not general retardation but a more differentiated curriculum adapted to their needs and abilities.

In regard to the under-age child, our data are much more favorable. Although cases of children young for their grade-levels can certainly be found, displaying immaturity and showing numerous signs of social maladjustment, this is not the general picture. A comprehensive study in Evanston, Illinois, by Vera Miller has shown that 113 pupils who were young for their grade-levels had a very favorable status, as compared with other pupils of their respective classes, in intelligence, academic standing, leadership, popularity with classmates, and personality ratings by teachers. The author concludes that her data "give little foundation for the concern that children younger than the average are injured from the standpoint of mental health by early admission to school." (24 — p. 261.)

Body size

In our culture, social problems arising from body size are confined largely to very small size in boys, extra tallness in girls, and obesity in both sexes.

Teachers have frequently observed that many boys who are very small for their age show signs of feeling inferior and may overcom-

[1] This is the position taken by Rogers from his Columbus, Ohio, study as quoted in *Identification of Maladjusted School Children,* a publication of the Federal Security Agency, Public Health Service, Monograph No. 7, p. 6.

pensate by extreme conscientiousness in schoolwork or by some kind of troublesome behavior. These observations are borne out by Dimock's study of three groups of thirty boys. These three groups were equalized in regard to chronological age, but one group was composed of boys *all* of whom were superior in height, weight, and strength; another one was composed of boys *all* of whom were average in these three traits; while the third group consisted of boys *all* of whom were inferior in height, weight and strength. From the results of a personality self-rating scale it was discovered that the boys in the third group were characterized by considerably greater amounts of feelings of difference, criticism of others, self-criticism, and inferiority attitudes. Also the boys of inferior size and strength had, as a group, many more unreciprocated friendship choices than was true of those in the other two groups, showing a higher degree of unrealistic appraisal of the attitudes of others (6).

These findings from group comparisons should not obscure the fact that some very small boys make good personal-social adjustments. The extent to which they do depends on how they have been taught (chiefly by their parents) to evaluate their small size, how much they have been compared unfavorably with other boys, how much they have been helped to succeed in physical activities (such as swimming, tennis, or skating) that do not put a premium on size, and also how much they have been helped to succeed in lines of endeavor other than physical activities (such as music, writing, and speaking). A good many small boys have grown up to be successful adults with their share or more of admirers and friends, when their development has been such that they have not devaluated themselves because of their size and have been helped to acquire compensating assets in both skills and personal qualities.

Apparently the main thing that an extra tall girl needs to learn is to accept the fact of her tallness and make the best of it rather than try to deny it by stooping over, or by developing exaggerated feelings of difference. Most people look upon personality assets and the ability to contribute to others as of much greater importance than any aspect of physical size, whether this aspect be favorably or unfavorably regarded.

The same can be said for cases of obesity. It is particularly important to develop in these individuals personal assets, ego-strength, and social skills, since clinical studies have shown that in many instances persistent overeating is a compensation for inferiority feelings and social failures.

Late physical maturation in boys

Several studies by Mary C. Jones (16-17) and by Mussen and Jones (26) have shown that boys who are late in reaching physical and sexual maturity are likely to encounter a generally unfavorable sociopsychological environment. As a group, such boys are found from adult ratings, from peer ratings, and from projective test data to be characterized — to a reliably greater extent than are early maturing boys — by immature social behavior, negative self-conceptions, feelings of inferiority, greater dependency needs, rebellious attitudes toward parents, and feelings of being rejected and dominated. It is important for teachers, and especially physical education teachers, to be sensitive to the social and psychological problems confronting late maturing boys and to try to help them attain the kinds of skills and attitudes that will reduce the severity of these problems. This point gains added emphasis from the fact that Mary Cover Jones' follow-up study of twenty late and early maturing boys into adult life has shown that, as a group, the late maturing boys were still characterized by more psychological handicaps than were those who matured early (16).

Physical defects and general health

It seems likely that the extent to which a physical handicap is a social barrier depends not so much upon the obviousness or the seriousness of the defect, as upon the extent to which it is irritating or obnoxious to others. For example, a habit spasm such as abnormal blinking or persistent sniffling is usually a greater social barrier than something much more serious, such as a paralyzed arm or being in a wheel chair — conditions which generally do not irritate others. In Jastak's report (p. 31) on social adjustments among children in Delaware's schools, he points out how facial blemishes, peculiar blinking, habit spasms, and unusual gait were involved in certain cases of isolation and rejection (13). On the other hand, in one of the writer's studies in several elementary school classes, no relationship was found between acceptability by classmates and number of tooth cavities, enlarged or inflamed tonsils, certain eye and ear defects, and extremes in basal metabolism. None of these conditions resulted in irritations in interpersonal contacts, although in a few instances the health implications were serious. Of course, in some cases such conditions as listed above could constitute social barriers. For example, serious eye defects such as being cross-eyed, or having severe loss of hearing, are obvious social handicaps. In one report by Lion, O'Neill, and Prager, case-study material is presented to show how cross-eyed children are frequently maladjusted in social groups, are hypersensitive, and may engage in antisocial acts as a means of retaliation for their interpersonal isolation (21). These authors also show how marked improvement in social adjustment can result from having the cross-eyed condition corrected.

That good general health conditions are associated with superior personal-social adjustments is substantiated in Hardy's study in which the data show that best-liked children have, as a group, much greater freedom from physical defects, better nutritional status, and superior general health ratings on several physical examinations (11).

Hardy's findings are completely supported in data reported by Jones from the California Adolescent Growth Study. As one phase of this study, ten of the strongest boys (determined by strength examinations at 17½ years of age) were contrasted with ten boys who were low on the same strength examinations. This contrast revealed that the boys high in strength were also generally high in other aspects of prestige, group acceptability, and personal adjustment. On the other hand, the boys low in strength were found to be generally low in interpersonal status and were characterized by feelings of inferiority and personal maladjustments. None of the low ones had a robust body structure and their health records were filled with physical difficulties (15). As Jones says: "Childhood diseases were numerous and severe in this group, with frequent colds, digestive upsets and other minor disorders during adolescence. In terms of their medical histories, nine of the ten cases would be classified as exceptionally subject to illness."

Jones points out that it is difficult to know to what extent physical deficiencies tend to produce social and personal difficulties, and to what extent the latter tend to produce the former. Probably there is always a reciprocal relationship between these two variables. However, there is a real possibility, as Jones suggests, that there is such a thing as "general fitness of the organism" which predisposes a person "by at least a small common tendency to both physical and psychological soundness. In the case of those who may have some kind of underlying biological weakness, they appear to be characterized not only by poor physical development and greater susceptibility to illness, but also by lack of vigor in social encounters and in meeting personal problems."

An interesting collaboration of Jones' data is found in a report on injury proneness among twenty-two pupils in a second grade at the University Elementary School of the University of Michigan. A careful record of all injuries and first-aid referrals throughout a school year showed that the most popular children (based on choices on four criteria) were hurt the least and the most unpopular ones were hurt the most. The socially isolated children also differed from the popular ones in that a higher proportion of their injuries had their origin in social conflict situations (9).

The foregoing analysis and summary of research data point to a fairly close relationship between physical and mental health. Obviously one of the first steps that teachers should take in trying to aid a child with personality difficulties should be to utilize all available resources for correcting physical defects and for building up health assets whenever weaknesses in these areas are found.

Special aids for the physically handicapped

In a good many instances it is impossible to correct a physical handicap. In such cases the objectives of mental hygiene can best be served by helping these handicapped individuals to make the best of themselves in spite of their limitations. Below are listed some suggestions for accomplishing this end in school situations.

1. Provide for their making some kind of contribution to their respective groups, including some ways whereby they can be of real service to at least a few others, such as helping certain pupils with a phase of school work.
2. Give recognition to their contributions but do not overpraise.

3. Expect them to perform according to the normal standards of their groups except in situations in which their handicaps constitute an insurmountable barrier.
4. In some cases that seem to justify it, teach them to perform well in a particular area in spite of their handicaps (such as playing baseball with only one arm), or to develop compensatory assets in other areas.
5. Teach them that their own acceptance of themselves as persons of worth and value is essential to their being accepted as equals by others.[2] One step in this direction is to help each one accept his handicap for what it is without trying to hide it or deny it, as evidenced by such behavior as: refusal to wear hearing aids or glasses or to take visual-training exercises when these are needed, a belligerent attitude toward anyone who mentions his particular handicap, compulsive and overcompensatory efforts to prove himself superior to others, and persistence in pursuing a type of work or vocational goal without adequate consideration of limitations imposed by his handicap.
6. Teach them to avoid at all costs both self-blame and self-pity, and to realize that many of the nonphysically handicapped have serious problems of other types.
7. Do not allow them to use their handicaps to gain advantages that would not ordinarily accrue to them, or to escape the normal consequences of their actions, as in the case of a boy who would frequently perpetrate some kind of annoyance upon others and when attacked would shout: "Don't touch me. I've got something wrong with my heart."
8. Finally, acquaint them through talks, class discussions, and readings with the many examples of people such as Glenn Cunningham and Franklin D. Roosevelt who have achieved great things in spite of serious handicaps. Such material, however, should also include examples of handicapped persons who have succeeded in the smaller niches of life.

---

[2] Some excellent material on this point is given in the reference at the end of the chapter by Ladieu, Hanfmann, and Dembo (20) in regard to this problem among seriously injured World War II veterans.

Appearance

Physical appearance as determined by grooming, dress, neatness, and cleanliness has obvious social consequences. Nothing about us is more evident to others or more quickly evaluated than our appearance. The boy or girl who is "good-looking" and is attractively attired has a marked advantage, particularly in middle-class groups; conversely, the child in these groups whose appearance is very bad has an almost insurmountable handicap.

These statements are borne out by several investigations among elementary school populations by Hardy (11), by Northway (27), and by Young and Cooper (33). In the latter study, an intensive analysis of physical attractiveness was made as a differentiating factor between fifty popular children and a contrasting group of isolated pupils. On the basis of several different rating procedures by school staff members, the popular children consistently showed statistically reliable advantages over the isolated pupils.

Among older subjects, personal appearance still plays a very favorable role in interpersonal affairs, but there is some evidence to indicate that a good many older adolescents are able to make more discriminating judgments than are children in regard to the relative importance of appearance.

This point is illustrated in Kuhlen and Lee's study of approximately four hundred pupils in grades 6, 9, and 12 in a community in upper New York state. These subjects responded to a sociometric test (including nine criteria) and also rated each other on various traits on a "Guess Who" type of measurement. Results showed that both sex groups rated "good-looking" as less important to popularity on the twelfth-grade level than on the sixth-grade level (19). Apparently the twelfth-graders placed greater relative value upon certain personality assets, such as friendliness and sociability, than did the sixth-graders. This finding may be regarded as encouraging to the child who is not physically attractive, but who has a good many favorable personality traits, since it offers a basis for believing that at older age-levels he may be evaluated more for personality assets than he is in childhood.

In regard to the importance of such appearance factors as tidiness and unkemptness among adolescents, data reported by Kuhlen and Lee and by Tryon show clearly that being tidy is very essential to acceptability for girls. In regard to boys, Kuhlen and Lee report that at the sixth-, ninth-, and twelfth-grade levels those boys who were most popular were also more frequently mentioned as being "neat and clean" (19). In Tryon's study, however, the trait of unkemptness was found to be valued quite favorably among twelve-year-old boys, but among fifteen-year-old boys untidiness was negatively related to all trait ratings implying social prestige (32).

In group discussions and in counselling work, particularly with adolescents, the point should be stressed that at least among psychologically mature people, physical attractiveness is judged not simply by body-form or features but by the effect created by the whole person. Beauty is much more than the summation of parts. This point is established in two studies among adolescents by Silverman (30) and by Perrin (28), in both of which ratings on attractiveness are shown to be very much influenced by more general qualities than such things as body-form, facial symmetry, or color of eyes or of hair.

These findings can be cited to reassure those children and adolescents who feel that they are doomed to social isolation, and particularly to heterosexual failure, because of some kind of defect in their physical structure. Apparently this pessimistic attitude is unwarranted if physical attractiveness is an attribute of a total person and not merely of his physical parts. It seems that with the maintenance of good grooming, the holding of positive self-regarding attitudes, and the development of resources for meeting the personal needs of others, there are very few individuals who would not be considered physically attractive by at least some of their associates.

INTELLECTUAL ABILITIES

Probably intellectual abilities have been studied more than any other trait or characteristic found among school populations. These studies have related varying degrees of intellectual competence to all other measurable variables in school groups, such as teachers' marks, social-class level of pupils' homes, drop-outs, participation in student activities, disciplinary records, and creative achievements in the arts. The chief focus in this chapter will be on the relationship between intellectual abilities and personal-social adjustments.

Intellect and personality

To what extent can teachers assume that those children who are intellectually bright also possess the personality assets necessary to good mental health? On a general group basis the answer is "very little." This is true whether a good personality be assessed by personality self-rating questionnaires, by teacher ratings, or by classmate choices of friends. Most of the correlations obtained between these three kinds of personality measurements, on the one hand, and I.Q.'s, on the other, have ranged between 0 and .40 with a median of about .30. Although this median shows a small degree of association between intellectual brightness and some kinds of personality assessments, it is obviously too small to have predictive value for individuals. In other words, a teacher can never assume that he has a reliable indication of the personality status or mental health condition of any child from knowing his I.Q. The same is true of academic competence as measured by standardized tests. Serious lack of social judgment and personal maturity in spite of high intelligence is shown in the following cases:

> A boy in the fourth grade (I.Q. 130) stood up and nominated himself for president of a classroom club. The teacher tried to ignore him but he insisted that his name be written on the board with the other nominees. He got one vote — his own.
>
> During an election in the third grade, a boy (I.Q. 121) said to another boy across the aisle, "Sonny, vote for me and I won't hate you any more."
>
> A boy (I.Q. 120) in the fifth grade said to another boy, "If you will be nice to me I'll give you 20 marbles every week."

Aside from distortions in personal growth, a few very bright children may find social adjustment with their age-groups difficult simply from the sheer fact of their intellectual superiority. Writing on this point, Hollingsworth says:

> The majority of children above 160 I.Q. play little with other children because the difficulties of social contact are almost insurmountable. Unless special facilities can be provided, these children tend to become isolates, a condition not conducive to leadership, except perhaps of a few rare sorts, later

> in life. Such children are ordinarily friendly and gregarious by nature, but their efforts at forming friendships tend to be defeated by the scarcity of like-minded contemporaries. The imaginary playmate as a solution of the problem of loneliness is fairly frequent, but far inferior to the real playmate, could one be found. Shaw makes Saint Joan say, "I was always alone." (12 — p. 588.)

In her discussion, Hollingsworth points out the fallacy of the common assumption that the very bright child, because of his brightness, will be able to take care of his personal-social needs, and so no special attention need be given him. This point is supported by Terman's follow-up study of gifted children into adult life, in which he found that those whose records were the poorest in regard to living up to their intellectual promise were characterized to a much greater extent than were the most successful gifted children by a variety of social and emotional handicaps, especially in regard to self-confidence, inferiority feelings, persistence, and drive toward well-defined goals (31). Presumably these personality limitations constituted the chief source of explanation as to why a few of the intellectually gifted children had a poor record of achievement in adult life.

In cases of very bright pupils who appear to be "always alone," a teacher can sometimes help them to attain some interpersonal satisfactions by doing something to bring two intellectually gifted pupils together, such as by assigning them to a joint research project, seating them near each other, suggesting to the mother of one of the pupils that she invite the other one to her home, or by putting both of them in the same subgroupings for classroom work. This suggestion is supported by the fact that several studies by Almack (1), Bonney (3), Dimock (6), and Seagoe (29) have shown substantial correlations (.46 to .57) between the I.Q.'s of mutual friends.

Data from contrasted groupings

Even though there is only a small correlation between intelligence and desirable personality traits on a total-group basis, and even though some very bright children have serious personal limitations, nevertheless, when intellectually gifted children (as a group) are contrasted with those of only average intelligence there are marked and consistent personality advantages in favor of those in the highly intelligent grouping. This is another significant finding from Terman's study of 1500 gifted children referred to above (31). As compared with children of average intellectual abilities, these very bright children were rated by teachers as being superior in social adjustments and in moral attitudes, they scored significantly higher on character tests, and had a much lower delinquency rate both in childhood and in adult life. Data from sociometric testing are also quite consistent in showing that those in the upper levels of choice-status have, as a group, reliably higher I.Q.'s than those in the lowest brackets of interpersonal desirability, as shown in studies by Feinberg (7) and by Grossman and Wrighter (10). In some studies, average I.Q. differences between upper and lower fourths in number of choices received have amounted to 15 points. It is very rare indeed for a child with an I.Q. below 85 in a typical public school class in this country to rank high on any choice-criterion involving either personal preference or a work-type activity. On the other hand, it is not unusual for a very bright child to be found in the lowest brackets on sociometric tests. This means that high intelligence is more widely distributed than is low intelligence throughout a personal-preference hierarchy. The same statement can be made in regard to academic achievement.

Social status of feebleminded pupils

That those with I.Q.'s below 70 are likely to be making extremely poor social adjustments in their classroom groups is shown from a study conducted by Johnson in 25 elementary school classes in which he isolated 39 pupils, all of whom were shown by a series of tests to have I.Q.'s of 69 or below (14). The acceptability of these pupils, along with others in their respective classes, was measured by a three-criteria sociometric questionnaire (like best, sit by, and play with), including both positive and negative responses. When the results were tabulated it was found that the 39 mentally deficient children had an average acceptance score that was much below the average of the rest of their classes, and that their average rejection score was four times higher. Although the pupils with I.Q.'s of 69 or below constituted only 5 per cent of the total population studied, they received 40 per cent of all the rejections.

That these feebleminded children were suffering in their personality development, from their very low social status in their respective classroom groups, is indicated by the fact that when the children were asked to give reasons for their preferences and rejections the most frequently mentioned reasons for rejecting the feebleminded pupils included references to such behavior as: rough, mean, bullies, teases, fights, misbehaves in school, poor sport, cheats, dirty, and smells. It is significant, too, that these kinds of behavior were referred to much more frequently as reasons for giving rejections than were any kinds of behavior directly implying that a child was considered "dumb," ignorant, or stupid. In other words, it seemed apparent that the main source of the social difficulties of the mentally handicapped pupils was not the simple fact of their low intelligence but rather the indirect effects which caused them to develop many kinds of obnoxious behaviors in an effort to overcompensate for their intellectual weaknesses.

Johnson's data (14) points to the conclusion that, from the standpoint of mental hygiene objectives, if mentally deficient children are kept in regular classes much more will need to be done than is usually done to help them attain some degree of social integration into their classroom groups. Otherwise they will need to be put into special classes, at least for academic subjects, so they will not be required to compete with normal and superior pupils. The latter plan has in recent years gained increasing adoption in many of our school systems.

A PROGRAM TO DEVELOP SOCIAL SKILLS

What has been said above in regard to the social and mental hygiene values of physical and intellectual abilities applies equally well to all other kinds of abilities, such as those in the areas of music, art, and dramatics. All socially approved abilities have contributions to make toward the goals of positive mental health for all children and youth. This being true, it will be appropriate to consider some general suggestions for promoting mental hygiene objectives through developing skills and abilities.

Opportunities for learning activities

In some schools the range of abilities in which a child can demonstrate his capacities is very limited. In a few schools academic abilities and outstanding athletic skills are about the only ones that receive much official recognition. What is needed is a wide range of activities and projects that provide for all socially approved abilities. A good school needs to provide for singing, dancing, playing of instruments, running, reading, hammering, storytelling, acting, painting, skiing, debating, writing, sewing, volley ball, etc., until all socially approved abilities and skills of which children and youth are capable are included.

Such examples as the following are familiar to all teachers who have had experience in a school with a flexible and varied curriculum:

> A fifth-grade boy with a relatively low I.Q. had attracted very little favorable attention until a project was started which involved some drawing and wood carving. His ability to draw boats and his ability to carve them out of wood brought him considerable praise and group recognition.
>
> An eighth-grade girl had never registered in her group until a hobby club was organized and her ability to take and develop pictures was integrated into her school program. Then she developed many personal relationships with other students.
>
> A high school freshman who had few social contacts or friends (none that were intimate) and was very much a "home-boy," came to the front when the school organized a game period during the noon hour. In this situation his skill in playing dominoes, checkers, chess, and various card games, which he had learned at home, soon made him a sought-after individual for the first time in his life.

The better schools today provide for the emergence of hundreds of such cases as those just cited. They provide for the development and the recognition of a wide variety of abilities through their regular classroom work, dramatics, auditorium programs, clubs, exhibitions of pupil-made products, and athletic activities. Even in these schools there are a good many pupils for whom no ability-avenues are provided. Furthermore, in some schools very little effort is made to give recognition to pupils whose abilities are fair but not outstanding. Of course there is nothing to be gained by playing up a thing for more than it is worth, but it is important to give some recognition to a wide range of abilities through teacher praise, auditorium programs, and school newspapers. The value for personality growth of any ability is greatly affected by the degree of prestige attached to it in a given situation.

It is certainly true that a child's respect from his classmates cannot be improved by official praise that is not merited. Neither can it be improved through any artificial situations that are arranged for this purpose. This latter point is illustrated in the case of a high school teacher who, thinking to help a timid girl in his class, told her ahead of time that he was going to call on her to recite on a certain topic and prompted her to prepare a good answer. The girl overresponded to this suggestion by making an elaborate preparation, and, when called on, made a lengthy recitation which bored the class. Furthermore, the other students suspected that she had been "tipped off." Needless to say, her group status was lower after this incident than before.

A teacher's efforts to help a child's social adjustment, whether through abilities or otherwise, should never be obvious to the rest of the group. Even grade-school children can "see through" some of the more obviously calculated efforts of teachers to help a particular child. A sixth-grade boy, for example, was overheard making the following remark to another boy regarding a third boy: "Let him alone — the teacher is trying to get him adjusted."

This does not mean that calculated efforts cannot, or should not, be made to help certain individuals; rather it means that such efforts should not be so obvious that other children can see that certain ones are getting singled out for special treatment.

Need for more than opportunities

Sometimes too much confidence is placed in simply giving an individual an opportunity to practice a social skill, under the assumption that the opportunity alone will be sufficient to call forth the appropriate behavior. The fallacy of this assumption is illustrated in the following examples:

A play-teacher gave the soccer ball to a second-grade rejected boy to carry out to the play group. (This was considered quite an honor among the boys.) When he got outside he held the ball and refused to throw it until the teacher commanded him to do so.

A fourth-grade boy who was an isolate was asked by the teacher to collect arithmetic papers from the other children. He grabbed the papers from their hands saying, "Give me that paper."

A socially inept girl in the seventh grade was elected secretary of a class club. Her first official act consisted of writing notes to three girls telling them they had been dropped from the club.

A high school girl who had never "belonged" in her school groups was appointed class treasurer by her class officers and the faculty sponsor to fulfill the unexpired term of a student who had left school. This girl attacked this assignment with dispatch, persistence, and directness — but untempered by social skills. She did not ask for dues; she demanded them. She expected immediate compliance, and if it was not forthcoming she pestered and annoyed those who didn't respond. She interrupted private conversations, and tapped students on the back at basketball games to tell them they had not paid their dues. In spite of all her efforts a good many dues remained uncollected at the end of the semester.

Personality maladjustment vs. lack of social skills

The above examples emphasize that some persons' lack of social adjustment is based on deep-seated personality difficulties which could be relieved only by various forms of protracted therapy such as individual counseling, interviews with parents, removal of handicaps, and environmental changes. Other persons, however, are low in group recognitions, not primarily because of serious personality defects but because of lack of training in social skills, or lack of opportunity for their particular skills to be known. It is important that teachers be able to distinguish between these two general types of socially incompetent persons. Otherwise methods will be used with some individuals which have little chance of accomplishing anything.

Provision for special coaching

Most teachers have observed cases of improved social adjustment resulting (partly at least) from special coaching in certain skills. They have seen children engage in less overcompensatory behavior after reading deficiencies have been removed; and they have seen progress in the social adjustment of certain pupils who have been helped in learning to play ball, wrestle, skate, dance, or speak in public.

Sometimes this better social adjustment is a consequence of working with a child on an individual basis rather than in a group setting. This is not saying that some persons can learn to swim without getting in the water — rather it is saying that some individuals need some kind of personal development before they can learn to swim when they do "get in the water." They need to learn certain skills that will afford them an advantage when they enter into group associations. The following examples illustrate the possibilities of special coaching:

> A first-grade boy was rejected by his classmates, as shown by the fact that he received a balance of negative over positive votes in a sociometric measurement. This boy's mother brought him in a car to and from school each day, he did not play with the other boys, and he was constantly talking about his music lessons. After the sociometric test, the teacher had a long talk with the boy's father, who was not aware of the boy's social failure at school. When he saw the problem he took immediate action. He kept the mother from taking the boy to school, he stopped the music lessons (which the boy was very willing to do), and he came home early three evenings a week to teach his boy to catch a ball, roller skate, and do other things that other boys were doing. He invited two boy neighbors over to make the learning situation more effective. The boy learned rapidly, and on a subsequent sociometric measurement, eight weeks later, his score rose from a small negative to a small positive degree of acceptance. Of course other factors besides the acquisition of physical skills were operating to produce the improved social adjustment of this boy.

> A tall, bright, socially inhibited girl in the second grade, who was sensitive about her height, was taught to knit by a college

> student who was working in the room. Then the teacher announced that all those who wished to learn to knit might form a club (to meet during activity period) and that the college student and this one girl would help them learn. The student let the girl do all the teaching and she did it well. The social foothold gave her a noticeable boost in self-confidence. She talked with other girls more, and on subsequent sociometric retest her peer acceptance was raised from the second to the third quartile.

> A fourteen-year-old oversized girl was made fun of because she couldn't swim, was "too fat," and was just an "old violin player." This girl was very capable for her age in playing the violin, but she did not play the kind of music that her age-grade contemporaries liked or appreciated; therefore they did not want her on school programs and some of them made fun of her musical ability. The classroom teacher held some conferences with this girl and with her parents in regard to her playing more popular music. As a result of these efforts this girl played "Alexander's Ragtime Band." This was enthusiastically received and proved to be an entering wedge for this girl in gaining a more favorable group position.

The latter case illustrates the possibilities of turning a technical skill into a social asset — without sacrificing the technical skill.

Social disadvantage of extreme individualism

The third case above illustrates the unfortunate social consequences that sometimes accrue from overconcentration on an individual-type skill, especially during childhood and youth. The pupil who excels in some form of individual endeavor may very frequently work alone, and when he demonstrates his talents he is very likely to do so by himself *in front of* others rather than *with* others. Although these conditions are generally advantageous for socialization, they are not always so, particularly when the person concerned spends a great deal of time on his specialty and becomes identified with it in the minds of others. He may acquire a nickname such as "the brain," "that kid who plays the piano," or "that Phi Beta Kappa guy." When this happens he is no longer thought of as a person but only in terms of his skill. The part has swallowed up the whole. The tail wags the dog.

Very often an excessive drive for individual achievement is an overcompensation for the lack of friendship and love. A person who is seriously lacking in these human satisfactions may say to himself: "I shall achieve; I shall become important; I shall be the best!" He goes on to tell himself that *then* they will notice him, *then* they will envy him. But what he really wants is that they should *like* him. When his achievements and recognitions fail to bring him the personal satisfactions he so desperately needs, his drive to superiority is likely to be intensified, with a consequent increase in his personal frustrations. Thus the dagger that was to slay his "enemies" becomes a sword of Damocles hanging over his own neck, constantly threatening to sever what few personal ties he has left.

REFERENCES

1. Almack, J. C., "The Influence of Intelligence on the Selection of Associates," *School and Society*, 16, 1922, 529-530.
2. Bedoian, V. H., "Mental Health Analysis of Socially Over-Accepted, Socially Under-Accepted, Average and Under-age Pupils in the Sixth Grade," *Journal of Educational Psychology*, 44, 1953, 366-371.
3. Bonney, Merl E., "A Study of Social Status on the Second-Grade Level," *Journal of Genetic Psychology*, 60, 1942, 271-305.
4. ———, "A Sociometric Study of the Relationship of Some Factors to Mutual Friendships on the Elementary, Secondary, and College Levels," *Sociometry*, 9, 1946, 21-47.
5. Buswell, Margaret M., "The Relationship Between the Social Structure of the Classroom and the Academic Success of the Pupils," *Journal of Experimental Education*, 22, 1953, 37-52.
6. Dimock, H. S., *Rediscovering the Adolescent*, Ch. III. New York: Associated Press, 1937.
7. Feinberg, M. R., "Relation of Background Experience to Social Acceptance," *Journal of Abnormal and Social Psychology*, 48, 1953, 206-214.
8. Frazier, A. and L. K. Lisonbee, "Adolescent Concerns with Physique," *The School Review*, 58, 1950, 397-405.
9. Fuller, E. M. and H. B. Baune, "Injury-Proneness and Adjustment in a Second Grade," *Sociometry*, 14, 1951, 210-225.

10. Grossman, B. and J. Wrighter, "The Relationship Between Selection-Rejection and Intelligence, Social Status, and Personality Amongst Sixth Grade Children," *Sociometry,* 11, 1948, 346-355.
11. Hardy, Martha C., "Social Recognition at the Elementary School Age," *Journal of Social Psychology,* 8, 1937, 365-384.
12. Hollingsworth, L. S., "What We Know About the Early Selection and Training of Leaders," *Teachers College Record,* 40, 1939, 575-592.
13. Jastak, J., *Human Relations in the Classroom,* Part II. Wilmington, Delaware: Delaware State Society for Mental Hygiene, Inc., 1944.
14. Johnson, G. C., "A Study of the Social Position of Mentally Handicapped Children in the Regular Grades," *American Journal of Mental Deficiency,* 55, 1950, 60-89.
15. Jones, H. E., "Physical Ability as a Factor in Social Adjustment in Adolescence," *Journal of Educational Research,* 40, 1946, 287-301.
16. Jones, Mary C., "The Late Careers of Boys Who Were Early and Late Maturing," *Child Development,* 28, 1957, 113-128.
17. ———, "A Study of Socialization Patterns at the High School Level," *The Journal of Genetic Psychology,* 93, 1958, 87-112.
18. Keislar, C. R., "Peer Group Ratings of High School Pupils with High and Low School Marks," *Journal of Experimental Education,* 22-23, 1954-55, 375-378.
19. Kuhlen, R. G. and B. J. Lee, "Personality Characteristics and Social Acceptability in Adolescence," *Journal of Educational Psychology,* 34, 1943, 321-340.
20. Ladieu, G., E. Hanfmann, and T. Dembo, "Studies in Adjustment to Visible Injuries: Evaluation of Help by the Injured," *Journal of Abnormal and Social Psychology,* 42, 1947, 169-192.
21. Lion, E. G., C. O'Neill, and R. E. Prager, "Strabismus and Children's Personality Reactions," *American Journal or Orthopsychiatry,* 13, 1943, 121-124.
22. McGraw, L. W. and J. W. Tolbert, "Sociometric Status and Athletic Ability of Junior High School Boys," *Research Quarterly,* 24, 1953, 72-80.
23. Meyerson, L. (ed.), "The Social Psychology of Physical Disabilities," *The Journal of Social Issues,* 4, Fall 1948, 115.
24. Miller, Vera, "Academic Achievement and Social Adjustment of Children Young for Their Grade Placement," *The Elementary School Journal,* 57, 1957, 257-263.
25. Morrison, Ida E. and Ida F. Perry, "Acceptance of Over-age Children by Their Classmates," *Elementary School Journal,* '56, 1956, 217-220.
26. Mussen, R. H. and Mary E. Jones, "Self-conceptions, Motivations, and Interpersonal Attitudes of Late and Early Maturing Boys," Child Development, 28, 1957, 243.

27. Northway, M. L., "Outsiders, A Study of the Personality Patterns of Children Least Acceptable to Their Age Mates," *Sociometry*, 7, 1944, 10-24.

28. Perrin, F. A. C., "Physical Attractiveness and Repulsiveness," *Journal of Experimental Psychology*, 4, 1921, 203-217.

29. Seagoe, M. V., "Factors Influencing the Selection of Associates," *Journal of Educational Research*, 27, 1933, 32-40.

30. Silverman, S. S., "Clothing and Appearance — Their Psychological Implications for Teenage Girls." New York: Bureau of Publications, Teachers College, Columbia University, 1945.

31. Terman, Lewis M., "The Discovery and Encouragement of Exceptional Talent," *The American Psychologist*, 1954, 221-230.

32. Tryon, C., "Evaluations of Adolescent Personality by Adolescents," *Monograph of Society for Research on Child Development*, No. 4, 1939.

33. Young, L. L. and D. H. Cooper, "Some Factors Associated with Popularity," *Journal of Educational Psychology*, 35, 1944, 513-535.

QUESTIONS AND EXERCISES

1. Consider various aspects of the problems created by over-age and under-age pupils in school classrooms, such as policies in regard to promotion, and in regard to admitting children in the first grade who are under six years old.
2. Cite some examples of late maturing boys who have made very poor personal-social adjustments and also some examples of such boys who have made very satisfactory adjustments. Try to find some evidence from these boys' lives which will throw some light on the large differences in their developmental level.
3. From the data and explanations given in this chapter what advice could you give a young person who is worried for fear a particular physical defect that he has will prevent him from having friends or being accepted as a leader?
4. Stimulate a class discussion on what is meant by physical attractiveness. Does there appear to be any difference in the criteria used by men as compared with that used by women?
5. Report to the class a case you know concerning a very bright child who is characterized by poor social insight into his personal affairs.

6. Which do you think suffers the most from failure in interpersonal relationships — a very bright child or a very dull child? Why?
7. Which kind of child is mostly likely to make a good social adjustment in a regular classroom — a bright child or a feebleminded child? To support your answer try to find data other than that given in this chapter.
8. Stimulate a class discussion on how special provisions may be made in a school for meeting the intellectual needs of bright pupils without doing damage to their personalities or social development.
9. State some criteria that a teacher can use to distinguish between a pupil who lacks social skills and one whose interpersonal difficulties are due to deep-seated personality difficulties.
10. Give examples of how children who possess marked individual abilities may be helped to integrate these abilities into group needs.

SELECTED FILMS

Teacher as Observer and Guide. 23 minutes. Deals with mental and social development of slow learners.

For Those Who Are Exceptional. 43 minutes. Presents methods of aiding pupils who have mental and physical handicaps.

OBJECTIVES AND GOALS 2

6

THE POSITIVE GOALS

IN THE PRECEDING CHAPTERS numerous mental health problems inherent in teaching situations have been presented. These problems have been dealt with from the standpoint of descriptions of the kinds of behavior involved, the kinds of measurements which can be utilized, and the kinds of teaching practices and school programs which are most likely to reduce the severity of these problems. In addition, considerable attention has been given to classroom procedures, subject-matter content, and teacher attitudes, which are conducive to the development of mental health values.

OF MENTAL HEALTH

In these discussions the term *adjustment* has been used many times. This is a very appropriate term to describe the various ways whereby people endeavor to arrive at satisfactory resolutions of their frustrations, internal problems, and interpersonal conflicts. Furthermore, it is a term that has a broad application, since adjustments may be on a low level — involving psychoneurotic and even psychotic behavior — or they may be on a high-quality level — involving psychological maturity and good judgment of social consequences. In discussing levels of adjustment, Shaffer and Shoben point out that "good adjustments" are integrative in the sense that they help satisfy all motives "as they function in an interrelated system, without overemphasis on one drive or the slighting of another" (4). Conversely, adjustments are nonintegrative because, even though they do reduce tensions temporarily in certain areas, they do not solve any real problems and "they make the accomplishment of other adjustments harder instead of easier" (p. 152). At another point in their discussion of adjustment, Shaffer and Shoben say: "People differ greatly in their tolerance of frustrations and conflicts, and in the types of adjustment mechanisms that they habitually employ. Such differences are variations in *personality*. The personality of an individual may be defined as his persistent tendencies to make certain qualities and kinds of adjustment." (p. 310.)

Certainly the objectives of mental hygiene require that the higher-level adjustments, of which Shaffer and Shoben speak, consist of something more than simply adapting oneself to whatever is found to exist. This kind of adjustment is based only on conditioning, habit formation, and conformity. Instead, we must think of the higher-quality adjustments as including critical judgments, value discriminations, and some orginality and daring.

In trying to achieve the goal of integrative adjustment as described above, we can be sure that one way *not* to accomplish this objective is to educate children to acquire a list of traits and virtues, each of which is to be diligently pursued as a particular goal. The weakness of this approach is that it puts emphasis on simply acquiring more and more of each trait or virtue, without regard to the dynamic interrelationships between them, and without regard to the complexities of life situations.

If a good personality is thought of as one in which a wide range of human needs and interests is satisfied, as opposed to a few, then it becomes evident that all traits must be balanced or integrated with others, or else the excessive pursuit of one kind of need may block out the satisfaction of others. A strong identification with modesty and humility as ideals can result in a serious reduction of satisfactions arising from legitimate self-assertion and aggressiveness. Likewise, an overly strong identification with the values inherent in hard work and ambition can lead to a blocking of friendship and love.

It can be safely said that all socially approved traits are to some extent in conflict with other equally desirable traits in nearly all situations. For example, the need for administering justice may be in conflict with the need for showing mercy; or, on the other hand, the desire to show sympathy may be in conflict with the need to administer justice. Standing up for one's beliefs may be in conflict with the need to be flexible, tolerant, and sensitive to the points of view of others.

Being honest may be contrary to the virtues of kindness and of consideration for others' feelings. Likewise a trait may be in conflict with itself in respect to its object of expression, as when a young person's sense of loyalty to his parents is in conflict with a sense of loyalty to a friend or to his clique; or when an employee's desire to be loyal to his employer is in conflict with his desire to be loyal to his labor union.

Furthermore, the mentally healthy and socially mature person must learn to integrate into his behavior some apparently contradictory traits and feelings. He must be able to hold attitudes of trust and love toward certain other people and yet also hold some feelings of fear toward these same individuals, for if there is no fear of what another person will think there can be but little respect for him.[1] Also the absence of fear of consequences (especially in childhood) from one's behavior toward a loving person leads to psychopathic personality traits and tends to produce the kind of person who expects the world at large to forgive him for his misdeeds as did his "loving" parents and teachers. The only alternative is that love and fear must be integrated into mutually supporting attitudes. In a similar vein the capacity for anger, along with generosity and sympathy, must be present in a mentally healthy person because the lack of anger means the absence of integrity, lowered self-respect, and a reduced ability to stimulate others to live up to their possibilities.

However, we should not think of a mentally healthy person simply in terms of absence of conflicts. This is too static and uninviting a conception, as Shoben has pointed out (5), and furthermore, is not in accord with the facts about socially mature people. The mentally healthy individual has conflicts, but he is usually able to resolve them in ways that further promote his social judgment and personal adequacy.

The goals of mental hygiene must be stated in terms of continual growth toward positive ends. The "good life" must be seen as a constructive attainment, not simply as the absence of bad traits; both physical and mental health must be viewed as a state of well-being and not simply as the absence of disease. Likewise, freedom

---

[1] This is the basis for the emphasis in Christianity on both love and fear of God.

is not simply the absence of restraints; nor is happiness simply the absence of sorrow.

In spite of this emphasis on the value of positive goals, as opposed to simply avoiding "various kinds of evils," the unfortunate fact is that from the standpoint of our present psychological knowledge, we know much more about how to help people to avoid the "various kinds of evils" than we know about how to help them attain the positive goals. This is true because we have much more research that is focused on people who have failed than on people who have succeeded. We know more about the developmental histories of delinquents, criminals, sex deviates, neurotics, and psychotics, than we know about the developmental histories of people who have led lives of unusual personal value, psychological maturity, and social significance. Writing on this point, Allport states that too many of our psychological theories of development are "based largely upon the behavior of sick and anxious people or upon the antics of captive and desperate rats," and that too few of them have been derived from the study of healthy human beings — "those who strive not so much to preserve life as to make it worth living." Allport continues: "Thus we find today many studies of criminals, few of law-abiders; many of fear, few of courage; more on hostility than on affiliation; much on the blindness in man, little on his vision; much on his past, little on his outreaching into the future." (1.)

Some general guidelines in regard to the nature of positive mental health goals for schools can be had by referring to the basic concepts presented in Chapter 1. These concepts placed emphasis on ego-strengthening, rational control of behavior, development of social interests, personality uniqueness, striving for self-realization (or self-actualization), orientation toward *becoming*, promotion of positive self-regarding attitudes, the attainment of satisfying interpersonal relationships, and group-belongingness.

From all the foregoing discussion it becomes evident that the goals of mental hygiene for schools are to be stated not in terms of specific habits, but of developmental levels; not in terms of a list of traits or virtues to be inculcated, but of stimulating critical analysis and social judgment; not in terms of what is to be avoided, but what is to be striven for.

These principles are incorporated into the content of the next four chapters, which are concerned with a description and analysis of major mental hygiene objectives for pupils in our elementary and secondary schools. These objectives are derived from the psychological sources reviewed above, and may be summarized as follows: Good mental health is based on (1) positive as opposed to rejecting attitudes toward one's self, (2) introjection of the most generally accepted social norms, together with sufficient adaptability to meet the demands of changing conditions and situations, (3) development of some social drive and social initiative, and (4) the acquisition of some group-centered and altruistic motivations. Thus these four major objectives begin with a solid base within ourselves and extend outward until we also have a solid base within the lives of others.

It is assumed that all these aspects of behavior are developing concomitantly rather than in any kind of sequence, and that all of these kinds of behavior are exerting reciprocal influences upon each other. It is also assumed that each of these behavior areas, regardless of its positive values, can be pushed too far and can be distorted in ways contrary to the ends of mental hygiene. Teachers, therefore, who are concerned about the mental health of their pupils, should not only understand the importance of the behavior objectives described in the four succeeding chapters; they also need to examine critically these objectives in order to realize their limitations and the conditions necessary for their optimal development. Considerations of this nature are also presented in the four chapters to follow.

REFERENCES

1. Allport, G. W., *Becoming*. New Haven: Yale University Press, 1955, p. 18.
2. De Haan, R. F. and J. Kough, *Helping Children with Special Needs*, Vol. II, Elementary Edition. Science Research Associates, Inc., 1956, p. 200.
3. Harsh, C. M. and H. G. Schrickel, *Personality-Development and Assessment* (2nd ed.), Ch's. IX and XII. New York: The Ronald Press Company, 1959.
4. Shaffer, L. F. and E. J. Shoben, *The Psychology of Adjustment* (2nd ed.). Boston: Houghton Mifflin Company, 1956.

5. Shoben, E. J. "Toward a Concept of the Normal Personality," *The American Psychologist,* 12, 1957, 183-189.
6. Symonds, P. M., "Normality," *Dynamic Psychology,* Ch. XXI. New York: Appleton-Century-Crofts, Inc., 1949.

QUESTIONS AND EXERCISES

1. Stimulate a class discussion on the various uses and criticisms of the term *adjustment.*
2. How do you evaluate the practice on the part of some school systems of using report cards that require teachers to rate their pupils on a list of personality traits?
3. Why can't the positive goals of mental hygiene be achieved simply by teaching children to avoid bad behaviors?
4. Write a paper or present an oral report in which you describe one or two children who you believe represent the highest levels of personality development. Do these children have positive assets that add up to something more than simply the absence of bad traits?
5. Consider how the mental hygiene goals presented in this chapter can serve to guide a teacher's thinking and actions in his work with children and young people.

7

SELF-ADJUSTMENT

PROBABLY almost all psychologists agree that good self-adjustment is fundamental to good social adjustment and to good mental health. By "good self-adjustment" is meant that a person is free from seriously disturbing internal conflicts, persistent worries, and pathological guilt feelings. Furthermore, on the positive side, it means that he likes and respects himself, can enjoy himself, and can throw himself enthusiastically into the *process* of living as well as into the pursuit of goals. Recently a great many psychologists have placed much emphasis on the importance of our self-regarding atti-

AND INDIVIDUALITY

tudes as a source of motivation in all of our behavior. What we think of ourselves is being regarded as a factor of primary significance in explaining both our personal and our social behavior. It appears that we are strongly inclined to respond to others in a manner that is a direct or indirect reflection of the way we regard ourselves.

In fact, Combs and Snygg go so far as to say that behavior is entirely determined by the "perceptual field" of the behaving organism (11). These authors state: "By the perceptual field, we mean the entire universe, including himself, as it is experienced by the individual at the instant of action. It is each individual's personal and unique field of awareness, the field responsible for his every behavior." (p. 20.) Combs and Snygg point out that accurate perception of the behavior of others is necessary for a realistic appraisal of the meaning of their behavior, since distorted perceptions lead to inappropriate responses regardless of what the objective facts may be. In extreme cases of perceptual distortion an individual responds much more to "pictures in his head" than to the social realities around him. They further elaborate their position as follows:

> The concept of complete determination of behavior by the preceptual field is our basic postulate. It may be stated as follows: All behavior, without exception, is completely determined by, and pertinent to, the perceptual field of the behaving organism. The perceptual field has also been called the personal field, the private world, the behavioral field, the psychological field, the individual's life-space, and the phenomenal field. The last term is derived from a school of philosophy known as phenomenology, which holds that reality lies not in the event but in the phenomenon; that is to say, in the individual's experience of the event. It will be recognized that this is essentially the position we have taken — that behavior is a function, not of the external event but of the individual's perception of it. (pp. 20-21.)

It is evident from the foregoing statements that, according to this psychology, the immediately determining factors in behavior are within the subjective experience of each individual. In other words, we respond to any stimulus-situation in terms of our interpretation of its meaning from our own private frame of reference. This is the only reality we can ever know.

Combs and Snygg, however, make it clear that not all aspects of one's total phenomenal field are equally effective in determining behavior. Of particular importance, they say, in the motivation of all behavior, are those parts of the phenomenal field perceived by an individual to be most characteristic of himself, or, more precisely, his *self-concept.* These authors define *self-concept,* as that aspect of a person's phenomenal field which is most vital or important to him, which is the very essence of "me," and which is a central frame of reference for understanding one's self and for directing behavior — especially when choices are made (p. 127).

This point of view is not altogether new, since numerous writers (Allport [1], Dai [13], Gordon [14], Lecky [16], and Rogers [19-20]) in psychology and sociology have emphasized the *personal frame of reference* as a basis for understanding why people behave as they do. Also Camilla Anderson, a psychiatrist, makes a strong statement supporting this view of behavior in the following quotation: "The pattern of life of every individual is a living-out of his self-image; it is his road-map for living. People can be counted on to behave according to their own patterns. This consistency is not voluntary or deliberate, but compulsive, and generally is outside of awareness." (2.)

When we think of the "self-concept" we should not think of it as a single, unitary concept that we carry with us in the same form wherever we go. Rather we should think of our self-concept as something that varies considerably under different circumstances. A person, for example, may have quite a different conception of himself as he engages in his usual roles in his family, in his social group, and in his work situation. The degree of personality integration that any individual possesses is in large measure due to the extent to which his various conceptions of himself in his major roles are consistent with each other.

Regardless, however, of degree of personality integration, it is the contention of numerous students of human behavior (as mentioned above) that each individual strives both consciously and unconsciously to maintain a consistent picture of himself in accord with the kind of person which he thinks of himself as being in his major life-roles.

This statement is meant to be true not only of those who have positive self-regarding sentiments but also of those whose self-concepts are negative and disparaging. In the former instance, the person who thinks of himself as being competent, courageous, friendly, or lovable, is characterized by behavior in accord with these conceptions. In the latter instance, the person who views himself as inferior, cowardly, reserved, hostile, or unlovable cannot help acting in such a way as to maintain these negative attitudes.

From what has been said, it is obvious that the kind of self-image which any person has of himself in reference to any situation is certain to be of first-rate importance in determining his social adjustment with others in this situation. To a large extent he is certain to respond to others, not simply according to the way they are, but also on the basis of subjective conditions within himself.

Furthermore, each individual is certain to respond to others very largely on the basis of whether or not they maintain and enhance his conceptions of himself. So likely is this to be true that we may set up as a principle: *The most important single factor determining how well we like others is the extent to which they help us to like ourselves.* This means that we are attracted to those persons who help us to maintain our conceptions of ourselves, or who inspire us to higher levels of achievement, aspiration, or self-evaluation. Their contacts with us sustain or increase our self-respect and bolster our ideal selves. In accord with this principle, studies on teachers' qualities liked by pupils have consistently shown that one of the major qualities most liked is a teacher's ability to stimulate pupils to learn and to achieve up to, or beyond, their expectations. "He made us want to amount to something" is a testimony sometimes given by students in regard to an admired teacher. On the other hand, we dislike or actively reject those persons whose associations with us cause us to lower our self-esteem, to achieve below our expectations, or to act contrary to our standards or values.

Our attitudes toward ourselves begin to take definite form in early childhood through parent-child relationships, especially those relationships which have a close bearing on how a child thinks his parents value him as a person. It seems certain that self-regarding attitudes acquired from the family are the most fundamental and the most persistent throughout life. However, our self-conceptions are also greatly affected by our experiences in a multitude of groups outside the home during childhood and in subsequent years. When changes do occur in our self-attitudes, these changes are not due to certain experiences as such, but rather to the way we *interpret or perceive these experiences* in relation to ourselves. A child, for example, may have a good many experiences involving either success or failure, praise or blame, but these experiences will not result in a significant change in his behavior unless they eventually cause him to give a different answer to the question: "Who am I?"

SIGNS OF NEGATIVE SELF-CONCEPTS

Children who have weak and self-devaluating attitudes are characterized by some, but not necessarily all, of the following kinds of behavior: They are seriously lacking in spontaneity and uniqueness, are very inept in responding to teasing and kidding, show numerous neuromuscular tensions, frequently associate with pupils who are considerably beneath themselves in personality maturity and general intelligence, sometimes do things in the nature of "boot-licking" or of "currying favors" from pupils of high prestige-status, engage in some kind of appeasement or apologetic behavior toward those whom they think they have offended, generally give in to others when opposed, occasionally make self-derogatory remarks such as "nobody likes me," usually reject a compliment on the grounds that it is not sincere or is not merited, and almost never enjoy themselves.

SIGNS OF POSITIVE SELF-CONCEPTS

Those children who have strong, self-accepting attitudes have a behavorial picture very much the opposite of that described above. Although there are variations from one individual to another and for the same individual between situations, by and large a pupil who has a healthy self-concept is characterized by the following:

1. He has some values and principles that he adheres to and that he is willing to defend — although he may modify them with new experiences and knowledge.
2. When he acts on his own best judgment he does not feel guilty or regret his actions when others let him know that they do not approve of what he has done.
3. He does not worry unduly over what is coming tomorrow or fret over yesterday's mistakes.
4. He maintains confidence in his capacity to deal with his problems even when failures and setbacks occur — does not become panicky or despairing.
5. He feels equal to others *as a person* — not superior or inferior — irrespective of differences in specific abilities, family backgrounds, or the attitudes of others toward him.
6. He takes it for granted that he is a person of interest and of value to others — at least to those with whom he desires to associate.
7. He can accept praise and compliments with ease and genuine appreciation.

8. He does not think of himself as queer, as abnormal, or as especially different from the great majority of others with whom he regularly associates.
9. He resists efforts of others to dominate him, especially of those who are his peers.
10. He can accept the fact (and admit to others) that he has on different occasions a wide range of feelings, impulses, and desires — some of which may be highly approved in his culture and some of which may be highly disapproved. It does not follow that he acts on all these feelings or desires.
11. When he finds in himself an aspect of behavior that he does not like because it is contrary to his concept of himself, he sets about to change it. He does not try to deny it, condone it, or engage in some form of overcompensation.
12. He can genuinely enjoy himself in a wide variety of activities involving work, play, self-expression, and companionship, or just loafing.

When all, or nearly all, of these characteristics are found in an individual, we have a person who has standards with regard to all sources of satisfaction whether these sources be food, clothes, books, shows, or friends. Everything external to himself is, in a sense, sifted or pretested before being allowed to enter and remain within his self-structure. He is selective; he is critical; he is demanding. Furthermore, if what is available in a particular environment falls too far below his standards or preferences, he can do without the attendant satisfactions without serious feelings of frustration. Of course there are limitations on how "choosy" a person can be, especially when physical needs are involved, and there is value in adaptability (as stressed in the next chapter), particularly when group needs or values are at stake. The chief point being made is that a person with a high sense of self-worth can be a real individualist; he can be highly selective in reference to what he responds to, but he can also tolerate frustrations in a particular area while he tries to bring this aspect of his environment up to his standards, or until he can go to another location where conditions for satisfying his preferences already exist. In reference to friendship, for example, a person of high self-integrity will not necessarily make close friends, or seek to be a leader, in a certain group just because he is there. If the total conditions are too far below his standards he may, instead, bide his time and tolerate some unfavorable circumstances until he can get into a group more compatible with his individuality.

SOME RESEARCH FINDINGS

Now that a description of individuals characterized by varying degrees of positive and negative self-feelings has been presented, it will be appropriate to review some research studies on this topic, particularly those which have the most pertinence to teachers.

Hartley has presented data from her study of preadolescent boys, which show that the boy who regards himself as being "different" from other boys is most likely to believe that other boys are unfriendly toward him, and furthermore, that these other boys are likely to feel he is unfriendly toward them. This feeling of difference undoubtedly creates real barriers in interpersonal relationships regardless of the extent to which real differences exist (15).

Hartley's data also show that those boys who indicate the largest differences between the kind of social adjustments they are making and the kind they *would like* to make, also receive below-average ratings on friendliness from their age-mates. Apparently this discrepancy between an actual and an ideal self constitutes another barrier to good interpersonal adjustments.

On the positive side, Hartley's study shows that those boys who indicate the greatest degree of liking for other boys also rank high in thinking that other boys are friendly toward them. Commenting on this finding, Hartley states that an individual's estimate of the friendliness of others is probably not very closely related to the objective facts in regard to the responsiveness of others to him, but rather is very much due to a "generalized personal tendency" within the individual. Concluding her remarks on this point, Hartley says: "We might say broadly, 'to the friendly boy, all boys seem friendly.'" (p. 46.)

From the foregoing evidence it seems to be true that those pupils who have good mental health and good interpersonal relationships with other pupils do not feel that they are different from others, do not sense a large discrepancy between what they *are* and what they *would like to be,* and look upon themselves as being regarded favorably by others.

These statements are supported in Taylor and Combs' study of over 200 sixth-graders, in which it is shown that those children who rate themselves favorably on a personality self-rating scale are much more willing to admit having common faults and weaknesses than are those who rate themselves low on the same scale (27). This finding is taken to mean that those children who are characterized by adequate self-feelings are more able to face facts about themselves, and that this more objective attitude toward themselves probably aids in making realistic and sincere social adjustments.

In a similar vein, Shiff's study of 141 high school students has shown that those students who *underestimated* their sociometric status, as determined by total choices received, tend to regard themselves as being below their group average in their acceptance *of* others and in their acceptance *by* others (22). In other words, they had a low opinion of their own choice-value to others, and they assumed that this derogatory attitude toward themselves was also held by others.

A series of studies among college students by Brownfain (7), Sheerer (23), and Stock (25) have shown significant relationships between the possession of positive self-concepts and being liked by others, and of holding favorable attitudes toward others.

Some investigations have indicated that highly intelligent children who are "under-achievers" are likely to be suffering from poor self-adjustments. Lecky was one of the first to point out that low academic achievement in a particular subject may be due to a child's definition of himself as a non-learner of this type of material (16). Following up this theme, Ann Walsh presents a summary of theories and investigations supporting Lecky's view; also she reports a study that she conducted on twenty elementary school boys with I.Q.'s over 120 who were "under-achievers" and who were matched with twenty other boys who had similar I.Q.'s but who were high-achievers. Using a projective-type test, her results showed that the low-achievers differed reliably from the high-achievers in: (1) feelings of being criticized, rejected, or isolated, (2) acting defensively through compliance, evasion, or negativism, and (3) being unable to express themselves appropriately in actions and feelings. These findings are interpreted by Walsh as being indicative of negative self-regarding attitudes on the part of the bright boys who were low-achievers (28).

Additional reports by Benjamins (4) and by Buckley and Scanlan (8) present data to show how an individual's feelings about himself have a direct bearing on his intellectual efficiency.

EGOTISM AND EXTREME MODESTY

High self-regarding attitudes should not be confused with conceit or egoism. The conceited individual is in a poor state of mental health since he is in a weak position in regard to both his internal and his external adjustments. He is overcompensating for some form of inadequacy and is notoriously inept in his assessments of others.

Since the conceited individual is constantly trying to satisfy his own needs at the expense of others, his chances of establishing rapport with them are practically nil. Even when he does manage to attract some favorable attention, his efforts to win approval are generally futile because he has nothing to offer but his own egocentric demands. His cupboard of supplies for others is indeed bare. He wants to be recognized, accepted, and loved, but he lacks the resources to win these coveted assets. His capital is meager and it earns no interest, because what little capital he has is hoarded within himself rather than invested in the open market of others' needs.

Aside from its interference in interpersonal affairs, conceit is undoubtedly one of the most vulnerable armors with which one can face life. The individual who has an inflated self-regard is generally easy prey for others who know how to cater to his weakness. He is highly susceptible to flattery and is likely to favor anyone (regardless of true merit) who knows how to mix the right kind of brew to feed his voracious ego.

At the opposite end of the scale from conceit and arrogance is excessive modesty or extreme humility. The second state may be as bad as the first. A deflated self may easily be as great a handicap in interpersonal relaltions as an inflated self. However, the evils of conceit have been far more emphasized in moral and religious circles than have the evils attendant upon a sense of low personal worth. The conceited person has been the well-deserved target of innumerable attacks, but not so with the excessively humble, self-effacing individual. On the contrary, he has on innumerable occasions been extolled and glorified. Self-denial has been held up as a cardinal virtue.

Those who have responded to this doctrine in its extreme form (partly due to inadequacies in their development and partly due to direct teaching), are ineffective in their personal relationships and frequently lead a neurotic style of life. They are ineffective because they cannot make themselves count in the social processes of which they are a part. They are so concerned with being humble that they lack the energy and the drive necessary to lead lives of social significance. They do not attract others to themselves because the person who looks down on himself stimulates others to do likewise, and it is extremely difficult for any normal individual to identify with another person who fundamentally rejects himself. There is nothing there to identify with. There is no stimulation; there is no upward pull. The cupboard of the self-effacing person, like that of the egotist, is also bare. One of the foundation stones for securing respect from others is respect for oneself.

Likewise, self-love is necessary before one can love another. The Biblical statement: "Love thy neighbor as thyself" certainly implies that self-love is a necessary forerunner of loving our neighbors. The individual who does not have a strong emotional attachment to himself does not have sufficient ego-strength to be able to love others. Furthermore, he is not likely to think of himself as a person worthy of being loved; so he finds it contrary to his nature either to give or to receive affection. It has been pointed out by psychoanalysts that those persons who cannot assert themselves against others, and who let others "run over them," are much more likely to suffer from guilt feelings than are those who do assert themselves. This is to be expected, since a weak, doormat type of person cannot have respect for himself; fundamentally he is ashamed of himself. The hostile feelings that he holds toward others are blocked from normal overt expression and are consequently turned in upon himself. He constantly berates and fights himself. Since no one can ever attack himself and win, it is not surprising that eventually he becomes ashamed of a self that loses every contest in which it enters. This persistent failure to be an effective person is the basis for his sense of guilt. He tells himself he is a no-good weakling. He has been tried and found wanting; he has not attained man's full estate; he is morally reprehensible, if not a sinner.

Sometimes the extremely humble, guilt-ridden person unconsciously develops various forms of hysterical and psychosomatic disorders which have self-punishing value, but which also gain him sympathy and attention and prove how much suffering he can stand. Through such avenues some individuals who regard themselves as very self-effacing actually satisfy egocentric motivations.

THE ROLE OF THE TEACHER

How can a teacher help promote positive self-feelings among his pupils? The answer to this question is as broad as the entire school curriculum. Every constructive experience a child has in school may help bolster his self-esteem if he can avoid unwarranted negative interpretations of these experiences. Certainly the successful learning of subject matter is one of the major ways whereby all pupils are helped in defining themselves as adequate, self-respecting individuals.

Another factor of general importance is the teacher's attitude of acceptance of the personal worth of all children, as revealed in his genuine interest in trying to promote the maximum growth of all of them. A warm, responsive attitude on the part of a teacher is of some value in fostering positive self-concepts in all pupils, but is especially important to those children who come from homes in which there has been a deficiency of love. Although a teacher cannot be a substitute parent, and cannot make up for the failures of parents, he can, nevertheless, give some emotional or ego support to those children who show obvious signs of self-devaluation. These signs can be detected not only by observing the kinds of behavior listed above in a preceding division of this chapter, but also by administering some of the personality measurements described in Chapter 11. A sensitive teacher can give emotional or ego support to those who need it most without singling them out for special treatment or favors. He can be responsive to all pupils, but with varying degrees of emphasis. Furthermore, the chief difference will not be in what the teacher does but in how the teacher's behavior is appreciated by different pupils.

It is not likely, however, that teacher-support alone will be sufficient to aid materially a self-rejecting child unless this child can also be helped to gain at least a few friends and some status among his classmates. In regard to aiding such a child to win friends, it is best to concentrate at first on helping him to gain one friend as opposed to trying to get him to be socially accepted on a group basis. This can be done by utilizing suggestions offered throughout this volume. In addition to what can be done in school to help a child win a friend, a teacher can sometimes suggest to a mother that she invite several children, one at a time, into the home and try to make sure that the visiting child has a good time. This will not likely happen unless the home has play equipment, records, games, and other resources whereby one child can entertain another.

NEED FOR SKILL-DEVELOPMENT PROGRAM

Regardless of what teachers or parents may do to help a self-devaluating child, the child must eventually prove himself to be a person of worth and value. He will not be given friendship or respect for nothing or out of sympathy. The first essential step for him is to raise himself in his own esteem. Aside from at least one friend who appreciates him as a person, he must be helped to gain status through demonstrated competencies. This means that a school must provide for recognition through a wide range of academic, social, and athletic skills; and that all pupils should be encouraged to participate in them and especially those pupils who are in greatest need of establishing status. A skill-development program, however, will not have maximum value for ego-building purposes unless several conditions are present.

Importance of skills with prestige

In the first place, it is important to recognize that some skills have much greater prestige value than others in particular groups. Among boys, for example, it is evident that skill in outdoor games "rates" higher than does ability in art or music or in reading and writing. Among most groups of adolescent girls it is also evident that skill in dancing and in entertaining others is recognized as more important to status with both sexes than is ability in sewing, cooking, or in outdoor games.

Importance of cooperative skills

Aside from depending too much on skills of low-prestige value there is the additional danger of concentrating too much on one kind of ability to the neglect of all others. This danger is especially great when the ability is one which can be engaged in alone.

Consider, for example, the case of Helen, a high school girl who is unusually talented in music. She spends nearly all of her time practicing at her piano to the serious neglect of her schoolwork and all other normal interests. She has only one friend in the student body and that is another girl who also has centered her entire life around music. Helen is characterized by nervous mannerisms, strong feelings of social inferiority, emotional instability, and practically no capacity to succeed with the opposite sex. The praise and recognition that she has received from her musical achievements have not brought her happiness or peace of mind. She is seriously lacking in ego-security; consequently she is unable to win friends because she is constantly seeking emotional support from others instead of being able to meet any needs in them.

Importance of individual skills

The danger of excessive dependence on an individual-type skill should not obscure the general value of such abilities in helping to build positive self-regarding attitudes. On the contrary, all children should be encouraged to acquire skills and interests that they can pursue alone, such as reading, music, arts and crafts, gardening, fishing, and hobbies of all kinds. Every child's development should include some emphasis on teaching him to live alone and like it. As he learns to enjoy himself he will come to think more highly of himself, and this attitude will be reflected in the responses of others toward him. Furthermore, he will not be among those pathetic human beings who are so utterly dependent upon others to show them a good time that they dread most of all having to spend an evening alone. The person who can sincerely say "I just can't stand myself" would no doubt be surprised to discover how many of his associates feel exactly the same way about him.

Importance of initiative

Another condition necesary for a good skill-development program is that considerable initiative be allowed. Training a person to read, to sew, to write, or to paint only under directions or under prescribed conditions does not contribute to self-confident attitudes as much as when his training allows him considerable leeway to do things his own way, to create, and to express his own individuality. This encouragement of initiative lays a broader foundation for confidence since "the self has been on its own" and therefore has acquired more assurance about meeting new situations. It follows, then, that children in school should be allowed to make many suggestions in regard to how they will do things; should be allowed to make some mistakes when these mistakes are not too costly; should be stimulated to be original in some of their ideas and projects; and should have opportunities to meet and deal with some new situations largely on their own.

Importance of challenging tasks

Finally, a skill- or ability-development program will not accomplish the purpose of building up positive self-feelings unless some of the tasks required for all children are sufficiently difficult to challenge their best efforts. How can a person have confidence in a self that has never been seriously challenged? Such an individual knows that he has never really proved his strength to himself or to others. He may have done some fairly difficult things, for which he may have been profusely praised, but he still knows that he did not exert himself much, and that compared with some others of his age or educational level, his achievements are only average. This is particularly true of exceptionally bright and ambitious young people. If they have never been seriously challenged, they may suffer from some feelings of uncertainty about themselves, in spite of a confident exterior, because they know they have never proved themselves by anything really hard for them. They wonder if they could achieve a very difficult objective.

Probably every teacher has observed increased pride on the part of those who have successfully completed a hard course of study in school. Also every teacher has probably observed the opposite result of lack of pride, or even disgust, on the part of those who have been associated with a course of study that did not amount to much, or that was considered easy to accomplish.

It seems likely that what some people mean who talk about "mental discipline" and "developing will power" in children has reference to the need of providing them with tasks sufficiently difficult to challenge their best efforts, in order to promote good work habits and to build up sufficient self-confidence to meet subsequent life-demands. The objective, however, is not to provide tasks on the basis of difficulty alone, without reference to their interest, utility, and adaptability to the individual participants. Rather, the problem is to arrange tasks that have these psychological advantages plus the additional advantage of difficulty.

The school that follows the doctrine of pursuing the spontaneous interests of children without insistence upon concrete and hard-earned achievements, or that has adopted the philosophy of keeping the children "happy" and defines happiness as lack of frustration, is indeed laying the foundation for weak and insecure personalities.

Moderate use of criticism and praise

Whether a teacher is trying to help children by showing genuine interest and acceptance, by aiding them to gain friends or by helping them to achieve recognition and status, he will accomplish more in stimulating the growth of positive self-concepts if he uses both criticism and praise only moderately.

Some criticism of children's behavior and work products is both desirable and necessary to stimulate maximum efforts. However, if criticism is to be most beneficial it should be given calmly and be focused on specific aspects of behavior or of work products, as contrasted with outbursts of general condemnation and name-calling. It is well-known that harsh and indiscriminate criticism is likely to undermine self-confidence in all but the most determined individuals, especially during childhood and youth. Furthermore, when a child is excessively criticized he is trained to depend on external approval for his behavior instead of building up internal standards of reference. He becomes "other directed" as opposed to "self-directed."

What about praise? Must this, too, be employed only moderately and with discrimination? Some teachers say they believe in "pouring on the praise" and that a child who lacks confidence or is self-devaluating can't be praised too much. This attitude is psychologically unsound for three reasons.

In the first place, some children who are praised beyond their merit are fully aware of this fact, and they are not slow to interpret this excessive praise as evidence that they must indeed be weak or their teachers would not be making so many efforts to build them up.

In the second place, the child who is the victim of undue praise may come to expect easy victories in every situation that he enters. Having been praised for little achievements it is indeed difficult for him to pitch his efforts to a higher level. What happens to an individual, who has been accustomed to unmerited praise, when he must be measured against more objective criteria outside the situations in which he has been stimulated to build up a false picture of his power and worth? Depending upon a variety of factors in each case, such a person may (a) readjust his self-evaluation and "make the grade," or (b) develop various forms of overcompensatory behavior to try to prove to himself and others that he is as strong as he has been led to believe or (c) become discouraged and frightened and withdraw from all conflicts — including retreat to the favored situation from which he came.

The third factor operating against the development of sound self-evaluation when praise is "poured on" without much regard for merit is similar to a point made above in regard to the ill effects of excessive criticism. This point is that the recipients of undue praise are likely to come to look upon external approval as the measuring rod for their actions, rather than building up some internal standards of reference. They seldom ask themselves whether they think something is good or right or proper; rather, the question before them is what will someone else think. If this "someone else" says it is "all right" or "swell," then they are completely satisfied. Their efforts have been praised — what more could anyone ask? Such people cannot develop genuine self-confidence because they have never been taught to have confidence in their own selves; instead their confidence has been placed in the "selves" of others.

Obviously what is needed is not to do away with either praise or criticism, but rather to use both in fair amounts, leaving many experiences that are neither praised nor blamed. This means that most of a child's behavior should be responded to by adults with a non-evaluative attitude. Teachers must learn to "accept" many statements and specific behaviors of children to build up some standards of their own, and before many years they will have developed some inner frames of reference in regard to what is good or bad for themselves. They will have something they can call their own, something to fall back on in new situations and emergencies. They will have confidence in their standards and therefore in themselves.

Importance of self-assertion

Another child-development factor of general significance in fostering positive self-concepts is the promotion of a fair amount of self-assertion against others. Some children have had affection at home, they feel ego-supported by their teachers, they have at least a few friends, and they can hold their own in several abilities, and yet they fall short of being characterized by strong self-regarding attitudes because they are afraid to assert themselves against others. They cannot resist another person of strong will; they find it very difficult to say "no" to anyone whose approval they desire; they seldom express their views when these views are contrary to a group trend; and they will generally "walk a mile" to avoid a fight.

What is the matter with such people? Of course, there are many causative factors in their background, but one thing which is quite universal is the lack of opportunity to learn to assert themselves against others without fear of serious retaliation. Very early in life they developed a fear of "talking back," of stating their own views, or of engaging in any minor deviations from the expressed wishes of their parents and teachers. They learned to "keep their mouths shut" regardless of how much they disagreed with things said and done; they learned to submit to the superior strength of their adult supervisors rather than run the risk of incurring their anger or punishment.

It is necessary, then, for teachers to accept some aggression from a child without returning "an eye for an eye and a tooth for a tooth." They must let him assert himself occasionally in minor matters without punishment. Also they must permit him to express some aggressiveness against other children, provided these expressions are not too frequent or too severe.

Reacting against these statements, some teachers will no doubt say, "If you give a child an inch in self-assertion he will take a mile." On the contrary, it is more likely that the child who takes a mile has never had an inch. That is, he has never had an inch under the right total conditions. There has never been a proper balance among love, firmness, and an objective interest in his development. Under such conditions the child senses that the leeway permitted him is not an evidence of weakness in his adult supervisors but rather a sign of strength. Only the strong have enough self-assurance to allow those under their control to become strong also.

A flexible balance between leeway and control should characterize a school's management of the social behavior of children and youth. An educational environment that promotes fundamental self-confidence is one in which pupils are allowed to make their wishes known — sometimes in opposition to those of the teacher, and are encouraged to express their views even when these views are contrary to prevailing opinion in a particular group. But the teachers and administrators in charge of the school must know when to "crack down" to prevent freedom from becoming license, or self-assertion from becoming domination.

Firm control when called for, to curb excesses, is essential to the development of genuine self-confidence, because the child who is allowed to "push adults around" is acquiring a very deceptive sense of power — his victories are being won against "straw men." This illusion of strength will certainly be shattered on numerous occasions when he tries to force his will on others who stand their ground and refuse to be dominated by a tyrant.

Importance of self-understanding

Finally the point should be stressed that there is a significant relationship between increased self-understanding and increased self-acceptance, and that when both of these factors are increased there is likely to be an improvement in positive behavior adjustments. These kinds of relationships have frequently been reported from studies on the effects of psychological counseling, as pointed out in a preceding division of this chapter. These findings are corroborated in a study dealing with changes in delinquent behavior among fifty-one boys and girls, conducted by Rogers, Kell, and McNeil (21). Ratings on self-insight obtained in reference to each subject included such factors as willingness to accept blame for difficulties, ability to sense the seriousness of problems, capacity to state assets and liabilities and to make calm and realistic judgments as to how behavior could be improved in the future. After approximately two years, follow-up data were obtained to determine what factors were most closely related to ratings on behavior improvements over this period of time. To the surprise of the investigators, the ratings on self-insight proved to be more closely correlated with the ratings on behavior improvement than any other factor studied.

Rogers, Kell, and McNeil were so impressed with their findings that they believed much more attention should be given to developing realistic self-regarding attitudes and self-understanding in delinquents, rather than depending so exclusively upon environmental manipulations as represented in foster home placements, economic assistance, probationary supervision, and efforts to improve family relationships. They believe that this objective of "insightful acceptance of self, and positive reorientation of self" can best be achieved through individual psychotherapy in clinics, through classrooms with specially trained teachers, through extension of counseling services in schools, and through group therapy carried on in schools or in conjunction with a recreational group.

Some other studies have also shown better quality adjustments to be associated with superior or improved self-insight. Norman, for example, found that among a group of seventy-two men, those who were characterized from his data as having an optimal amount of self-insight were also, as a group, the ones who were most desired as friends and companions by their associates (17). Likewise Austin and Collins have shown that it is possible to bring about some positive personality gains (as measured by self-ratings and case-history material) through a nine-month course in psychology on the high school level (3).

From these kinds of evidence it seems certain that any avenue that a school can use to help children and young people gain greater self-understanding and self-acceptance will contribute to building stronger self-regarding attitudes. From the standpoint of the classroom teacher, the most specialized means for accomplishing these objectives lie in the use of the discussion exercises and materials described in Chapter 13. From the standpoint of school administration, the most specialized means for increasing self-understanding consists of guidance services, and particularly those which include psychological counseling.

REFERENCES

1. Allport, G. W., *Personality — A Psychological Interpretation,* Ch's. VI and VII. New York: Henry Holt and Co., Inc., 1937.
2. Anderson, C. M., "The Self Images: A Theory of the Dynamics of Behavior," *Mental Hygiene,* 36, 1952, 227-244.
3. Austin, H. T. and F. I. Collins, "An Experiment in Improving the Personality of High School Seniors," *Journal of Educational Psychology,* 31, 1940, 550-553.
4. Benjamins, J., "Changes in Performance in Relation to Influences upon Self-Conceptualization," *Journal of Abnormal and Social Psychology,* 45, 1950, 473-480.
5. Berger, E. M., "The Relation Between Expressed Acceptance of Self and Expressed Acceptance of Others," *Journal of Abnormal and Social Psychology,* 47, 1952, 778-782.
6. Brandt, R. M., "Self: Missing Link for Understanding Behavior," *Mental Hygiene,* 41, 1957, 24-33.
7. Brownfain, J. J., "Stability of the Self-concept as a Dimension of Personality," *Journal of Abnormal and Social Psychology,* 47, 1952, 597-606.
8. Buckley, H. and K. Scanlan, "Faith Enough for Both," *Childhood Education,* 32, 1955-56, 230-232.
9. Cogan, L. C., A. M. Conklin, and H. L. Hollingworth, "An Experimental Study of Self-Analysis, Estimates of Associates, and the Results of Tests," *School and Society,* 2, 1915, 171-179.
10. Cohen, L. D., "Level-of-Aspiration Behavior and Feelings of Adequacy and Self-Acceptance," *Journal of Abnormal and Social Psychology,* 49, 1954, 84-86.
11. Combs, A. W. and D. Snygg, *Individual Behavior* (2nd ed.). New York: Harper and Brothers Publishers, 1959.

12. Cowen, E. L., F. Heilizer, and H. S. Axelrod, "Self-Concept, Conflict Indicators and Learning," *Journal of Abnormal and Social Psychology*, 51, 1955, 242-245.
13. Dai, B., "A Socio-Psychiatric Approach to Personality Organization," *American Sociological Review*, 17, 1952, 44-49.
14. Gordon, T., *Group Centered Leadership*. Boston: Houghton Mifflin Co., 1955.
15. Hartley, Ruth Edith, "Sociality in Preadolescent Boys," *Contributions to Education*, No. 918. New York: Bureau of Publications, Teachers College, Columbia University, 1946.
16. Lecky, P., *Self-Consistency — A Theory of Personality*. New York: Island Press, 1945.
17. Norman, R. D., "The Interrelationships among Acceptance-Rejection, Self-Other Identity, Insight into Self, and Realistic Perception of Others," *Journal of Social Psychology*, 37, 1953, 205-235.
18. Perkins, Hugh V., "Changing Perception of Self," *Childhood Education*, 34, 1957, 82-84.
19. Rogers, C. R., "Some Observations on the Organization of Personality," *The American Psychologist*, 2, 1947, 358-368.
20. ———, *Client-Centered Therapy, Its Current Practice, Implications and Theory*. Boston: Houghton-Mifflin Co., 1951.
21. ———, B. L. Kell, and H. McNeil, "The Role of Self-Understanding in the Prediction of Behavior," *Journal of Consult. Psychology*, 12, 1948, 174-186.
22. Schiff, H., "Judgmental Response Sets in the Perception of Sociometric Status," *Sociometry*, 17, 1954, 207-227.
23. Sheerer, E. T., "An Analysis of the Relationship Between Acceptance of and Respect for Self and Acceptance of and Respect for Others in Ten Counseling Cases," *Journal of Consulting Psychology*, 13, 1949, 169-175.
24. Spivack, Sarah S., "A Study of a Method of Appraising Self-Acceptance and Self-Rejection," *Journal of Genetic Psychology*, 88-89, 1956, 183-202.
25. Stock, D., "An Investigation into the Interrelation Between the Self-Concept and Feelings Directed Toward Other Persons and Groups," *Journal of Consulting Psychology*, 13, 1949, 176-180.
26. Stotland, Ezra and Alvin Zander, "Effects of Public and Private Failure on Self-Evaluation," *Journal of Abnormal and Social Psychology*, 56, 1958, 223-229.
27. Taylor, C. and A. W. Combs, "Self-Acceptance and Adjustments," *Journal of Abnormal and Social Psychology*, 16, 1952, 89-91.
28. Walsh, Ann M., *Self Concepts of Bright Boys with Learning Difficulties*. New York: Bureau of Publications, Teachers College, Columbia University, 1956.

29. Wylie, R. C., "Some Relationships Between Defensiveness and Self-Concept Discrepancies," *Journal of Personality*, 25, 1957, 600-616.

QUESTIONS AND EXERCISES

1. Discuss critically the idea that all behavior is determined by an individual's perceptional field. How does the role of past experience enter into this conception of causation?
2. Analyze some of your own actions from the point of view stated in Question 1. Can you see how your behavior would have been different if your perceptional field had been different?
3. Analyze yourself, or some other person, to try to understand how a negative, or devaluating self-concept, can influence behavior in unfortunate ways.
4. Discuss the differences between egotism and a strong, positive self-concept.
5. Confer with an experienced teacher to find out what he or she has done to try to help children characterized by very low or negative self-concepts.
6. Select a child who fits quite well the description given in this chapter of a person with high, positive, self-regarding attitudes, and find out all you can about his background in an effort to understand his present self-adjustment.
7. Discuss the material of this chapter in relation to the question of what kind of teacher is best liked. From this frame of reference, point out some mistaken notions about what kind of teacher is best liked.
8. Write a brief paper, give an oral report, or stimulate a class discussion on the statement: "We like other people to the extent that they help us to like ourselves better."

SELECTED FILMS

The Eye of the Beholder. 25 minutes. Excellent presentation of how the same events may be perceived very differently from different personal frames of reference.

Feeling of Rejection. 18 minutes. Very clear portrayal of the personal tragedies likely to be experienced by those who are not permitted to develop positive, self-regarding attitudes.

Overdependency. 32 minutes. Illustrates on the adult level the kind of personal frustrations that result from lack of self-confidence and denial of self-realization on a mature level.

Preface to Life. 29 minutes. Excellent in showing need of letting a child find his own ways of self-realization as opposed to domination from parents.

8

CONFORMITY, ADAPTABILITY,

HOW ARE CONFORMITY and adaptability related to the attainment of sound mental health? The answer to this question is primarily in terms of the need for introjection of behavioral norms in regard to style of dress, beliefs, morals, values, etc., as a basis for socialization within a particular culture. However, in this chapter the problem of degree of conformity within school situations is primarily focused not on the prevailing mores of our major cultural norms, but on a wide range of subcultural and peer-group behaviors bearing on fads, social interests, and personal values.

AND MENTAL HEALTH

Undoubtedly all experienced teachers have witnessed the compulsive desires of many adults to "go along with" clique-defined behaviors, have been distressed at pupils' hurt feelings arising from interpersonal conflicts over the struggle for group status, and have also been pleased to see some phychological gains arising from the pressure to conform.

In other words, conformity has both negative and positive aspects. Probably the major positive value of conformity is in the fact that a considerable degree of acceptance of the customs and values of a group is one of the conditions for attaining security and status in this group. Furthermore, a fairly high degree of conformity to those expectations and standards considered most important in a particular population is necessary for mutual trust. Although some differences will be tolerated in most groups, while other differences will be encouraged and still others will be enjoyed, there still must be an extensive and solid foundation in similarities and in feelings of oneness, before strong interpersonal attachments can develop, or before leadership influences can be exerted. Just as an individual must be basically *at one* with himself (not torn by conflicts and doubts) in order to like and respect himself, so the members of a group must have a large common ground in customs, interests, and values before they can develop strong interpersonal attachments or a high degree of trust. Otherwise there are always feelings expressed in reference to a particular individual that he is "not one of our kind," "he doesn't belong," or "he doesn't know us."

Although a considerable degree of conformity is basic to a socially acceptable personality and to leadership influence, and therefore is essential to the mental health of the great majority of children and adolescents in our schools, this conformity does not play a highly discriminating role in determining either interpersonal attractions or status after its primary contribution is made. Within a population which is fairly homogeneous in regard to conformity-demands, such as most school groups, individual personality characteristics and abilities become of major importance in determining varying degrees of positive and negative feelings and of respect among the members.

IMPORTANCE OF ADAPTABILITY

One outstanding fact about conformity which most teachers have probably observed is the fact of conflicting expectations in different groups in which we all participate. In a complex society such as ours, conformity can never be simply a matter of routine. The kind of behavior needed to be highly regarded in one group may run counter to what is needed in another group. This fact emphasizes the importance of adaptability.

Although there are large differences in the extent to which individuals in our culture find it possible, expedient, or desirable to adopt contrary behavior patterns in order to conform to the expectations of the many groups in which they move, it seems safe to say that these differences are a matter of degree only. Even within the same group a good many adaptations are generally necessary to conform to the shifts of emphasis in approved behavior on different occasions and in varied circumstances.

In fact, a person who is seriously lacking in adaptability is likely to be considered inhuman, insensitive to the responses of others, and something of a bore in most situations. He is rigid, and is therefore either unaware of, or is unyielding to, the finer shades of behavior expectations which are found in all group situations except those in which stereotyped responses are sufficient. Thus the rigid person is characterized by a high degree of egocentricity, since he persists in living a certain style of life irrespective of the wishes, needs, and inner feelings of his associates.

The adaptable person, on the other hand, is sufficiently attuned to the responses of others and to the feeling tone of situations that he can sense what kind of behavior is most appropriate and can respond accordingly. He can "fit into" a wide range of social situations. He always knows "what the score is." He has the security arising from group rapport; he has the strength arising from flexibility.

In the more personal affairs of life the adaptable individual is the one who can shift his plans when circumstances change and can do it without a lot of complaining; he can make the best of any bad situation; and he can tolerate for a time people he doesn't particularly like for the sake of attaining a useful objective, or simply for the sake of being polite. When his group decides to play a game that he does not like to play he nevertheless plays it to the best of his ability. When he is not chosen for the leadership role that he expected to get he nevertheless participates, and without pouting. When he does not get to make the oral report that he wanted to give, or when his part in a dramatization is shifted, he tries to understand why this thing happened and accepts it without anger or without a feeling that he is being discriminated against.

VALUES OF CONFORMITY AND ADAPTABILITY

On the nursery school level, both Koch (14) and Lippitt (15) found that those children who received the highest number of positive choices in sociometric-type tests were characterized by quick, unobtrusive adjustment to the daily run of situations, such as complying with requests, waiting turn, and listening attentively. By contrast, the low-choice children were characterized much more by unadaptive behavior such as refusing, dawdling, and silly acts.

Likewise, from a five-year follow-up study of approximately eighty children from the nursery school into the elementary grades, Van Alstyne and Hattwick report that one of the most certain conclusions from their teacher ratings is that those children who were most consistently classified as being "well adjusted" in their groups were also characterized on the rating scales as being "adaptable and flexible." Under this general heading were included such specific traits as being responsive to suggestions, being willing to lead or to follow according to the necessities of a play situation, and being quick to accept new ways of doing things (27). Also, in a population of several hundred adolescent boys Dimock has found that popular boys were rated by their adult leaders as being much superior to unpopular boys in such conforming-type behavior as "cooperates and helps willingly" and "observes rules and regulations."

Of course, we would not expect to get the kind of findings reviewed above in a school, or in any other organization, in which most of the children were strongly antagonistic to the requirements of a situation or to certain persons in positions of authority over them. In such instances those who defy the rules and show the most aggression against those in charge are often the ones who are most respected by the group members.

Additional studies among college students and adults by Burks (5), Gibb (11), and Terman (25), have produced data that emphasize the importance to successful interpersonal relationships, and to leadership roles, of the general trait of social adaptability. In these studies this trait was evidenced by a sense of fitness of responses to varied situations as contrasted with formalized responses and rigidity.

CONFORMITY IN CLOTHES

Conformity in clothes is one of the more obvious requirements for in-group acceptance. The child or adolescent whose clothes are definitely substandard, particularly in middle-class school groups, has a very serious social barrier against him and one which is likely to cause him many mental and emotional strains. Unless this barrier can be removed it is not likely (although not impossible) that any other corrective measures will improve his group status.

Conformity in clothes, however, should not be thought of simply in terms of neatness, style, or attractiveness. On the contrary, conformity may demand some dress effects that are bizarre, unkempt, and unhealthy.

Some of the peculiar demands of conformity in regard to clothes are found in fads. Even small children sense the importance of dressing according to the latest flair, such as wearing a certain color of hair ribbon or a special kind of cap. A mother of a first-grade boy bought him a new suit with attractive suspender buttons on the pants. The boy gave the pants a quick glance and flatly announced, "Don't think I am going to wear that thing until you take those buttons off. I am not going to wear suspenders." The mother felt it was necessary for the boy to wear suspenders. A conflict ensued which was finally resolved by putting the buttons on the inside of the trousers and under a shirt and a sweater, thus making sure that the suspenders were well hidden from the view of the other boys in his class.

That the clothes prescribed by group pressures may be contrary to health standards is illustrated in the case of a second-grade group of boys who formed a little clique that was quite powerful in controlling affairs among the boys. During a cold spell a mother brought her boy's jacket to school at noon so he could wear it home, but her son refused to put it on. The mother could not understand his reaction. During her conflict with the boy, the leader of the clique came by and observing his pal in difficulty he announced to the mother: "The brave boys in here are tough and they don't wear much clothes." Not wanting her boy to be branded "a sissy," or to lose his group status, the mother took the jacket home but made her son promise to hurry home as fast as he could.

On older age-levels, especially through adolescence, the emphasis on conformity in dress and other aspects of personal appearance is equally as strong, if not stronger, than during childhood. In Tryon's study of adolescents the most acceptable twelve-year-old boys were those whose appearance was somewhat unkempt, whereas among the girls of this age-level a neat appearance was very closely associated with popularity ratings (26).

It is interesting to note that conformity in dress frequently embodies contradictory behavior. On some items of dress it is important that an individual wear almost exactly what other group members are wearing, but on other items it is equally important that he not closely duplicate the appearance of others. It is, for example, essential at a particular time that an adolescent girl wear silk stockings of a certain shade because this is the shade "all the others are wearing," but she would likely be embarrassed to find a duplicate of her dress adorning another girl, especially if the occasion were somewhat formal. Conformity, then, is not always a matter of "doing what others do," but rather following social definitions — some of which are contradictory to each other — from the standpoint of overt behavior.

All experienced school people are aware that clothing fads, especially on secondary school levels, may become unduly oppressive and may also be ridiculous from an adult point of view. In such circumstances it is important that members of the school staff do not underestimate the importance of the clothing fad in the social psychology of the students, and do not make fun of their desire to belong to particular cliques. On the positive side it is equally important that efforts be made to reduce the oppressive nature of the conformity pattern. Such efforts are most likely to be successful through group discussions in homerooms, clubs, and physical education classes, and when the content of these discussions is not entirely on clothing fads but also on such general topics as "Ways to Have an Interesting Personality." When such discussions are well conducted they may reduce the emphasis on overt conformity and call attention to the many ways in which students can be constructively different.

CONFORMITY AND PRODUCTIVITY

The pressure of group conformity is an important factor in determining the amount of work that is done in a wide range of situations. How great this pressure is depends primarily upon such factors as the degree of in-group feelings among the group members, how long they have been together in a particular work situation, extent of personal identification with the task-objective, and the degree to which they hold antagonistic as opposed to cooperative attitudes toward their leaders or directors.

The imporance of group sentiment in determining production

has been emphasized in studies of industrial work units (19). These investigations clearly show that work-units, through informal communications, soon develop definitions in regard to what constitutes a "day's work," and that a person who does not conform quite closely to this definition is likely to feel the sting of social disapproval soon by being the object of such epithets as "eager beaver," "rate buster," or the "slave," while those who persist in doing less than the group definition calls for are likely to be derided as "chiselers."

These studies also show that sometimes an individual who is rejected by his fellow workers will strive extra hard to become one of the very best producers in his unit. This extra efficiency nets him a feeling of superiority over his associates, may bring him additional financial rewards, and may also be the lever whereby he is able to pry himself out of his present situation into another group or into a supervisory position.

Probably every experienced teacher has observed these social processes operating in classroom groups and in the school as a whole. They have seen how students' academic efforts are affected by class and school attitudes in regard to the importance of learning and the prestige attached to grades. They have seen bright students refrain from doing their best work lest they be branded as "book-worms," "grinds," or "mark-scrubbers." They have known cliques that have influenced all their members to a low level of academic achievement by conferring prestige on "get-by" attitudes. Also they have seen some bright students who study extra hard to compensate for interpersonal failures, and who apparently hope that their diligence will, like that of the industrious workers mentioned above, enable them to gain a position of superiority over their classmates or to be promoted out of the group that has rejected them.

The foregoing remarks should not give the impression that the demands of conformity must necessarily lower productivity. This is only half the story. Conformity demands may raise productivity when a group's level of aspiration is high.[1] An individual who is inclined to

[1] Some studies in factory situations have shown that group productivity can be significantly raised under proper leadership which stimulates worker participation in setting production goals. See J. G. Miller, *Experiments in Social Process* (New York: McGraw-Hill Book Company, 1950), Chapter 6.

work below his capacity may be stimulated to unusual efforts when he finds himself in a group in which productive effort is one of the important conditions for high status. It is, therefore, of first-rate importance that schools and particular classes become places where productive effort has prestige value in the peer culture of their students.

The achievement of this objective is affected by many factors. Chief among these are: the cultural level of the homes from which the students come, the long-range occupational objectives of the students, and the extent to which the students are ego-involved in academic learnings as a result of their participation in helping to determine the nature and content of these learnings. According to several experimental studies by Berkowitz (2), by Berkowitz and Levy (3), and by Dittes and Kelley (10), the extent to which a high expectancy-level existing in a particular class would operate to induce all class members to work up to their maximum would depend primarily upon their degree of pride in class membership, their feelings of mutual interdependence for achieving group rewards, the extent to which they perceived group goals as being important to themselves either now or in the future, their feelings of interpersonal acceptance by their classmates, and the degree to which the class members perceive that all of them, as opposed to only a few, can share in group rewards.

Particularly in their work with pupils who are low-achievers it is important for teachers and guidance personnel to recognize that low achievement may be as much a result of group processes as of individual weaknesses. Certainly both of these sources should be investigated. Sometimes the only way an individual can be "pulled up" is to take measures to raise the expectancy-level of the group he is in. A number of suggestions bearing on this objective are given at the end of this chapter.

CONFORMITY, ADAPTABILITY AND WEAKNESS

In certain remarks made above it was implied that conformity and adaptability may, under certain conditions, represent serious weaknesses from the standpoint of personality development and mental health standards for individuals. If we ask directly "Is this true?" the answer is very definitely in the affirmative. The "certain conditions" under which this is true are primarily (1) when these traits are acquired to an excessive degree and (2) when they represent a lack of personal integrity.

The individual who endeavors to adapt himself to all shades of opinions and standards with which he comes into contact is soon likely to find himself without genuine admirers in any camp. He lacks the strong, positive, self-regarding attitudes emphasized in the preceding chapter. Tolerance must be viewed, not as the lack of opinions or standards, but as a sincere attempt to understand or to appreciate the views and behavior adjustments of those who differ from us. Understanding and appreciation need not lead to acceptance of ways that differ from our own. The person who prides himself on being broad-minded may be so broad that he lacks depth and convictions, and therefore has no cutting edges to his personality. Such a person may have a good many like-minded friends, but he is generally regarded as ineffective since he does not try to influence, stimulate, or inspire others.

The weakness of excessive conformity has been frequently pointed out by writers in psychology, psychiatry, and mental hygiene, such as Cantor (6), Gross (12), Redl and Wattenberg (18), and Sarbin (21). These writers have discussed the variety of meanings which may be associated with such terms as *conformity, normality,* and *adjustment,* and have made it clear that all three of these generally desirable objectives may be severe sources of frustration to individual initiative and leadership when too great emphasis is placed on being like others, being "normal," or being well adjusted to a relatively low-level environment. In other words, social security or group approval may be purchased at too high a price in terms of other values that may be lost.

However, it is well to point out that moderate degrees of conformity and adaptability are not necessarily handicaps to originality and daring. On the contrary, it is far nearer the truth to say that good social adjustment lays a solid foundation for constructive originality and creative endeavors. A strong sense of ego-security arising from good group status often provides the basis for the courage necessary to dare to be different in some constructive manner. Such an individual can afford to risk losing (perhaps only temporarily) some positive feelings from others, since he has enough of both personal and social strength to have some reserve to trade on. The insecure person, too, may have a strong motivation to be different, and he, too, may be different in some very constructive ways; but, on the other hand, he is often different in unsocial and antisocial ways such as negativism, indiscriminate rebelliousness, fighting, or delinquency.

It can frequently be observed that many insecure persons are the very ones who are most slavish in conformity. Having only a poor and shaky hold on the prize of interpersonal acceptance, they dare not risk deviation from well-defined norms lest their grip become even more uncertain. Their superconforming behavior may be a defense against anxiety. As long as they can be supergood they can keep their own hostile impulses in check and they avoid retaliation from others. Also we may suspect that many people who are strongly attached to rules, regulations, and ceremonies, and to all kinds of highly prescribed situations where nothing unexpected can happen, are suffering from anxiety about their competence in spontaneous social relationships.

In his study of dominance and submission among 130 college women, Maslow described the very submissive type of woman as "oversocialized," in the sense that she had so completely introjected social norms that she was extremely inhibited; she was highly conventional in regard to etiquette, sense of humor, esthetic tastes, and religious and moral attitudes (16). Typically this kind of woman was rigid and tense. She lacked what Maslow calls "psychological freedom." Her self was hemmed-in on all sides by her fears of making a mistake and her anxieties over her interpersonal failures.

We would not expect leadership or social innovations to come from the kind of people described in the preceding paragraphs. Their personalities do not provide the kind of soil from which courage and originality spring. Their lives are dominated by the need to conform, to please, to protect their weak selves. Good social adjustment, then, is not the handicap to creative individualism that it is sometimes thought to be. Instead it can and should provide the firm foundation needed for constructive deviations from social norms. Just as a military commander is more likely to risk forays into enemy territory if he knows he has an adequate and safe base of supplies, so a person is more likely to offer leadership toward some positive social contribution when he has a strong base of group belongingness from which to operate.

We cannot assume, however, that all those who have a firm foundation in social security will go beyond this level and actually achieve a noticeable degree of originality or uniqueness. They will do so only if they have the kind of development which *permits* and *stimulates* the growth of all kinds of abilities and personal assets.

In fact, from the standpoint of one significant view on personality, we can say that only as individuals vary from complete conformity can they be said to have "personality." This view is emphasized by Stagner (1937) when he states that "personality depends upon individual differences to nonadaptive behavior" (24—p. 7). This means that an individual will stand out and make an impression on others to the extent that he is *unique.* Perfectly adaptive behavior is that which exactly fits the requirements or expectations of a particular situation. It is complete conformity. This makes for security and safety but does not contribute to "personality" as defined above.

The person who goes to a meeting or to a party and dresses, talks, and otherwise conducts himself in very close accord with the social definition of the proper thing to do at that time and place, will certainly not be criticized nor will he make enemies, but neither will he be likely to attract others. He will not be thought of as having an interesting personality. A good many persons will not even remember that he was there. He will fit so well into the social background that, like a chameleon, he will not be noticed.

Uniqueness, however, is seldom effective when it is due to calculated efforts to be unique. The person who tries hard to be peppy, different, and fascinating is not likely to succeed with any but the most gullible. Genuine uniqueness must be the product of personal integrity, real interests, and spontaneous expressions of a *self* that is actually *there* rather than a manikin-type self that is paraded for a particular occasion.

An example of this latter point is found in the case of a rejected sixth-grade girl who lacked personal integrity. This girl was observed by the writer to use varied behavior, such as aggressive fighting, crying, pouting, telling "tall tales," apologetic behavior, ingratiating behavior, cleverness, laughter, and unusual generosity, under varying circumstances as she writhed and turned in her futile efforts to wring some satisfaction from her social environment. She was willing to try anything that she thought might "work" even temporarily, but she continued to be rejected.

SUGGESTIONS FOR SCHOOL PROGRAMS

One conclusion that the foregoing discussion leads to is that teachers and school administrators need to have a good appreciation of the fact that all pupils, and especially those above the level of the primary grades, have a peer culture to adjust to as well as an adult culture. Fortunately these two cultures are, for most children and youth, far more alike than they are different. Outside of delinquent gangs, those who are most respected by their peers are much more likely to be characterized by adult-approved traits than by behavior contrary to adult standards.

However, it is well-known that there are some real and persistent differences between the conformity-expectancies of many groups of children and youth, on the one hand, and adult groups on the other. This is true not only in regard to clothing and health standards as previously described, but also in regard to safety precautions, vocabulary, and recreational pursuits. A strong clique may confer prestige value upon such generally disapproved behaviors as reckless driving of automobiles, swearing and obscene language, stealing, and truancy from school. There are cases of high school girls who have submitted to overt sex relations, even though the act was repulsive to them, simply because it was the kind of behavior defined as necessary to belong to a particular club.

Shobbs mentions the case of an elementary school boy who he says was "babyish" at times, although he frequently performed well in leadership roles, and was always chosen in sociometric tests by the more influential boys. When this boy was questioned about his "babyish" behavior he replied: "You gotta do this to have friends. If you just do your work and don't make some fun in class, the fellows think you're a sissy." (22.)

The chief problem in all such cases involving so-called babyish behavior is to try to keep the child from overadapting to certain aspects of his peer code to the point that he fails to acquire a sense of responsibility from the adult code. This is a problem on all age-levels. Smucker, for example, has shown from his studies of cliques on a college campus that a good many students are more loyal to the values of cliques and other subgroups than to the standards associated with the college as a whole or with administrative policies (23).

Undoubtedly the greatest problems arising from conflicting loyalties between peer codes and adult codes occur in those families, schools, or churches in which a great deal of emphasis is placed on the validity of adult codes, together with strongly disapproving attitudes toward any peer-group codes that are at variance with those of the adults. Under such conditions a child or adolescent may, on the one hand, overconform to adult values and become supergood and morally rigid, and as a consequence be "out of step" in many ways with most of his peers; on the other hand, he may rebel against adult values and become a delinquent.

A guiding principle for adults, then, is to adopt "live and let live" attitudes in regard to peer-group codes vs. adult codes. Both are essential to the integrated or balanced development of children and youth. Both must be introjected simultaneously; otherwise there is certain to be marked imbalance one way or the other. If these kinds of attitudes prevail, and if children and youth are allowed many constructive ways for establishing personal identity and achieving normal sex roles, the danger of their adopting antisocial peer-behavior codes will be minimized.

Keeping a pupil with his peer group

One way whereby teachers can show that they recognize the importance of the peer culture is not to do things that have the effect of pulling a pupil apart from his classmates so that he is made to appear different or superior in ways which are resented by his age-mates.

An example of this kind of teacher behavior is found in the case of a fifth-grade girl. This pupil was among the higher ones in her class in choices received on several sociometric measurements. She also gave many choices to others. Yet, in spite of this generous flow of choices both to her and from her, it was evident to the teacher and several student observers who were assigned to this room that there was some kind of psychological barrier existing between this girl and the other pupils. She was seldom observed in any personal relationship with other children. She was not in a clique. She nearly always walked to and from school alone. That she herself was aware of her lack of intimacy with other children was indicated by her response to a questionnaire on wishes. She stated as her first wish: "I wish I had one true friend."

This girl was intelligent, highly responsible, and competent in her schoolwork. She was a little on the sober side, and gave the impression of being older than her chronological age. Naturally the teacher and the student observers were curious as to why there was such a discrepancy between the sociometric choices and the overt consummation of feelings between this girl and her classmates. After considerable checking of observations it was decided that the psychological barrier existing in this case was the fact that the teacher had frequently used this girl to help other pupils in their academic work, had often appointed her to do things in the room, and had on numerous occasions put her in charge of the class when she (the teacher) had gone out of the room. It seemed that the other children had come to regard this highly responsible girl as the teacher's assistant rather than one of them. She had been pulled apart from the normal social processes of her peers. She was respected by them and no doubt liked by most of them, but she was apparently regarded as living on a different level. This point was strikingly illustrated when one little boy in a group of which she was chairman referred to her as "mother."

Unfortunately there was not sufficient time left in the school term to check the validity of this conclusion, but it seems reasonable, and it is in accord with observations of other group leaders on similar cases. Coyle, for example, cites the case of a girl who was not well accepted in a Y-Teen club in spite of many favorable qualities, due, she believes, to the fact that this girl assumed too much of an adult role in the group (7—p. 124). She often reminded the other girls of how certain kinds of behavior "would look." This girl had to take considerable family responsibility at home, so she apparently transferred this role to the Y-Teen club. Coyle states that adult leaders frequently welcome the kind of "assistance" in group control that this girl offered, but without realizing the effect upon the individual who is allowed to perform in this capacity. What is needed, she says, is to help such a person take an equal and cooperative role with his peers.

Another procedure sometimes used by teachers, which often creates a psychological barrier between an individual and his group, is that of holding up one child as an example, especially when the example bears on personal conduct. Generally no harm is done when the kind of behavior referred to is such relatively unimportant things as having a clean desk or sitting straight, or when some particular ability is praised. However, considerable harm may be done to a student's acceptability-status by holding him up as an example of such behavior as courtesy, responsibility, diligence, honesty, or obedience. Most students have some ego-involvement in these kinds of behavior, so that when one person is officially designated as being superior to others in his group in these conduct areas, the others feel a threat to their self-regard, which in turn produces feelings of antagonism toward the source of the threat. Furthermore, excessive praise of a child or a young person for adult-approved behavior serves to intensify differences between adult and peer-group codes. This is likely to be most true among older children and adolescents.

Particularly among high school students, teachers should be careful not to put a student "on the spot" by making him appear "too good." An example of what may happen is found in the case of a high school English teacher who greatly praised a boy's theme. This happened two more times within a period of two weeks. The third time she called on him to read his theme, he said he didn't have one. The teacher was obviously hurt and disappointed. The boy offered no explanation; he said he just didn't have it. The teacher probably never understood why her prize pupil "let her down." Her academic background, and perhaps, too, her lack of group-belongingness during her childhood and adolescence, made her oblivious to the social forces operating in the little group in front of her.

The need for respecting the peer culture is also present in many efforts to make some kind of special provisions for an exceptionally bright student, such as excusing him from certain class recitations or allowing him to leave the room to go to the library when others do not go. Although such efforts are highly commendable, they should be managed through official announcements and under conditions that are open to anyone who can qualify, in order that the intellectually gifted child does not appear to his classmates to be a recipient of special favors.

Fostering individual uniqueness

Recognition of the importance of the peer culture does not mean, however, that individual uniqueness should be played down or discouraged. There is no need for one of these objectives to crowd out the other. Although it is frequently (but not always) true that a child who persists in some kind of peculiar behavior, or who refuses to "go along with" major group-activities, will experience considerable isolation, the teacher, nevertheless, can show this child that he is interested in him and respects his right to be different. Furthermore, the teacher can usually aid such a child to pursue his particular interests (when they are not antisocial) by helping him find reading materials, by conferring with his parents about his needs, or by helping him to see how he might incorporate his special interest into his schoolwork requirements.

In considering all cases of group-norm deviations, the first responsibility of a teacher is to try to determine if the deviation is some kind of compulsive revolt based on hostility or fear, or instead is an expression of genuine uniqueness springing from strength and integrity. Obviously it is the latter kind of deviation which should be stimulated when it is not present and encouraged when it is discovered. In addition to teacher support for these kinds of deviations, efforts should also be made to create a classroom climate that is tolerant of, if not favorable to, eccentric individuals who are honestly trying to be themselves rather than rubber stamps.

What should a student do who would like to attain some status and personal acceptability in a school group, but who finds that he cannot attain these goals with most of the members because they engage in practices that he believes to be immoral, such as dancing, swearing, gambling, and drinking? It seems that the best counsel he could be given would be not to condemn overtly the behavior he disapproves, and not to forfeit his integrity by doing things against his principles. Rather he should maintain a tolerant, nonjudging attitude toward the behavior of which he disapproves, and at the same time prove himself to be a cordial, interesting, and helpful companion to other students. Also he can be counseled to try to make an objective analysis of the disapproved behavior to see if all of it is as bad as he has been taught to believe.

Striving for high group-expectancy

Obviously, if peer codes are as important in determining all kinds of behavior as has been emphasized in this chapter, it must follow that one of the most effective means of raising the level of conduct of individuals is to try to establish conditions that will raise the level of peer-code expectancy. So often have the limitations and crippling effects of conformity been pointed out that it is often overlooked that the desire to conform can pull people up as well as down. As mentioned previously in this chapter, conformity can elevate as well as degrade in respect to any behavior standard. This is a matter of common observation in regard to highly courageous military units, highly productive work units, and highly successful sport teams. Who does not know of at least some individuals who have been inspired to behave on a more demanding level than ever before in their lives because of their desire to live up to a particular group expectancy?

All this emphasizes the importance of building up groups with high morale and in-group pride. How can this be done, especially in schools? This is too large a question to be considered in detail in this discussion, but the suggestions listed below are especially pertinent. Those in charge of a group, such as school administrators and classroom teachers, should make every effort to:

1. Set a high level of work-expectancy which is stimulating to all levels of ability.
2. Get those students of high sociometric status to identify with the school and with academic success.

3. Build up a high degree of mutually reciprocated interpersonal relationships.
4. Help students see the long-range benefits or objectives of their schooling.
5. Help students to have a large part in managing their group affairs, including their academic learnings, and provide for some cooperative endeavors.
6. See to it that adult-approved values are rewarded in peer-group living, but at the same time allow considerable leeway for some peer-group values that may be at variance with adult-approved conduct.
7. Provide for a wide distribution of different kinds of academic and social rewards so that all pupils can see the possibility of gaining some status and personal satisfactions.

One limitation that must always be considered in evaluating the importance of group-inspired behavior is that such behavior may be pretty well tied to only this one group. Unless the members involved introject the kind of behavior emphasized and set up some individual standards which they regard as their own, there may not be much transfer of a particular level of behavior-expectancy to other groups. This applies to both socially approved and socially disapproved behavior.

Flexible school program

Although a school program should be characterized primarily by stability and predictability, since these characteristics are regarded as essential to the development of stable and secure personalities, it is also important, in the interests of promoting adaptability, that provisions be made for a considerable amount of flexibility. This means that routines will not always be followed, well-laid plans will sometimes be changed, and occasionally rather striking innovations will be introduced. These points apply not only to school administration practices but also to classroom management. Both administrators and teachers should be sufficiently spontaneous to be able to shift their plans when circumstances change. The "show" does not always have to go on exactly as planned.

A school or a class is not likely to be too inflexible if the pupils or students are allowed responsible roles in determining what goes on. One of the conditions making for undue rigidity in any situation is that only a few at the top of the administrative hierarchy have anything to say about what goes on within the group.

The writer was in a second-grade room one morning before school and heard the teacher state briefly what she had planned for the first hour. However, just before the bell sounded a boy came up to her with excitement written all over his face and announced that he and several other pupils had prepared a puppet show illustrating one of the stories in their readers, and that they would like to put it on for the class right then. The teacher immediately shifted her plans and allowed the pupils the first fifteen minutes to present their puppet show.

We do not have adequate data with which to assess reliably the extent to which a flexible school program contributes to the development of an adaptable personality. From our general knowledge of development, however, we do have reason to believe that a flexible program in any situation will tend to develop more adaptable persons. One reason for this belief is that such a program puts emphasis on *experience* as opposed to simply written or verbal appeals. This does not mean that the academic curriculum has no contribution to make toward the development of adaptability and tolerance, but rather that educators interested in these objectives should place their chief reliance on promoting a total school program that incorporates adaptability on an experience basis.

Instruction on intelligent adaptability

Although it is difficult to determine just how much contribution to adaptability is made by instruction, via lectures, readings, discussions, etc., we have reason to believe that such approaches can have some value when they are directed toward the objective of building up attitudes favorable to accepting changes in all areas of life. Courses dealing with large social and economic problems are particularly appropriate for this purpose, but so also are those which deal with the personal and social problems of individuals, such as certain courses in home economics, in English, in psychology, in sociology, and in religion.

Through such courses, as well as in discussion groups in clubs and churches, young people should be helped to think through some of the conflicts in values and in overt behavior which they are faced with now, and which they will continue to face in subsequent years. Some of these conflicts are well stated in the following quotation from a psychiatrist, Kindwall:

> Furthermore, the child, as he grows up, must inhibit his natural tendencies to acquire the things he wants by direct action; yet he must maintain his capacity and zest for competitive struggle for the goods of this world, in which struggle he must draw a line of hair-like fineness between what is moral and what is immoral or "wrong." And although he must acquire property and wealth, if possible, he must also be altruistic, generous, noble. He must be constantly exposed to sex stimulation through visual, aural, and olfactory channels, and he must take a manly interest in the other sex in order to be acceptable socially, yet he must remain continent, or find his sexual outlets under a cloud of such conflicting rules, traditions, and emotions that the light of reason never penetrates. He must have strong drives, be aggressive and alert, yet conceal these drives, as much as possible. He must have a deep respect of the truth, yet learn to suppress, deny, or distort it on innumerable occasions. On such foundations does our civilization rest. If a man cannot make these fine distinctions, he is called a "rigid personality," and it seems to be true that such personalities are more liable to mental or emotional derangement. Rigidity, indicating strength in mathematics, thus becomes weakness in life. (13.)

A psychoanalyst, Franz Alexander, has pointed out the persistent need of adaptability in our rapidly changing culture and has emphasized that "the instrument of flexible adaptation is the conscious ego" (1). In other words, we cannot expect to develop adaptable people simply by routine training, by conditioning, or by habit-formation. In addition, we must have intelligent understanding of ourselves, of our conflicts, and of the social pressures under which we live.

Need of stimulating leadership

One of the areas in which overconformity is most serious is that of leadership roles. Although it is very important that any person who aspires to be an effective leader in a particular group should acquire a considerable degree of "membership character" in this group (by becoming *like* the members in as many ways as possible), it is equally important that he also, as Brown has put it, "represent a region of high potential in the social field" (4—p. 344). By this is meant that he should be a source of stimulation for ideas, plans, and activities. In other words, he must not only conform and adapt himself to what he finds, but must also *lead.*

A classroom teacher who finds out what his pupils want to study, or what their needs are, has discharged only about half of his responsibility. He has yet to *stimulate* them to see problems and needs and to want to acquire interests and skills of which they are not yet aware. He must not only know the minds of his pupils, but must also represent a region of high potential in the social field of the classroom.

Especially in such academic areas as the social studies, as well as in cocurricular activities, teachers can help pupils to see that effective social leadership depends upon both membership character and the capacity to stimulate. They must help pupils to see that so-called leaders who only conform and adapt to what they find, and cannot stimulate beyond present levels, soon become mere figureheads; and that, on the other hand, those so-called leaders who try to stimulate without first having attained a certain minimum degree of membership character, soon find themselves without a responsive audience.

It is essential, too, that teachers help pupils to see that conformity on the part of some leaders, or would-be leaders, may be a disguise to fool people. Examples of this kind of behavior can be obtained, not only from the pupils' experiences, but also from such larger areas as political campaigns and the practices of members of the Communist Party who are taught to hide their party identity by acting, dressing, and living generally just like the average American. Conformity may, indeed, conceal as much as it reveals.

REFERENCES

1. Alexander, Franz, "Mental Hygiene in the Atomic Age," *Mental Hygiene,* 30, 1946, 529-544.
2. Berkowitz, L., "Effects of Perceived Dependency Relationships upon Conformity to Group Expectations," *Journal of Abnormal and Social Psychology,* 55, 1957, 350-354.
3. ——— and B. J. Levy, "Pride in Group Performance and Group-Task Motivation," *Journal of Abnormal and Social Psychology,* 53, 1956, 300-306.
4. Brown, J. F., *Psychology and the Social Order.* New York: McGraw-Hill Book Co., 1936.
5. Burks, F. W., "Some Factors Related to Social Success in College," *Journal of Social Psychology,* 9, 1938, 125-140.
6. Cantor, Nathaniel, "What Is a Normal Mind?" *American Journal of Orthopsychiatry,* 11, 1941, 676-683.
7. Coyle, G. L., *Group Work With American Youth.* New York: Harper and Bros., 1947.
8. Crutchfield, Richard S., "Conformity and Character," *The American Psychologist,* 10, 1955, 191-198.
9. Dimock, H. S., *Rediscovering the Adolescent,* Ch. VI. New York: Association Press, 1937.
10. Dittes, J. and H. Kelley, "Effects of Different Conditions of Acceptance Upon Conformity to Group Norms," *Journal of Abnormal and Social Psychology,* 53, 1956, 100-107.
11. Gibb, C. A., "The Principles and Traits of Leadership," *Journal of Abnormal and Social Psychology,* 42, 1947, 267-284.
12. Gross, A. A., "The Manners and Morals of Adjustment," *Mental Hygiene,* 23, 1939, 445-455.
13. Kindwall, J. A., "The Aims of Psychiatry," *Mental Hygiene,* 21, 1937, 353-372.
14. Koch, H. L., "Popularity in Pre-School Children: Some Related Factors and a Technique for Its Measurement," *Child Development,* 4, 1933, 164-175.
15. Lippit, Rosemary, "Popularity Among Pre-School Children," *Child Development,* 12, 1941, 305-332.
16. Maslow, A. H., "Dominance, Personality, and Social Behavior in Women," *Journal of Social Psychology,* 10, 1939, 3-39.
17. Navarra, John Gabriel, "Rebellion Against Rigidity," *Childhood Education,* 33, 1956, 22.
18. Redl, F. and W. W. Wattenberg, *Mental Hygiene in Teaching.* New York: Harcourt, Brace & Co., 1951.
19. Roethlisberger, F. J., *Management and Morale.* Cambridge: Harvard University Press, 1941, p. 194.

20. Rooks, M. M. and Mary Northway, "Creativity and Sociometric Status in Children," *Sociometry,* XVIII, 1955, 194-201.
21. Sarbin, T. R., "Adjustment in Psychology," *Character and Personality,* 8, 1940, 240-249.
22. Shobbs, N. E., "Sociometry in the Classroom," *Sociometry,* 10, 1947, 154-164.
23. Smucker, O., "Near-Sociometric Analysis as a Basis for Guidance," *Sociometry,* 12, 1949, 326-340.
24. Stagner, R., *Psychology of Personality* (1st ed.). New York: McGraw-Hill Book Co., 1937.
25. Terman, L. M., "Psychological Approaches to the Biography of Genius," *Science,* 92, 1940, 293-301.
26. Tryon, C., "Evaluations of Adolescent Personality by Adolescents," *Monograph of Society for Research in Child Development,* No. 4. Washington: National Research Council, 1939.
27. Van Alstyne, D. and L. A. Hattwick, "A Follow-up Study of the Behavior of Nursery School Children," *Child Development,* 10, 1939, 43-70.

QUESTIONS AND EXERCISES

1. Much has been said in recent years about our children and young people being pressured into too much conformity. Since this is a controversial question it would be good for a class debate or panel discussion, in order to bring out the many different interpretations of this topic.
2. Can you set up some criteria whereby you can judge whether or not adaptability in a given individual is an indication of personality strength or weakness?
3. How should teachers and other school officials deal with clothing fads that are considered to be ridiculous or contrary to health standards?
4. Find examples on your campus, in your local schools, or in your community, of groups whose insistence upon certain standards have helped many individuals raise the level of their performance or of their conduct in order to conform to these group expectancies.
5. Stimulate a class discussion on how schools can recognize conformity demands, and at the same time provide for individuality and uniqueness.

6. Set up some criteria for judging whether nonconformity in any individual personality is an indication of strength or of weakness.
7. What kind of qualities are most needed in teachers and other adults for them to help young people strike a reasonable balance between loyalty to peer codes and introjection of adult codes?
8. Find additional reading materials that could be used to help young people think through some of the conflicting demands of our society.

SELECTED FILMS

Individual Differences. 25 minutes. Illustrates two contrasting approaches a teacher may use in dealing with a child who is different from his classmates.

Each Child Is Different. 17 minutes. Points out differences between children in a fifth-grade class and indicates best teaching practices to follow.

Children Growing Up with Other People. 23 minutes. Has special value in showing need of holding onto individuality while adapting to group demands.

9

INITIATIVE, SOCIAL DRIVE,

FROM THE STANDPOINT of some of the major values in American culture, a mentally healthy person is characterized by sociability, drive, and social initiative. From numerous sources in business, education, religion, and civic groups, emphasis is placed on the importance of doing things, contacting people, seeking new relationships, being active in the community, and joining various groups. This kind of emphasis obviously places much value on extroverted personality characteristics. In other words, it seems apparent that in our culture most individuals who are considered to be

AND MENTAL HEALTH

mentally healthy are those who have not only good self-adjustment and a fairly high degree of conformity and adaptability, but also considerable social initiative. They are active and sociable people.

Our society, especially during and since the days of the westward movement, has long been characterized by aggressive activity. Most of our paramount values have had their roots in the adventurous spirit, in daring, and in numerous forms of *doing* as opposed to the more quiet pursuits of thinking, reading, and artistic expression. Progress has frequently been defined in terms of more intense activity to get things done, make things bigger, increase membership rolls, and raise or spend more money. Oftentimes an honored citizen is described as "a go-getter." One of the most consistent themes of advertising, in all its branches, is that of showing how a particular product promotes vigorous living or aids in getting ahead of others. It seems likely that one of the reasons for the lack of respect for old age in our culture is that the later years of life are generally characterized by a slowing down of all activities. The old person is no longer "on the go" — so "what good is he?" seems to be a common attitude.

Most of our churches, too, place a large emphasis on expression of religion through some form of activity such as attending church meetings, participation in money-raising campaigns, teaching classes, singing in the choir, making furniture for the nursery department, etc. These forms of religious expression seem to predominate over those of a more quiet nature such as Bible reading, meditation, and prayer. Those who become leaders in churches and receive the most public recognition are likely to be those who have shown the most initiative in getting things done.

This cultural theme is clearly evident in our schools, from the primary grades through our colleges, as evidenced by the strong orientation toward knowledge for use in practical projects and for getting ahead in the world, as opposed to orientation toward learning for its own sake, contemplation, search for truth, or interest in theory. In our elementary and secondary schools there are strong influences operating to induce pupils to be aggressive in competing with others, to do things for public display, and to possess the kinds of personal qualities associated with having a "lot of pep" and social aggressiveness.

In this chapter attention will be centered on questions and issues involved in an evaluation of social drive and initiative from the standpoint of mental health objectives in our schools.

INTERPERSONAL QUALITY OF RELATIONSHIPS

At the outset, the point must be clearly expressed that no assumption should be made that the more social initiative a child has the more he approaches the goals of positive mental hygiene. Rather, attention must be focused not only on the need of social contacts and initiative but also on the interpersonal quality of the relationships established. Several research investigations have reported data showing that, generally speaking, a moderate amount of social initiative results in better group adjustments than either a very small or a very large amount. For example, Koch's study in a nursery-school population showed that a high degree of withdrawal behavior, as well as a high degree of social initiative (expressed in attacking behavior), were both fairly well correlated with unpopularity (18). Other studies among children of preschool and of elementary school ages by Green (10) and by Van Alstyne and Hattwick (32) have shown that one of the traits most clearly differentiating between those making poor and those making good interpersonal adjustments is that of extreme submissiveness to frustrating or unpleasant situations. These studies point out that some quarreling and "making up" should be regarded as an essential part of the socializing process, since such behavior can help children to learn to minimize their grievances and to develop a "give and take" attitude. Another investigation by Northway and Wigdor has shown that nearly all of the isolated and rejected children included in their study could be described as being either very recessive and socially isolated, or, on the other hand, characterized by antagonistic aggressiveness such as in noisy, rebellious, and boastful behavior (24).

Studies among adolescent boys by Dimock (7), and among young men in college dormitories by Bonney, Hoblit and Dreyer (5) and by Kidd (17) have all presented data that emphasize the interpersonal rejection of the overly aggressive, domineering, attention-demanding type of individual. These studies are equally clear in showing the weak social position of the overly submissive person who is so lacking in ego-strength that he is unable to exert enough social initiative to hold his own in the interpersonal milieu of his respective groups.

That in general a moderate amount of aggressiveness in social contacts represents a more effective kind of social adjustment than either a very low or a very high frequency, within a given population, is indicated from Jennings' study (15) in the New York State Training School for Girls. Here it was found that although a group of forty-three most acceptable girls made about twice as many social contacts as did a corresponding group of least desired girls, there was very little difference in this respect between the high-choice girls and the average for the total institutional population. In other words, the best-liked girls certainly could not have been spotted simply by observing which ones were most active in contacting others, but, on the other hand, they definitely showed more social initiative than the least-liked girls.

However, as stated above, the major emphasis should be on

quality rather than *quantity* of social contacts. Some individuals are characterized by a very high degree of social initiative, including some antagonistic aggressiveness, and yet are highly respected and have many friends within a particular group. How is this possible? The answer generally is that they have counterbalancing personality assets, or their strong social drive is focused on group-centered objectives, or they have both of these advantages.

An example of how all these psychological factors may be found in one individual is seen in a case reported by Hartley (12). This case, an eleven-year-old boy designated J.O., is described as being very socially aggressive and at times dominating, and yet he stood high among the other boys in his club in both personal acceptability and leadership status.

J. O.'s extreme sociality was evidenced by the fact that he was in almost constant contact with all the major aspects of his immediate environment. He was outstanding not only in his group in being absorbed in his work materials, but also in the amount of contacts he made with other boys. He initiated activities, made suggestions on nearly everything that came up for discussion, assumed leadership roles, and did everything with zest and enthusiasm. When new boys entered the club he did not make a fuss over them, but he included them in his invitations for different activities, and also listened to their suggestions He seemed to have a need constantly to keep in contact with others through some form of interpersonal exchanges, and these exchanges were by no means always kindly and pleasant. Many of them involved aggression and dominance. He sometimes "bawled out" other boys, called them derogatory names, and criticized their work. Also he was frequently involved in overt fighting — including pushing, hitting, shoving, and destruction of another boy's materials. How could a boy engage in so much hostile aggressiveness and yet stand so high in the estimation of his peers? Hartley points out several factors which worked in J. O.'s favor:

First, he was not only aggressive against others but was also at other times helpful, sympathetic, desirous of pleasing, and stood for fair play. He volunteered to help other boys with the things they were working on; he expressed sincere regret when he hurt another boy, saying: "I'm sorry; I didn't mean to hurt you." He appeared to enjoy having other boys share with him in using something he had made, as when he invited two other boys to play with him in a fort that he had constructed. His standing for fair play was shown in one incident in which he ran to help a boy who had called for his aid in a fight, but quickly left the fray when the third boy involved called "no fair."

Second, J. O. could accept aggression as well as give it. He could accept aggressive acts against himself without getting mad, pouting, holding grudges, or crying. He could not only dish it out; he could also take it.

Third, he was adaptable since most of his aggressive behavior was "tempered to the situation." Also he was very flexible in adapting his behavior to different kinds of boys.

Fourth, he was outstanding in making contributions to his various groups. He started new activities, suggested interesting things to do, and was "in" on practically everything that went on around him.

This case illustrates that although a certain kind of behavior may be considered, from a mental health point of view, to be generally favorable or unfavorable, its evaluation in particular individuals must include an analysis of its interrelationships with other personality and situational variables.

A further illustration of this point is found in another case representing personal qualities exactly opposite to those shown by J. O. This case is an elementary school girl who was highly preferred on a wide range of sociometric measurements, involving both friendship and abilities, over a period of six years. Yet she was a true introvert in the sense in which Jung originally used this term. Her "true introversion" was shown by the fact that she was emotionally sensitive and subjectively orientated, but at the same time was not seclusive and did not suffer from feelings of inferiority. She made very little effort to contact other children or to win their friendship, yet she was always friendly when others contacted her. She never rebuffed or snubbed another child, never picked quarrels, never sought an argument, and never intentionally antagonized others. She was a quiet, peace-loving child who did not strive to be recognized, did not push herself, and was not socially aggressive; yet she did not shun people, and she certainly was not lacking in self-assurance. She was physically attractive and dressed well, always pleasant and cheerful, highly responsible in group obligations, capable in all academic subjects, and performed well in dramatizations.

This case presents a caution to those who are oversold on the value of social aggressiveness from the standpoint of both achieving personal happiness and attaining group status. Those who are socially weak, and who have been unduly impressed with the swath cut by the extreme extrovert, may develop a compulsive drive to "get into things" at any cost. Others, though, who have more poise and self-resources may win out over their driving competitors simply by biding their time, by not being anxious, and by quietly developing many personal qualities which carry their own weight without being forced upon the attention of others. The first kind of individual says: "I shall make people notice me if I have to knock them down to do it!" The second says: "I shall develop such assets that others will be attracted to me." The first acts like a charging bull, the second like a magnet.

TALK AND SOCIAL INITIATIVE

One of the most obvious ways whereby people show that they are sociable is through talk, and in no behavior-area is the interpersonal quality-level more important. Here, again, the point of chief significance is not sheer amount of talk but its communicative value to others. This point is substantiated in a research investigation reported by Rosenthal in which he contrasted the language structure used in interviews by twenty sociometrically high children and twenty who were very low on the same choice-criteria (27). The author concluded that the highly chosen children did not use more words than the low ones, but the statements of the high children had greater communicative value and showed more variety and vividness of expression.

In studies by Jersild (16), and by Winslow and Frankel (34), it is pointed out that one of the reasons why some individuals are rejected in particular groups is that they talk too much from egocentric motivations. In Jersild's study, involving pupils in four elementary school classes, it was observed that those children who were most loquacious in the classroom discussions were frequently ignored and sometimes avoided by other children outside the regular class sessions. The conclusion was drawn that the extent to which these pupils participated in the group discussions seemed to be determined considerably less by each individual's ability to contribute than by his desire to be heard. In other words, the most talkative pupils were apparently compensating for some kind of personal maladjustment (16).

We should not assume, however, that those who talk a great deal in group discussions, or in any other situation, are certain to be compensating for an inner need, or that their greater frequency of talking is resented by others in this situation. Much depends upon the extent to which their verbal contributions are directed toward group objectives, and also to the extent that they are liked or disliked as total persons. As a matter of fact an individual may talk a great deal more than anyone else in his group and yet be highly respected and well-liked provided that what he says is stimulating, interesting, or amusing to the others present. His remarks must be appropriate to a particular problem to be solved or to a particular social atmosphere prevailing at the moment, or in accord with the feelings of his particular companions. Such a person can attain an intimate rapport with others, especially with his close associates. But this does not mean that he never talks about himself, since, if he has positive self-regarding attitudes, he takes it for granted that his activities and experiences carry normal social value to others when presented in the appropriate social context.

Teachers can help pupils to make their verbal communications more effective and acceptable by the methods described in Chapter 13 dealing with the uses of group discussions. Also some teachers use story-writing and role playing to help students learn how to make conversations more stimulating and mutually satisfying.

However, it is safe to say that socially effective and pleasing talk is not the result of any special training, or of reading a book on *The Art of Conversation,* but is the outgrowth of mature personality development. The child who engages in an excessive amount of irrelevant, boring, egocentric talk needs help in building up his ego resources by all the means suggested throughout this book.

SEX DIFFERENCES

When considering the goals of mental health within the areas of sociality and social initiative, the matter of sex differences becomes important, since our evidence is quite consistent in showing that boys, as a group, are characterized as being more socially aggressive in some kinds of behavior than are most girls.

In studies of groups of young children reported by Goodenough (8), Green (10), Landreth (20), and Muste and Sharpe (22), boys as compared with girls are shown to be characterized by more antagonistic aggressiveness, more outbursts of anger, and especially by greater use of physical force as contrasted with verbal attacks, in settling arguments and conflicts.

In a similar vein, several investigators — Bonney (3), Kuhlen and Lee (19), and MacFarlane, Honzik, and Davis (21) — have presented data showing that when pupils on the elementary and secondary school levels are asked to rate each other on a prepared list of traits, the ones upon which the boys receive much higher frequencies than the girls are such traits as: *quarrelsome, restless, wiggly,* and *enjoys fighting.* Furthermore, junior high school boys in one study (Hicks and Hayes [13]) were shown to excel girls in both "desirable" and "undesirable" classroom verbal responses and, in another study, to engage in more "show off" behavior in classroom situations.

That aggressive behavior in boys, if not too extreme or obnoxious, may be more tolerable and acceptable than when found in girls is indicated by Tryon's study of personality trait ratings among 350 adolescents in the public schools of Oakland, California (31). These students rated each other on twenty traits through the use of a "Guess Who" measurement which requested them to write under each trait-description the names of those students who they considered fit the various trait-descriptions best. From these data Tryon was able to arrive at a number of trait-clusters consisting of three or four or more traits which were sufficiently correlated with each other to warrant the conclusion that these particular traits are quite likely to be found together in the same individual. Since one of the twenty traits involved "popularity" it was possible to relate some of the trait-clusters to this one variable of "popularity."

When this was done in reference to twelve-year-old boys, it was evident that the kinds of traits most clearly associated with popularity at this age-level included such characteristics as daring and willingness to take chances, leadership in some group endeavors, active participation in games, and friendly attitudes toward others. To a lesser degree the most popular twelve-year-old boys were also characterized as being restless, talkative, attention-demanding, and bossy at times, and as being willing to compete in physical combat when necessary to defend themselves.

These same boys were again rated by their adolescent peers three years later, when they were fifteen years old, and very much the same syndrome of traits was found to be associated with high ratings on popularity.

Popularity and masculinity

Tryon states that it was evident from staff observations that the above cluster of traits was closely linked with masculinity and the attainment of good heterosexual adjustment (31). It should be noted that those who stood highest in masculinity, as well as in popularity with both sexes, were not those who were simply *friendly,* nor those who were simply *aggressive,* but rather those who possessed a combination and integration of these two major characteristics.

From these data we may conclude that the kindly, friendly boy will frequently be liked by his associates, but he will not generally be accepted into the higher ranks of group prestige unless he is also characterized by such traits as courage, the disposition to stand up for his rights, the capacity to assume some kind of leadership role, and the ability to play vigorously in one or more group games.

The fact that, among both twelve- and fifteen-year-old boys, the trait of friendliness was found to be incorporated in the syndrome of traits related to masculinity deserves special emphasis because it means that the masculine boy is not generally a bully, nor one who rides roughshod over the feelings and interests of others. Instead, he is characterized by cordial attitudes toward his associates and a sincere personal interest in them.

Popularity ratings in 12-year-old girls

When Tryon assembled her data in regard to the trait clusters found to be correlated with popularity among twelve-year-old girls, she found some striking differences from the corresponding data for boys (31). Notably there was much less emphasis on such aggressive traits as daring, taking chances, leadership, and active participation in group games. Other traits that these 350 adolescent raters regarded with less favor in girls than in boys included: restlessness, talkativeness, attention-demanding and bossy behavior, and overt physical attacks on others.

What kinds of behavior were found to be most closely related to popularity ratings among the twelve-year-old girls? Primarily a cluster of traits including enthusiasm, happiness, sense of humor, cheerfulness, and friendliness. In other words, from Tryon's data we may say that the most popular twelve-year-old girl is the one who is characterized by not being bold, loud or bossy, nor overly aggressive, especially in overt physical contacts. Rather, she is amiable, cordial, cheerful, and conforming, and yet shows enthusiasm for living and participates eagerly in many group activities, especially those of a social nature.

From the above descriptions it is evident that the chief contrast between twelve-year-old boys and girls is that the boys are expected to be both aggressive and friendly, whereas the girls are expected to be primarily friendly and sociable.

Popularity ratings in 15-year-old girls

When the personality trait ratings were obtained on the girls in Tryon's study on the fifteen-year-old level, some significant changes were evident as compared with the corresponding ratings obtained on the twelve-year-old level (31). The principal change noted was a shifting of the girls' ratings so that the most popular girls were described by trait-clusters more closely resembling the traits associated with popularity among boys. This shift was evidenced by the fact that the ratings of the girls gave more favorable emphasis to such socially aggressive behavior as daring, leadership, and jocularity. Gone was the twelve-year-old prototype of a demure, docile miss.

Instead, the most popular girls in the older age-group showed much more of the qualities of good fellowship and good sportsmanship as exhibited by boys. Also these highly rated girls were observed by staff members to be above their group averages in organizing group activities, doing things to "pep up" parties, and seeing to it that both boys and girls had good times at social functions. Also, restlessness, talkativeness, and activity in games and various forms of attention-getting behavior, although not highly approved, were regarded with more tolerance than was true on the younger age-level.

The significance of this shift is not altogether clear, but it may be interpreted to mean that the girls were less certain of their roles than the boys were. It may be that they sensed that our society gives greater recognition to extroverted than to introverted behavior characteristics. It may also be that the shift noted is just a normal aspect of greater social maturity and, consequently, has no special significance. However, if this viewpoint is accepted, it is difficult to explain why a similar shift was not found for the boys.

As far as the boys were concerned, the chief difference shown over the three-year period was in the greater value placed on personal appearance. This was undoubtedly due to greater heterosexual interest. Other traits which were evaluated somewhat differently by boys over the three-year period were boisterousness, defiance of adult regulations, and extreme output of energy. Although these traits were not disapproved by the older boys, on the other hand, they were not given the prestige-value accorded to them on the twelve-year-old level. Could these modifications, too, be related to increasing heterosexual sensitivity? Could this be an example of the "taming of the male" by the female of the species? A case might be made out here for saying that during the early adolescent years most boys shift somewhat toward the standards and desires of girls in order to be better accepted by them, while at the same time most girls are making an even greater shift toward masculine values in order to be better accepted by the boys. This seems like a plausible interpretation of Tryon's data.

It may be that this kind of compromising on the part of both sexes is essential to good heterosexual adjustment, and that those who make the most effective compromises are the ones who succeed the best (assuming other necessary qualifications) in their relations with the opposite sex as well as in adult life, including marriage. The psychological gulf between the sexes is often rather wide; only those who are willing and able to build at least part of the bridge across this gulf should expect the satisfactions attendant upon happy inter-sex relations.

Commenting on her finding in regard to the relatively greater shifting of girls' trait-ratings toward those of boys, Tryon points out that this finding must mean that the girls did more adapting than the boys and consequently went through a period of more drastic psychological changes and confusion. That this was probably the case is attested to by the systematic observations made by members of Tryon's staff. Summarizing and interpreting these observations, Tryon says:

> At about age thirteen (eighth grade) the majority of the girls exhibited behavior suggestive of emotional upheaval characterized by desultory interest in the objective environment; unorganized, unoriented activity; excessive response in the form of screaming and giggling to mild, ordinarily ineffective stimuli; and excessive, egocentric interest in their own persons. The writer would hazard the opinion that this behavior was symptomatic of changing values. After about a year and a half most of the group had subsided into a fairly adult pattern. Boys as a group did not manifest any comparable degree of disorganized activity though they were similarly observed over a period of seven years (from eleven to seventeen). (31 — p. 80.)

These findings in regard to the shifting of girls' values and behavior toward masculine patterns are substantiated in a study reported by Smith in which girls between eight and fifteen years of age were found to give progressively more favorable personality trait ratings to boys, although no such trend was evident in the boys' ratings of girls (29). Likewise, in Terman and Miles' investigation of masculinity and femininity they found that girls made the most feminine scores (on paper and pencil testing instruments) at the eighth-grade level, and thereafter their scores veered toward masculine norms until early maturity (30). No such trend was evident in the case of boys. Further substantiation for this same phenomenon is found in a study reported by Harris and Tseng from the responses given by 3000 pupils from the third through the twelfth grades to a sentence-completion measurement which was designed for the purpose of testing intra- and intersex attitudes (11). These responses showed that above the sixth-grade level, girls clearly expressed more negative attitudes toward girls, but a corresponding trend was not found for boys. Finally, Susan Gray has reported a study among sixth- and seventh-grade students, using an anxiety scale and a "Guess Who" type reputation instrument constructed to measure what these students regarded as sex-appropriate behavior for both sexes (9). From these data the author concludes that the most approved social role for the early adolescent girl is more confused and contradictory than is true for a boy of the same age-level.

Educational implications

These findings place added emphasis upon the importance of sixth- through ninth-grade teachers' being sensitive to the struggles of early adolescents as they try to establish personal identity and find acceptable social roles. Apparently, from the above data, most girls need more adult patience and understanding than most boys, and they need many opportunities to explore numerous social roles under a permissive type of control, lest they strike out with blind trial-and-error behavior just to see what will happen.

From the standpoint of mental health, what should be the goal of teachers in respect to helping early adolescent girls achieve a satisfactory sex role? The answer is to help them to maintain and enhance their femininity without adopting an extreme type of adjustment. For example, a girl who is encouraged by direct and indirect suggestions to maintain herself in a role that is too prim and lady-like, too reserved and "hard to get," and who is taught to be very proper about many little things, is not only likely to develop an inhibited personality, but is also likely to be avoided by boys. She is too different from them for mutual grounds to be easily established. On the other hand, the girl who is encouraged (or allowed) to adopt a role that is too raucous, tomboyish, socially aggressive, and "tough," is likely to develop an unfeminine personality which will cause her to be unattractive to boys from a true heterosexual standpoint, although she may have a good many superficial friendships among them. She cannot draw boys to her on a more intimate basis because she has too little femininity to offer. She has overadapted toward the masculine end of the scale. She can be a good sport with boys, but she can seldom win their hearts. The goal, then, for those responsible for adolescent girls should be to help them develop the capacity for good fellowship and emotional rapport with boys, but at the same time help them to hold to their birthright of femininity. Since the need of balancing these behavior patterns is accelerated during the early adolescent years, and since most girls have very little (if any) intelligent guidance on what their heterosexual goals should be, it is not surprising that many of them are characterized by some degree of emotional upheaval and confusion.

In the case of boys at all ages, and particularly so during early adolescence, it is very important that they be provided with constructive outlets for daring and aggressiveness, since these traits possess high prestige-value as badges of masculinity. However, it is important to help adolescent boys to see that this is not the whole story about masculinity. According to Tryon's data cited above, adolescents themselves, of both sexes, see the masculine boy not only as possessing such traits as courage, aggressiveness, and physical skills, but also as being characterized by genuine friendliness and sensitivity to the personal-social needs of others (31). Presumably it is the aggressive, friendly boy who succeeds best in winning friends and admirers among other boys, and also in establishing intimate rapport with girls.

EDUCATIONAL PRACTICES AND OBJECTIVES

In the foregoing discussion some educational implications of sex differences in aggressiveness were pointed out. We may now turn to further considerations of educational practices and objectives that are related to promoting mental hygiene values in the entire area of sociality and social initiative.

Introverts or extroverts?

Should teachers try to make all children extroverts? Even though this question has already been partially answered in the negative in a preceding division of this chapter, it would be well to recognize (as stated at the beginning of this chapter) that the aggressively orientated individual, if he is not personally obnoxious, is highly approved in our culture. This fact alone would tend to promote feelings of adequacy and of good self-adjustment in those who initiate and promote social contacts. The more extroverted individuals are swimming in the main current of our social value-system, whereas the more introverted ones are generally regarded as having been stranded in some of the eddies and shoals bordering the main stream.

However, the evidence previously reviewed in this chapter makes it plain that the race for personal and social status does not always go to the swift nor to the most determined. By no means do those who contact the most people, go to the most meetings, or start the most projects, always succeed over those of somewhat lesser initiative, either in gaining friends or in achieving leadership status.

From her extensive studies of the processes of socialization among children, Northway makes the point that it is not at all necessary or desirable to try to make everyone an extrovert, even though our civilization does place great emphasis on extrovert qualities (23). She states, "With children perhaps the most unfortunate thing we do is to insist that they must drive towards winning friends and influencing people."

One factor that might reduce emphasis on this drive in some peoples' minds is the knowledge that in winning friends, as in many other endeavors, "trying hard" may be the most important thing in producing failure. Straining and compulsive effort in social relations result in unfortunate psychological effects and are most likely to bring scorn from others rather than the approval that is sought.

Pursuing Northway's point further, she makes the observation that as long as society needs artists, thinkers, and quietly effective people, as well as salesmen, leaders, and flamboyant figures, it is most important for schools and other agencies to help a child form the kind of adjustment that is most *adequate for him* (23). "The youngster with his few loyal friends, a socialized point of view, and ability to play his part in a group may be as adequate and happy a person as the very highly acceptable child who is the center of the group."

It is important to note the qualifications in this quotation. There would seem to be no justification for assuming that our artists, scientists, thinkers, and writers should be consigned to a role in life which precludes their being successful persons as well as successful in achievement. As Northway puts it, those who engage in the more individualistic and quiet pursuits of life can nevertheless be so developed that they have some social interests, can enjoy the fruits of friendship and love, and can experience a sense of belonging in certain groups of their choice (23).

Consequently, when it is said that a child should be helped to form "the kind of adjustment that is adequate for him" this must not be taken to mean that he should be permitted to stabilize on a level that may subsequently bring him recognition or wealth, but that will almost certainly result in psychic pain and endless frustration when he is expected to mesh his personality with the personalities of others, or when he tries his hand at the difficult roles of marriage and parenthood.

Importance of humor

Everyday observation indicates that humor is a jewel of great price to those who would be considered sociable. He who lacks this quality to a marked degree is likely to be called a "dead head," a "sour puss," or a "drip." A friendly contact falls short of its full measure of value without a smile, a sparkle of humor, a joking remark, a little kidding, a little element of change or variety. By such means do we introduce a genuine personal element into contacts with others. Without these qualities (excepting situations involving sorrow) a relationship with another is in danger of being simply a matter of routine or of being on a purely business basis. A person with a good sense of humor is constantly lifting the routine of living to a little higher level of satisfaction. He contributes to the well-being of others by stimulating buoyant feelings in them, and also by creating the impression (whether true or not) that he is enjoying their company. Others are drawn to him because he helps them feel better about themselves. The sad, complaining, depressed type of person, on the other hand, is very generally avoided because he does not contribute to the well-being of others.

In their pamphlet called *Sociometry in Group Relations* the staff composing the Intergroup Education Committee states that one of the most marked characteristics of those teachers who were able to promote unusually good social relationships in their classrooms was the quality of "warmth" in their responses to the children — particularly as shown by their being "animated, receptive, and given to quick humor — even at their own expense" (14).

Since humor is a highly valued human quality, it is not surprising that some children and adolescents (as well as adults) overplay their parts. They tell too many stories, pull off too many stunts, and engage in too many efforts to be clever. Their sense of timing is often bad, as well as their sense of appropriateness.

It is well-known, too, that smiling and laughing are not always the badges of cheerfulness or of friendliness which they are generally supposed to be. They may be overdone to the point of weakness; they may be motivated by an effort to win favors; or they may be a cover-up for feelings of insecurity.

What can schools do to promote the development of a sense of humor? Can such a delicate flower be deliberately cultivated? Would it be destroyed or distorted by calculated handling? There would seem to be no cause for concern on this point if those who do the promoting are not too awkward in their approach. Probably the most important thing is that teachers should set an example in the use of a sense of humor, and should create the kind of a group atmosphere in which humor and other efforts to be amusing are not only permitted but encouraged. A far cry is this from the schoolrooms, particularly those of previous generations, in which laughter and amusement were practically excluded from the teachers' definition of the learning-situation. To these teachers (and to some today) learning was looked upon as a grim affair which must not be diluted by the spirit of play, and certainly not by levity.

It is a highly welcome change today to see many schools allowing children and adolescents to tell stories and jokes, to introduce "wise-cracks" into serious discussions, to laugh uproariously on occasions, to draw cartoons of the teacher without being punished, to do some things "just for the fun of it," to write humorous themes in English and to learn to laugh at some of their foibles and mistakes instead of rationalizing them and building up defenses in an effort to keep in line with an overly serious, overly moral behavior-code which predominates in too many classrooms.

It seems likely, too, that the quality of humor may be promoted indirectly through recreational periods and play activities that are conducted primarily for the purpose of their being enjoyed, rather than primarily to meet curriculum requirements or to beat others.

Group activities and cooperative endeavors

Our present evidence is overwhelming in showing that socialization and constructive forms of social initiative can be markedly increased through group activities and various kinds of cooperative endeavors. This is true on all levels of our educational system.

One of the most extensive studies that has been conducted among elementary school pupils is one reported by Wrightstone, Rechetnick, McCall, and Loftus in which it was shown that children participating in activity-type programs, involving considerable group work, were reliably superior to comparable pupils in traditional-type schools, in the extent to which they engaged in *cooperative, self-initiated,* and *leadership* activities (35).

On the high school level, Cook has shown that the friendship index in a tenth-grade class was approximately doubled during a school year in which these students engaged extensively in recreational events and in cooperative World War II service projects (6). Similar testing with this same group the preceding year, when group activities were not carried on, showed no such gains. A corresponding study by Amundson showed large gains on a friendship index in a tenth-grade homeroom over a year's time when these students engaged in many cooperatively planned recreational events and school service projects. A control group that did not participate in such activities showed only minor changes on the same measuring instrument (1).

Inadequacy of group associations

However, it is easy to overestimate the value of simply increasing group associations or interpersonal contacts as a means of promoting mental health values. Although numerous studies have shown that such propinquity is a basic condition determining interpersonal attractions, we cannot assume that close physical proximity is an adequate condition for such attractions to be consummated. We know from a wealth of data that some children, adolescents, and college students may come together in the same classroom day after day for a semester, or longer, and still some of them may be practically unknown to others in this class at the end of the semester. Others who do become better known, still do not have anyone with whom they can enjoy reciprocated interpersonal associations. Even when numerous cooperative activities are utilized in a group over a period of time, some of the more maladjusted individuals will show very little measurable improvement in winning friends, gaining admirers, or in attaining any form of leadership status. This point is supported in studies among elementary school children reported by Olson (25) and by Singer (28). In each of these studies concentrated efforts were made to help socially maladjusted pupils, and although some gains were registered, there were in each population some pupils who made little or no improvement over a period of a semester or longer. Improvement in these studies was assessed by such instruments as personality self-rating scales, teacher ratings, and sociometric choice-status.

Another study carrying similar implications as those just reviewed is reported by Walker (33). She provided for an experimental group of 40 third-grade pupils to participate in a carefully planned physical education program throughout the year, and compared them on several measurements with a control group of 60 third-graders who did not take part in this program. The results showed the experimental group to be reliably superior to the control group on a motor-skills test, but there was not a reliable difference between the two groups on a personality self-rating scale, on a teacher rating scale, or on choices received on a sociometric friendship test.

The inadequacy of group socializing experiences for meeting many personality needs of some individuals is further emphasized in three studies by Angell (2), by Bonney and Nicholson (4), and by Phillips (26), in which children who had had either nursery school or kindergarten training, or both, were tested for social adjustment in subsequent elementary school grades with comparable groups of pupils in the same grades who had not had either nursery school or kindergarten training. The evidence from all three studies is clear in showing that there was not a reliable difference between the groups having had preschool training and those not having had such training on personality self-ratings, teacher ratings, and sociometric tests.

From the above evidence, it seems clear that teachers could easily expect too much in the way of personality development from group activities, team play, and cooperative endeavors. In spite of the undoubted value of these socializing experiences for many children, they leave some mental health problems untouched. Some children do not need more social participation, but more help in resolving internal conflicts. Some do not need more freedom, but more firm control; some need not more activity or social contacts, but more help in knowing how to establish closer relationships with just one other person. Some need not more initiative and aggressiveness, but more self-insight and capacity for self-enjoyment. Furthermore, it is well-known that children's personality problems that are due to serious home conflicts are seldom alleviated by group experiences at school or elsewhere.

From these statements it naturally follows that a school's socialization program should be supplemented by numerous means for reaching the peculiar needs of individuals, as through parent-teacher conferences, visiting teachers, counselors, school psychologists, and cooperative arrangements with community clinics. Unless some form of therapeutic help can be obtained for the child with serious personality problems, there is reason to believe from our present evidence that more and more social experiences simply reinforce his conception of himself as a failure in group situations. This reinforcement, plus the fact that he gains no additional insight into the nature of his difficulties, generally has the effect of causing him to fixate on a low level of personal adequacy.

It should be stressed, however, that if a teacher is sensitive to the needs of individuals and not just to "group needs" or to "the needs of six-year-olds," he can frequently manage things so as to provide for many differentiated roles to fit the needs of particular pupils.

REFERENCES

1. Amundson, C. L., "Increasing Interpersonal Relationships in the High School with the Aid of Sociometric Procedures," *Group Psychotherapy,* 6, 1953-54, 183-187.
2. Angell, Dorothy B., "Differences in Social Behavior Between Elementary School Children Who Have Attended Nursery School and Those Who Have Not Attended Nursery School," Unpublished M.A. thesis, North Texas State College, 1954.
3. Bonney, Merl E., "Personality Traits of Socially Successful and Socially Unsuccessful Children," *Journal of Educational Psychology,* 34, 1943, 449-472.
4. ——— and E. L. Nicholson, "Comparative Social Adjustments of Elementary School Pupils with and without Preschool Training," *Child Development,* 29, 1958, 125-133.
5. ———, R. E. Hoblit, and A. H. Dreyer, "A Study of Some Factors Related to Sociometric Status in a Men's Dormitory," *Sociometry,* 16, 1953, 287-301.
6. Cook, L. A., "An Experimental Sociographic Study of a Stratified 10th Grade Class," *American Sociological Review,* 10, 1945, 250-261.
7. Dimock, H. S., *Rediscovering the Adolescent,* Ch. VII. New York: Association Press, 1937.
8. Goodenough, F. L., *Anger in Young Children.* Minneapolis: The University of Minneapolis, 1931, p. 278.
9. Gray, Susan, "Masculinity-Femininity in Relation to Anxiety and Social Acceptance," *Child Development,* 28, 1957, 202-214.
10. Green, E. H., "Friendships and Quarrels Among Preschool Children," *Child Development,* 4, 1933, 237-252.
11. Harris, D. B. and S. C. Tseng, "Children's Attitudes Toward Peers and Parents as Revealed by Sentence Completions," *Child Development,* 28, 1957, 401-411.
12. Hartley, Ruth Edith, "Sociality in Preadolescent Boys," *Contributions to Education,* No. 918. New York: Bureau of Publications, Teachers College, Columbia University, 1946.
13. Hicks, J. A. and M. Hays, "A Study of the Characteristics of Two Hundred Fifty Junior High School Children," *Child Development,* 9, 1938, 219-241.
14. Jennings, H. H., "Sociometry in Group Relations — A Work Guide for Teachers," *American Council on Education.* Washington, D.C., 1948, 85.
15. ———, *Leadership and Isolation* (2nd ed.). New York: Longmans, Green and Co., Inc., 1950, Ch. VII.
16. Jersild, A. T., "A Study of Elementary School Classes in Action," *The Advanced School Digest of Teachers College.* Columbia University, June, 1940, 129-131.

17. Kidd, J. W., "An Analysis of Social Rejection in a College Men's Residence Hall," *Sociometry,* 14, 1951, 226-234.
18. Koch, H. L., "Popularity in Pre-School Children: Some Related Factors and a Technique for Its Measurement," *Child Development,* 4, 1933, 164-175.
19. Kuhlen, R. G. and B. J. Lee, "Personality Characteristics and Social Acceptability in Adolescence," *Journal of Educational Psychology,* 34, 1943, 321-340.
20. Landreth, C., "Factors Associated with Crying in Young Children in the Nursery School and the Home," *Child Development,* 12, 1941, 81-97.
21. MacFarlane, J. W., M. P. Honzik, and M. H. Davis, "Reputation Differences Among Young School Children," *Journal of Educational Psychology,* 28, 1937, 161-175.
22. Muste, M. J. and D. F. Sharpe, "Some Influential Factors in the Determination of Aggressive Behavior in Pre-School Children," *Child Development,* 18, 1947, 11-28.
23. Northway, Mary L., "Outsiders," *Sociometry,* 7, 1944, 10-25.
24. ——— and B. T. Wigdor, "Rorschach Patterns Related to the Sociometric Status of School Children," *Sociometry* 10, 1947, 186-199.
25. Olson, W. C., "Improvement of Human Relations in the Classroom," *Childhood Education,* 22, 1946, 317-325.
26. Phillips, G. J., "Kindergarten Training as a Factor in the Social Adjustment of a Selected Group of Young Children," Unpublished M.A. thesis, Eastern New Mexico University, 1953.
27. Rosenthal, F., "Some Relationships Between Sociometric Position and Language Structure of Young Children," *Journal of Educational Psychology,* 48, 1957, 483-497.
28. Singer, A., "Certain Aspects of Personality and Their Relation to Certain Group Modes, and Constancy of Friendship Choices," *Journal of Educational Research,* 45, 1951, 33-42.
29. Smith, M. B., "Comparison of the School Progress of Boys and Girls in American Public Schools," *The Southwestern Social Science Quarterly,* 28, 1948, 303-312.
30. Terman, L. M. and C. C. Miles, *Sex and Personality.* New York: McGraw-Hill Book Co., 1936, Ch. VII.
31. Tryon, C., "Evaluations of Adolescent Personality by Adolescents," *Monograph of Society for Research in Child Development,* No. 4. Washington, D.C.: National Research Council, 1939.
32. Van Alstyne, D. and L. A. Hattwick, "A Follow-up Study of the Behavior of Nursery School Children," *Child Development,* 10, 1939, 43-70.
33. Walker, J. C., "The Effect of Physical Education Upon the Social

Behavior of Third Grade Children," Unpublished M.A. thesis, Illinois State Normal University, 1953.

34. Winslow, C. N. and M. N. Frankel, "A Questionnaire Study of the Traits That Adults Consider to be Important in the Formation of Friendship with Members of Their Own Sex," *Journal of Social Psychology,* 13, 1941, 37-49.

35. Wrightstone, J. W., J. Rechetnick, W. A. McCall, and J. J. Loftus, "Measuring Social Performance Factors in Activity and Control Schools of New York City," *Teacher's College Record,* 40, 1939, 423-432.

QUESTIONS AND EXERCISES

1. Under what conditions can a person have a high degree of social drive and social initiative and still be able to establish satisfying and reciprocated interpersonal relationships?
2. From the standpoint that "we like people who help us to like ourselves better," why is the overly aggressive, dominating type of person so generally disliked?
3. On the basis of the same principle (Q. 2) why is the overly submissive, subservient type of person also generally disliked?
4. Point out ways whereby both kinds of individuals mentioned in Questions 2 and 3 can be helped through the school program. What kinds of teacher aids and activities are most likely to be useful in such cases?
5. Do you think most of our schools are too dominated by a feminine psychology?
6. What kinds of things have many schools done in the past thirty years that have helped to make them more compatible with masculine needs and desires?
7. Stimulate a class discussion on what schools and other agencies could do to help boys and girls, especially in early adolescence, to think through the problems associated with learning sex roles that are most appropriate in our society.
8. Also discuss how teachers and counselors can help children and adolescents to appreciate the contributions and the inherent values of many different kinds of personalities, as opposed to stressing some one kind as better than all others.

9. Cite an example from your experience of a teacher, a parent, or a leader of a youth group who placed entirely too much confidence in group socialization as a means of correcting personality maladjustments in particular individuals.

SELECTED FILMS

Age of Turmoil. 20 minutes. Shows emotional instability in early adolescence.

From Sociable Six to Noisy Nine. 22 minutes. Shows age differences in socialization.

Social-Set Attitude in Adolescence. 22 minutes. Deals with heterosexual problems and offers some guiding principles.

Socialization. 15 minutes. Illustrates how the socialization level of an adult can be traced back to childhood.

And So They Grow. 28 minutes. Shows how many aspects of socialization can be promoted in a year-round school-sponsored recreational program.

10

GROUP-CENTERED AND

THE PERSONAL, social, and moral importance of altruistic and group-centered behavior has been stressed in countless sources. It is one of the major themes of the Bible and especially of the teachings of Jesus. It finds a modern expression in the writings of persons representing numerous fields of knowledge, such as in psychiatry in Blanton's *Love or Perish,* in religion in Fosdick's *On Being a Real Person,* and in psychology in Montagu's *The Direction of Human Development.* Also a strong emphasis on the importance of objectively orientated social interests for mature

ALTRUISTIC BEHAVIOR

personality development is found in the writings of Adler (1-2), Fromm (15-16), and Sorokin (41), as shown in Chapter 1. Considered from the frame of reference from which this book is written, the higher levels of positive mental health cannot be attained without some introjection of moral and social values. Numerous writers in the areas of psychology, sociology, psychiatry, religion, and mental hygiene, such as those mentioned above, have reported case studies and various forms of scientific evidence in support of the thesis that a major factor in mental and emotional illness is excessive self-centered orientation. They have shown, on the other hand, that a major factor in enthusiastic living and positive mental health is a strong identification with goals or values that are larger and more socially significant than one's own private or selfish interests.

Objectively orientated social interests go beyond what would normally be expected from self-adjustment, conformity, tolerance, sociality, or social aggressiveness. However, sufficient emphasis has been given in the preceding sections to make it clear that a fairly high degree of these types of behavior constitutes a favorable base from which altruistic and group-centered motivations may be fostered. It is clear, though, that these kinds of motivations must be *developed.* It is well-known that an individual may be characterized by a high degree of self-regard, conformity, and sociality, and yet have very little interest in or concern for the welfare of others.

SOURCES OF SOCIAL INTERESTS

Can human beings have a genuine, objective interest in others — an interest that is not simply some form of sublimation of biological urges, tissue needs, or disguised selfishness? It is the belief of this writer that such an interest is possible, although it is not necessary to assume that when such an interest is present it is the only motivating factor operating. All motives are mixed in regard to sources and goals. All that is being contended is that a person can be so developed that he is sensitive to the responses of others, and that from this sensitivity he can be motivated to act in behalf of others. In terms of the self-concept theory he comes to think of himself as one who responds to the material and psychological needs of others. When he makes such a response he experiences self-approval; when he doesn't make such a response in a situation in which he perceives the need, he experiences some degree of discomfort since his self-concept has not been supported or enhanced.

Going back to the point made above, it is the position of this writer that sensitivity to others, and the capacity to experience some degree of personal satisfaction in responding to other people, are qualities that, though not specifically inborn, are certainly not contrary to our original endowment and can readily be developed through proper social stimulation.

A number of psychologists, particularly Allport (5), Asch (7), Gibson (17), and Maslow (27), have in recent years presented critical reviews of various doctrines on the origin of social motivations. In all of them they have emphasized that such motivations are either natural to the human organism or are derived from social learnings, as opposed to their being simply indirect sources of satisfaction of primary tissue needs or compensations for infantile frustrations. Furthermore, they maintain that the development of such interests does not depend upon first defeating or repressing certain so-called instincts or natural impulses. The following quotation from Asch is a good statement of the view that our capacity for enjoyment of interpersonal responses should be regarded, not as something derived from the gratification of physiological needs, but as spontaneous and natural expressions of our *human* nature.

> As soon as he is capable, the child forms an unfeigned interest in persons. This interest does not fade as "primary" needs are satisfied. On tne contrary, our interest and enjoyment in people flourish when we are not under the pressure of deprivation. Half-starved and exhausted persons do not present a model of sociability. Just as the satisfaction of bodily needs is not the sole reason for interest in the surroundings, so is it not for our relations to persons. Social interest does not need the support of an "original" instinct of gregariousness or the "reinforcement" of food and drink. The sources of social interest are always present and are created anew at each moment. (7—p. 236.)

SOME FALSE FRONTS

It is well recognized that what appears to be altruistic and group-centered behavior may be due primarily to egocentric motivations. Genuine, objective interest in others cannot be assumed simply from observation of overt behavior. In this area of conduct, as in most others, there are numerous false fronts.

In the first place, we know that generous behavior may be an effort to buy friendship. Every experienced teacher has probably had a few pupils at different times who have tried to win a place for themselves in their groups by giving other children presents, money, candy, fruit, etc. Not possessing the necessary personal assets to win friends, they hope that material possessions freely offered will be a satisfactory substitute. Probably they have heard that "everybody loves a cheerful giver." On sociometric testing, such a child is frequently found to be an isolate or a reject, since the other children are able to "see through" his motivations and to recognize that his generosity is a gesture of weakness and an effort to buy their friendship. This kind of child was described in Chapter 2 as being the result of distorted parent-child relationships.

Among her seventeen nursery school subjects Koch (24) found a small negative correlation (—.30) between likability, on the one hand, and the frequency of offering gifts and of making flattering remarks, on the other (24). Thus even among these preschool children there was a small tendency to dislike those who were too effusive with either gifts or words.

Parallel evidence is reported by Newstetter from his study of three groups of boys in a summer camp. He presents data to show that the extent of cordial behavior that a boy showed *toward* other boys was not nearly so good an indication of their acceptance of him for a tent-mate as was the extent of cordial behavior that he *received* from the other boys (33). In other words, this study emphasizes that the kind of impression that a child is making on others in his group can be much better determined by observing how the group members *treat him* rather than by how *he treats* the group members.

From her study of eighty girls in a summer camp, Northway states that one of the girls most rejected by other campers was characterized by a great deal of "present-giving and superhelpfulness in the camp." (34 — p. 53.) Such cases illustrate how "doing good to others" may be motivated primarily by egocentric needs. In addition to their use as a means of trying to wring some favorable responses from others, "good deeds" may also be employed as a basis for dominating or controlling others. A child or an adolescent may help another pupil with his lessons, defend him in a fight, or aid him in a conflict with a teacher primarily with the thought in mind of being able later to force favors from this pupil. Such tactics are sometimes used as a means of securing votes in an election. Unfortunately the developmental level of some pupils is such that, as Shoben has stated, they "form the scheme that interpersonal relationships are essentially matters of traded favors, and that, instead of basic trust, the proper attitude is one of getting as much as possible while giving no more than necessary" (38).

Another distortion of social service behavior is found in those pupils who volunteer for extra work in classroom activities, committees, or clubs, but who have very little genuine interest in either the work or the objective involved. Instead, they hope to satisfy their need for recognition or to use their extra work as a springboard for other positions of power. Such pupils will work hard as long as their selfish goals are being realized. When this is not the case their efforts quickly fade.

Acts which, on the surface, are presumably an indication of group-centered interests may actually be motivated primarily by a desire to be superior to or to outshine another person who is regarded as a rival for group approval. An instance of this nature was observed by a third-grade teacher. There were two girls in his room who were competing for popularity and prestige, and on several occasions they had done things which appeared to the teacher to be efforts to outshine each other in being useful to the class. One such instance involved the bringing of flowers. One of the girls brought a floral arrangement, and this fact was mentioned to the class by the teacher. The next day the other girl brought a much more elaborate one. She had never brought flowers before.

Finally, social service behavior may be heavily motivated by a need to compensate for pathological guilt feelings due to feelings of rejection, sex complexes, or very severe religious teachings. Examples of this kind of behavior may be found among some early adolescents who show an exaggerated concern over the moral welfare of other students, or who loudly proclaim their identification with high-sounding and frequently unrealistic vocational goals whereby they may "serve humanity" in some humble capacity.

Sometimes an individual who suffers from guilt and inferiority feelings will be characterized by an unusual amount of service behavior in a particular group, as in the case of a boy who plays the role of a perpetual underdog in a boys' gang by frequently being useful to the other members in subservient ways. Many classrooms and school clubs have a few pupils who fill similar roles.

Teachers and counselors can sometimes help this type of pupil to see that an excessive desire to please others is an admission of a weak self, and that a weak self, like a doormat, is convenient to step on but does not arouse respect, admiration, or affection. As pointed out in Chapter 7, others are not proud to be associated with such a person because his presence does not compliment them; he does not support or enhance their own self-respect. Such a pupil needs to be helped, not only to see his fundamental mistake, but also to learn to do some positive things to *please himself*, and to do them with sufficient skill and enthusiasm to attract others to join him.

SOME POSITIVE CORRELATES

In the preceding section some false fronts and distorted motivations in altruistic and group-centered behavior were noted. We shall now consider some of the positive attributes and correlates of such behavior.

High interpersonal acceptance

In the first place, we are confident that those individuals who are outstanding in their identifications with group values are much more likely to stand high in interpersonal desirability than are those who rank low in such behavior. Evidence bearing on this point is available for research reported from groups of elementary school children, adolescent-age subjects, and college students.

In several studies among primary-grade pupils it has been shown that those children who rank high as desired associates are, as a group, markedly superior to those who rank low as desired associates in those kinds of behavior which involve voluntary contributions to a group purpose or a class objective, such as offering assistance, giving suggestions to help solve a problem, contributing materials, and participating whole-heartedly in whatever the majority of a group decides to do (provided there is no violation of their standards or values).

In a study by Austin and Thompson approximately five hundred sixth-graders were asked not only to make friendship choices but also to give reasons for their choices (8). An examination of these reasons shows that one of the major characteristics of those pupils most desired as friends was some kind of objectively centered, social interest such as being kind, generous, cooperative, agreeable, and loyal. This finding is sharpened by a follow-up study of these same pupils after an interval of two weeks when they were asked to indicate any changes that had occurred over this time-interval in their friendly attitudes toward other pupils and to give reasons for these changes. An examination of these reasons shows that nearly a third of them could be classified under headings that indicate or imply a *lack* of genuine concern for others such as being conceited, bossy, underhanded, discourteous, unkind, and selfish.

On the adolescent level, Jennings has presented some very pertinent data dealing with behavior differences between forty-three "overchosen" and forty-one "underchosen" girls in the New York Training School for Girls (20). One of the most pronounced differences between these two contrasted groups of girls (based on housemother reports) was in reference to interest in group objectives and concern for others. The high-choice girls were frequently characterized as being very cooperative, as volunteering to do more than their own share of work, as being willing to accept minor roles so that others could have the limelight in certain activities, and as being motivated to do numerous things to help certain "problem girls," such as playing up the good points of these girls to others, trying to get them some recognition, helping them to control their tempers, and expressing solicitude for their welfare to the staff psychologist.

The low-choice girls were seldom or never characterized by these kinds of behavior. Instead they had very high frequencies in such behaviors as antagonistic aggressiveness, forcing another girl to wait on them, passive or active resistance to the activities of a particular group, and numerous kinds of pernicious conduct such as spreading untrue rumors, encouraging other to disregard institutional rules, and complaining about other girls to the staff psychologist.

In commenting on her findings in reference to the behavior differences between her socometric groupings, Jennings concludes that her data show that most isolates or near-isolates are primarily "self-bound" (p. 204) as contrasted with most of the highly chosen individuals who are characterized by such capacities as: "an unusual sensitivity and orientation on their part to the elements of the total situation"; an ability to "contribute constructively to enlarge the social field for participation of other citizens"; an ability to be "creative improvers of others' situations as well as their own"; and an ability to display a high *esprit de corps* through which they enhance the general tone of the special milieu about them. (20 — p. 165.)

Aggressiveness, self-assertion, forthrightness

Another point of which we can be quite confident is that altruistic and group-centered behavior need not be thought antagonistic to or contrary to the kinds of behavior discussed in the preceding chapters on Self-Adjustment and on Social Drive and Social Initiative. As a matter of fact, all these kinds of behavior may very well support each other. This point has been stressed in reference to good self-adjustment in a preceding division of this chapter. We may now press this point further and consider some relationships between concern for others and such traits as aggressiveness, self-assertion, and forthrightness.

From her intensive study of social behavior among two groups of nursery school children, Murphy found a positive correlation of .40 between aggressive and sympathetic behavior (31—p. 274). Although this coefficient would not be considered very high with most data, it should be regarded as quite high in this instance in view of the contradictory types of behavior that were correlated.

Murphy reports that one boy who had the highest score for frequency of conflicts with other children also had the highest score for sympathetic responses — the latter being shown by such behavior as offering a new child a toy, comforting a child who was hurt, and showing warmth and resourcefulness in helping others out of difficulties (31). In other words, this boy who was the "biggest fighter" was also the "greatest sympathizer." (p. 138.)

Of course not all the children studied showed such a marked integration of these two kinds of behavior as did this particular boy. There were several others who received high ratings on aggressive behavior and low ratings on sympathetic behavior, and there were also a few who had outstanding sympathy scores and very low aggression scores (p. 252).

The general trend of Murphy's data, however, as shown by the analysis of individual cases as well as by the .40 coefficient mentioned above, was in the direction of emphasizing that sympathetic and aggressive behavior is more likely to be found together than to be found separately, i.e., both types of responses are often found in the same child (31).

Murphy interprets this finding as being due primarily to the fact that our culture emphasizes both cooperative and aggressive behavior, and that most young children become sensitive to this dual set of values and begin to incorporate both of them into their own behavior. She also surmises that the child who is able to do this in a fairly well-balanced manner is the one most likely to be considered "well adjusted" in our culture.

Other nursery school studies by Horowitz and Smith (19) and by Muste and Sharpe (32) have supplied data which support Murphy's finding, since both these investigations have reported positive correlations between various kinds of "combatant behavior," aggressiveness, and self-assertion, on the one hand, and various forms of sympathetic, affectionate, and protective behavior, on the other.

We cannot assume, however, that these correlations between aggressive and sympathetic behavior are due entirely to learning of these different social behaviors. It is also possible to regard these findings as being due to a large degree to constitutional differences in endowment with energy. Allport (3) has made this point in his review of Murphy's book. He says that "A child of high energy and marked reactivity will make many contacts with his fellows. He will (by virtue of this hyperkinesis) be found in more social situations than an inactive child, in some of which he will (by chance alone) be causing distress and in others responding to distress. In short, the children's differential levels of temperamental kinesis alone would guarantee the correlation" — (meaning the .40 reported above).

Regardless of the degree of emphasis placed on learning vs. constitutional factors in determining the presence of both sympathetic and aggressive behavior in the same individual, teachers can be assured that such an integration exists in a good many pupils. This appears to be true not only of nursery school pupils but also of older-age children, adolescents, and adults.

In one of the writer's studies of elementary school pupils, the finding was revealed that a *combination* of aggressive and friendly traits was much more characteristic of socially acceptable pupils than of those who were low in interpersonal desirability (11). Also it will be recalled from the preceding chapter that the most popular boys in Tryon's study of adolescents were those who were *both* aggressive *and* friendly (43). It is worth noting, too, that in his study of psychologically mature adults (designated self-actualizing people), Maslow has found these highly selected persons to be characterized not only by the capacity to be friendly, generous, and loving but also by the capacity to be self-assertive and aggressive in the pursuit of their own interests (27).[1]

In a preceding division of this chapter, data were presented from Jennings' study in the New York State Training School for Girls showing that the high-choice girls were much more characterized by altruistic and group-centered behavior than were those of low-choice status (20). This, however, is not the whole story. Many of these high-choice girls were also outstanding in various forms of aggressive behavior such as refusing to follow requests of persons in authority, initiating innovations without permission, and engaging in retaliatory behavior such as "getting even" with another girl considered to be unfair, or making caustic remarks about her in the presence of others. Furthermore, some of these highly chosen girls were outstanding in taking a definite stand for what they considered to be right, offering severe criticisms of certain girls of whose conduct they disapproved, and demanding (when the occasion required it) that all members of a group "get going" on an assigned task (p. 203).

A questionnaire study on traits liked and disliked in friends, conducted by Winslow and Frankel among 200 college students, has also shown that most of these students saw no conflict between a person's being friendly and also being frank in expressing his opinions, as well as being critical at times of the ideas and actions of others (45). In fact many of these students indicated that they wanted their best friends to be self-assertive in standing up for their beliefs and in expressing sincere criticisms.

In line with the above findings is a report on the number of "positive" and "negative" approaches made by four teachers in four different classrooms, as given by Jersild (21). He found that in one

[1] This finding supports Maslow's thesis, as outlined in Chapter 1, that the most adequate satisfaction of higher-level needs must be built on satisfaction of lower-level needs.

of these classes the teacher was scored by observers as using "negative" approaches almost twice as often as "positive" approaches. However, in spite of her greater use of reproof as compared with praise, this teacher is described as being "exceedingly well-liked by her pupils." Jersild states that evidences of the pupils' fondness for this teacher appeared frequently in records of the research staff, and that even a casual visitor could sense that a friendly and cooperative spirit prevailed (21). The "negative" responses of this teacher are said to have occured primarily when individual children lagged through inattention or lack of preparation. "The class as a whole seemed to appreciate the teacher's efficiency in putting the pupils on their mettle. There were no evidences of tension or resentment, and at other times the very pupils who were reprimanded felt free to joke with the teacher and to call upon her for help."

In the case of this teacher we see how aggressive and sympathetic responses may be integrated in promoting a group-centered objective. Also we see how a person may be critical, forthright, and demanding of other individuals, and at the same time be well-liked by these persons. Apparently what happens in such cases is that the person who is well-liked in spite of his critical and demanding attitudes, in the first place, wins personal identification through admiration of his ability; in the second place, he wins affection through his genuine interest in others and his effective efforts to help them; and in the third place, he aids others to think better of themselves by stimulating them to higher levels of achievement from which they derive self-pride.

Evaluative comments

From the foregoing evidence it seems clear that, from the standpoint of mental hygiene objectives, teachers should regard genuine social-service motivations as springing from strong personalities. In other words, the development of objectively orientated social interests must also include the development of positive self-regarding attitudes, courage, integrity, and aggressiveness. An individual with a strong personality is not primarily characterized by being nice, polite, and agreeable; rather, he makes himself *count* as an effective person in all his groups. When altruistic and group-centered motivations are developed in such an individual, we can have considerable assurance that he will make contributions to the lives of others with whom he associates; and he will thereby become a stronger and more mentally healthy person.

PROMOTING ALTRUISTIC BEHAVIOR

As stated above, we should regard objectively orientated and persistent concern for others as being incorporated into a healthy, vigorous personality rather than growing out of the neurotic soil of overcompensations for inferiority and sublimations for guilt feelings. However, the point has also been stressed above that genuine concerns for others do not necessarily grow out of a strong personality; these concerns must be developed. Although we do not possess a large amount of dependable knowledge on just how group-centered motivations emerge, we are reasonably confident that they are the product of certain kinds of developmental histories.

The suggestions offered below include the more important developmental conditions which our present knowledge would indicate to be specifically related to the stimulation of objective concern for others.

Showing genuine interest in pupils

The influence of personal example is well-known. Teachers who wish to develop social interests in children and youth should begin by examining their own behavior on this point, and should ask themselves the question: "To what extent do I demonstrate genuine interest in and respect and concern for my pupils?" More specifically, each teacher should ask himself:

Do I really try to understand why a child has done something wrong instead of jumping to my own conclusion and meting out punishment?

Am I as courteous and considerate of personal feelings in speaking to pupils as I am in speaking to my adult friends?

Am I willing to give at least a little of my time and energy to help certain pupils who are having academic or personal difficulties?

Do I exert my best efforts for the whole class and occasionally "go the second mile" in trying to promote maximum growth in all pupils?

Do I lend a sympathetic ear to pupils' complaints and troubles, show a reasonable tolerance for their failures and weaknesses, and maintain a cheerful optimism in regard to their long-range possibilities for personality growth?

It would be too much to expect that all teachers could actually answer these questions with a very high degree of objectivity, but at least the point must be emphasized that group-orientated motivations are *caught* as well as taught. In fact it seems very doubtful that such motivations can be taught unless they are also *caught* both consciously and unconsciously from the social climate of groups in which people live. With children, especially, this social climate must be created very largely by adults.

The influence of personal example is an aspect of our general psychological knowledge bearing on the tendency of any kind of behavior to elicit like behavior in others. This principle is illustrated in a study reported by Anderson on forty-nine kindergarten children in which he found a statistically reliable tendency for dominative behavior in one child to incite dominative behavior in another child with whom he is in contact, and likewise for cooperative behavior to incite corresponding behavior in others (6). Anderson quotes other studies on small children which support these findings.

We would not, however, always expect to find a close association between the kind of behavior exhibited by a particular person and the kind shown by others whom he contacts. Referring specifically to the influence of personal example, it is well-known that in spite of frequent emphasis on this source of personality and character formation, it is nevertheless true that personal example is ineffective with large numbers of children and youth. This ineffectiveness seems to be due primarily to the fact that the children or young people do not *like* or *admire* the *adults* whose conduct they witness. In other words, introjection of the behavior standards of others implies some degree of identification with these persons. However, even when identification is present there may be only a small degree of actual behavioral change due to the many conditions and factors that are operating to limit behavior change.

Role of punishments and rewards

Various forms of punishments, such as criticisms, scoldings, physical restraints, and withholding of privileges or gains, play a part in fostering other-centered attitudes. This is true because judiciously administered punishments generally help to prevent a child from becoming unduly self-satisfied and self-centered; they help him to realize his shortcomings and the ways in which he displeases others.[2]

Symonds (42) and Reik (37) have both emphasized that the completely self-satisfied person cannot love. Such a person feels no genuine, subjective need for others. He does not sense discontents and weaknesses within himself; therefore he lacks the incentives necessary to seek psychological satisfactions from the responses of another.

The person who is highly self-satisfied with his beauty, his intelligence, or his personality may so overvalue these assets that he is not sensitive to serious flaws in his make-up, and so is not aware of his need to find complementary support in the friendly, loving responses of others. His arbitrary definition of his own self-adequacy automatically excludes others from an intimate place in his life.

Obviously, however, punishments and criticisms, no matter how judiciously applied, could never be expected by themselves to lay a foundation for the development of social interests, or for establishing affiliative relations with others. They define only what a child should *not* do, and they help him to realize his inadequacies.

Of much greater positive value are various types of rewards in helping a child to introject group-centered standards of conduct. We certainly cannot assume that social attitudes will "just naturally" put in their appearance any more than we can assume that critical understanding will appear from the sheer fact of inheriting a complex central nervous system. Social attitudes, like intelligence, must not only be cultivated; they must also be found rewarding in the general run of

[2] See Chapter 2 for a more detailed statement on desirable kinds of punishments.

experiences. They must be praised occasionally and they must on the whole bring a person more satisfactions, as he defines them, than would accrue to him if he acted almost entirely on egocentric motivations.

From the standpoint of school situations, this means that children who wait in line must not be deprived of their place by other more unscrupulous pupils who may dash in ahead of them. It means that those who play unfairly in games must not be allowed to win. It means that those who perform acts of kindness or thoughtfulness must be praised occasionally by teachers — not, as a rule, in front of a group but privately. It means that the school must provide many opportunities for children and youth to attain group recognition and academic success by working *with* and *for* other pupils in addition to whatever they achieve on an individual basis.

We can hardly expect many pupils to develop altruistic motivations, if, in their particular school situation, they see that practically all the rewards, in the way of both group recognition and academic success, go to those who work only for themselves all the time.

In-group security for all children

One of the conditions which help to foster objectively orientated interests and responsive attitudes toward others within a particular group is the fact of having, to at least a fair degree, feelings of in-group security. Those who feel that they have some belongingness in a situation, and are appreciated for their contributions and their personal worth, are much more likely to have genuine identifications with group-centered interests than are those who are isolated or rejected. This point has been established in numerous studies that have shown positive relationships between acceptance by peers and degree of concern for others and for group objectives.[3]

An illustration of this point in regard to the lack of group-centered interests on the part of socially insecure young people is given by Lois Meek, in her discussion of material collected on 100 boys and 100 girls of secondary school age, over a seven-year period,

[3] The material presented in the earlier section of this chapter from Jennings' study is especially pertinent to this point.

by the staff of the Institute of Child Welfare of the University of California (29). In reviewing the data on different degrees of responsibility found among these young people, Meek says: "Those who were absorbed by their desire to achieve status with their peers were the least responsible from any adult point of view. They were no longer impressed by what adults thought was the right thing to do, if it differed from what peers did. They were also too distracted by their personal and immediate concerns to see a situation in an objective manner." (p. 64.)

From the standpoint of improving group-centered motivations it seems that the greatest emphasis should be placed on that kind of group security which arises from *being needed* by others. The more a person feels that he is genuinely needed and is making a contribution to at least some others in his group, the more he is likely to feel that he *belongs* there, that he has some status. From these antecedents we have reason to believe that group-centered behavior will arise in increasing amounts in some individuals.

To be effective in this respect, however, it is essential that an individual feel that he is needed or valued *as a person,* and not simply as a performer of menial services for the benefit of others. He must believe that he is respected as a human being of worth in the eyes of other group members, as opposed to being tolerated simply for what he can *do* that is of value to others. His group security must be based on personality rather than service values; but these two values are not necessarily mutually exclusive. They may, and often are, found together.

A particular area in which the attainment of genuine group status has been shown to have marked value in promoting group-centered behavior is that of rehabilitation of delinquents. An example of what is meant is found in an account of work being done for so-called "bad boys" in Public School 37 in New York, as described in 1945 by McCormick (28). The boys in this school are sent there from other schools in the city because of their extremely bad conduct, such as beating and knifing other children, vandalism, and assaulting teachers.

When a new boy enters this school he is usually surly, defiant, and ready to cause trouble as he has in other situations; but under the influence of the good morale of the other boys, the smaller classroom groups, the personal interest of staff members such as Mrs. Lillian Rashkis (the principal), and many opportunities to engage in significant group achievements, his attitude generally changes within a few weeks. Here at last he finds himself valued for his abilities and personal assets, not only by his peers but also by adults whom he likes and admires. As one boy put it when asked how he accounted for his good record in the school: "Well, I never was in a school before where they needed me."

The importance of providing all group members with opportunities to be needed is sometimes not appreciated by those who have strong social service motivations, since they are so anxious to do good "unto others" that they cannot see that "the others" must also have opportunities to *serve* and not merely to *be served.* Burnham has suggested that the golden rule should be taken not only directly but also reversed, by which he means that we should want not only to do unto others as we would have them do unto us, but also to give others a chance to render service unto us (12 — p. 225). Particularly is this true of those who have generally been forced into some kind of inferior role and have felt insecure and unappreciated. They need to be *needed* before they can develop the ego resources necessary to objective concern for others.

From the preceeding discussion the conclusion is drawn that teachers can promote feelings of in-group security by fostering many forms of interdependence among pupils. Sometimes the virtue of independence is played up so much that teachers lose sight of the need for mature forms of dependency. A mentally healthy person not only knows how to "hoe his own row" and to work alone, but also knows how to depend on others for advice and assistance and for emotional support. He recognizes his limitations in certain areas, he is eager to utilize the contributions of others, and he enjoys the interpersonal values arising from cooperative efforts with his associates. The psychological ground created by these kinds of satisfactions affords a fertile soil for the growth of altruistic and group-centered motivations.

Practical service projects

It seems evident that an effective means of encouraging feeling-responses for others is to provide for a wide range of practical service activities in which children and young people are stimulated to participate. Some of these can be in the classroom and can include such things as writing letters of sympathy to pupils who are sick, helping children who have been absent to catch up in their work, and aiding newcomers to make an easier adjustment to their new school.

Marshall describes the social service projects engaged in by pupils in one school (26). These projects included acting as telephone clerks, assisting in office work, helping teachers of younger children during the noon hour, helping with the school milk program, keeping sidewalks cleared of safety hazards, decorating the nursery in a children's hospital, presenting a choral program in a home for the aged, and sending toys for boxes to be sent to children in foreign countries. The obvious advantage of all such projects is that they call for overt performance and actually doing something for others, as contrasted with simply having altruistic feelings. The chief limitation of such projects is that the social-service behavior induced under supervision may not transfer to other situations or conditions.

Two organizations that are especially helpful to schools in providing an experience basis for social service motivations are the Junior Red Cross (headquarters in Washington, D.C.) and the Citizenship Education Project of Teachers College, Columbia University.

Sometimes a practical service project is centered on the one individual. In such instances the objective is to get one or more pupils to aid a particular individual in some special way appropriate to his need. Ordinarily only pupils possessing considerable group status and personality maturity are asked to participate in such projects, but sometimes a whole class, other than the individual being helped, may be involved. Here are two examples of such endeavors.

In a fifth-grade class there was a girl of quite limited mentality who was becoming the object of class ridicule. One day when this girl was absent, the teacher had the class discuss the matter of individual differences and the need of tolerance and sympathetic understanding for differences of all kinds. Only one reference was made to the mentally retarded girl, but the teacher reported that nearly all the pupils responded by being more considerate of this child's limitations.

A girl transferred at mid-term to a high school in Texas from a school in one of the New England states. She was quite unhappy over the move and took out her hostility toward the situation by making numerous unfavorable comparisons between the way things were done in the Texas school as contrasted with the way these things were done "up North." She was rapidly getting herself into a rejected social position when the physical education teacher conferred with several of her girls possessing high personality maturity and group status; she asked them if they could be friendly with this new girl and invite her to one of their group parties and also to join the girls' athletic association. These girls followed the teacher's suggestion, and the new girl responded by accepting both invitations and by gradually changing her attitude from one of hostility and unfavorable comparisons to one of friendliness.

Other examples of the use of this procedure may be found in a report by Johnson (22) in reference to several adolescent boys, and in reports by Price (36) and by Sorokin (40) in regard to particular projects of this nature with a few selected college students.

Verbal and written sources of stimulation

Probably the most generally employed procedure for teaching altruistic and group-centered behavior is using various types of verbal and written approaches, such as instruction and selected readings and discussion. Churches, schools, clubs, and homes all try to inculcate unselfish motivations by the direct-telling method, by discussion of problem-situations as they arise, by appropriate readings, and by conferences with recalcitrant individuals. From the widespread use of these methods it is evident that many people have considerable faith in these approaches.

What do we know about their effectiveness in promoting group-centered motivations? Actually we have very little scientific information on this point. However it does seem reasonable to believe that both verbal and written appeals have a part to play in a total program designed to develop interest in and concern for others. Some people can be helped to understand better their need for others, some can be helped to generalize from one experience to other similar experiences, and some can be made more sensitive to others' problems.

Ojemann's work with story materials in the elementary grades, described in Chapter 13, has shown the possibility of increasing children's sensitivity to the feelings and problems of other children (35).

Jones' study of the transfer effects of several programs dealing with training in personal conduct has emphasized that discussion may be most effective when closely linked with some form of related experience (23). Using pupils in eight public school classes in New Haven, Connecticut, Jones set up an experimental program to determine which of several methods of teaching desirable conduct could be shown to be most effective as measured by objective tests, given at the beginning of the school year and again at the close of the school term in June. Three methods used were, first, direct participation in experience projects without any planned discussion; second, planned discussions with no correlated firsthand experiences; and third, a combination of direct experience and discussion. There were six trained classes and two control groups. The program in the experimental groups consisted of units of work so selected that they could be adapted to some kind of direct experiencing, or planned discussion, or both. These units of work centered around the choosing of leaders, a Halloween unit on respect for property, attitude toward the police, a Thanksgiving project on trusteeship, a Christmas unit on giving and receiving, health and accident-prevention, fire prevention, use of the library, gambling, good sportsmanship, honor in examinations, and international friendship.

The beginning and end tests in this study consisted of tests on honest and dishonest behavior, tests of cooperative and noncooperative behavior, and tests of moral knowledge and self-evaluation. The material involved in these tests did not parallel in any exact way the content taught in the various units and projects mentioned above. Consequently the factor most involved in the experiment was the degree of transfer from the teaching situation to the test situations.

On the whole there was not much improvement in conduct as a result of any one of the three methods described above, but there was some reliably measured improvement, especially as a result of the experiences-plus-discussion method. The children in these groups exceeded those in the control group in nine out of twelve comparisons, and these differences are shown to be statistically reliable.

One of the most significant findings of Jones' study was that the kinds of experiences that the children had in the projects listed above, unaccompanied by discussion, did not result in any more improvement in conduct, as measured by the objective tests, than did discussion of similar kinds of moral behavior unaccompanied by any correlated experiences (23). This finding is contrary to the frequent emphasis in some educational literature on the value of experience *per se* as almost the sole foundation of a child's education. Commenting on this point, Jones says that apparently the children involved in the direct experiences "became so interested in each project for its own sake that the activity became an end in itself — a process of doing in specific situations without sufficient attention to the significance of the doing in terms of generalizations and applications to new situations." (pp. 186-187.)

In one of his discussions of the role of factual information in improving intercultural and interracial relationships, Allport gives due credit to all the well-known limitations of this approach, and yet he holds to the view that the giving of information and the discussion of this information, do constitute valuable aids in promoting more tolerant and accepting attitudes among diverse groups (4). He makes the point that since "people are not wholly irrational" it is reasonable to assume that accurate information will play some part in undermining unfounded beliefs and in correcting muddled ideas.

We must also consider that the effects of information and discussion on conduct may be long-delayed, and therefore do not show up on the short-term studies that have often been made in this area. Continuing this point, Allport expresses the belief that the value of information in regard to minority groups "may consist in driving wedges of doubt and discomfort into the sterotypes of the prejudiced. It seems likely, too, that the greater gains ascribed to action and project methods require sound factual instruction as underpinning. All in all we do well to resist the irrationalist position that invites us to abandon entirely the traditional ideals and methods of formal education. Facts may not be enough, but they still seem indispensable." (p. 375.)

If we accept the view of human nature that people *can* become more intelligent about their behavior, *can* learn to generalize from their experiences, and *can* through the proper approaches be made more sensitive to the needs of others, then we shall not pin all our hopes for character development on such processes as conditioning and specific habit formation. Instead, we shall believe that children can not only have experiences, but also be helped to *understand* the significance of these experiences; we shall believe that children can not only be trained, but also be educated.

Education in democratic leadership

It seems doubtful that any one thing is more important to the development of group-centered attitudes than is education in the philosophy of democratic leadership. This appears to be true because of the wide application of this particular philosophy, and because of the close similarity between it and objective interest in others. Furthermore, it seems likely that one of the most persistent characteristics of those individuals who are considered to have good mental health is that their relationships with others are permeated by the democratic conception of leadership.

The basic idea of democratic leadership is contrary to long-standing conceptions in regard to the function of a leader. In the minds of large numbers of people, a strong leader is one who tells others what to do. He determines policies, he persuades or forces others to abide by *his* decisions, and he drives through to his objectives with little or no attempt to profit from ideas of others in his own group or to consider objectively opposing points of view. The authoritarian type of leader has little faith in the capacity of the average person to have ideas or to contribute anything beyond doing what he is told. In such a situation practically all the initiative and spontaneity that emerge from a group must come from the one leader, or from him and a few of his trusted advisors. The authoritarian leader thinks of leadership skill as consisting primarily of artful techniques of "putting over" his ideas on others, of outsmarting those who disagree with him, and of persuading the members of a group that what he, the leader, wants is just what they *should* want. He thinks of the personal qualities of a strong leader as consisting chiefly of cleverness, dominance, and aggressiveness.

Democratic leadership, on the other hand, provides for each member of a group, at one time or another, to assume a leadership role. The dichotomy between "the leader" and "the led" is broken down. There are no members who are followers and nothing more. Leadership is conceived in terms of degrees of influence. A few generally exert a good deal more influence than others, but all are given opportunities and are stimulated to make contributions. There is a constant respect for the minds and personalities of all group members. Initiative and spontaneity may spring from anyone in the group.

The individual — such as a classroom teacher, a club director or a school administrator — who is appointed or elected to head a particular group, and who is committed to democratic leadership, does not set out to "sell" a batch of self-made plans, nor does he scheme for subtle ways to manipulate a group with such finesse that the members will not know they have been manipulated. Instead he leads the group into a high degree of individual participation in both policy-forming and in the carrying-out of plans. He honestly and sincerely *depends* upon the group members for assistance in determining objectives, planning activities, solving special problems, and in evaluating achievements. He does not place false or exaggerated values on "independence in judgment" or on "capacity to make one's own decisions."

In terms of personal qualities he places greatest emphasis on such traits as modesty, sensitivity to the responses of others, ability to listen, skill in arousing ideas and participation from others, and respect for the unique capacities of all persons both great and small. This means that he has much more to offer than is generally implied by the hackneyed phrase "ability to get along with people."

This does not mean, however, that the democratic leader has no ideas or plans; nor does it mean that he is lacking in self-confidence. Rather it means that he is sincerely willing to integrate his ideas with those of others in order to achieve more satisfactory results for all concerned, himself included. Furthermore, it means that he has such a high degree of self-assurance and personal security that he does not feel threatened when others offer ideas supplementary to his own or in contradiction to them.

Group-centered leadership, as the term applies, is leadership directed toward the maximum development of a total group rather than the promotion of the interests of one person (such as the leader), or the promotion of one segment in the group against another. The aim of democratic leadership is not to dethrone any person or any clique which has previously had power, but to achieve a better distribution of influence, power, and rewards so that *all* members will be enriched by the contributions of *all* members. Then everyone in a group will be more adequate and more secure, and therefore more able to produce and to create. This emphasis on total group-centeredness does not mean that all members are to become more alike in ideas and skills. On the contrary, democratic leadership assumes that people will become more diversified in their thinking and in their talents as their respective contributions are utilized. Given the known facts about individual differences, any plan that is designed to promote maximum participation of all members of a group is certain to result in greater diversifications in both personality and productivity.

Furthermore, a democratically managed group is almost certain to be a *dynamic* group, in the sense that it will be constantly changing and developing as the members interact upon each other. When people are stimulated to achieve and to create, and when they experience interpersonal satisfactions, the tendency is to want more and more of these very things. Democratic leadership, then, must be prepared to provide for constantly expanding needs, wants, and expectations.

In concluding this topic it is appropriate to emphasize that democratic, or group-centered, leadership is an attainment based on some special insights and social skills, and cannot be assumed to be easily acquired. Nor can it be assumed that as one moves away from autocratic leadership he automatically moves into democratic leadership. As Lewin has pointed out, a person who does not have the positive insights and skills necessary for real democratic leadership, but who tries to give up an autocratic type of leadership, is much more likely to move into a *laissez faire* type of group management which essentially amounts to no leadership at all (25). Just as a good personality is not due simply to the absence of bad traits, so group-centered leadership is not simply the absence of individual domination.

Although the development of the necessary skills and insights for democratic leadership is no doubt possible for most children and adolescents — and can also be achieved on the adult level, as shown in reports by Celia Baum (9), by Bavelas and Levine (10), and by French (14) — teachers should not expect all students to respond favorably or effectively to this kind of leadership training. This limitation is due to personality maladjustments in some students, such that they are unable to rise to the level of group-centered orientations. They are bound to their own egocentric needs as Prometheus was bound to his legendary rock. Such students will need some form of psychological treatment and family readjustment before they can muster the resources for either altruistic or group-center motivations.

More detailed suggestions for developing democratic skills in classroom settings are given in Chapters 12 and 13 in this book, and in a volume by Cantor (13).

REFERENCES

1. Adler, A., *Social Interest.* New York: G. P. Putnam's Sons, 1939.
2. ———, *What Life Should Mean to You.* Boston: Little, Brown and Co., 1931.
3. Allport, G. W., "Review of 'Social Behavior and Child Personality,' by L. B. Murphy," *Journal of Abnormal and Social Psychology,* 33, 1938, 538-543.
4. ———, "Techniques for Reducing Group Prejudice," Ch. XXIV, *Forms and Techniques of Altruistic and Spiritual Growth* (ed. P. A. Sorokin). Boston: The Beacon Press, 1954.
5. ———, "Basic Principles in Improving Human Relations," Ch. II, *Cultural Groups and Human Relations.* New York: Bureau of Publications, Teachers College, Columbia University, 1957.
6. Anderson, H. H., "Domination and Social Integration in the Behavior of Kindergarten Children in an Experimental Play Situation," *Journal of Experimental Education,* 8, 1939, 123-131.
7. Asch, S. E., *Social Psychology.* Englewood Cliffs, N.J.: Prentice Hall, Inc., 1952.
8. Austin, M. C. and G. C. Thompson, "Children's Friendship: A Study of the Bases on Which Children Select and Reject Their Best Friends," *Journal of Educational Psychology,* 39, 1948, 101-116.

9. Baum, Celia F., "Developing Competencies in Democratic Group Leadership," *Journal of Educational Sociology,* 30, 1597, 275-282.
10. Bavelas, A. and K. Lewin, "Training in Democratic Leadership," *Journal of Abnormal and Social Psychology,* 37, 1942, 115-119.
11. Bonney, M. E., "Personality Traits of Socially Successful and Socially Unsuccessful Children," *Journal of Educational Psychology,* 34, 1943, 449-472.
12. Burnham, W. H., *The Normal Mind.* New York: Appleton-Century-Crofts, Inc., 1924.
13. Cantor, N., *The Teaching-Learning Process.* New York: Henry Holt and Co., Inc., 1953.
14. French, J. R. P., "Retraining an Autocratic Leader," *Journal of Abnormal and Social Psychology,* 39, 1944, 224-237.
15. Fromm, E., *Man for Himself.* New York: Rinehart and Company, Inc., 1941.
16. ———, *The Sane Society.* New York: Rinehart and Company, Inc., 1955.
17. Gibson, J. J., "The Implications of Learning Theory for Social Psychology," Ch. VIII, *Experiments in Social Process* (ed. J. G. Miller). New York: McGraw-Hill Book Co., 1950.
18. Hollister, W. G., "The Risks of Freedom-Giving Leadership," *Mental Hygiene,* 41, 1957, 238-244.
19. Horowitz, E. L. and R. B. Smith, "Social Relations and Personality Patterning in Preschool Children," *Journal of Genetic Psychology,* 54, 1939, 337-352.
20. Jennings, H. H., *Leadership and Isolation,* Ch. VIII. (2nd Ed.). New York: Longmans, Green and Company, Inc., 1950).
21. Jersild, A. T., "A Study of Elementary School Classes in Action," *The Advanced School Digest of Teachers College.* New York: Columbia University, June 1940, 129-131.
22. Johnson, Alvin D., "An Attempt At Change in Inter-Personal Relationships," *Sociometry,* 2, July 1939, 33-48.
23. Jones, V., *Character and Citizenship Training in the Public Schools.* Chicago: The University of Chicago Press, 1936.
24. Koch, H. L., "Popularity in Pre-School Children: Some Related Factors and a Technique for Its Measurement," *Child Development,* 4, 1933, 164-175.
25. Lewin, Kurt, "Pyschology and the Process of Group Living," *The Journal of Social Psychology,* 17, 1943, 113-131.
26. Marshall, M., "Learning to Serve," *Childhood Education,* 28, 1951-52, 166-169.
27. Maslow, A. H., *Motivation and Personality.* New York: Harper and Bros., 1954. Ch's. IV, V, VII, X.

28. McCormick, E., "They Can Be Made Over," *Survey Graphic*, 34, 1945, 127-140.

29. Meek, L. H., "Personal-Social Development of Boys and Girls With Implications for Secondary Education," Progressive Education Association, Committee on Immediate Social Relations of Adolescents, under Auspices of Committee on Workshops, 1946, p. 243.

30. Menninger, K. and J. L. Menninger, *Love Against Hate*. New York: Harcourt, Brace and Co., 1942.

31. Murphy, L. B., *Social Behavior and Child Personality: an Exploratory Study of Some Roots of Sympathy*. New York: Columbia University Press, 1937.

32. Muste, M. J. and D. F. Sharpe, "Some Influential Factors in the Determination of Aggressive Behavior in Pre-school Children," *Child Development*, 18, 1947, 11-28.

33. Newstetter, W. I., "An Experiment in Defining and Measuring of Group Adjustment," *American Sociological Review*, 2, 1937, 230-236.

34. Northway, M. L., "Appraisal of the Social Development of Children at a Summer Camp," *University of Toronto Studies, Psychology Series*. Toronto: The University of Toronto Press, 1940.

35. Ojemann, R. H., "Changing Attitudes in the Classroom," *Children*, 3, 1956, 130-134.

36. Price, Louise, "Sociometric Practices on the Campus," *Sociometry*, 3, 1940, 192-200.

37. Reik, T., *A Psychologist Looks at Love*. New York: Farrar and Rinehart, 1944.

38. Shoben, E. J., "Toward A Concept of the Normal Personality," *The American Psychologist*, 12, 1957, 183-189.

39. Smith, M., "Group Centered Behavior," *Journal of Social Psychology*, 37, 1953, 237-247.

40. Sorokin, P. A. (ed.), *Forms and Techniques of Altruistic and Spiritual Growth*, by J. M. Thompson. Boston: Beacon Press, 1954, Ch. XXVI.

41. ———, *The Ways and Power of Love: Types, Factors, and Techniques of Moral Transformation*. Boston: Beacon Press, 1954.

42. Symonds, P. M., *Dynamic Psychology*, Ch. XIX. New York: Appleton-Century-Crofts, Inc., 1949.

43. Tryon, C., "Evaluations of Adolescent Personality by Adolescents," *Monograph of Society for Research in Child Development*, No. 4. Washington, D.C.: National Research Council, 1939.

44. Turner, W. D., "Altruism and Its Measurement in Children," *Journal of Abnormal and Social Psychology*, 43, 1948, 502-516.

45. Winslow, C. N. and M. N. Frankel, "A Questionnaire Study of the Traits That Adults Consider to be Important in the Formation of Friendship with Members of Their Own Sex," *Journal of Social Psychology*, 13, 1941, 37-49.

QUESTIONS AND EXERCISES

1. Cite examples from your own experience, or from public life, of persons who have good self-adjustment in the sense that they have very few inner conflicts, but seldom or never show any concern for others or for group objectives. Do you consider these people normal? Why or why not?
2. Stimulate a classroom discussion on the validity of the idea that social sensitivity is a primary disposition of the human organism.
3. What criteria can you set up for judging whether an act of social service is prompted primarily by egocentric motivations as opposed to genuine interest in others?
4. Can you see how the kind of data reported by Helen Jennings from the New York State Training School for Girls could be used to support some of our moral and ethical teachings?
5. Should a teacher be surprised to find within a particular child some rather contradictory behavior, particularly in reference to aggressive and sympathetic acts? How should a teacher view such contradictions in overt behavior? How do such contradictions bear on the principle of personality integration?
6. How do some of the findings of this chapter bear on the common assumption that the way to be well-liked is not to be critical or demanding of others but instead to concentrate on pleasing them?
7. Mention things you have known teachers to do which you believe would run counter to their teaching of altruistic attitudes to pupils.
8. Also mention some of the things you have known teachers to do which you believe helped support the teaching of genuine concern for others.
9. Mention examples of efforts in schools and other agencies to teach verbally altruistic and group-centered attitudes under conditions in which these attitudes were not being supported or reinforced. Point out *all* the conditions which should be present before we would expect such teaching to be effective.

10. Observe a teacher who uses democratic leadership with the main objective in mind of noting how this kind of leadership promotes group-centered attitudes.

SELECTED FILMS

Everyday Courtesy. Deals with manners among adolescents.
Let's Play Fair. Shows importance of taking turns and of sharing.
The Other Fellow's Feelings. Brings out need of trying to understand how others are responding.

MEASUREMENT 3

11

INTERPERSONAL ASSESSMENTS

In the preceding chapters many kinds of behavior adjustments among school children have been described. These accounts reveal a wide range of problems that a teacher encounters in his regular teaching duties. Numerous suggestions have been given for dealing with the difficulties presented. However, in order to work most successfully with these kinds of problems, on both a preventive and a corrective basis, a teacher needs more than descriptions. He also needs measurements and other forms of personality assessments of both individual and group adjustments. Without such aids

OF PUPILS' PERSONALITIES

he cannot make use of much of our scientific knowledge relating to the promotion of mental health values in schools.

Several published reports have pointed out the contributions to mental health objectives which can be realized from the use of various kinds of personality assessments of pupils. Herrick and Knight in a journal article describe the values to be gained by teachers from intensive analysis of pupil behavior episodes (16). In Hoyt's study of two junior high schools he found that although greater knowledge of pupils' characteristics on the part of teachers did not result in better academic achievements on the part of their pupils, there was a reliable tendency for increases in teachers' knowledge of pupils' abilities and traits to be associated with improved attitudes of the pupils toward teachers (17).

Brandt and Perkins present some summary findings from sixteen research studies that have been conducted as a part of the child-study program (involving more than 40,000 teachers) under the direction of the Institute for Child Study of the University of Maryland. These investigations show that most teachers who have participated in this program have become more objective in evaluating a child's behavior, and have made increasing use of positive, as opposed to negative, ways of dealing with children (7). Other findings reveal that:

> teachers become warmer and more accepting in their attitudes toward children;
>
> their judgments regarding the seriousness of children's behavior tend more and more to coincide with judgments of mental hygiene authorities;
>
> these teachers show a greater sensitivity to human development principles, such as those which deal with the uniqueness of the individual and the multiple causes of behavior.

Although testing and rating instruments, inventories, and other forms of assessments have genuine contributions to make toward the better total development of children, these approaches can easily be overdone, too much can be expected of them, and data-gathering may become an end itself rather than a means of helping pupils. Information about children, no matter how scientifically obtained, does not result in anything better for the children unless it is utilized by a sensitive and professionally minded teacher. Scientific methods never substitute for genuine concern and warm human relationships.

It is the purpose of this chapter to describe the most typical means whereby teachers can achieve more objective and complete knowledge bearing on the personal-social adjustments of pupils. Each type of assessment will be described, with a statement of the conditions under which it can be most reliably obtained and effectively used.

RECORDED OBSERVATIONS

One of the oldest methods of studying the behavior of individuals is the recording of observations. When teachers record their observations of particular children, these records are then available for subsequent analysis for the purpose of discovering major characteristics and trends. An additional advantage is found in the fact that when teachers begin to notice one or two pupils closely enough to write down some things about them, they generally become more observing and analytical of other pupils as well, since they begin to realize how easy it is to look at a group of children day after day and yet not *see* any one of them accurately enough to understand his particular social role in the class. A second-grade teacher, for example, who started taking notes on a girl who was shown to be an isolate on a recently administered sociometric test, noticed for the first time that this girl associated entirely with boys before and after school and during noon hour. She remarked: "Funny I didn't notice that before, but I didn't."

Anecdotal records

One of the ways most frequently recommended to study the interactions between an individual pupil and his immediate associates is to keep a record of significant episodes in his daily behavior. Such a record is usually referred to as an anecdotal record or a behavior journal. This record, however, is not equivalent to a case history. It is, instead, a study device whereby teachers can achieve a better understanding of child behavior. It is meant to be a continuous and cumulative record of behavior samples throughout a school year and from year to year.

Due to the pressure of other duties most teachers lack the time and energy to keep a good representative sampling of behavior episodes on more than two or three pupils during any given time-interval, such as one semester, although an occasional note may be made on a much larger number. However, an intensive study, even when limited to one child, can result in increased understanding of other pupils since such an effort nearly always makes a teacher more sensitive to the personal-social adjustments of all pupils.

The main thing that a teacher needs to learn about recording anecdotes or episodes in a behavior journal is to write down only what a child *did* or what *happened* in a certain situation without coloring the statement with a value judgment or an interpretation. The purpose of this type of recording is to help the teacher to become more objective and analytical in regard to a child's social behavior. This means that a teacher must look at his recordings to see if what he has written is actually what the child did, or is instead the teacher's *reaction* to what the child did. Such words or phrases as "stubborn," "smart aleck," "friendly," "sweet child," "silly," "very cooperative," etc., should not be included in an anecdotal record since these are all expressions that state a teacher's *reaction* to a child, and not a description of a particular overt act. Instead, such statements as the following are desired:

> Jane got in Mary's seat before school and refused to get out of it in spite of several requests by Mary.
>
> Robert went around the room during noon-hour, stopping in front of several girls, making faces at them and trying to snap them with a rubber band.
>
> When no one in history class indicated a desire to look in a reference book to find out when the Lewis and Clark expedition started, Elizabeth volunteered to do it even though she already had another assignment.

The above statements, however, do not mean that there is no place for a teacher to express his evaluations and feelings in regard to what he observes and records. Such expressions are essential to growth of insight into a child's motivations, and are an aid to the teacher in achieving a more objective understanding of the child's feelings. The only requirement is that the record of what happened be kept separate from the evaluations or interpretations. Below are several examples:

Situation	*Interpretation*
Jack arrived at school at the usual time (very early), entered the room to find five or six children grouped in front of the Horse Club bulletin board. Before waiting to see what they were saying, he walked straight to Bob (his mutual friend) and kicked him in the back with his knee. Bob said: "That hurt." A fight followed.	Just the day before, Bob had added some new kodak pictures to the bulletin board. Jack felt that he was playing second fiddle to Bob since Bob's pictures were attracting attention and favorable comments. Jack must be "It" *all* the time.
During the noon hour on the same day, Jack cornered four little first-grade boys on the playground. He slapped or popped his hands together in their faces in a threatening manner. The little boys ran away from him.	Jack had to be "Big Shot" over someone. Since he had failed to be sufficiently noticed during the morning, he ran his bluff on the younger and smaller boys.

Many other anecdotal records were obtained on this boy, all showing him to be a very aggressive and dominating child.

Corrective efforts

Obviously the primary value of anecdotal records is to help a teacher in planning corrective efforts especially adapted to each child's needs. In acting upon this fact the teacher of the above class planned for Jack to participate in a wide variety of activities from which he could receive legitimate recognition. Special efforts were made to have him do things *with* one or two other children, rather than simply performing by himself. For example, he and the other boy, Bob, mentioned above in the anecdotal record, kept up the special bulletin board on horses, since each of them had expressed an interest in horses and, also, since each one had chosen the other one in a recently administered sociometric test.

During one semester, this boy participated in 34 planned activities with one or more other pupils. Subsequent anecdotal records, as well as other kinds of evidence, revealed that he made some progress in curbing his hostile aggressiveness. This was particularly shown by an increased amount of voluntary, constructive participation in class activities.

Keeping the records and journal

A teacher's recorded observations will be a better source of objective data about a particular child if the suggestions listed below are followed:

1. Observe a child in a wide range of situations in the classroom and on the playground, so that the record will reveal the many-sided nature of this child as he interacts with different persons in varying circumstances.
2. Do not let any child know that a record of his behavior is being kept. All writing should be done when pupils are not in close proximity, and the record should not be left on the desk where some children may look at it.
3. Give dates of all observations and include names of all children immediately involved in a situation that is being recorded.

4. Especially when studying a child who is considered to be a problem, do not be so blind to his "good side" that only negative or derogatory notes are recorded about him.
5. Three or four anecdotes a week that are quite revealing about a child's personal-social adjustments are better than a larger number that are less significant.
6. When recording something a child said, try to quote his exact words rather than paraphrase.
7. When there is considerable uncertainty about the meaning of a particular behavior episode, it is better to withhold interpretative comments until more observations are made and recorded; otherwise there may be a strong tendency to accept the first interpretation as the only right one. Furthermore, a teacher should not feel that he must make an interpretative comment about every recorded observation. The chief objective should be to try to detect developmental trends.
8. Remember that an adequate evaluation of any aspect of behavior depends upon supplementary knowledge about the child, such as can be obtained from standardized test scores, medical histories, family relationships, etc.
9. Although most teachers probably prefer to study a child who is considered to be a problem, it is also recommended that they occasionally concentrate on a child who is making an average or a superior adjustment, in order to achieve a more detailed understanding of "normal children," and also to pick up suggestions that may be used in working with a maladjusted pupil. Some writers recommend that a teacher start a behavior journal with a child who is making a fairly satisfactory group adjustment so that the task of analysis and interpretation will not be too difficult in the beginning stages of child study.
10. The problem of learning what kinds of behavior to take notes on can probably best be solved by (1) reading references such as *Helping Teachers Understand Children* (29), (2) having a supervisor or a consultant work with teachers on this point, and (3) by small teacher-discussion groups in which examples of anecdotal records are presented and evaluated in the light of appropriate readings and consultant services. As pointed

out in *Helping Teachers Understand Children* (p. 37) one of the most essential things that must be accomplished is to get teachers to look for incidents that reveal interests and problems of the children themselves, and not simply those which bear most directly on teacher concerns such as academic deficiencies and violation of rules.

Evaluation

There is no doubt that a well-kept behavior journal on one or more pupils for a period of several months or longer can be a source of real professional growth for a teacher, especially if he has some help in refining his technique and in interpreting his findings. The chief limitations of this procedure are (1) the fact that intensive and extensive observations, together with recordings, can generally be made on only a few pupils, (2) the difficulty of *selecting* the behavior episodes to record, i.e., of deciding which ones are significant enough to put in the behavior journal, and (3) the danger that a teacher may become so absorbed in "studying the individual" that he loses sight of the larger complex of interpersonal relationships in which the child is embedded and from which he derives in large measure his individual characteristics, and (4) that a teacher may become so busy studying a particular child that he never finds time to initiate anything to help the child achieve a better adjustment.

TEACHER RATINGS OF PUPILS

One of the most persistent activities of teachers is that of evaluating their pupils in all aspects of growth, including their personality traits and their interpersonal relationships. Remarks such as "Mary is so immature for her age," "Henry is the most responsive child in my room," are frequently heard in school hallways or in other situations where teachers talk with each other.

What can be gained by making these kinds of evaluations more systematic and comprehensive, as through the use of rating scales? The answer is, in the first place, that a well-developed rating scale affords a much more comprehensive picture of a child's personality traits than the kinds of statements quoted above. In the second place, a rating scale provides for indicating *the degree* to which a child possesses a particular behavior characteristic. In the third place, a rating scale is a record that can be filled out and used by a number of teachers during any one year, and over a period of years.

It is common practice for school systems, especially the larger ones, to prepare their own rating scales for teachers to use in making their evaluations of pupils' behavior adjustments. One advantage of this practice is that such "homemade" scales may be better adapted to particular local needs and objectives. Furthermore, if the teachers in a school system develop their own pupil rating scales, or help materially in doing so, they will be more ego-involved with these instruments and therefore most motivated to make professional use of the ratings for their teaching.

Nevertheless, there are many school systems that prefer to buy a ready-made rating scale, since such scales are generally the product of more intensive study and research than is feasible for the staff of a school system to devote to such a project.

Published rating instruments

One scale that is well adapted for use in the elementary school is the *Haggerty-Olson-Wickman Behavior Rating Schedules.** This scale is composed of two parts: "Schedule A: Behavior Problems Record" and "Schedule B: Behavior Rating Scale." [1]

"Schedule A" consists of a list of fifteen behavior problems such as cheating, marked overactivity, bullying, and imaginative lying. The teacher checks each child on each of these kinds of problems on a scale of frequency ranging from "never occurred" to "frequent occurrence."

"Schedule B" consists of a list of thirty-five questions about the intellectual and the personal-social behavior of pupils. An example of the items on this scale is:

Does he lack nerve, or is he courageous?

White-livered, Fearful	Gets "cold feet"	Will take reasonable chances	Resolute	Dare-devil
(4)	(3)	(1)	(2)	(5)

[1] Published by World Book Company, Yonkers-on-Hudson, New York, 1930.

Another teacher-pupil rating form has been prepared by the Committee on Human Development of the University of Chicago under the direction of Robert J. Havighurst.[2] This instrument, referred to as the "Behavior Description Chart," embodies the more recently developed procedures for constructing rating scales, including the forced-choice technique. This technique requires a teacher to check one of five items (listed under each of the 18 groupings) which a particular child is *most like* and one which he is *least like*. An example of one of these groupings is:

A. Makes sensible, practical plans
B. Breaks rules
C. Needs much prodding
D. Dislikes criticism
E. Accepts responsibility when it is assigned to him.

From this "Behavior Description Chart" five scores can be obtained, namely: leadership, withdrawn maladjustment, aggressive maladjustment, masculinity, and maladjustment. This chart appears to be very useful in locating those children who are regarded by teachers as outstanding in leadership, or in aggressive maladjustment, or in withdrawal maladjustment.

Making personality-trait ratings

The principal objective in personality-trait rating is to obtain as sincere and objective an evaluation of each pupil as possible. It should be clearly recognized that a rating is simply a recorded, subjective judgment of the rater, and that this judgment is determined (1) by observed behavior in a particular child, (2) by the personality make-up of the teacher doing the rating, and (3) by various social-psychological conditions within the larger school situation — such as who will see the ratings, administrative practices in regard to promotions, and the kinds of classroom objectives emphasized by supervisors. Nevertheless, teacher ratings should be regarded as having a contribution to make to better understanding of children and to better professional develop-

[2] Published in *Studying Children and Training Counselors in a Community Program,* edited by Robert J. Havighurst, "The Youth Development Series," Number 2, University of Chicago Press, 1953.

ment of teachers — the conscientious use of a rating scale stimulates a teacher to think more definitely about the personality assets and liabilities of pupils. Teacher ratings will generally be more objective if the suggestions listed below are followed.

1. *Try to avoid the "halo effect."* This means try to avoid rating a pupil high in all traits or in all kinds of situations simply because you are very favorably impressed with a few things about him. Of course, a child or adolescent may actually deserve very favorable ratings on a wide range of different kinds of behavior, but a teacher must be sensitive to the possibility that a few traits such as industriousness, high verbal intelligence, politeness, or neatness may be shedding a kind of halo over all the rest of this individual's behavior.

The halo effect may be reduced to some extent by rating all pupils on one trait before going on to successive traits or types of situations listed on the scale. This tends to break up the tendency to generalize one's judgments from one item to another when rating one person on the entire scale at one sitting. The main thing necessary, however, for counteracting the halo tendency is the realization that it is rare indeed to find any person who is outstanding in all socially approved kinds of behavior. In fact, psychological studies have consistently shown that it is characteristic of well-adjusted individuals to have some behavior trends that are deviations from the standards set up for good psychological or social development.

2. *Try to avoid the weakness of undue generosity.* The point here is that experience with raters has shown that a large proportion of them will rate everybody in a group either average or above average in all traits listed on a rating scale. This is regarded as undue generosity, since some individuals in any population are almost certain to be low in at least a few kinds of behavior. Unless ratings are discriminating in reference to both favorable and unfavorable characteristics they lose much of their value. Although it may be laudable under some circumstances to give others "the benefit of the doubt," this is not the kind of attitude which results in the most accurate appraisal of a child. If subsequent teachers, supervisors, and guidance personnel are to make maximum use of teacher ratings, these persons must be made aware of each pupil's weaknesses and limitations as well as his strengths.

3. *Try not to be influenced by preconceived notions in regard to what pupils are supposed to be like who belong to certain ethnic groups or social classes.* The emphasis here is on trying to break through stereotypes. This is admittedly very difficult to do because of long-standing attitudes and emotional involvements, and to the fact that the community frequently holds prejudiced ideas and resorts to stereotyping. However, the conscientious teacher must be sensitive to this factor as a source of unfair or inaccurate ratings. Sincere effort must be made to counteract the influence of preconceived or prejudiced ideas about pupils belonging to certain categories, (1) by keeping an anecdotal record on one of these pupils as a means of inducing greater objectivity, (2) by asking oneself in regard to all ratings, but especially in regard to unfavorable ratings given to a minority-group pupil, "Is this rating based on actual observations of this child's behavior or is it based on my assumption of what he does or does not do?"

4. *Try not to be influenced by ratings given by previous teachers.* This is another difficult assignment. In fact, some teachers say they do not want to see a previous teacher's ratings for fear of being biased either toward or against particular pupils. Although this point of view can be appreciated it is an attitude that is contrary to the objective of obtaining maximum results from the scientific study of children and adolescents. Teachers, along with all other professional workers, must learn to utilize data obtained from other professional workers without being so influenced by this information that they lose confidence in their own ability to make an independent judgment. Furthermore, it is well established that ratings are of most value for adequate appraisal of a person only when ratings on the same traits are obtained from several independent raters.

Teachers may be helped to make sincere and independent ratings if they can understand that different persons will almost certainly be differently impressed by the same individual in regard to some behavior characteristics — due to personality differences among the raters and to wide differences that frequently exist in their opportunities to observe a particular person. These differences not only are inevitable but also are essential to an adequate understanding of pupils. In fact some rating scales are designed so that the various ratings cannot be averaged or summed in any way, but rather so that all the ratings given on a particular item are shown on a pupil's rating sheet and preserved for the permanent record; in this way the range and variability of his ratings can be seen. One essential condition for obtaining sincere and independent ratings from all teachers is that there not be any threat arising from an administrative attitude implying that a teacher who gives low ratings to pupils has failed to perform his duties properly.

PERSONALITY SELF-RATING SCALES

One of the most frequently used instruments for studying the personal-social adjustments of pupils in school is some form of self-rating inventory containing questions that are to be answered by *yes, no* or *?* (to indicate uncertainty of response). These inventories usually consist of somewhere between 100 and 200 questions bearing on a wide range of topics such as inferiority feelings, relationships with parents, worries, attitudes towards age-mates, fears, feelings of personal adequacy, mood fluctuations, etc.

A typical example of a personality self-rating scale is the *California Test of Personality*.[3] This test is available in different forms for all levels of our school system, including primary, elementary, intermediate, secondary, and the adult. Every test on these levels gives a total score as well as a subscore in the general areas of self-adjustment and social adjustment. In addition, each of these two general areas is subdivided into six trait-areas, such as (under Social Adjustment): Social Standards, Social Skills, Freedom from Anti-Social Tendencies, Family Relations, School Relations, and Community Relations.

Several examples of questions that are asked under Social Skills for the primary grades are:

Do you talk to the new children at school? Yes – No

Do you say nice things to children who do better than you do? Yes – No

Do you sometimes hit other children when you are playing with them? Yes – No

[3] Published by the California Test Bureau, 5916 Hollywood Boulevard, Los Angeles 28, California.

Honesty and accuracy of responses

After reading these three items many teachers will probably ask whether children can be depended upon to answer such questions honestly and accurately. The answer is that, in so far as honesty is involved, it seems likely that the great majority of children, under favorable testing conditions, do answer such questions honestly. The primary basis for this statement is the fact that when good rapport exists between pupils and teachers, practically all pupils mark a few questions in an unfavorable manner, some mark a good many in this manner, and a few score themselves low on a majority of all the questions. This is what we would expect from our general knowledge of personality traits and behavior characteristics.

In regard to the accuracy or the validity of pupil responses to personality questionnaires, our best answer is to admit that some of these responses (many of them in cases of a few pupils) are not accurate or valid since they are at marked variance with other evidence in respect to the overt behavior of particular children. This variance, however, should not be regarded as sufficient grounds for rejecting personality self-ratings, since the chief purpose of these questionnaires is not to obtain objective data on the overt behavior of pupils, but rather to obtain subjective data on how each pupil feels about various aspects of his personality. If they give honest responses a teacher has this subjective data and can use it as an additional basis for understanding the pupils in his class.

Even when a child's answers to particular questions are obviously at variance with known facts about his behavior this does not mean that such responses are worthless to a teacher, since these responses are frequently quite revealing about certain psychological conditions within this child. For example, a second-grade boy who was shown by numerous observational records to be involved in more fighting and quarreling than any other child in his class answered *No* to the following two questions on the *California Personality Test:*

Do the boys and girls often quarrel with you?
Do you sometimes hit other children when you are playing with them?

Are these obviously inaccurate responses of any value to the teacher of this child? The reply must be in the affirmative, since these answers are revealing in regard to this boy's inability to face his weaknesses and his strong desire to put up a good front irrespective of the facts about his behavior. Observational data had indicated that he was very defensive in reference to his feelings and his overt behavior. These findings, together with the self-rating responses, made it clear that one of the objectives in counseling should be to try to get him honestly to accept his hostile feelings and the fact of his antagonistic behavior. That these efforts produced some desired effects was indicated five months later when the *California Test of Personality* was readministered and the boy answered many questions in a more realistic manner, resulting in a 30 percentile drop in his total score.

Examining answers and obtaining follow-up data

Although total scores on a personality self-rating scale are useful in showing a pupil's over-all evaluation of his personal-social adjustment, it is equally important, as implied in the example given above, for a teacher to examine responses to particular questions (especially those which anecdotal records and other evidence point to as having unusual significance for a particular child). He should also obtain follow-up data on these questions after an interval of several months or more.

This point is further illustrated in the case of the boy Jack who was mentioned in the anecdotal records given in a preceding division of this chapter. Since there had been some indications that Jack's trouble at school stemmed from his home situation, his teacher was especially interested in noting how he answered certain questions bearing on home relationships. That this area did represent a sore spot in his life was indicated by his answering *Yes* to the following questions:

Is there someone at home who does not like you?
Is there someone at home so mean that you often get angry?

Conferences with Jack revealed that this *someone* was an older sister who was frequently put in charge of Jack when the mother left home.

In follow-up contacts with this boy's family the teacher did not mention the big-sister problem, but instead she concentrated on getting the father to see that he should spend more time with his son. When Jack took the *California Personality Test* again six months later he answered *No* to both of the home-questions listed above.

Advantages and disadvantages

The scope of this discussion does not allow for a detailed examination of the merits and weaknesses of personality self-rating scales, but a listing of advantages and disadvantages will call attention to topics that may be pursued further by those who wish to study these instruments more thoroughly.

The chief advantage of personality inventories are that (1) they serve as screening devices for discovering children with problems who might not otherwise be discovered, because the answers to these questionnaires reveal feelings and attitudes which are not always evident in overt behavior; (2) they afford a basis for conferences with individuals; (3) they help in confirming or in questioning other kinds of personality evidence obtained by teachers and counselors; (4) they can be used through tests and retests over any given interval to help evaluate the success of any kind of school effort planned as an aid in personal-social development.

The disadvantages or limitations usually listed for self-rating questionnaires are that: (1) they are weak from the standpoint of possessing external validity; (2) they can be easily faked unless full cooperation of the subjects is obtained; (3) the results may be materially affected by mood fluctuations in some subjects and by peculiar conditions at the time and place of testing; (4) some subjects (even though they are honest) cannot give accurate evaluations of themselves because of unconscious motivations or defenses, because of being extremely self-analytical, or because of their lack of a clear association between feelings and language symbols; and (5) the answers to a series of questions (even though they are categorized into traits) do not reveal how different aspects of an individual's personality are related to each other, nor do they reveal how he expresses his positive traits in overt behavior or how he controls his negative traits.

Other self-rating instruments

In addition to the *California Personality Test* mentioned above, there are a large number of other similar questionnaires available for use in schools. Space in this volume does not permit an evaluation or even a listing of all these scales, but some of the more recently published self-rating instruments that teachers are most likely to find useful will be mentioned.

For example, one designed for use in grades 4 to 8 is the *SRA Junior Inventory.*[4] This is a problem checklist which yields scores in the areas of: Things in General, My Health, About Myself, Getting Along With Other People, About Me and My School, and About Me and My Home.

Two self-rating scales made for use in junior and senior high schools are the *SRA Youth Inventory* which is similar in design and in scope to the *Junior Inventory* mentioned above, and the *Thurstone Temperament Schedule*[5] which provides scores for the following traits: active, vigorous, impulsive, dominant, stable, sociable, and reflective.

Two recently published scales are designated *Child Personality Questionnaire* for ages 8 to 12, and *The High School Personality Questionnaire*[6] for ages 12 to 18. These scales yield scores on 12 and 14 traits respectively, including emotional maturity, extraversion, level of anxiety, ego-strength, and superego-strength.

Those who are interested in more comprehensive listings of personality self-rating instruments, and in their critical evaluations, will find such material well presented in references by Buros (10), Ferguson (13), Guilford (15), and Super (34).

CONFERENCES WITH PUPILS AND PARENTS

One of the ways whereby teachers have always sought to obtain a better understanding of their pupils is by a conference with individual pupils or with one or both of a pupil's parents, or better still,

[4] Published by Science Research Associates, 57 Grand Ave., Chicago 10, Illinois.
[5] *Ibid.*
[6] Published by the Institute of Personality and Ability Testing, 1602-04 Colorado Drive, Champaign, Illinois.

with both a pupil and his parents. It is of greatest importance, however, not that a conference is held, but rather *how it is conducted.* If the question is asked: "What is the greatest criticism to be made of teacher-sponsored conferences?" — the answer undoubtedly is: "The teacher talks entirely too much." Why is this a bad thing? Unfortunately the teacher who talks too much cannot make much progress, if any, in understanding the child or the parent being interviewed.

This tendency of teachers to dominate a conference is a natural carry-over from their usual roles as instructors and disciplinarians. Unless a teacher can give up these roles temporarily he will never be able to learn much from a conference. Unless he can learn really to listen and be sensitive to the *feeling* responses of a child or a parent, he will continue to maintain a psychological wall between himself and those whom he is presumably trying to understand.

At the outset of a conference, a teacher should have as his major purpose the attempt to establish rapport with the mind of the one being interviewed. In order to do this he must not make threatening or derogatory remarks, or make a lengthy statement (more than a minute or two) about anything. Such beginnings put the one being interviewed in a defensive mood or in a passive mood in which he expects simply to be "talked at." Instead, a teacher should begin a conference in a relaxed manner and assure the child or parent being interviewed that this is his opportunity to state his case if he has complaints to offer, to ask for information, or to express interests and needs that are not now being adequately realized in the school situation. The teacher may, of course, ask questions to clarify points and to call forth responses that are necessary to a better understanding of the pupil or the parent, but he should not press for answers and should be very sensitive to maintaining the kind of rapport essential to effective communication.

It is important to emphasize that not all teacher-sponsored conferences should be held with those individuals, either pupils or parents, who are in some kind of difficulty with the school. In fact, if conferences are held only on this basis they will not be able to accomplish the kind of purposes discussed above, since a stigma would soon grow up around teacher conferences. Instead, conferences should be held with every pupil and his parents if time is available. It is becoming increasingly recognized that many teachers and other school personnel have spent so much time conferring with problem pupils that not nearly enough extra time has been given to those who are highly capable, ambitious, and well adjusted; yet the fruits of extra efforts with the latter are likely to be much greater than with problem pupils.

A teacher's conference with a parent affords a unique opportunity to gain understanding of a child. It is unique because of the highly significant role for good or for evil which a parent plays in the life of a child, as described in Chapter 2. What suggestions apply particularly to making a teacher-parent conference successful?

In the first place, a teacher must realize that the success of such a conference depends primarily on him since he is the professionally trained person, and since he has the official responsibility for the child's education while he is in school. Therefore, he must have some guiding principles for conducting conferences or many of them will fall far short of possibilities.

The basic principle, as stated above, is to begin with the parent's own story, comments, or questions rather than with a prepared speech. Whatever the parent says should be followed up with serious consideration; it should never be ignored because it seems irrelevant to the teacher. If the parent is critical and questions some of the teacher's methods the teacher must explain his theory and his procedure; he should never imply that the parent is "out of line" or is stupid for asking such questions. He should not show anger or obvious irritation; neither should he give explanations in a technical vocabulary that the parent does not understand. Instead he should rely heavily on illustrations from pupils' work to make his meaning very clear. A teacher should by all means avoid acting superior by "talking down" to a parent, by giving him direct advice, by brushing aside his questions, or by interrupting him while he is talking. On the other hand, a teacher should not act inferior to parents from a wealthy or socially prominent family. He should not let such parents "push him around" or force him to make concessions for their child. However, he should not argue with these people any more than he should argue with any other parents, since arguments do not generally result in better understanding. Instead he should explain his position and try sincerely to answer objections with examples and with evidence, and if the parents are still not satisfied, he should refer them to one or more members of the administrative staff who are more responsible for school policies than are classroom teachers. A secure teacher, however, is not afraid to say "I don't know" or "I may be mistaken about the value of this approach" or "I'll find out more about this issue and we can discuss it again later." Most parents who come to a conference with considerable hostility will "cool off" and become quite reasonable when they discover that their views are taken seriously and given a fair hearing.

What is discussed in a conference with a parent should be confined to this parent's immediate family. This means that other children should not be talked about, and remarks should be made neither about other teachers nor about people in the community. Occasionally a parent will endeavor to get a teacher to compare one child with another, to run down another teacher, or to make some derogatory remarks about the way a particular family treats their children. If a teacher falls into this trap, not only are his statements likely to get back to the one talked about, but such unprofessional conduct undermines the teacher as one in whom parents can confide. Nothing is more essential in the long run to successful teacher-parent conferences than the firm belief on the part of parents that what they tell a teacher is in confidence and will not be repeated to make a "good story" or to satisfy someone's appetite for gossip.

A conference confined to the immediate family of the parent (or parents) present, and in which good rapport is established, can result in new insights into the behavior adjustments of a child in school. This will be most true only if the teacher can learn to listen sincerely to the parent and, as previously stated, can detect the underlying feelings that the parent holds toward the child. More specific objectives include finding out what home-interests a child has which could be utilized at school, what problems are encountered in homework, what vocations or ambitions the family thinks are appropriate for the child, who are his best friends, and what he likes and dislikes most about his school situation.

In discussing these and similar topics, such as those relating to methods of punishment and concepts of right and wrong, the teacher should never presume to tell a parent what he or she should do. Any topic bearing on the child, his family, and his school can be discussed for better mutual understanding, but as Langdon and Stout put it:

"Only the parents themselves can figure out what *they* can do with *their* child in *their* home." (22 — p. 101.)

Finally, as a word of caution against too optimistic expectations, especially on the part of beginning teachers, the point should be made clear that not all conferences, even when conducted by the best qualified teachers, are successful. This means that a teacher who has some apparently futile conferences should not begin to think he is a failure in this area. All professional people have to learn to take some failures "in their stride." Parents, too, need to be reassured that in spite of mistakes they can be basically good parents. They, as well as teachers, need to know that it is not the separate acts but the pattern of life that counts.

SELF-EXPRESSIVE PRODUCTIONS

It has become increasingly recognized in recent years that one of the ways whereby a teacher can find clues to better understanding of children is careful observation of their self-expressive productions and behavior, such as revealed in artistic and written forms and in spontaneous play. When children are allowed to express their ideas and feelings through clay modeling or in finger paintings or drawings, they are revealing something about themselves. Likewise, when they write stories or themes on topics of their own choosing or engage in unsupervised play, they give indications of factors or trends in their personalities. In the cases of many children nothing especially unusual is revealed in any of these activities since there is nothing particularly unusual in their personality make-ups. However, in the cases of a few children these kinds of activities are more revealing than anything else.

The value of all self-expressive media as sources of personality studies is that they permit each individual to reveal unique things about himself. In most instances these are the kinds of things which cannot be found out in any other way, partly because they are so uniquely individualistic and partly because the psychological conditions revealed are so little understood by each person that he himself cannot clearly state them in either a verbal or a written form.

These statements obviously imply that if a teacher is going to make use of self-expressive media in understanding personality he must know what to look for and what to be sensitive to. For psychologically untrained teachers there will be serious limitations to their ability and their confidence in interpreting the significance of a child's self-expressive productions or activities. However, in regard to artistic and written expressions, most professionally trained teachers should be able to do the following:

1. Notice unusual or bizarre productions and try to relate these to other evidences of personality trends in a particular child, such as those obtained from observations, self-rating scales, conferences, etc. However, the teacher should not assume that all peculiar or odd productions are indicative of an abnormal personality, since these may be sincere expressions of genuine uniqueness without abnormality.
2. Persuade a child to talk about what his productions mean to him in order to get additional insight into his subjective world.
3. Show the most significant materials to a school counselor, to parents, or to the staff of a child-guidance clinic (depending upon which persons or agencies seem most appropriate) for aid in interpretation.
4. Plan for additional teaching situations with similar stimulation in order to see if the same kinds of unusual or bizarre productions reoccur with the same pupils.
5. Finally, never criticize, denounce, or ridicule a child's self-expressive productions regardless of how shocking or immoral these are considered to be. Instead, regard them as *possible* indicators of serious personality problems that a particular child has not been able to reveal in any other way.

The problems that may be revealed in the self-expressive productions of pupils are most likely to be ones involving some kind of sexual difficulty, repressed hostility (especially toward parents), and some form of poorly understood fears or anxiety states. An example will make this discussion more definite.

A first-grade teacher noticed that whenever the pupils were stimulated to make drawings of anything that they wanted to make, a certain boy always drew pictures that included several objects of destruction, such as guns, hammers, and knives. In one picture he drew a picket fence and between each pair of pickets he showed the protruding muzzle of a gun. When the teacher induced this boy to talk about the picture he said that when he drew it he thought about being a policeman when he grew up so he could "shoot people dead." He further stated: "I know the kids in here don't like me, but I don't care; I'll show 'em, I'll throw 'em down and stomp on 'em."

This evidence of extreme hostility led the teacher to investigate the boy's home situation. When she did, she found that his father was dead and that he and his mother were living with his paternal grandparents. His mother worked and the grandfather, who had almost complete responsibility for the boy, was very strict with him and frequently whipped him severely.

It seemed clear to the teacher that this boy had carried over into the school situation his hostility toward his grandfather, and that this carry-over was causing him to imagine that all the other children were against him. That his feeling of class hostility was largely a projection of his own feelings of hostility toward them was clearly evident from the results of a sociometric test which showed him receiving a few positive choices and no rejections.

It is not known whether the teacher's efforts made any difference in this boy's home situation, but there is no doubt but that her follow-up of his art creations did make a big contribution to her understanding of his personality. As a consequence she had several conferences with him, during which she assured him that the other pupils were not against him. Also, she placed him in groups with the pupils who had chosen him and changed his seat so he could sit near one of them. Furthermore, she tried in numerous ways to be a kind of substitute parent to him. It is the judgment of the teacher that this boy improved in both self- and social adjustment throughout the school year. The destructive theme almost completely disappeared from his drawings.

Other similar uses of elementary school art in personality diagnosis are given by Myron Cunningham (12). She cites the case of a second-grade teacher who had a very bright girl characterized by poor interpersonal relationships with her classmates, and whose drawings were always stilted and precise delineations of conventional scenes. When this girl drew pictures of her home situation she included her parents but never herself. Conferences with this child revealed that she had such a low conception of her own worth at home that she could not see herself as a family member. Cunningham states that through follow-up contacts with the parents this second-grade teacher persuaded them to be less strict and less demanding of their daughter.

Teachers who wish additional examples and more extended discussions of the use of childrens' self-expressive productions in personality study, and in individual therapy, will find very helpful materials in the following: Bernard's *Mental Hygiene for Classroom Teachers*,[7] Chapters 13 and 14; in Buhler's *Childhood Problems and the Teacher*,[8] Chapters 1 and 15; and *Fostering Mental Health in Our Schools*, Chapter 15.[9]

In addition to the more objectified forms of self-expression just considered, some children reveal significant subjective conditions within themselves through the spontaneous play they engage in, such as before school or during lunch periods when their activities are not supervised. Under these conditions some children who are struggling with emotional problems will "act out" these problems in their play. This acting out may take various forms, such as unprovoked attacks against others, indicating hostility trends; talking about and dramatizing unusual fears, indicating anxiety states; constantly playing the role of some well-known comic strip character, indicating exaggerated fantasy identification; frequently taking an opposite-sex role, indicating rejection of own sex; or frequently accusing other children of being a fraidy-cat or a sissy, indicating projection onto others of their own feelings of inadequacy.

In concluding these remarks about the use of self-expressive productions and activities as sources for understanding the personalities of individual children, it is important to point out that the role of a teacher in this area is not the same as that of a psychotherapist or a psychiatrist. The chief difference is in regard to depth of diagnosis and degree of individual therapy. Whereas the specialist in diagnosis and therapy uses various types of tests, conference techniques, and other clinical procedures to induce a child to reveal his unconscious motiva-

---

[7] McGraw-Hill Book Co., New York, 1952.

[8] Henry Holt and Co., New York, 1952.

[9] 1950 Yearbook of the Association for Supervision and Curriculum Development of the National Educational Association, Washington, D.C.

tions, a teacher deals only with those feelings and motivations which are either voluntarily expressed or are ready to be expressed when an appropriate medium is supplied. As Dorothy Baruch puts it: "The teacher deals with conscious feelings that are there, ready to come out if the letting is sanctioned." (39.) She goes on to say that an essential function of the teacher is to help an emotionally disturbed child to realize that it is "all right" to give some form of overt expression (exclusive of attacking others) to his hostilities, guilt attitudes, fears, and feelings of inadequacies. Baruch continues by pointing out that when a child is allowed to objectify his feelings in some form of overt expression and realizes that his expression is approved by the teacher, he develops a greater sense of power over his impulses and consequently acquires a better acceptance of himself. This psychological condition, once attained, aids greatly in establishing a solid foundation upon which group-orientated socialization efforts to help the child can take root and grow.

SOCIOMETRIC MEASUREMENTS

During the past twenty years a large body of literature has grown up in reference to the uses of sociometric measurements. One of the areas of application of the concepts and methods discussed in this literature has been school classes.

The key idea of sociometry is that behind every formal organization, such as a class or a club, there is an informal, spontaneous organization consisting of interpersonal attractions and repulsions, and that this unstructured organization greatly affects the functioning of the formal organization as well as playing a significant role in the personal successes and failures of the group members. The primary purpose of sociometry in a school situation is to obtain quantitative data on these attraction-repulsion patterns and to evaluate these data in terms of mental hygiene objectives, from the standpoint of individual class members and from that of group management.

Types of sociometric measurements

The three principal kinds of sociometric measurements are: (1) testing on specific criteria which are functional in a particular group,

(2) sociometric questionnaires, and (3) measurements of reputation. In utilizing specific criteria that are functional in their particular classes, teachers may ask pupils to state their preferences for other classmates with whom they would prefer to work in studying a unit on transportation, in putting on a one-act play, in preparing an oral report in history, etc. Sometimes criteria of a more personal-social nature are used, such as, "Who would you like to sit near?" or "Who would you like to have in your play group?" When a teacher uses specific criteria that are related to on-going activities in his class, he should definitely plan to form groups or make other social arrangements which are indicated by his findings as being desirable.

Sociometric questionnaires are instruments that ask each child in a class to respond with varying degrees of positive and negative feelings to all other members of his class. This is generally done by giving each pupil a list of the names of all his classmates and asking him, as in the *Ohio Social Acceptance Scale,* to indicate how he regards them: (1) My very, very best friends, (2) My other friends, (3) Not friends, but okay, (4) Don't know them, (5) Don't care for them, (6) Dislike them.[10]

Another questionnaire is the *Classroom Social Distance Scale* published by the Horace Mann-Lincoln Institute of School Experimentation of Teachers College, Columbia University. Although sociometric questionnaires have the advantage of measuring each pupil's generalized personal feelings toward others, and although they have the additional advantage of squeezing out all the positive and negative feelings existing between the members of a class, they lack the specific functional utility of the first type of testing discussed above.

Measurements of reputation are instruments for obtaining data on how children regard each other in reference to certain kinds of traits or behavior characteristics. An example of such an instrument is given by Cunningham and Associates in their *Understanding Group Behavior of Boys and Girls* (pp. 419-422).[11] Several of the items from this are:

---

[10] Published by Division of Elementary Supervision of the State Department of Education, Columbus, Ohio.

[11] Published by Bureau of Publications, Teachers College, Columbia University, New York, 1951.

Here is someone who likes to talk a lot, always has something to say.

Here is someone who always tries to keep himself (or herself) neat and clean and tidy-looking.

Here is someone who is always telling others what to do, bossing them.

Under each item a space is left in which the pupil is to write the name of each classmate who he thinks fits the descriptive statement.

Another reputation measurement is *The Ohio Recognition Scale for Intermediate Grades,*[12] and a third one is found in *Studying Children and Training Counselors in a Community Program* (pp. 135-136).[13] This latter instrument is particularly useful in locating those pupils who are considered by their classmates to be outstanding in social leadership, aggressive maladjustment, withdrawn maladjustment, and in friendship. It is designed to be used in conjunction with the "Behavior Description Chart" referred to in a preceding section of this chapter in the discussion of teacher-pupil rating scales.

Uses of reputation measurements

Teachers who make use of reputation measurements are nearly always surprised at the kind of reputation that some pupils have. These surprises usually motivate them to observe certain children more critically and in a wider variety of situations. One fifth-grade teacher, for example, was at a loss to explain why a certain boy whom she regarded as an almost model child was listed under several unfavorable trait descriptions by eight different pupils on a reputation instrument. A few days later she had an answer to her question when she saw this boy in the corner of the playground with four girls hitting and kicking him in a united attack. When these girls were asked to explain their behavior they said, "He says bad words to us on the school bus, and we told him if he didn't quit doing it we were going to beat him up." This teacher was impressed with how much contrast there can be in a child's reputation as viewed by an adult observer and as viewed by his age-mates.

---

[12] Published by the Division of Elementary Supervision of the State Department of Education, Columbus, Ohio.

[13] The University of Chicago Press, The Youth Development Series, No. 2, 1953.

The point must be emphasized that the major purpose in administering such measurements as those discussed above is to discover more accurately those pupils who are making favorable impressions upon their classmates in regard to certain traits or kinds of overt behavior, in order that their skills and personal assets may be utilized more effectively in group processes, and that corrective efforts may be more specifically directed toward the needs of particular individuals. All this is especially necessary at early age-levels since it is well-known that a child's reputation follows him from grade to grade through the school system. In fact, his bad reputation may easily become magnified beyond legitimate facts. In such instances his reputation is more a product of group processes than of his own behavior.

A teacher may often need to realize this fact in understanding what appears to him to be a large discrepancy between the actual traits or behavior of a particular child and the way he is regarded by many of his classmates. He also needs to realize, however, that the way these other classmates treat this particular child will be determined more by the "picture in their heads" in regard to him than by the way he actually is. This means that in trying to change a child's bad reputation some efforts must be directed toward helping all the members of a class to develop more objective attitudes toward each other, and some must be directed toward changing the child himself.

Object of sociometric testing

If we confine our attention to the first kind of sociometric testing discussed above, namely that which obtains choices for a designated purpose within a particular class, we can say that a sociometric test measures the *choice-status* that each individual has in a tested population at a given time and in reference to a stated choice-criterion. It is a measure of person-to-person responsiveness in which each group member renders a judgment in regard to the desirability or undesirability of certain other members for a specific purpose, activity, or relationship. This statement clearly assumes that the members of a group hold *preferences* toward each other. Although this assumption is probably quite generally accepted, it is sometimes denied by those people who directly state or imply that everyone in a given group should like everyone else in it. The fallacy of this position is pointed out by Mary Northway when, in speaking of an individual who pretends to like everybody, she says: "He cannot; and if he tries to do so, he develops a superficial pseudo-socialization which has little meaning; or when he fails, is nagged by a remorseful sense of guilt." (25—p. 42.) However, as Northway also points out, it is important not to substitute preferences for justice or confuse it with prejudice. In other words, we can be fair, honest, and generous toward people whom we would not *prefer* to associate with for any purpose. Since, as stated above, sociometric testing is designed to measure the interpersonal preferences among the members of a group, such testing should not be assumed to be measuring attitudes like sympathy, generosity, or altruism.

It is important to note that any one sociometric test is only a *sampling* of each individual's choice-status with his peers. Other testings with different criteria than the one used, and at different times, will produce a somewhat different picture for most group members.

It seems clear that each person's choice-status in a particular group is greatly affected by the extent to which he is viewed by the others as possessing the kind of skills and values most important for successful achievement and overt social adjustment in this group. This is especially true when the choices are made in regard to partners or associates for some kind of group activity. It is less likely to be true when the choice-criterion has no direct reference to a group function, but instead is of a highly private or personal nature such as "best friends" or "ones I like to confide in." Obviously choices made on such criteria as these have an individual frame of reference and in most cases would certainly be motivated by more strictly personal feelings and needs than by considerations of group needs or group values. In either case, it is clear that the sociometric measurement is a highly *social* measurement in the sense that it is always getting at feelings or judgments that individuals hold *toward each other* rather than toward themselves. It is indeed an interpersonal measurement.

However, these measurements also reveal some important *subjective* qualities within the individual doing the choosing. In the first place, it is important to point out that a sociometric test does not ask a child "With whom do you play?" or with whom he does anything or has any kind of relationship *now*. Rather, he is asked with whom he would *like* to play or to have any other type of association or relationship in the *future.* Thus the emphasis is on what he would like *to become.* Northway has pointed out that every normal child is much more interested in what he is *to be* than in what he *has been;* thus the sociometric test, properly given and utilized, is a means whereby he may more fully *be* himself (p. 44) and more completely *reach* his social goals (25).[14] Thus a sociometric test measures not only each individual's *choice-value* among his immediate associates, but also from the standpoint of the psychology of the chooser, each person's subjective interpersonal *aspirations or wants.*

The pupil who chooses others who are much higher than himself in the social group structure may receive no reciprocations, and yet we should not regard this unrealistic choosing as a total loss either to the group or to the individual who does it. Instead, we should view such choosing as an indication that this individual still has a high aspiration level in regard to his *future* interpersonal possibilities. He still has enough "choice-daring" (Jennings [20 — p. 360]) to believe that he *could* be accepted as an associate by the ones he prefers. He has more healthy psychological resources to work with for his eventual social improvement than does a pupil who lacks any upward identification or social aspiration. The latter type of child consistently chooses only those who are on his own choice-status level or below it. He shows the psychology of defeatism as far as interpersonal mobility is concerned, especially when his own choice-status is very low.

It is important, then, for a teacher to study a child's social *wishes* or aspirations as well as his *choice-value,* especially in those cases in which a child's aspirations are very much higher or very much lower than his own sociometric position.

Significance of number of choices

Helen Jennings has emphasized that the number of choices a person *gives* in a sociometric test is an indication of his emotional need for others (20). In her study in the New York State Training School for Girls, Jennings found no relationship between the number of choices

---

[14] This emphasis in sociometric testing is obviously in accord with Allport's thesis in his *Becoming,* as summarized in Chapter 1.

that a girl gave to others and the number that others gave to her. This means that some girls gave only a few choices but received many in return, while some gave many choices but received only a few or none. Jennings concluded that a girl's responsiveness toward others was determined by a need so central to her personality that she was motivated to try to fulfill it regardless of the extent to which the immediate environment offered opportunities for its objective realization (p. 86). In other words, the extent of a girl's positive and negative responses toward other girls in this institution was determined not primarily by how much the others *needed her* but by how much she *needed them.* Furthermore, her level of responsiveness toward others was found to be quite constant over a period of nine months, irrespective of actual success or failure in overt interpersonal associations.

These findings, together with similar results obtained in school populations,[15] emphasize that the number of choices a person *gives* on a sociometric test, especially when related to the number received, is an additional index to the subjective needs and aspirations of the choosers.

Furthermore, the generally low or zero relationships that have been found between the number of choices given by the pupils in any class and the number that they receive emphasize that a teacher cannot accurately judge how well a child is accepted by his classmates simply from knowing his attitudes or feelings toward others. Instead, he must find out how *others* feel toward the child. Although there is surely some relationship between the way a person feels toward others and the way they feel toward him, this reciprocal relationship is certainly much too small to be depended upon for predictive purposes — at least in so far as this relationship is measured by number of choices given and number received on sociometric tests.

Teachers, too, should be cautioned against assuming that the number of choices given on a sociometric test is always a reliable index to a child's interpersonal need for others. There are exceptional

[15] In dealing with this point, the writer has run correlations between number of positive choices given and number received in twenty-five elementary and junior high school classes. The obtained coefficients have ranged from −.30 to .35 with a median of .10.

cases of pupils who will give no positive choices to others, and if rejections are asked for, will reject most of their classmates; yet this kind of choice-behavior does not appear to represent their inner feelings, since observations and conferences will nearly always reveal strong desires for intimate contacts with at least some other pupils. In such instances we must regard the antagonistic choice-behavior as an ego-defense mechanism whereby an insecure self is striving "to keep the score even" by rejecting others whom he thinks are rejecting him. As a matter of fact, the records will nearly always show that this child is not rejected nearly so much as he imagines, and he may even receive a few positive choices. Such information can serve as a basis for a conference with this child in which, without revealing any actual data or names, the teacher can help the child to see that the other pupils are not nearly so hostile toward him as he imagines, and that his own attitude stands in the way of his achieving what he most desires.

Factors affecting interpersonal attractiveness

It seems certain that the most general reason, and possibly the only reason, why one person is attracted to another is that there is a fulfillment of some kind of need. If the truth of this statement is accepted, then it would follow that the person with the most diversified capacities for meeting needs in others should receive the greatest number of choices on sociometric measurements. One line of evidence supporting this view is the finding that the person of high choice-status is generally characterized as being both *aggressive* and *friendly* in his relationships with others.[16] Through such traits as enthusiasm, drive, initiative, daring, and dominance, he attracts some who need to identify with the strong, and he attracts others who need his contributions to a common endeavor. Through such traits as kindness, sympathy, good humor, and genuine interest in others, he attracts many who need his particular kind of friendliness to raise *their* self-esteem and to fill *their* need for companionship. In other words, those individuals who are both aggressive and friendly are possessed of a wide range of human resources from which others may draw aid, comfort, and stimulation.

[16] See Chapter 10 for data bearing on this point.

Furthermore, those who have abilities, whether intellectual, physical, musical, or otherwise, are obviously in possession of important resources for meeting human needs if they are motivated to use their abilities toward this end. Even, however, when they use their abilities for selfish ends they will generally attract a few on the basis of genuine admiration, and a few others on the basis of the weak identifying with the strong. Our evidence indicates, though, that the possession of any ability in increasing amounts beyond the average necessary for success in a particular group does not mean corresponding increases in social effectiveness or personal desirability, although it may in some cases mean increased individual productivity. On the other hand, those who are definitely low in an ability valued in a particular group have a decided handicap in winning a favorable status on any ground.

When we have talked about the resources of an individual to meet human needs, we have considered only half the picture. The other half consists of the variety and the quality-level of the needs of all members of a particular group. The achievement, by any person, of high sociometric status in a given population is not due simply to what he has to offer, but also to what his associates *perceive* to be their needs, i.e., their needs which they believe can be fulfilled through personal or leadership channels.

In any typical classroom group, we would expect to find a wide range in both kind and quality in the perceived needs of its members, even in reference to any given individual. For example, in the case of one highly chosen sixth-grade girl whom the writer studied (and also her choosers) it seemed evident that a few chose her on several sociometric tests because they admired her for her oral and writing abilities, a few because she was influential in including them in her clique, a few because they shared mutual interests in hobbies, one because she could generally count on this girl to help her in arithmetic, two because they would like her to choose them since she was "so pretty" and wore such nice clothes, and one because she liked to have someone in her group who would "always do her part" and "had ideas."

Obviously this girl had a good many human resources to be able to arouse so many different kinds of motivations in her choosers. Obviously, too, these sixth-graders had a good many different kinds of personal-social needs which they were seeking to fulfill through their associations with this girl. Of course, all the pupils who chose this particular girl were at the same time choosing other pupils through whom they were expecting to satisfy the same and other needs.

Thus high sociometric status is seen as an *integration* of individual human resources and the perceived needs of the group members. Likewise, a person who is generally very low in sociometric status is in this condition either because he has few resources to offer others, or because those resources he does have are not perceived as needed by the members of the group he is in. In the first instance, the individual must be changed if his status is to be improved; in the second instance, the attitudes of the group members may be changed to include this individual's contribution within the field of their perceived needs.

From the many different kinds of motivations inherent in sociometric choosing, it is easy to understand why there is no one type of individual who is always highly chosen; the wide range in personal differences and perceived needs within a group would naturally mean that there is a considerable range in the kind of individuals who are most sought after for interpersonal associations. When the demands made by specific leadership roles are considered, this diversity becomes even greater, since in technical-type roles and in emergency situations a person may be chosen for a leadership assignment without much reference to the personal-social needs of the group members. Furthermore, when the differences between groups are also included, it is easy to see that we are not going to come out with a particular list of traits, or any combination of traits, that are certain to be characteristic of those persons who are highly chosen.

Personalities of individuals of varying choice-value

One conclusion from the above analysis is that not all those who are highly chosen are shining examples of "good personalities." Children who are sociometric stars frequently have rather serious personality faults and weaknesses, both as viewed by their peers and as viewed by their adult supervisors; however, those who are in the upper fourths of sociometric distributions are characterized, as a group, by many more personal-social assets than those in the lowest fourths of the same distributions. There will, however, be certain individuals in these lowest fourths who are characterized by some very favorable personality traits, both as viewed by their age-mates and as viewed by their teachers.

These findings place the major emphasis upon the desirability or the social effectiveness of a total person in a particular kind of situation rather than on a list of traits. It is one's desirability *as a total person* for certain kinds of personal relationships or group endeavors that is measured by a genuine sociometric test.

Aside from the fact that some socially disapproved traits can be "successfully carried" by strong personalities, there is another important reason why some rather serious deviations in personal traits and social behavior are found in some individuals of high-choice rank. Reference is made to the fact that the kinds of persons who are highly chosen depend to a large extent upon the personal-social maturity level of the choosers. If we hold to the theory mentioned above in regard to sociometric choices being directed toward those who are perceived as meeting various kinds of needs within the group members, then it would naturally follow that the highly chosen are to a considerable extent a mirror of the choosers. The quality-level of the one is certain to be reflected in the other.

Those who are psychologically adequate and secure direct a large proportion of their choices to others who are likewise adequate and secure. Their interpersonal attractions are based primarily on ego satisfactions and self-realizations. They desire to affiliate with another person chiefly because of such factors as pride in this person's abilities and achievements, shared interests and values, cooperative efforts carrying mutual benefits for both, mental stimulation, and persistent concern for the other person's happiness and self-enhancement. Likewise, in selecting leaders the adequate and the secure direct nearly all their choices to those whom they believe will represent their group to the best advantage for all.

On the other hand, it is well-known that there are many people whose interpersonal attachments and selections of leaders are heavily determined by immature and neurotic conditions within themselves. They tend to seek from others only the lower level or more basic satisfactions such as sex, security from physical or social harm, comfort and reassurance, and personal prestige values; or, in more extreme cases, even punishment, domination, and abuse to assuage feelings of guilt and worthlessness.

To the extent that lower-level motivations are operating in sociometric choosing, we would expect to find some individuals receiving more choices than an objective appraisal of their personal and social worth would warrant. The degree to which such lower-level motivations are operating in any particular testing situation can be known only through a rather intensive knowledge of the personality needs of the choosers. This calls for more study of the peculiar satisfactions arising from the interpersonal attachments within a group than is generally available. Such studies would seem to be a most fruitful area for psychological investigation.

Raising the quality-level of preferences

If we ask a general question in regard to how more members of more groups may be developed so that they are capable of higher-level interpersonal attachments, and of objectively motivated leadership choices, the answer would seem to be twofold. In the first place, we must concentrate more on the development of individuals who have feelings of personal worth and of self-adequacy, and who are characterized by reasonable amounts of conformity, adaptability, social aggressiveness, and group-centered motivations — characteristics which have been considered in detail in Chapters 7 through 10. In the second place, we must endeavor to achieve much greater interpersonal satisfactions in groups, and a much greater utilization of human resources for the attainment of group objectives.

As classroom groups (and all others in churches, clubs, and elsewhere) are more effectively managed from the standpoint of sociometric objectives and of democratic values, we would expect not only an increase in group productivity, but also an increase in the capacities of the group members to make more free and more mature choices of each other in both friendship and leadership situations.

Thus we see the close relationship that exists between the psychological qualities of individuals and the social-psychological qualities of the groups of which they are members. As individuals, whether children or adults, acquire more resources for meeting their own needs as well as the needs of others, they help to raise the quality-level of every situation they are in. Then, too, as the human dynamics residing in a particular group are stimulated and utilized, this group becomes a more fertile social field in which its members can grow into the full stature of human beings who are both liked and admired by their associates.

Value of sociometric data to teachers

From the foregoing analysis it will be clear that teachers who administer sociometric tests will find in them a rich source of information about individual pupils and group processes. Generally they are stimulated by these data to see some pupils in a new light. Also, they can measure the effects of their socialization efforts over any stated period of time, as shown in studies by Atkins and Riggs (1), by Olson (27), and by Rosenthal (30). Another use of such data is in the arrangement of sociometrically formed groups which are frequently more harmonious and productive than other kinds of grouping, as shown in Chapter 12. An additional use is possible through the study of degrees of acceptance between subgroups already existing in the classroom, such as bus versus town students and members of different ethnic groups.

Sociometric data are also useful in guidance work with individuals, not only in regard to personality problems, but also in regard to academic difficulties and the desire to drop out of school before the legal age limit. A pupil who is an isolate or a reject in one or more of his school groups may be so disturbed by this fact that he engages in various kinds of overcompensatory behavior and is unable to concentrate on his academic work.

That such children are often motivated to drop out of school early is substantiated in a study by Kuhlen and Collister which reports the rates of drop-outs among more than 400 sixth- and ninth-graders in New York State between 1942 and 1948 (21). Since extensive sociometric data had been obtained on these students in 1942, it was possible to relate their acceptance by their peers to their drop-out records. When the sociometric scores obtained in 1942 on those who subsequently dropped out of school were compared with the scores made by those who graduated from high school, the data were highly consistent in showing that those who dropped out were (as a group) definitely in the category of being unpopular with their classmates when they were either in the sixth or the ninth grades. Although there were certainly other factors operating to cause these pupils to drop out of school, it is also reasonable to assume that lack of peer acceptance played a part since there is a strong tendency for people to withdraw from situations in which they find that they are not liked or appreciated. It seems certain that efforts to help some pupils with their academic problems are largely wasted unless something can also be done to help them relieve their anxieties about their interpersonal adjustments.

Finally, the results of sociometric measurements may be useful in dealing with certain kinds of problems involving discipline and group control. Several kinds of situations illustrating this point are presented below.

Sometimes a teacher will notice that a few pupils get blamed by other pupils for nearly all bad situations or rule-infractions. Such reports are most likely to come from the playground or from any unsupervised activity. In such instances sociometric data would be useful, since it is very likely that the "overly blamed" child would be shown to be a group reject. An example of this kind of behavior was observed by the writer in a fourth-grade class in which the teacher was making an effort to find out who had written a note with some offensive words in it. Several pupils immediately volunteered the information that Bob had written it; but Bob, a group reject, was not in school that day.

Britt quotes a study in which an elementary school teacher, just previous to a physical drill, carefully instructed several very popular children to make some rather awkward mistakes during the exercise (9). Immediately afterward the teacher asked the pupils to write the names of those children who had interfered with the smoothness of the drill. She discovered that nearly all the pupils listed the names, not of the popular pupils who had actually made the mistakes, but of unpopular children who had made no obvious errors (p. 123).

Unwarranted favorable responses are just as worthy of notice by a teacher as are "overblaming" attitudes. Some children are so supported by the interpersonal networks in their classrooms that they can "do no wrong." This kind of support may be observed in operation when students evaluate each other's oral reports. The writer has been present in several classrooms when very unpopular children have made reports, and has noted the whispering, shuffling of feet, and lack of attention while the reports were in progress — in marked contrast to the eager attention and highly favorable comments following a report by a sociometric star.

Another possibility for use of sociometric data is found in the fact that such information may be utilized to help locate danger spots in human relations before these relationships become dangerous or disruptive. The data that are most pertinent for this purpose include rejections as well as positive choices. The kind of situations meant here will be illustrated by several examples.

In a junior high school, sociometric testing in eighteen homerooms showed that in two of these rooms the extent of positive choosing between the students was much lower than in the other rooms, and the number of rejections was noticeably greater. A follow-up on these two rooms revealed that the teachers in charge were well aware that the students were uncooperative toward each other, and at times disruptive and hostile. In fact, one of them had already told her principal that "something ought to be done" about her homeroom group "before they exploded."

In these two rooms the sociometric data (particularly the large number of rejection responses) shed a lot of light on why the teachers in charge of them were having trouble. It is reasonable to assume that if this kind of information had been obtained on these groups earlier something might have been done to forestall these very bad interpersonal situations. As it was, one of these groups was allowed to "rock along" until the end of the school year, but the other one was broken up by shifting some students out of it and some new ones into it.

One of the principles of successful social control is to be able to anticipate trouble and to correct the disruptive forces before a crisis situation is created. In the area of human relations, it seems evident that one of the best ways to abide by this principle is periodically to obtain sociometric data (including rejection responses) from the members of particular groups.

A third type of problem involving discipline and group control is found in those instances in which teachers or counseling personnel wonder how much a certain child's antisocial conduct is affecting other children. A situation of this kind in a high school was the concern of a guidance director. He knew of two girls in this high school who had bad reputations in regard to personal conduct, and he also knew that these girls were rather aggressive in the student body and had on several occasions tried to be nominated or elected to leadership positions. He wondered how much influence they had in the student body. Since he knew that several sociometric-type tests had been given in some classes and homerooms, he consulted the teachers who had conducted these measurements. He found data available on these two girls from two classes and from their homerooms. In all these groups the girls were shown to be very low in number of choices received for any purpose or activity. This information afforded considerable reassurance to the guidance director that these two girls did not constitute a center of influence in the student body.

In other situations certain students who are known to engage in various forms of antisocial conduct may nevertheless prove to be centers of influence. When this is shown to be the case, such students obviously cannot be ignored, and furthermore, a teacher or counselor may find it futile to work directly against them.

This situation is illustrated in a case reported by Cook from a study in a small Midwestern high school (11). As a part of some socializing activities introduced into this school, an effort was made to induce an aggressive clique leader by the name of George to identify with more socially acceptable modes of personal attitudes and conduct; but these efforts completely failed, according to Cook's judgment, because he and his co-workers had proceeded "on a false premise," namely, that they could persuade George to change his personal behavior by bringing official pressure to bear on him. This pressure was ineffective because the boy was a star in every sport and had great prestige in the school at large; he could afford to be indifferent to the opinions of many of his classmates and of his teachers. "Neither class nor teacher had anything to offer him that he wanted, no way to motivate status striving, to shake his supreme self-confidence, hence the learning (or integrative) process could not get started. Our mistake was not to recognize his solid anchorage in the school and to work from this angle." This case serves to emphasize a principle of importance in group management, namely the need to work *with* or *through* a group's accepted leaders, and to avoid working directly against such persons.

A situation illustrating the validity of this point is found in the case of a sixth-grade class whose regular teacher became ill, and whose place was taken by a substitute teacher who did not understand how to work with the leaders of the class. Instead, she did numerous things to antagonize these leaders in her efforts to control the class. She "bawled them out" in front of others, made one of them sit in a corner, and ridiculed one of them before the class for taking a girl to a picture show. These coercive efforts finally resulted in so much "bad blood" between her and the class that she had to give up teaching. Another substitute teacher was called in but she "inherited" so much of the antagonism aroused by the preceding teacher that she voluntarily withdrew in less than a week.

The third teacher called in had a good understanding of group processes, and she knew what had happened to the two preceding substitute teachers. What did she do? The first time she appeared before the class she told the pupils that since she was a new teacher she would like to get their help in finding out what work they had covered and what plans they would like to make for the next week or two. In order to "find out these things in the quickest time" she asked the pupils to list the names of three or four other children whom they thought would be the best qualified to work with her for the purposes mentioned above. The pupils responded and, of course, the ones receiving the highest number of votes were the generally accepted leaders of the class.

The teacher selected the five pupils receiving the highest number of choices and proceeded immediately to meet with them around her desk while the rest of the class members were given seatwork to do. Out of this conference the teacher not only found out something about where the class was in the various textbooks, but she also followed up their suggestions in regard to laying tentative plans for a field trip, and for organizing a classroom club which was to have elected officers and was to meet every Friday afternoon. Everything went quite smoothly in this class for the rest of the school year. Although this condition was due to numerous factors, it seems certain that one of the most important of these was the teacher's ability to work *with* rather than against the accepted leaders of the class.

REFERENCES

1. Atkin, E. M. and L. A. Riggs, "More Sociometric Experiments at School No. 45," *Baltimore Bulletin of Education,* 23, 1945-46, 3-7.
2. Barr, John, "A Multi-Question Sociometric Procedure," *Personnel and Guidance Journal,* 33, 1955, 527-530.
3. Bieker, H., "Using Anecdotal Records to know the Child," Ch. XII, *Fostering Mental Health in Our Schools,* Washington, D.C., 1950 Yearbook of the Association for Supervision and Curriculum Development of the N. E. A., 1950.
4. *Bonney-Fessendon Sociograph* with manual, published by California Test Bureau, 5916 Hollywood Boulevard, Los Angeles 28, California.
5. Bowes, F. H., "The Anecdotal Behavior Record in Measuring Progress in Character," *The Elementary School Journal,* 39, 1939, 431-435.
6. Breen, L. C., "Diagnosis of Behavior by Finger Painting," *Elementary School Journal,* 56, 1956, 321-324.
7. Brandt, R. M. and H. V. Perkins, "Teachers Change as They Study Children," *Childhood Education,* 34, 1957-1958, 218-220.
8. Brieland, D., "A Variation of the 'Guess Who?' Technique for the Study of the Adjustment of Children," *Journal of Educational Research,* 45, 1952, 385-390.
9. Britt, S. H., *Social Psychology of Modern Life.* New York: Farrar and Rinehart, Inc., 1941.
10. Buros, O. K. (ed.), *The Fourth Mental Measurements Yearbook.* Highland Park, N.J.: The Gryphon Press, 1953.
11. Cook, L. A., "An Experimental Sociographic Study of a Stratified 10th Grade Class," *American Sociological Review,* 10, 1945, 250-261.
12. Cunningham, Myron, "A Realistic Emphasis on Art," *Childhood Education,* 32, 1956, 223-229.
13. Ferguson, L. W., *Personality Measurement.* New York: McGraw-Hill Book Co., 1952.
14. Gronlund, N. E., *Sociometry in the Classroom.* New York: Harper and Brothers, 1959.
15. Guilford, J. P., *Personality.* New York: McGraw-Hill Book Co., 1959.

16. Herrick, V. E., and J. Knight, "Child Study and the Improvement of the Educational Program," *Elementary School Journal*, 51, 1950-51, 371-379.

17. Hoyt, K. B., "A Study of the Effects of Teacher Knowledge of Pupil Characteristics on Pupil Achievements and Attitudes Towards Classroom Work," *Journal of Educational Psychology*, 46, 1955, 302-310.

18. Jarvie, L. L. and M. Ellingson, *A Handbook on the Anecdotal Behavior Journal*. Chicago: The University of Chicago Press, 1940.

19. Jennings, H. H., "Sociometry in Group Relations — A Work Guide for Teachers." Washington, D.C.: American Council on Education, 1948.

20. ———, *Leadership and Isolation* (2nd Ed.). New York: Longmans, Green and Co., 1950.

21. Kuhlen, R. G. and E. G. Collister, "Sociometric Status of Sixth and Ninth Graders Who Fail To Finish High School," *Educational and Psychological Measurements*, 12, 1952, 623-637.

22. Langdon, G. and I. W. Stout, *Teacher-Parent Interviews*. Englewood Cliffs, N.J.: Prentice-Hall, Inc., 1954, p. 356.

23. Martyn, Kenneth A. and Harold J. Bienvenu, "The Parent Conference — Progress Report, Not Psychotherapy," *Elementary School Journal*, 57, 1956, 42-44.

24. Maves, H. J., "Contrasting Levels of Performance in Parent-Teacher Conferences," *The Elementary School Journal*, 58, 1958, 219-224.

25. Northway, M., *A Primer of Sociometry*. Toronto: University of Toronto Press, 1952.

26. ——— and Lindsay Weld, *Sociometric Testing — A Guide for Teachers*. Toronto: University of Toronto Press, 1957.

27. Olson, W. C., "The Improvement of Human Relations in the Classroom," *Childhood Education*, 22, 1946, 317-325.

28. Peller, L. E., "Models of Children's Play," *Mental Hygiene*, 36, 1952, 66-83.

29. Prescott, D., *Helping Teachers Understand Children*. Washington, D.C.: American Council on Education, 1945.

30. Rosenthal, S., "A Fifth Grade Classroom Experiment in Fostering Mental Health," *Journal of Child Psychiatry*, 2, 1953, 302-329.

31. Russel, D., "What does Research Say About Self-Evaluation," *Journal of Educational Research*, 46, 1952, 561-567.

32. Sells, S. B., "Observational Methods of Research," *Review of Educational Research*, 18, 1948, 425-447.

33. Strang, R., "The Interview," *Review of Educational Research*, 9, 1939, 498-501.

34. Super, D. E., *Appraising Vocational Fitness*. New York: Harper and Brothers, 1949.

35. Symonds, P. M., "Studying the Individual Through Projective Techniques," *Modern Educational Problems,* The Report of the 17th Educational Conference of the Educational Records Bureau and the American Council on Education, 48-60.
36. Travors, Robert M. W., *Educational Measurements.* New York: The Macmillan Co., 1955, pp. 10-125.
37. Tryon, C., "Studying the Behavior of Children," *Elementary School Journal,* 42, 1941-42, 241-254.
38. ———, *How to Construct a Sociogram,* Horace Mann-Lincoln Institute of School Experimentation, Bureau of Publications, Teachers College, Columbia University, 37, 1947.
39. ———, "Mental Health in Modern Education," Ch. VII, *The Fifty-fourth Yearbook of the National Society for the Study of Education,* Part II. Chicago: University of Chicago Press, 1955.

QUESTIONS AND EXERCISES

1. Arrange with one of your local schools to observe a child during play periods or during the lunch periods, for the purpose of taking some anecdotal records on his behavior. Report to the class on how this experience helped you to understand this child better. Did you have difficulty in objectively putting down "only what happened" free from your judgment?
2. Try to find a teacher who has kept some anecdotal records and ask him to come to the class to tell how he has used such data.
3. Obtain a teacher-pupil rating scale used in your own or a nearby community and spend some time in class analyzing its contents and how it could best be used. Also obtain copies of the rating scales mentioned in this chapter.
4. Try to get a teacher, an administrative official or a counselor in your local schools to come to class and tell how personality self-rating scales are used by him to understand his pupils better.
5. Plan role-playing skits before the class for the purpose of demonstrating some good and bad practices in teacher-parent conferences. Provide for class discussion of each demonstration.
6. Try to get someone in your local schools, or in a nearby clinic, to come to class and tell how he has utilized self-expressive productions of children as a source of personality diagnosis.

7. Arrange for a committee of class members to obtain some sociometric data in one or more classes in the local schools. Present a summary of findings to the class and discuss the values of this kind of testing.
8. Try to get someone who has utilized sociometric data with his class or other kind of group, to come to your class and tell how these data have been of value to him in working for mental health objectives.

SELECTED FILMS

Child in the Middle. 18 minutes. Illustrates the use of parent-teacher conferences in solving a problem with an elementary school child.

Facing Reality. 12 minutes. Good example of use of teacher-pupil conference.

Learning to Understand Children, Part I: A Diagnostic Approach. 21 minutes. Very good illustration of several ways of understanding a socially maladjusted pupil; Ada Adams, a high school girl, is studied through school records, observations, home visits, and conferences.

Learning to Understand Children, Part II: A Remedial Program. 23 minutes. In this section of the film various procedures are followed to help Ada, showing how accurate diagnosis can lead to effective action.

Your Child Is a Genius. 13 minutes. Points out value of creative expression in personality diagnosis and development.

Know Your Children. Shows how to make a sociometric study of a class.

CLASSROOM MANAGEMENT 4

12

PUPIL PARTICIPATION AND

NUMEROUS REFERENCES have been made in the preceding chapters, both directly and by implication, to the need for various kinds of pupil participation in the learning process as a necessary condition for achieving the objectives of mental hygiene. Even some of the methods of personality assessment described in Part Three require pupil participation on a responsible level; this is most true of sociometric measurements. It is now time to consider directly pupil participation in classroom management, and especially those kinds of participation which are achieved through various

CLASSROOM GROUPING

forms of classroom grouping. As stated in the preface to this volume, if a teacher is going to do anything effective toward mental health goals he must do so primarily through classroom management, since in his role as a teacher he is in charge of a group, or is in group situations, practically all the time he is on duty.

Maximum development of the abilities and personal qualities of all pupils requires that they assume many responsible roles in all aspects of classroom affairs. This kind of classroom management capitalizes upon the psychology of ego-involvement as a source of motivation; furthermore, it provides a basis for stimulating the growth of all the positive goals of mental hygiene presented in Part Two. When pupils take many active roles, both individually and in collaboration with others, in all phases of their school work, they have numerous opportunities for developing self-confidence, for learning the constructive values of conformity and adaptability, for acquiring skill and balance in exercising social initiative, and for experiencing satisfactions in working *with* and *for* classmates as opposed to working against them.

The kind of classroom management under consideration is the kind which demands a high degree of ability on the part of the teacher to direct the skills and interests of pupils into problem-solving and creative endeavors. Major factors in this ability are: the teacher's attitude toward pupils as shown by his faith in their capacities to manage many of their classroom activities, his confidence in their ability to develop intrinsic interests, his skill in establishing friendly relationships with pupils, and the extent to which he can achieve a permissive type of classroom control.

MAJOR KINDS OF CLASSROOM CONTROLS

By permissive control is not meant a passive, do nothing, *laissez faire* kind of control, but rather one under which children sense that they have a wide latitude in which to ask questions, make suggestions and criticisms, initiate activities, and express sincere feelings. Permissive control *is* a form of *control.* It does not mean "turning children loose to do as they please." It is a type of control requiring a high level of self-confidence on the part of the teacher and also a high level of insight into the motivations and capacities of children. Probably the chief weakness in the permissive type of classroom management is that some teachers have not taken a strong enough role in helping children to select an appropriate task and to move forward toward its completion. Only a teacher who is a persistent source of stimulation to pupils can be successful as a leader under permissive class management. The emphasis must always be on responsible pupil participation, not on "turning the class over to the students."

Satisfying human relationships require not only responsible effort but also a considerable volume of friendly intercourse even in work-type situations. It seems very doubtful that the objectives of mental hygiene can be attained with anything like maximum effectiveness unless instructional activities are supported by a considerable amount of definitely friendly contacts between pupils and teachers. According to some reports, this is an area in which many teachers show marked limitations. In his *Teaching-Learning Process* Cantor states that, although most teachers hold favorable attitudes toward pupils and toward their work, a good many of them reflect attitudes in their classrooms which preclude any feeling of friendliness toward children (5 — p. 19). He writes: "Carson W. Ryan, who visited schools throughout the United States in a study of the class atmosphere, concluded, 'Simple friendliness in the schoolroom would seem to be one of those easily attainable and obviously desirable conditions for any human enterprise having to do with good mental health, but the visitor to schools finds it in shockingly few of the places he visits.'" (p. 19.) Good human relations, however, should never be allowed to pervert or undermine the achievement goals necessary to a work situation, such as happens when a teacher allows his personal feelings for a pupil to influence his evaluation of this pupil's academic work via grades, or to motivate him to grant certain children special privileges.

Speaking generally, all groups must be predominantly either a work-type group with the objective of achieving or producing something; or they must be of a social nature with no stated objective but simply for interpersonal enjoyments.[1] If the predominant characteristic of a group is not well defined and its organization fluctuates between that of the work type and that of a social nature, the group will soon "fall apart" since its core, or the purpose for which it was originally composed, will be unclear. In other words, a social structure must have certain primary characteristics or it will disintegrate, the people involved in it will leave, or their relationships will become very frustrating or chaotic.

Teachers, for example, have found that a certain amount of friendly talk among pupils in a classroom and a certain amount of such things as entertainment stunts, parties, jokes, and kidding are necessary to good morale and to good social development of children and young people. However, beyond this "certain amount" such activities begin to undermine a "work atmosphere." If allowed to go too far the primary structure of the class may be so destroyed that little work is accomplished even by those who would like to achieve something.

It is apparently quite important that the principal nature of a group structure be well defined shortly after people first come to-

[1] See Jennings' discussion of this topic under the classification of socio and psyche groups listed at end of this chapter (15).

gether, otherwise it may be very difficult subsequently to establish the kind of structure originally desired. The participants in a situation must be able to sense what kind of a social whole they are involved in or they soon become confused (or create confusion), as evidenced by such remarks as "what goes here?" or "what's the score here?" Once this primary structure is realized and accepted, some deviations from it of an opposite nature are readily tolerated and are definitely expected in most work situations. Beginning teachers have frequently been warned that on the first day of school they must establish firm control and set a strong work atmosphere, with greater permissiveness coming later.

VALUES OF PUPIL PARTICIPATION

In a series of journal articles devoted to research findings on responsible pupil participation in classroom learnings, Thelen and his graduate students at the University of Chicago present evidence dealing with contrasting conditions found in classrooms dominated by teacher planning, as compared with those classrooms in which there is a large amount of pupil-teacher planning.[2] These studies present considerable evidence bearing on the value to total child development of mutually shared efforts and of positive interpersonal feelings between pupils and teachers. In making a summary statement from the various researches conducted under his direction, Thelen points out that these studies have shown that a teacher's behavior in large measure determines the quality of emotional conditions in a classroom (25 — p. 31). Moreover, the learning of certain social attitudes and human-relations principles is very much affected by teacher-pupil interactions.

This point is substantiated by evidence from several of the above studies showing statistically reliable differences in favor of the more student-centered classes in respect to their showing fewer manifestations of anxiety and unproductive tensions, and in regard to fewer hostile feelings among pupils and between pupils and teachers. Elaborating on this latter point, Flanders (one of Thelen's students) concluded from his study that pupils who were anxious about their

[2] In *Journal of Educational Research,* 45, Oct.-Nov., 1951-1952.

relationships with their teacher were more concerned with the problem of adjusting to their teacher than with the problem of achievement (8).

Perkins (another of Thelen's co-workers) concluded from his analysis of students' statements about their academic work that in "student-centered" classes there was more evidence of achieving insight into concepts, and of looking at problems in an objective as opposed to a self-involved manner (21).

Several investigations in the above-mentioned series, especially those by Bovard (3), McKeachie (18), and Rehage (22), report evidence showing "student-centered" classes to be superior to teacher-dominated classes in reference to several kinds of behavior patterns essential to a mentally healthy individual; namely, spontaneity, initiative, and uniqueness. These behaviors were evidenced by the greater frequency of unusual remarks and unpredictable responses, by more willingness to deviate from group norms, and by starting more things on their own.

Of particular interest on the latter point is Rehage's study of two eighth-grade social studies classes, one of which had a large amount of teacher-pupil planning, whereas the other one (established as a control group) was entirely teacher-controlled (22). Results showed that although there was not a significant difference between these two classes in amount of factual subject matter learned, there was an obvious contrast in group behavior. Whereas those in the teacher-pupil planning class initiated and carried out four rather substantial group projects, requiring much group cooperation and expenditure of energy, nothing of this kind happened in the control group.

CRITICISMS OF PUPIL PARTICIPATION

Not all studies on the values of pupil participation in classroom management, group problem solving, committee work, and class projects show as favorable results as those reviewed above. In fact a comprehensive survey of the literature, such as that presented by Bonner in his *Group Dynamics — Principles and Applications,* especially in Chapter 8, "Group Dynamics in Education," makes clear the point that there are a good many variables that must be considered in evaluating all of the more recent efforts to give students more active roles in their education.[3] Considering particularly the evidence bearing on the value of the lecture method as compared with various types of group-centered teaching on the college level, Bonner states in his Chapter 8 that, although the group-centered approaches have shown some real advantages in humanizing education, some students in particular colleges have shown strong preferences for the lecture method because they believe it prepares them better for comprehensive examinations that they are subsequently expected to pass. Bonner also makes the point that some students become dissatisfied with a type of teaching that places a large amount of emphasis on arriving at group consensus, or that tends to give the group a centralized or dominant influence in determining the learnings that are arrived at. Another frequently voiced criticism of student-centered or nondirective type of teaching is that it is too time-consuming for what is accomplished.

These negative reactions no doubt spring, in some students, from objective evaluations, while in other students these kinds of reactions to group-centered teaching spring largely from personality characteristics. Regardless of the source of the dissatisfaction, it seems likely from our present evidence that any teaching procedure that permits a large amount of student participation, particularly in the form of verbal expressions, will arouse disapproval from some students, and will not result in satisfactory learnings of any kind from *all* students. But this is only half the story. The same thing can be said for any other kind of teaching, as is well shown in P. E. Jacob's, *Changing Values in College, An Exploratory Study of the Impact of College Teaching.*[4]

The significance of all this is that no teacher should rely on any one teaching procedure; instead he should utilize a variety of approaches and methods, including lectures, discussions, oral reports, gathering of firsthand information, research projects, questioning of students, role playing, etc. Diversification of teaching methods is necessary to promote the mental health objective of maximum self-realization for all students, since it is well-known that every class is composed of students who are characterized by a wide range of differences in levels of competence, interests, attitudes, and personality traits.

[3] New York: The Ronald Press Company, 1957, p. 531.
[4] New York: Harper and Brothers, 1957.

UTILIZING SUBGROUPING

One of the ways most frequently used by teachers to increase responsible pupil participation is that of subdividing an entire class into smaller units usually consisting of two to six individuals. Below are several most commonly used bases for determining these units.

1. *Teacher judgment.* The teacher puts those pupils together (as on a committee) whom he feels, on the basis of his records and personal knowledge, will work well together for a given purpose. The particular value of this basis for grouping is that a perceptive teacher can sometimes sense that two or more children would profit from associating with each other when these children themselves are not aware of it.

2. *Similarity in abilities.* The teacher puts those children together whose test results and other performances show them to be fairly similar in such subject-matter areas as reading, mathematics, science, or English. The obvious advantage of this kind of grouping is that both personal and intellectual growth can generally be most effectively stimulated through associations with others who are not too far from one's own level of competence.

3. *Similarity in interests.* The teacher finds out from the pupils who are in a particular class what special aspect of the subject they would like to concentrate on for a project, or a written or oral report. Those who indicate interest in the same topic are asked to work together. This kind of grouping frequently results in a high level of cooperative effort and of personal growth due to similar motivations. Furthermore, pupils of a wide range of abilities are sometimes brought together, thus providing opportunities for bright, average, and dull pupils to learn from each other.

4. *Sociometric choices.* The teacher administers a sociometric test such as described in Chapter 11, and then utilizes the data to form subgroups that have a sufficient degree of interpersonal rapport to provide a basis for cooperative and productive efforts. The chief values of sociometric groupings are that the interpersonal bonds existing among the members of each subgroup make possible a higher degree of mutual support and harmonious effort than is generally found in other kinds of groupings. How these particular values can

be obtained through sociometric groupings is described for teaching reading (Cornelius [6]), for teaching physical education (Bonney and Burleson [2] and Todd [24]), for teaching English (Brickell [4] and Hatfield [13]), and for teaching a wide range of subjects on the junior high school level (Forlano and Wrightstone [9]).

Each of these forms of grouping, when properly managed, makes for a wider distribution of responsibilities, more provisions for individual differences, and greater opportunities for unique expressions than is possible when a class is held together as one unit all the time. This is not to say, however, that a teacher should have nothing but group work. This would be a mistake since there are numerous times when a class can be taught as a total unit and, furthermore, there are also numerous times when children need to work alone. Classroom management that stimulates a wide range of interests, temperaments, and abilities cannot be rigid, but must be flexible according to developing situations and sensitive to the values of all ways of learning.

A teacher's first experience in group work

The report given below was written by a high school mathematics teacher. It is pertinent to the present discussion because it shows a teacher's first experience with group work and illustrates how such grouping may contribute to increased motivation and academic achievement, in addition to the more distinctly personal-social values of increased development of individual talent and of cooperative efforts and mutual aid.

> The class which met for plane geometry at period five was a most unsatisfactory collection of students. This was partly due to the fact that most of them were coming directly from lunch and partly to the fact that there seemed to be absolutely no social ties among the students. At the end of the first six-week period of the Fall term there was a much higher percentage of failures than in the other two classes of plane geometry I taught in periods one and two.
>
> About two weeks before time for the second six-week test, the students were asked to make choices as to whom they would like to work with. It was explained that each group

would be working up some project for review. There was a flare of interest that was totally foreign to this class.

When the choices were tabulated, I was quite surprised to see that some students were rejected by certain other students. One of these was a boy whom I would classify as the laziest boy in class.

After the groups had been set up, the class was given 15 minutes during the latter part of each class period for four days each week. This time was used for decisions as to what the groups could work up as a means of review. Some were more enthusiastic than others and planned to get together at lunch period, at a study hall period, and even outside of school.

One group worked up a set of multiple-choice exercises. A girl who had not been chosen at all could type, so she cut a stencil of the exercises. Another girl in the group, who worked in the office, ran enough mimeographed copies for every class member.

The "lazy" boy turned out to be quite good at drawing figures, and made three large posters for his group to use on "their day." Other members of the group each had questions to ask orally about the figures. This period proved highly entertaining as well as informative.

Still another group had put questions requiring one-word answers on slips of paper, and students drew a slip from the box and answered the questions.

Each group made much of keeping up with the average score made by its members and comparing these with averages of other groups.

Needless to say, there were fewer failures in this class when the six-week tests were scored than in either of the other two classes. The number of failures on the test alone had been reduced from 21 to 5 percent.

When the students were asked to make choices for the same purpose four weeks later, only one person received a rejection. She was outstandingly smart but was slightly overbearing. However, several students did choose her. Every person got at least one choice and the "lazy" boy got three!

This account illustrates how group work can encourage the utilization of a wider range of abilities and promote more cooperative efforts than is generally possible in the traditional total-class recitation procedure.

Principles for composing subgroups

If subgroupings are to promote maximum productive efforts and human-relations values, they should be formed according to certain guidelines. Most of these guidelines, which are listed and described below, apply to any kind of grouping except that based entirely on ability, but some of them apply only to sociometric grouping.

1. When either the teacher or pupils are inexperienced in group work it is best to begin on a small scale, such as by having this type of work only once or twice a week or for only part of a period. Also, in beginning this kind of work it is important that the teacher help a class to decide quite definitely what the groups are going to do when they come together. Furthermore, the size of the groups should be kept quite small — probably not more than three or four members.

2. Closed cliques should not be allowed to form separate groups by themselves. To prevent these cliques from becoming more and more isolated from the rest of the group, a few other students should be put in work-groups with these clique members. Probably the best students to choose for this purpose are those who are fairly strong socially and have indicated a preference for at least one member of the clique.

3. Especially during the early stages of grouping students who differ in regard to sex, race, or family backgrounds, it is important to place more than one student representing a particular difference in a group with others. For example, if girls and boys have not previously worked together in groups it is wise to put two or three girls rather than one in a group composed mostly of boys. In regard to grouping those individuals who are likely to be considered in an inferior category by the majority group, it is very important, especially at first, to select only those from the "inferior category" who are the best or strongest representatives of this category.

4. In placing students who are unchosen on a sociometric test or who are obviously ignored by others, it is best not to put more than

two of these in any one group of five or more students. Usually each group of five or more students should be composed of a few highly chosen individuals, one or two who are unchosen or low, and the rest of average interpersonal status. In cases of poorly chosen, unchosen, or rejected children, the teacher's judgment must often be the determining factor in placing a particular child. Such a pupil is likely to fare better in a group in which at least one or two of the other members are characterized by a high degree of personal adequacy and security. These self-confident individuals have sufficient ego-strength that they *can* be genuinely interested in really trying to include a weak person in a group endeavor, and *can* respond to a generally rejected person on the basis of what he *is,* regardless of stereotypes held against him. The fact that self-confident individuals can do these things is no guarantee that they will; nevertheless they are more likely to than are insecure individuals. Certainly two or more pupils who reject each other should never be put together, since they do not identify with each other and therefore are not motivated to work together.

5. When sociometric data are used every pupil should be grouped with at least one whom he chooses. In doing this it is probably more important to pay attention to *reciprocated* choices than to the order of choices, i.e., whether a choice is a first-, second-, or third-level preference is probably less important than the fact of reciprocation.

PROBLEMS IN GROUP WORK

Probably most teachers who have conducted some form of group work have found that this kind of classroom management does not always produce the educational and human relations values that are anticipated. There are numerous reasons for these disappointments, including personality and professional weaknesses within particular teachers, as well as limitations within the teaching environment. Some conditions which frequently result in frustrations in group work are: the kind of task selected for this type of work may not be one that is well suited for cooperative efforts, or it may be too easy, or it may be poorly defined, or it may be of interest to the teacher but not to the pupils, or it may be one requiring more concentration than a particular subgroup has time or ability to deliver.

Examples of kinds of tasks most appropriate for classroom group work are: planning for a field trip, mutual aid in doing some practical thing like directing games or presenting a demonstration of how to do something, creating a one-act play or skit or mural, developing an oral report in which several persons tell about different parts of a fairly large topic, developing one or more solutions to a defined problem arising out of academic work or from school experiences, and listing problems which the class as a whole should consider.

Another problem closely related to that of inappropriate task assignment is found in those situations in which too much dependence is placed on group discussion or group agreement, or on good human relations, when what is needed is a digging up of pertinent facts or the utilization of special skills possessed by certain group members. Harmonious agreement or ability to get along with others can never be substituted for necessary knowledge and skill. In a definitely work-type situation good human relations must help promote, and not interfere with, the major work objectives. This point is given research support in a study of 14 high school basketball teams reported by Fiedler, Hartmann, and Rudin in which it is shown that the more effective teams (determined by win-loss records) conferred the greatest status on task-centered boys, while the less effective teams conferred the greatest status on warm-relationship-oriented individuals, that is, those who were friendly and very likeable but not necessarily the best players (7). These remarks emphasize a point previously made; namely, that group work may be overdone to the neglect of individual work. It is just as possible for a person to become overdependent upon a group as to become overdependent upon himself. In the first instance he becomes too "other-directed," and in the second instance too "self-directed."

Some teachers who are unaware of the need of a proper balance between group work and individual effort go to the extreme of having nothing but group work. Unless this kind of a program is under unusually expert guidance it is likely to result, not only in a reduction of individual effort, but also in a serious lack of stimulation to intellectual growth. We cannot expect a pupil's peers of approximately the same age and educational level to supply the kind of stimulation which should come from a well-informed teacher. The chief contributions of group work are in the area of cooperative learning and mutual aid rather than advanced intellectual stimulation. This distinction should be made clear, especially to older-age students. In his report on student evaluations of small-group work at Teachers College, Columbia University, Watson points out that although a large majority of these students gave such work a "warm general endorsement," one of the chief sources of criticism was "lack of stimulation" (26). Watson points out that he and his staff had tried to make it clear to these students that the primary objectives of work in small groups were to promote interpersonal satisfactions and cooperative learnings rather than intellectual stimulation, but apparently some of his students did not get this distinction, or if they did, they did not believe that they needed the kind of satisfactions or learnings which were supposed to be gained from work in small classroom groups. This does not mean that they actually did not need these things, since it is well-known that some persons who are most deficient in interpersonal and cooperative skills have developed strong psychological defenses against recognizing these deficiencies.

Another problem which is sometimes encountered in group work is that of the dominating person who does too much talking during discussion or planning sessions. Except in cases of deep-seated personality maladjustments, this problem can often be met through using role-playing as a training device or through a teacher conference with the overtalkative child. Also this problem, along with others, can often be attacked by having the students evaluate their own group-work experiences in class discussions following such activities. The teacher should feel free to bring in suggestions for improvement which do not occur to the students. In some groups this evaluation can be promoted by the use of checklists or rating scales whereby each group member rates the others on the items listed.

Occasionally a very bright student is found who feels that group work is a waste of time for him since he can do his work by himself. The chief answer to this problem seems to be for the teacher to hold a conference with such a student and try to get him to see the importance of intellectually capable students learning to collaborate with others in their thinking and in their activities. Just because a bright student can meet academic requirements by his own isolated efforts is not sufficient justification for a school's not trying to develop in him some cooperative attitudes and practices. It is well-known that one of the sources of occupational failure among some intellectually superior individuals is their inability to engage in cooperative efforts with others.

Finally, teachers should note that it is harder to conduct group work in some classes than in others, due to the composition of particular classes in regard to antagonistic cliques or to unusual intragroup differences. Although students of rather wide ranges of abilities and backgrounds can work together in classroom groups, there are limits beyond which cooperative efforts become extremely difficult.

This problem is illustrated in a high school speech class in which there was a rather unequal distribution of the sexes — there being 8 boys and 28 girls. This made the formation of groups for putting on plays difficult, since most plays involve both male and female characters. In addition there were students in the class whose academic standing varied all the way from sophomore to senior level. Furthermore, there was in this class a strong, disruptive clique that had been a problem for several years; the nine members of this clique were noisy, belligerent, and uncooperative in all school affairs. The teacher felt that the dissension caused by this clique, plus the unequal sex distribution, plus the wide range of academic standing, prevented the class from producing for public presentation more than one one-act play, whereas other classes taught at the same time produced three such plays. In these other classes the sociometrically formed groups worked effectively even though four groups were working at the same time in the same room. They did not have the handicapping factors mentioned above.

A teacher who tries group work in a class that happens to be characterized by some socially disintegrating factors should not be discouraged over the possibilities of such work in other classes which may afford more fertile soil for the development of interpersonal relations and effective group action.

REFERENCES

1. Bennett, Margaret E., *Guidance in Groups.* New York: McGraw-Hill Book Company, 1955.
2. Bonney, W. C. and R. M. Burleson, "Socializing Techniques," *Journal of Health, Physical Education and Recreation,* 25, 1954, 40-41.
3. Bovard, E. W., "The Psychology of Classroom Interaction," *Journal of Educational Research,* 45, 1951-52, 215-224.
4. Brickell, H. M., "What You Can Do With Sociograms," *The English Journal,* 39, 1950, 265-267.
5. Cantor, N., *The Teaching-Learning Process.* New York: The Dryden Press, 1953.
6. Cornelius, R., "Reading with Six-Year Olds," *Childhood Education,* 26, 1949, 162-163.
7. Fiedler, F. E., W. Hartmann, and S. A. Rudin, "The Relationship of Interpersonal Perception to Effectiveness in Basketball Teams," Bureau of Research and Service, College of Education, University of Illinois, Urbana, Illinois, *Technical Report No. 3,* 1952.
8. Flanders, N. A., "Personal-Social Anxiety as a Factor in Experimental Learning Situations," *Journal of Educational Research,* 45, 1951-52, 100-110.
9. Forlano, G. and J. W. Wrightstone, "Measuring the Quality of Social Acceptability Within a Class," *Educational and Psychological Measurement,* 15, 1955, 127-136.
10. Forlano, G. and J. W. Wrightstone, "Sociometric and Self-Descriptive Techniques in Appraisal of Pupil Adjustment," *Sociometry,* 14, 1951, 340-350.
11. Greenblatt, E. L., "Two Additional Studies in the Dynamics of School Social Structure of Classroom Seating and School Dances," *Journal of Educational Research,* 47, 1953, 261-270.
12. Gronlund, N. E., *Sociometry in the Classroom,* Ch. VIII. New York: Harper and Brothers, 1959.
13. Hatfield, W. W., "A Versatile Procedure," *English Journal,* 33, 1944, 428-432.
14. Hopkins, L. Thomas, "Classroom Climate Can Promote Creativeness," *Educational Leadership,* 8, 1956, 279-282.
15. Jennings, H. H., "Sociometric Differentiation of the Psychegroup and the Sociogroup," *Sociometry,* 10, 1947, 71-79.
16. Lewin, K., R. Lippitt, and R. K. White, "Patterns of Aggressive Behavior in Experimentally Created Social Climates," *Journal of Social Psychology,* 10, 1939, 271-299.
17. Lorge, I., "Groupness of the Group," *Journal of Educational Psychology,* 46, 1955, 449-456.

18. McKeachie, W. J., "Anxiety in the College Classroom," *Journal of Educational Research*, 45, 1951-52, 153-160.
19. Nelson, E. F., "Sociometric Techniques for Student Teachers," *Journal of Home Economics*, 41, 1949, 244-246.
20. Otto, H. J., "The Use of Social Criteria in Grouping Children at School," *Childhood Education*, 22, 1946, 326-329.
21. Perkins, H. V., "Climate Influences Group Learning," *Journal of Educational Research*, 45, 1951-52, 115-119.
22. Rehage, K. J., "A Comparison of Pupil-Teacher Planning and Teacher-Directed Procedures in Eighth Grade Social Studies Classes," *Journal of Educational Research*, 45, 1951-52, 111-115.
23. Strevell, W. H. and Pauline Oliver, "Grouping Can Be Flexible Within the Classroom," *The Nation's Schools*, 59, 1957, 89-91.
24. Todd, F., "Sociometry in Physical Education," *The Journal of the American Association for Health, Physical Education and Recreation*, 24, 1953, 23.
25. Thelen, H. A., "Experimental Research Toward a Theory of Instruction," *Journal of Educational Research*, 45, 1951-52, 89-93.
26. Watson, G., "An Evaluation of Small Group Work in Large Classes," *Journal of Educational Psychology*, 44, 1953, 385-408

QUESTIONS AND EXERCISES

1. Stimulate a class discussion on the psychology of learning which supports the need of responsible participation as a basis for good teaching.
2. Also discuss the various ways in which the kinds of participation described in this chapter are necessary to the achievement of mental hygiene objectives in schools.
3. Point out examples of teachers you have known who seemed to have a misconception of what is meant by permissiveness in the classroom.
4. Observe the different groups you are in and note the major social structure prevailing in them; also observe the relationship between these prevailing social structures and the effectiveness of each group. Do some groups seem to be ineffective because an inappropriate social climate is allowed to be too dominant?
5. Stimulate a class discussion on the kind of conditions which should exist in a class in order for group work to be most profitable.

6. Why are a variety of teaching methods necessary to accomplish the goals of mental hygiene?
7. State the particular contributions that can be made to mental health objectives through the use of classroom subgroups.
8. Observe a classroom in your local schools in which subgrouping is utilized as a basis for learning. Confer with the teacher about the values of this kind of work for the better total development of children.
9. Describe a classroom program that would provide maximum values through both individual and group work.
10. Invite a teacher who has had trouble with group work to come before your class and describe his problems, and see how much the members of the class can help him determine the reasons for his difficulties.

SELECTED FILMS

Broader Concept of Method, Part I. 13 minutes. Reveals weakness of teacher-dominated class in arousing interest in students.

Broader Concept of Method, Part II. 19 minutes. Shows how pupils can be brought in on responsible planning and learning activities.

Learning Through Cooperative Planning. 20 minutes. Demonstrates how elementary school children can take considerable responsibility for their learning.

Importance of Goals. 18 minutes. Stresses importance of goals to obtain responsible participation from pupils.

Effective Learning in the Elementary School. A fifth-grade teacher relates how she made her work more functional and meaningful to her pupils.

Skippy and the Three R's. 29 minutes. Very good in showing how a first-grade teacher found and developed abilities and interests in all of her class, and especially with one boy.

13

GROUP DISCUSSION AND

TWO OF THE NEWER aspects of classroom management which have real contributions to make toward the goals of mental health in education are group discussion and role playing. These two kinds of activities help children to develop confidence in expressing their thoughts and feelings, to learn adaptability in reference to contrary views and different types of behavior adjustments, to exercise initiative and spontaneity in interpersonal and group situations, to increase their incentive to solve group problems, and to enlarge their capacity for understanding the feelings of others.

ROLE-PLAYING ACTIVITIES

The kinds of attitudes, insights, and skills which grow out of adequate training in group discussion and role playing are important, not only for the mental health of individuals, but also for the healthy functioning of our society. A democratic organization, whether it be a small unit or a nation, must depend upon all forms of discussion as a means of resolving conflicts between individuals and between groups. Discussion in its broadest sense includes many forms of expression, such as: interchange of ideas among several individuals, prepared speeches in which various points of view are contrasted, formal debates between persons representing opposing positions, printed documents in which issues are stated and evaluated, and groups formed for the purpose of considering a particular topic. As stated above, a democracy is committed to the principle that all conflicts, whether personal, political, religious or economic, should be resolved through discussion as opposed to some form of force or coercion based simply on superior power. The significance of this principle is underscored by the fact that suppression of free discussion is one of the foundation stones of all dictatorships.

Certainly our schools are missing one of their major assignments if they do not give continuous support to the kind of attitudes and behaviors necessary for building up dependence on discussion as the way to resolve conflicts. This cannot be well done if important matters affecting school practices are determined by administrative fiat; nor can it be well done if teachers, in their academic instruction, assume an authoritarian role, pretend to know the one right answer to everything, spend practically all their time quizzing pupils on factual material in textbooks, and permit no criticisms or interchange of ideas.

Discussion, and especially group discussion, presupposes interchange of ideas and mutual stimulation. In a school setting this is the chief contrast between a discussion and a recitation. Whereas the latter is usually a "re-citing" of information already known from reading a textbook, a discussion is not a question-and-answer period, it is not tied to a textbook, and its chief purpose is not the teaching of information. Instead, a well-conducted discussion is one in which a topic or a problem is *explored* for alternative answers or solutions, and is led by a person who knows how to instigate participation of maximum quantity and quality. This means that in order to have a genuine discussion a group must develop, or be presented with, a question or an issue that is controversial, that permits more than one solution, and that arouses thinking and a problem-solving attitude. In our elementary and secondary schools such topics are most likely to emerge in the teaching of literature, social studies, the various sciences, and in the management of clubs and other cocurricular activities. Although all teachers have probably held innumerable class recitations, not all of them have conducted group discussions, and probably only a few have utilized role playing.

THE ROLE OF THE LEADER

The success of any discussion group is greatly affected by how well the leader plays his role. Whether this leader be the teacher or a student who is being trained for this role, he must learn how to stimulate and how to control the discussion process.

At the outset, the chairman or group leader must make it clear that he is not in the usual role of an instructor, since he is not to ask questions or to answer questions except occasionally when a technical point arises which only he can answer. Neither is he to pass judgment on the merits of a member's responses by such remarks as "That's right," "I agree with that," or "That sounds ridiculous." Instead, he should constantly induce the members to respond to each other's remarks and get them to assume responsibility for "carrying the discussion." If the chairman (especially when the chairman is the teacher) falls into the trap of answering questions or of passing judgment on statements made, he soon finds himself maneuvered into the role of an instructor; then the group members assume less and less responsibility for developing their own ideas and working out their own solutions to a problem. When this happens there is not only poorer problem-solving but also less development of individuality.

This does not mean, however, that a discussion chairman should never call on a group member. This is desirable when the chairman knows that a particular group member who has not talked should have a contribution to make because of his special skill, knowledge, or experience. Even then the individual called on should only be asked if he would like to say something. He should not be urged. In any case, calling on discussion group members should rarely be done.

In addition to presenting the problem and playing his proper role as guide and instigator rather than instructor, a chairman may promote discussion participation by subdividing the group members into "buzz groups." In using this procedure the chairman simply asks those who are sitting near each other to turn around and face each other and thus form a small subgroup of three, four, or five persons who are to engage in a brief "buzz session" on a stated topic. This stated topic is generally one which has grown out of some preceding group discussion, and is one which arouses a rather wide range of responses in the way of suggestions or alternative solutions.

The "buzz group" procedure has advantages over total-group discussion since it encourages much greater participation of all members. A pupil who is one of three, four, or five other persons is forced into a more responsible position and is practically certain to be given a chance to make a contribution. However, in a total group of thirty or more he is less evident as an individual, and may more easily slide into the periphery of group activities unless he is strongly motivated or is verbally aggressive as an individual.

The usual procedure is to allow the "buzz group" about 5, 10, or 15 minutes, depending upon age-level and difficulty of the topic, and then ask each of these groupings to select someone, frequently called a *recorder,* to report to the whole class the results of his group's deliberations. This brings all the suggestions together and also provides realistic experiences for many pupils in summarizing and in oral reporting. By requiring that the "buzz groups" select a different person each time the reporting is done, a teacher may also insure a wide participation in this type of experience.

ROLES OF GROUP MEMBERS

Effective group discussion can also be facilitated by training the group members for the different roles or functions that they may perform in different discussion situations, and at different times in each situation. The purpose of such training is to help pupils understand the ways in whch they can promote a good discussion, and also to help them understand why certan kinds of behavior hamper profitable discussion.

What are some of the approved functional roles of discussion-group members? The following are among a good many others listed by Benne and Sheats:

1. Suggesting new ideas in regard to goals and procedures.
2. Asking for factual information on points made by others.
3. Giving factual information on points before the group.
4. Elaborating on points and suggestions made by others.
5. Encouraging or praising points of view stated by others.
6. Harmonizing several conflicting points of view by showing how they might be reconciled. (2.)

The above authors also list eight different kinds of group behavior that interfere with the progress of a discussion. Five of these are:

A. The *aggressor* may work in many ways — deflating the status of others; expressing disapproval of the values, acts, or feelings of others; attacking the group or the problem it is working on; joking aggressively; showing envy toward another's contribution by trying to take credit for it; etc.

B. The *blocker* tends to be negativistic and stubbornly resistant, disagreeing and opposing without or beyond "reason" and attempting to maintain or bring back an issue after the group has rejected or by-passed it.

C. The *recognition-seeker* works in various ways to call attention to himself, whether through boasting, reporting on personal achievements, acting in unusual ways, struggling to prevent his being placed in an "inferior" position, etc.

D. The *playboy* makes a display of his lack of involvement in the group's processes. This may take the form of cynicism, nonchalance, horseplay, and other more or less studied forms of "out of field" behavior.

E. The *dominator* tries to assert authority or superiority in manipulating the group or certain members of the group. This domination may take the form of flattery, of asserting a superior status or right to attention, giving directions authoritatively, interrupting the contributions of others, etc.

The above list of interfering behaviors, together with others which experienced teachers will be able to add, points up the fact that the success of a group discussion does not depend simply upon having a good chairman, a good topic, and good procedure, but also upon the personality-maturity level of the group members. This close interaction between group processes and the psychology of the individual engaged in these processes has sometimes been overlooked by writers dealing with the values of the discussion method. In some groups (regardless of age-levels) an objectively orientated discussion is much easier to achieve than in others, because of a much greater proportion of members characterized by a higher level of personal-social maturity.

To what extent can our children and young people be helped to improve their performance in conducting group discussions, either as chairmen or as members? The answer seems to be that from our present experience and evidence we are confident that nearly all of them can be helped to some extent — a few can be helped greatly and another few can probably be helped very little unless they can receive some psychological or psychiatric aid toward better self-adjustment. Those who have attained fairly good psychological adjustments, and so need only *skill training* in discussion, are helped most through teacher instruction on discussion-group roles, pupil discussion of these topics, selected readings, and role playing.

That even small children can be trained to be *conscious of* and *critical of* their own group processes is indicated by the statements below taken from a class discussion among ten-year-olds in response to the question: How can we improve our performance in group work?[1]

SUSAN: *Choose a good planning leader, not just the person you like.*

ANN: *Give your attention to the one that's talking.*

GEORGE: *Don't be afraid to speak up. The idea you're thinking of may be the one the class will want to use.*

TOM: *Take everyone's ideas.*

HOWARD: *Don't have the planning too long.*

MARGARET: *Yes, but before you stop be sure everyone knows how to get started on what you've planned to do.*

Such statements reveal differentiations in intellectual and personality development, as opposed to stereotyped or biased responses.

MATERIALS USED IN DISCUSSING PERSONAL PROBLEMS

Although it is readily agreed that teachers are not therapists, this fact does not mean that competent teachers can do nothing in regard to

[1] Ruth Cunningham *et al.*, "Leadership and the Group," *National Education Association Journal,* 37, 1948, 502-03.

the more personal problems and emotional needs of children and young people. As a matter of fact, efforts of this nature are being made now by a good many teachers — efforts consisting principally of reading stories and showing films that present problem situations for group discussion. In addition to these more frequent activities there are also a good many three- and six-hour courses in psychology on the high school level, and a few on the junior high school level.

One of the most commonly used sources of story material is *Human Relations in the Classroom, Course I,* by E. E. Bullis and E. E. O'Malley, published by the Delaware State Society for Mental Hygiene, 1404 Franklin St., Wilmington 35, Delaware, 1948. The stories and discussion questions included in this book are written for various levels ranging from the upper elementary grades through junior-senior high schools.

The Child Welfare Research Station of the University of Iowa, under the direction of Ralph H. Ojemann, has prepared some story materials which are designed especially for use in the elementary grades. Like the Bullis stories, these too are accompanied by a series of questions which are to help guide the teacher's efforts in making the stories most meaningful and functional for children. These stories have been especially written for the purpose of presenting conduct situations to school children.

Both the Bullis and the Ojemann materials are reviewed and evaluated in a publication of the Committee on Preventive Psychiatry of the Group for the Advancement of Psychiatry of Topeka, Kansas.[2] In this publication the materials by Ojemann are commended because they are not structured simply for a course in human relations but are, instead, orientated toward "humanizing" all content that deals with behavior, and are to be taught as learning exercises about human behavior rather than as sources for therapy. Furthermore, these materials are commended because they are clearly written, do not stress moralizing, place constant emphasis on multiple causation of behavior, and show how values are distributed as opposed to simply a dichotomy of "right" and "wrong." Also, the reviewing committee mentioned above commended Ojemann for his numerous studies con-

[2] *Promotion of Mental Health in the Primary and Secondary Schools: An Evaluation of Four Projects.*

ducted to find evidence on the transfer or carry-over values from using his discussion materials.

The National Conference of Christians and Jews (381 Fourth Ave., New York) publishes a series of pamphlets which contain material of value to teachers for the purpose under discussion. Two of the most pertinent ones are *Feelings are Facts* by Heaton and *Role-Playing the Problem Story* by Shaftel.

Another source which provides booklets on a wide range of topics dealing with personal-social and emotional problems is Science Research Associates (57 Grand Ave., Chicago 10). These booklets are written on the level of junior-senior high school students. Several of the titles are *Building Your Philosophy of Life, Getting Along with Others,* and *Growing Up Socially.* A pamphlet listing all available booklets can be secured from the company.

A series of books, called the "Golden Rule Series," has been prepared by the American Book Company (55 Fifth Avenue, New York) to serve as a basis for instruction and discussion of moral, personal, and conduct problems. On each grade-level there is also a *Teacher's Edition* which offers numerous aids and suggestions for teaching the story materials included in the "Golden Rule Series."

Two sources of films of the nature under consideration are Young American Films, Inc. (18 E. 41st St., New York 17) and Test Film Department of McGraw-Hill Book Co., New York. Several titles in the "Young America Series" are *The Bully, The Other Fellow's Feelings,* and *The Outsider.*

In reference to the courses offered in psychology mentioned above, a recent survey in this country shows that in nearly all of our states some high schools offer such courses, but that less than five per cent of high school students are enrolled in them (13). This survey also includes a statement on the objectives of high school psychology courses as determined from textbooks and from teachers. These stated objectives show much agreement in stressing the aim of helping students understand themselves and their personal-social problems, and of increasing their ability to live harmoniously with others. In one instance, at least, a psychology course is being offered on the eighth-grade level. A report of this effort, together with a summary of major topics covered and student evaluations, is given by the teacher, Joseph B. Patti (33).

MENTAL HEALTH VALUES

What are the mental health values to be obtained from pupil discussions of stories, reading materials, and films bearing on personal-social problems? Undoubtedly one of the chief values is the development in children and young people of greater understanding of themselves and of others. As this understanding increases it would presumably lead to greater insight into their own motivations and those of others, and thus contribute to more rational control of conduct. This would not always be true, and it would be easy to overestimate how much such discussion would result in changes in attitudes or in overt behavior. However, it can be shown from research evidence that children can be educated to be more analytical toward behavior motivations.

Reference is made particularly to the work of Ojemann, previously mentioned in this chapter, at the University of Iowa Child Welfare Research Station. The chief objective of Ojemann's effort has been to develop materials and methods that teachers can use to stimulate children to take an analytical attitude toward behavior, i.e., an attitude that is orientated toward discovering the *motivating* as opposed to the *surface* causes of behavior (30). The chief means whereby this objective is accomplished is (1) through the preparation of stories and other written materials to be used in classes, (2) through well-directed discussions following these materials, and (3) through the special training of teachers in the *causal* as opposed to *noncausal* approach to human behavior.

In a series of follow-up studies conducted by Ojemann and his co-workers, involving experimental and control groups, considerable evidence is presented to show that elementary school children can be taught to *think* about their social environment; they can be taught to respond to annoying and disruptive behavior on the part of their classmates with understanding and constructive suggestions rather than with blame and punishments (26, 27, 21). This evidence is based on teachers' verbal reports, results of tests especially constructed to obtain the measurements needed, and the carry-over of the instruction into new situations, such as dealing with problem cases coming before pupil councils.

In addition to this kind of research evidence there are also many observational reports from teachers and supervisors bearing on the values to be obtained from pupil discussions of personal-social problems. What have been the values most frequently mentioned from these sources?

In the first place, there has been considerable emphasis placed on pupils' greater understanding and acceptance of themselves, and on increased understanding of others. A good many reports have stressed how some pupils are relieved to find out that they can talk quite frankly about their emotional problems (involving chiefly fear and anger) without arousing disgust and hostility. Also they are often relieved to discover that many other children or young people have fears and personal difficulties similar to their own. Psychologically this kind of result should be considered a large gain since one of the most fertile sources of maladjustments is unwarranted anxieties (including guilt feelings) about one's personal adequacy as compared with one's associates. A well-conducted discussion, however, should not leave the impression that there is necessarily something wrong or bad about being different from others. In fact, the very opposite impression should be encouraged in order to promote uniqueness and to help those who are different in certain respects to feel more comfortable with themselves, or even to be proud of their differences.

Especially for those persons who are inclined to be inhibited and self-devaluating, more frank expression of feelings aids their personality development, because such expressions are ego-building — they are self-assertive and they reinforce the integrity of the self rather than deny it. Furthermore, such expressions help to differentiate one's self-feelings, making them more clear-cut, and thus promoting a more adequate self-identity. As an individual becomes more intrinsically honest he comes to like himself better and he finds others have more respect for him too. On the other hand, people who, through external pressures or internal fear, are unable to express their honest feelings, are likely to experience a growing sense of personal inadequacy, a blunting of personality into stereotyped and highly conforming responses, followed by a loss of self-respect and of respect from others.

Our point is very well supported by Dorothy W. Baruch, a consulting psychologist, in *Mental Health in Modern Education:*

> Most teachers still hold the impression, and work sincerely on the basis of a faulty impression, that to help a child grow into a healthy, kindly, wholesome, well-wishing, and socially minded human being, the essential step is to keep him acting exclusively along positive lines. With enough practice or repetition (in good Thorndike fashion), learning will take place. Similarly, if "bad" feelings are allowed into the picture, they will be practiced. Then they will become set.
>
> This is untrue. Feelings can become set most deeply when they are *not* openly faced or brought out, when they are shoved into the unconscious, out of sight. As Weiss and English have said about anger, "Latent hostility and repressed aggression are to be found in every neurosis." Such feelings, when blocked so that they are not expressed against an outer target, are often turned inward hurtfully against the self. Among other disturbances, they then produce psychosomatic illnesses. Miller and Baruch, for instance, found actual evidence of this in 92 per cent of the allergic children whom they studied. Long ago, Wickman pointed out that children, by withdrawing, by closing inside, and by being too "good," could develop even more serious emotional problems than by being too "bad."
>
> Not that we are advocating being too "bad." This does no good either. Acting out feelings that are terrifying or troubling can make these feelings become even more terrifying or troubling so that they remain quite unresolved. This occurs especially if the acting out is such that it gets the person into real difficulty or produces too grave a load of anxiety, guilt, or fear. On the other hand, bringing troubled feelings to light and practicing or using them, as it were — *steering them out through safe action-pathways* — this is another matter. It is the soundest means of prevention and of assuring emotional health. (46 — pp. 162-63.)

A second kind of value that observational evidence has stressed in regard to the values to be derived from pupil discussions of personal-social problems is a noticeable improvement in rapport between teachers and pupils. This is the point most frequently mentioned by teachers with whom the writer has worked in using the University of Iowa story materials. One teacher who had used the story-discussion procedure once a week for a semester said that she felt for the first time that she really "belonged to the class." Another one received a pleasant surprise one day when two boys stopped after class and said "We think you are the best teacher we have ever had." Since this was the first time in her twenty years of teaching that she had received such a compliment she eagerly asked "Why's that?" "Because," the boys replied, "You let us tell bad things we have done and you don't scold us or punish us."

There is, of course, a time and place for punishment, but the theory behind the story-discussion teaching is that as unpleasant feelings and antisocial motivations are analyzed in a permissive atmosphere, it is much more possible to think clearly about them and how they may be redirected.

The much closer communication that may develop between teacher and pupils as a result of the use of stories and dramatized incidents dealing with personal-social behavior is further illustrated in the following statement from a report by Ojemann and Emrich:

> Another type of effort noted is illustrated by the example of a third-grade girl who had been in the program but a short time. One day she came to the teacher she had the previous semester with a written account about a girl who was not getting along well with the other boys and girls in her grade. She asked the teacher if she would read it to the boys and girls and see what they would suggest. It didn't take the teacher long to discover that the story was about the child herself. She had been rather unhappy in the new group but instead of brooding over the situation or trying to solve it by fighting the other children she had thought of another way. She had begun to learn to assist in guiding her own development. We have had quite a few examples of children coming to the teacher in similar ways. (32 — p. 5.)

In commenting on this statement the above authors observe that the greater tendency for some pupils to confide more in their teachers was probably due more to changes in the teachers than to changes in the pupils.

A third value that is generally observed to be directed from well-conducted discussions bearing on conduct problems is that they serve as an excellent avenue of communication between pupils and teachers in regard to a wide range of topics and problems such as existing attitudes toward children of different races, or attitudes toward children who engage in some form of morally disapproved behavior such as stealing, lying, and cheating. Also, insight may be gained by teachers into pupils' aspirations, fears, hopes, home conflicts, and heterosexual interests. These kinds of closer contacts with the minds and hearts of children have frequently been mentioned by teachers who have stimulated discussions based on stories, role-playing episodes, and films.

It is generally recognized by both teachers and administrators that one of the basic reasons for disciplinary problems and conflicts between subgroups within a school is the lack of adequate communication between the school officials, on the one hand, and the pupils, on the other. It is also generally recognized that the most effective way to deal with any problem is to "nip it in the bud." This, however, cannot be done unless there is some way to know where the buds are and what they are composed of. Certainly one of the best ways is through the kind of discussions described above. They open up many avenues of communication, and they reduce secrecy and distrust. Among the teachers with whom the writer has collaborated with story-discussion materials, there have been three instances in which problems involving stealing and sexual misbehavior were effectively handled because certain pupils volunteered to the teachers information that they thought the teachers should know in order to help the individuals involved. This kind of thing had never happened before.

One of the principles developed by social psychologists for the practical resolution of such problems as delinquency, riots, and industrial conflicts is that of anticipating trouble and taking countermeasures before the trouble becomes too big to handle. It seems that the schools, through the proper use of discussions, have at their disposal an effective means of acting on this social-psychological principle.

EVALUATIONS BY GROUP DISCUSSIONS

Many teachers use group discussion as a means of evaluating class activities. Sometimes this is done informally and at irregular intervals by simply asking the class as a whole if they have any suggestions for improving a particular kind of group endeavor. Sometimes it is done at stated intervals, and sometimes it is done even more systematically in regular planning sessions or by using some kind of evaluation check-lists or rating forms. When such evaluations are well conducted and are sincere and critical, they help to lay the foundation for sound mental health.

In the first place, they put emphasis on the value of rational processes in solving interpersonal and intergroup problems. Time and again the weakness of prejudiced attitudes, superficial judgments, and inadequate knowledge are brought to the fore in evaluative comments. As stated before, it is one of the main theses of this book that a psychologically mature person in our culture must rely heavily upon rational processes as a basis for determining his attitudes and for directing his overt behavior. It is well-known that this end is not achieved simply by acquiring factual information but must be supplemented by appropriate experiences. One kind of "appropriate experience" for this purpose is provided through evaluative sessions since each participant can be helped to learn really to *listen* to critical comments of others relative to his behavior in group situations. Also he can learn to be more objective about his own contributions and about the quality of performance of a group he is in.

Another value to personal development to be derived from well-conducted evaluation sessions is found in the fact that they afford a constructive outlet for aggressive and self-assertive needs, especially for those pupils who are not able to satisfy such needs through athletics and other physical skills. One of the important traits needed for both good self-adjustment and good social status in our culture is at least a normal capacity for overt expression of aggressiveness. Otherwise, aggressive needs are likely to be turned inward resulting in guilt feelings and inferiority reactions. It should be noted, too, that aggressiveness expressed through evaluations of some kind of class work is much more likely to be orientated toward group-centered objectives than is aggressiveness expressed through more individualistic endeavors, such as reciting right answers in class.

CONDUCTING EVALUATIVE SESSIONS

Like all other educational endeavors, the use of discussion for evaluating group work or other types of class activities will not promote mental hygiene objectives unless certain conditions are present. One of these conditions is that much attention must be given to *quality* as opposed to mere *quantity* of production. This point must be emphasized many times throughout a school year, especially during evaluation periods. Attention must be directed time and again to the questions of how *well* a group or an individual performed a task and of how it might have been done better. As the school year goes along, progressively higher levels of achievement should be expected in regard to ability to make definite plans, to assume responsibilities, to exercise leadership roles, and to perform as contributing members of group discussions. It seems that one of the most serious criticisms of group work in our schools at all levels, including college, is that such work very often remains *on the same level* over long periods of time. When this happens, such work becomes routinized and soon reaches a dead-end in so far as it contributes to personality development, the acquiring of cooperative skills, or the refinement of thinking processes.

It is important, for example, to help pupils see that sheer amount or frequency of talking in a discussion is not the thing of chief value. Instead, emphasis should be placed on saying something that contributes to an issue before a group. Some teachers have been led to believe that a good discussion is one in which everyone talks. By itself this is obviously a superficial criterion. The more this kind of evaluation is applied in a classroom, the more we would expect to find a blunting of intellectual and personal qualities rather than their refinement. Although wide participation is desirable, the major emphasis should always be on "talking only when you believe you have something to say that will aid in answering the problem before us."

It is important to note, too, that regardless of the topic before a group there will nearly always be some who have much more to contribute than others, and they should be expected to talk more. Overparticipation should not be thought of simply in terms of frequency of talking, but primarily in terms of talking too long on a point, saying irrelevant things, repeating things already said, making personalized remarks, and otherwise talking just to be heard rather than really to contribute.

Another particular point upon which some pupils will need help is in how to give criticisms of another person's remarks without arousing personal antagonisms. This could well be a topic for pupil discussion. It is likely that such discussions held among pupils from about the sixth grade on up through our school system would result in such suggestions as the following:

1. Give criticisms in a calm tone of voice.
2. If possible, mention something in the other person's remarks with which you can agree before pointing out disagreements.
3. Always criticize what the other person *said* and not him personally.
4. State that you might have misunderstood what the other person said and that you would like for him to correct you if he is being misinterpreted.

Another condition for a well-conducted discussion is that the pupils feel free to express honest opinions and to differ with each other and with the teacher. There must be a permissive atmosphere free from threat; otherwise maximum growth toward effective individuality is thwarted. Sometimes teachers are told that one of the criteria for a good discussion is reaching a fairly uniform consensus in reference to an issue or a problem. Although it is true that we must all frequently abide by the expressed will of the majority, especially when some form of action must be taken, it is nevertheless equally true that teachers must forever be alert to the danger of smothering minority opinion and of blotting out the genuine contributions of unusual individuals. A teacher's measure of success in promoting effective and interesting personalities is to a large degree determined by the extent to which he encourages *differentiations* in the thinking and in the behavior of individuals. As far as discussion groups are concerned, this principle can often be observed by encouraging minority as well as majority reports on topics that have become important to a particular group and upon which there has been considerable disagreement.

A final condition necessary for a well-conducted evaluative session is that pupils, in their assessments of the value of any particular project or unit of work, be helped to understand that immediate interest is not an adequate basis for judging the worth of a classroom endeavor. Instead, emphasis must also be placed on *future needs* and also on what they *ought to know* and *ought to be able to do* because of their *obligations* to their classroom group, their school, their community, and the hopes of a "free world."

It is sometimes stated that "children live in the present." This must be recognized as only a half-truth, since it is very evident that practically all normal children, and especially the more intelligent ones, also *live in the future,* in the sense that aspirations for the future play an important part in their present endeavors. Such children and young people can be genuinely motivated to learn materials or skills that they can see will help them to *become* more adequate persons. A good many pupils will certainly not be stimulated to higher-level aspirations if they are allowed to believe that the only things they should be expected to work on are those things which they happen to like *right now.*

ROLE PLAYING FOR THE CLASSROOM

Role playing is increasingly being used as an aid in classroom teaching and management. This procedure is an *action* method whereby the participants are stimulated to imagine themselves in certain specified roles which they are to act out in response to others who are included in the role-playing sociodrama. However, these "specified roles" are described only in a general sense. The way any role is played — what is said or done — is left up to the spontaneity of the individual players. Definite structuring would defeat the purpose of role playing. It is in this respect that role playing differs most from the usual kind of dramatizations given in schools. Whereas the typical dramatizations are taken out of a book, sociodramas are taken out of the present or the anticipated experiences of the group members. As one fifth-grade child is reported to have put it, sociodrama is "'a new way to learn things' in which we 'take things out of our lives' and 'show each other, and everyone tells what he sees from' what is portrayed."[3]

When role playing is well done, it induces a higher degree of ego-involvement than is generally possible through discussion alone. There is a greater participation of the total organism, involving thoughts, feelings, and neuromuscular adjustments.

Values of role playing

More specifically, from the standpoint of healthy personality development, it seems clear that role playing has some particular contributions to make because it:

1. Contributes to growth in spontaneity and flexibility, since the participants must learn to break some habitual patterns and instead try to respond as they believe another person, whose role they are playing, would respond.
2. Promotes rational control of conduct, since the participants as well as the other group members are able to see, through varying enactments of the same role by different individuals, that there are *alternative solutions* to all problem-situations dealt with.
3. Promotes understanding of self and of others, since some individuals see their own adjustment problems mirrored in a role-playing episode, and since those who participate must try to identify themselves with the attitudes and feelings of other persons whose roles they are taking, such as other classmates, teachers, parents, or school and civic officials.
4. Promotes the development of a variety of social skills (depending on what kinds of problems are dealt with), such as greater skill in proper social behavior, or in winning cooperation from another person, or in leading a group discussion, or in being a contributing member of a discussion.

[3] *Fostering Mental Health in Our Schools,* Yearbook of the Association for Supervision and Curriculum Development of the National Education Association, Washington 6, D. C., 1950, p. 262.

5. Provides a permissive atmosphere in which to explore a variety of solutions to a problem-situation, since in role playing the participants are not "playing for keeps" but are engaging only in reality-practice. This means less ego-defensiveness, less feeling of threat in regard to making mistakes, and therefore more freedom to respond in a creative manner.

Conditions for successful role playing

The above-mentioned values of role playing in personal development will not, however, be realized unless certain conditions are present. The more important of these conditions are listed below.

1. The problem-situation that is to be role-played should be one which has emerged from a group's experience, or one which is very likely to be encountered in the near future, or one which is quite similar to the kinds of experience most of the group members are involved in. To the extent that these conditions are not met, role playing will simply be an entertainment stunt with little or no lasting values.

This emphasis on group experience indirectly implies that matters of a highly personal nature should not be role-played before a group. To do so could easily hurt the individuals involved. Role playing, as a form of sociodrama, implies a reference to a group or collective interest as opposed to psychodrama, which implies a reference to the *psyche* or private world of an individual who is the center of treatment in a psychodramatic production.

2. There should be a "warming-up" period previous to the actual role playing in order to stimulate the group members to develop the kind of thought and feeling responses appropriate to achieving rapport with the particular roles to be played. This is usually done through a brief discussion, which includes a consideration of the nature of the problem-situation, the character roles to be included in it, and emphasis on the importance of each participant's being able to *feel* his way into the role he volunteers to play. One value in asking for volunteers is that such persons will presumably be more ready to identify themselves with particular roles than will those who are simply assigned. Without a warming-up period, a role-playing session

is likely to be superficial, mechanical, and consequently not contribute to any of the values listed above.

3. There should be a discussion and evaluation of a role-playing episode immediately following its conclusion. It is usually best to let the actors evaluate their own performances first. Then additional comments should be encouraged from the group members concerning how well the roles were played toward resolving the problem-situation involved in the acting.

One of the chief advantages of role playing is that it presents a concrete action-basis for discussion, as opposed to simply a verbal description of a problem. This fact generally insures that the remarks made will be definite and clearly understood by everyone. Ordinarily after 8, 10, or 15 minutes of discussion it is appropriate to ask for new volunteers to show how they would play the roles under consideration. This necessarily brings out alternative solutions.

4. Finally, role playing will not be effective if it is overused, if it is employed as a time-killer or as a cure-all procedure, or if a learning attitude is not the predominant orientation of the pupils.

Typical problem-situations for role playing

In the kindergarten and lower grades, role playing is frequently used as training procedure in helping to prepare children to meet successfully a wide range of practical situations such as:

Crossing streets.
Taking turns at the drinking fountain.
Sharing of play and work materials.
Learning how to greet their mothers, introduce them, and seat them when they come to a classroom social event.

In the middle and upper elementary grades role playing is often used in regard to such problems as:

Conflicts between classes over the use of playground space.
Proper conduct in the lunchroom and in the hallways.
Learning to be a good discussion group leader.
Conflict situations (which are not too intimate) between children and parents, between brothers and sisters, or between children of neighboring families.

The effects of excessive teasing, or of the spreading of a malicious rumor, or of intolerant treatment of a newcomer into a class.

On the junior and senior high school levels some typical situations for role playing are:

Trying out various approaches to prospective employers.
Learning of social etiquette practices in a wide variety of circumstances with age-mates of both sexes and with adults.
Resolving conflicts that develop during small group and committee work.
Trying out various solutions for resolving conflicts between differing ethnic groups, or between adolescents and their parents.

REFERENCES

1. Arnhotter, E., "Social Drama for Retarded Adolescents," *Exceptional Children,* 21, 1955, 132-134.
2. Benne, K. D. and Paul Sheats, "Functional Roles of Group Members," *Journal of Social Issues,* 4, 1948, 41-49.
3. Boer De, J. J., "Implications of Group Dynamics for English," *English Journal,* 41, 1952, 239-244.
4. Bovard, E. W., "The Psychology of Classroom Interaction," *Journal of Educational Research,* 45, 1951, 215-224.
5. Boyd, G. A., "Role Playing," *Social Education,* 21, 1957, 267-269.
6. Brown, I. S., "How We Act in Groups," *Childhood Education,* 27, 1950-51, 156-160.
7. Bullis, H. E. and Cordelia W. Kelly, *Human Relations in Action.* New York: G. P. Putnam's Sons, 1954.
8. Cunningham, R. and others, "Group Creates Its Climate," *Educational Leadership,* 5, 1948, 358-362.
9. ——— and Associates, "Leadership and the Group," *National Educational Association Journal,* 37, 1948, 502-503.
10. Daniel, E., "Learning the Skills of Cooperative Planning," *Educational Leadership,* 5, 1948, 322-327.
11. Driver, H. I., "Learning Self- and Social Adjustment Through Small Group Discussion," *Mental Hygiene,* 36, 1952, 600-606.
12. Elliott, L. H., "Teaching for Life Adjustment," *Elementary School Journal,* 51, 1950-51, 152-156.
13. Engle, T. L. and M. E. Bunch, "The Teaching of Psychology in High School," *The American Psychologist,* 11, 1956, 188-193.

14. Hardiman, R. and J. T. Robinson, "The Social Roots of Learning," *Educational Leadership,* 7, 1949-50, 159-164.
15. Harris, F. E., "Techniques for Guiding Group Experiences in the Classroom," *Elementary School Journal,* 49, 1948-49, 32-36.
16. Hertzman, J., "Developing a Mental-Hygiene Curriculum in a Public-School System," *Mental Hygiene,* 36, 1952, 569-588.
17. Hyder, L. D., "Life Adjustment Through Literature," *The English Journal,* 40, 1951, 28-33.
18. Johnson, L. H., "Abuses of Group Discussion," *School and Society,* 85, 1957, 324-326.
19. Kean, C. D., "Some Role-Playing Experiments with High School Students," *Group Psychotherapy,* 6, 1954, 256-265.
20. Kelly, E. C., "How the High School Can Educate for Human Understanding," *School Review,* 57, 1949, 353-357.
21. Keltner, John, *Group Discussion Processes.* New York: Longmans, Green and Company, 1957.
22. Koenig, F. G., "Group Therapy Experiment in a City Elementary School," *Understanding the Child,* 18, 1949, 40-44.
23. Lewit, E. E., "Effect of a 'Causal' Teacher Training Program on Authoritarianism and Responsibility in Grade School Children," *Psychological Reports,* 1, 1955, 449-458.
24. Lippitt, Rosemary and Catherine Clancy, "Psychodrama in the Kindergarten and Nursery School," *Group Psychotherapy,* 7, 1954, 262-290.
25. Mann, John H., "Experimental Evaluations of Role Playing," *Psychological Bulletin,* 53, 1956, 227-234.
26. McNiel, B., "Development at the Youth Level of Conception of the Causes of Behavior and Effectiveness of a Learning Program in This Area," *Journal of Experimental Education,* 13, 1944, 81-85.
27. Morgan, M. E. and R. H. Ojemann, "The Effect of a Learning Program Designed to Assist Youth in an Understanding of Behavior and its Development," *Child Development,* 13, 1942, 181-194.
28. Nichols, H., "Role-Playing in Primary Grades," *Group Psychotherapy,* 7, 1954, 238-241.
29. Ojemann, Ralph H., "Changing Attitudes in the Classroom," *Children,* 3, 1956, 130-134.
30. ———, "Research in Planned Learning Programs and the Science of Behavior," *Journal of Educational Research,* 42, 1948, 96-104.
31. ———, A. Nugent, and M. Corry, "A Study of Human Behavior in the Social Science Program," *Social Education,* 11, 1947, 25-28.
32. ——— and Dorothy Emrich, "Development of Mental Hygiene Approach to Behavior at the Elementary Level," Mimeographed report distributed by the Iowa Child Welfare Research Station, State University of Iowa, Iowa City.

33. Patti, J. B., "Elementary Psychology for Eighth Graders?" *The American Psychologist,* 11, 1956, 194-196.
34. Pressey, S. L. and D. C. Hanna, "The Class as a Psycho-Sociological Unit," *The Journal of Psychology,* 16, 1943, 13-19.
35. Rosenthal, S., "A Fifth-Grade Classroom Experiment in Fostering Mental Health," *Journal of Child Psychiatry,* 2, 1953, 302-329.
36. Scheidlinger, S., "Should Teachers be Group Therapists?" *Progressive Education,* 32, 1955, 70-74.
37. Shellhammer, L. B., "Solving Personal Problems Through Sociodrama," *The English Journal,* 38, 1949, 503-505.
38. Slovertz, Frank and Alice Lund, "Some Effects of a Personal Developmental Program at the Fifth Grade Level," *Journal of Educational Research,* 49, 1956, 373-378.
39. Sobel, M. J., "Socio-Dramas: An Aid in Classroom Discipline," *Clearing House,* 26, 1951, 235-238.
40. ———, "Socio-Dramas: In the Classroom," *Social Education,* 16, 1952, 166-168.
41. Stavsky, W. H., "Using the Insights of Psychotherapy in Teaching," *Elementary School Journal,* 58, 1957, 28-35.
42. Stiles, Frances S., "Developing an Understanding of Human Behavior at the Elementary School Level," *Journal of Educational Research,* 43, 1950, 516-524.
43. Thelen, Herbert A., *Dynamics of Groups at Work.* Chicago: University of Chicago Press, 1954.
44. Zander, A. and R. Lippitt, "Reality-Practice as Educational Method," *Sociometry,* 7, 1944, 129-151.
45. ———, *How to Use Role Playing and Other Tools of Learning.* Chicago: Adult Educational Association, 1955.
46. ———, *Mental Health in Modern Education,* Ch. VII, The Fifty-Fourth Year Book of the National Society for the Study of Education, Part II. Chicago: University of Chicago Press, 1955.

QUESTIONS AND EXERCISES

1. Point out how a well-conducted group discussion contributes more to the goals of mental hygiene than does a recitation period.
2. Try to arrange to have some direct experience in leading a group discussion in a church, a club, a local school, or as chairman of a subgroup in your class. Evaluate your performance on the basis of the criteria given in this chapter, or, better still, have a qualified observer evaluate your efforts.

3. If the class has not utilized "buzz groups" it would be desirable for the members to organize such groupings to discuss some topic in mental hygiene, and also to demonstrate the use of this teaching method.
4. During your class discussions try to analyze your own role on the basis of the material given in this chapter from Benne and Sheats. Does this material suggest any ways whereby you could improve your role as a class member?
5. Find out if a teacher in your community is using any of the story-discussion materials or films described in this chapter. If one is located, try to be present when such materials are being used with children.
6. Do you have a clear distinction in your mind between moralizing and Ojemann's objective of developing a *causal* approach to human behavior?
7. How does your own observation agree with Baruch's statement that the release of "bad feelings," under certain conditions, may reduce rather than strengthen these feelings?
8. In what respect does role playing contribute to personality development more directly than do group discussions?
9. Choose a typical school situation involving a mental hygiene objective, such as a teacher-parent conference, and have several groups of students role-play this situation. Discuss and evaluate the performances on the basis of the criteria given in this chapter.

SELECTED FILMS

Let's Discuss It. 29 minutes. Good for demonstrating right and wrong ways to conduct a group discussion.

How to Conduct a Discussion. 24 minutes. Clear presentation of principles to follow in stimulating discussion.

Role Playing in Guidance. 14 minutes. Demonstrates procedure of role playing with one boy who needs counseling.

Role Playing in Human Relations. 15 minutes. Demonstrates use of role playing to help develop insight into interpersonal relationships.

GROUP MORALE AND COHESION

5

14

DETERMINING FACTORS IN

DURING THE PAST twenty-five years there has been a marked acceleration of research activities in the general area of group morale, the social aspects of leadership, and the relationships between the productivity or efficiency of a group and such social factors as the cohesiveness and the interpersonal responsiveness of its members. These kinds of studies in business and industrial organizations have stressed the importance in production of a greater degree of responsible participation on the part of employees, and the value of genuine teamwork between employers and the

CLASS SOCIAL CLIMATE

workers.[1] These kinds of investigations have also revealed the critical roles played in productivity by group sentiments, clique organizations, and the extent to which the official leader of a group is sensitive to the feelings and the wishes of the persons under his direction.

Studies in military units, too, such as those by Berkowitz (4) and by Goodacre (20-21) have focused attention on numerous social factors in morale and efficiency. Chief among these are: interpersonal acceptance among the men of a unit, feelings of mutual respect and understanding between an official leader and the men assigned to him, and the degree of ego-involvement felt by the men for task objectives.

Experimental and systematic studies of morale and group cohesiveness, such as those by Hemphill (25) and by Libo (33), have included all the points listed above. In addition, they have stressed

[1] See references at end of chapter by Homans (26), by Mayo (34), by Roethlisberger and Dickson (40), and by Van Zelst (43).

the value of general feelings of pleasantness in reference to membership in a particular group, the role of homogeneity of members in regard to such variables as socio-economic status and attitudes, the need of a group's having primary significance for its members with reference to their central values, and the importance of linking up a group's activities with high-level principles and with persons of prestige. These contributions relative to group morale and efficiency will serve as an orientation to this chapter, which is devoted to a consideration of the more general conditions affecting the social climate of a class.

Sensitive teachers have always been aware that classes differ in the extent to which various influences, some obvious and some subtle, are operating to determine the over-all tone or spirit of a class. These influences are felt to be closely related to in-group feelings, cooperative attitudes, interpersonal attractions, seriousness of purpose, and enthusiasm for group objectives. These variables constitute what is referred to in this discussion as the "social climate of a class." These kinds of group dynamic factors are what lead some teachers to say: "This is the worst class I've ever had," or "This class has never been a group," or, in an extremely good situation, "These pupils are so eager to learn and work together that teaching them is a joy." In discussing this topic, Kurt Lewin puts emphasis on the role of the teacher when he says: "It is well-known that the amount of success a teacher has in the classroom depends not only on her *skill* but to a great extent on the *atmosphere* she creates." (32 — p. 74.)

IDENTIFICATION WITH GROUP OBJECTIVES

Good class morale depends heavily upon a high degree of feelings of identification with group objectives on the part of the members. It will be recalled from Chapter 10 that one of the major goals of mental health education, as defined in this book, is the development of group-centered motivations. Such motivations promote feelings of identification with group purposes.

One of the most obvious evidences of goal-orientated activities in a classroom is found in those verbal expressions and overt efforts which clearly indicate that the pupils are eager for their class, and for subgroups within the class, to succeed in all collective endeavors such as games, dramatic productions, and assembly programs. When this in-group pride exists to a marked degree, most pupils are likely to be quite critical of any classmate who does not do his best, who shirks his responsibility, or who "lets the group down" in any way — such as not knowing his lines in a play, marching out of step in the band, or "clowning" his assignment in a game or a public performance. Also a group with high morale will be characterized by more arguments and vigorous discussions of any topic bearing on a class project or class objective than will a group of low in-group feeling. In the latter type of group, where little disagreement is shown, there may be a superficial appearance of harmony which is often misjudged as evidence of a cooperative spirit. Teachers and supervisors should be alert to the fact that expressions of differences — arguments and heated discussions, even including emotional outbursts — are found only among those members who care very much about their group. This is true, however, only when these expressions are aroused over group problems or goals as contrasted with interpersonal conflicts.

The foregoing obviously means that the members of a cohesive, high-morale class are not only strongly concerned about attaining group objectives, but they are also very much interested in influencing each other to "get in line" and to support whatever is a predominant group demand or expectation. This sometimes means considerable pressure to conform. As pointed out in Chapter 8, when conformity is overemphasized individualism is thwarted. The best way a teacher can deal with this problem is to help a class understand that a strong group is built not only on similarities but also on the different contributions of all individual members.

Degree of identification with group goals is particularly shown in the care with which class members select individuals for leadership roles such as officers and chairmen of committees. When a condition of low morale exists there is very little concern as to whether or not the individuals chosen are qualified to perform the required functions. In fact, a group reject may occasionally be elected to an important position. Also, if the poor morale is partly due to the denial of interpersonal satisfactions within the official functioning of the group, then the members may seize upon every opportunity offered them for selecting leaders to express their personal preferences irrespective of the pertinence of these preferences to the leadership roles involved.

Even when a condition of fairly good morale exists, many children often need guidance in selecting the best-qualified class members for leadership roles. Teachers have frequently observed that in some classes and clubs a few popular individuals are elected or chosen for nearly every leadership situation, even though there are frequently other pupils as well or better qualified for some of the roles than are the popular individuals. This kind of condition results in passivity on the part of many pupils and resentment on the part of a few who desire more recognition. When this kind of situation exists, guidance in discriminative choosing should be introduced. This kind of training can begin in the first grade by having children state the qualifications for the various elective and appointive roles in the class. When some reading ability is attained, particularly on the second-grade level, the teacher can write these qualifications on a chart or on the blackboard and check them later to see if various pupils have performed their duties according to the listed qualifications.

An example of the outcome of this kind of training is found in the election of a class librarian for a fifth grade. As soon as the need for someone to fill this position was evident, the teacher asked the pupils to consider what kind of person would make a good librarian. Several things were mentioned, but the chief point made was that the person elected should be one who was "good in his studies" so that he would have time to take care of his duties. A boy and a girl were nominated. One of the highly accepted boys in the class got up and said: "All of us boys like David (boy nominee) but I think we should vote for Helen because she always has her work done ahead of time, and so would have time to be a good librarian. David is not so good in his studies." Helen was elected.

These pupils had had considerable guidance in selecting the most qualified individuals for official positions. However, they did not select each other for any responsibility without regard for personal likeableness. It was quite evident over a period of a year, during which data were collected in this class, that a child's personal acceptability was always a kind of background factor entering indirectly into all selections for roles involving particular skills or leadership functions. Apparently a rough estimate of minimum personal attractiveness was prerequisite for consideration for any capacity involving representation of the group. Helen, for example, although not one of the highest in her class on any personal-preference criterion, was also not one of the lowest.

Degree of group-centered motivation is reflected in productivity. In school situations this aspect of morale, however else it is evidenced, must also be reflected in academic achievement. A class cannot be said to have good morale unless all or most of its members are motivated to achieve or surpass grade-level expectations. Such achievement-motivation shows acceptance of the school's standards, introjection of academic values, a willingness to work for group-defined objectives even when these may not be in accord with personal wishes, and a desire to hold the respect of classmates. One of the most reliable signs of poor morale in a school situation is a resistant or "don't care" attitude in regard to the kind of learnings expected there. It naturally follows, then, that anything a teacher can do to increase pupils' interest in learning is a contribution to the social-psychological climate of the class.

Feelings of identification with a group are stronger when the members know that this group is highly regarded by important individuals and organizations in the larger community, such as a city, a state, or a nation. This point is well illustrated in the efforts of many out-of-school groups to establish and to improve their prestige rankings by playing up the names of outstanding sponsors. How can this type of influence be utilized in school situations? Chiefly by teachers and other school personnel helping our children and youth to realize the vital importance of academic education to all aspects of our society, including the survival of our way of life against international communism. In doing this, the names of individuals and organizations of high prestige in our culture can readily be brought to bear on this objective. In addition to emphasizing the significance of formal education in our society, administrators and teachers can utilize every means to promote the prestige of the school in their particular cities and neighborhoods (1) by involving important individuals in numerous aspects of the school program, including classroom participation in areas of special interests and competence, (2) by obtaining recognition of all aspects of the school program in local newspapers, (3) by obtaining the support of significant community organizations for such school activities as music festivals, band trips, and science fairs, and (4) by doing everything possible to make the school building and grounds clean, impressive, and beautiful.

Finally, the identification that members feel with a group is indicated to a considerable extent by their regularity of attendance. In school populations this point is evidenced in the extent to which unexcused absences and truancy constitute a problem. This is also substantiated by the extent to which pupils attend school-sponsored, out-of-class, or after-school events, such as club meetings, parties, dances, and athletic games. The more pupils identify themselves with their school the more they want to become a part of all of its activities.

PERSONAL ACCEPTABILITY AND LEADERSHIP ROLES

Numerous studies bearing on leadership and social interactions in groups have shown that group morale is very much affected by the extent to which various kinds of social satisfactions and rewards are distributed throughout a group as opposed to being concentrated in a few individuals. This point has been presented in Chapter 10 and is further elaborated and supported in studies by Coch and French (15) and by Kahn (29). As pointed out in Chapters 12 and 13, there is considerable evidence to show that the social climate of a group is more positive and more in accord with mental hygiene principles when social satisfactions and avenues of recognition are widely distributed among the members of a group rather than concentrated in a few hands. Shared satisfactions and responsible participation result in greater ego-involvement in a situation where these values are experienced. This involvement results in greater feelings of personal worth, and these feelings in turn are important ingredients for creating a positive social climate.

The child who is persistently "left out" of his school group will nearly always develop some bad attitudes toward himself and toward others. He will probably acquire some of the self-defensive mechanisms described in Chapters 3 and 4. Also, he will be frustrated or delayed in achieving his higher-level needs, as described by Maslow.[2] Frequently his condition is made worse by the fact that he directs most of his positive feelings and social desires toward others who are highest in social recognition in his group, and does not direct positive feelings toward other classmates who are low in social status. Like all others who are weak, incompetent, or insecure, he does not identify with those whom he regards as being equally bad off as himself. He is not proud of them any more than he is proud of himself, and he does not profit psychologically from associations with them. He aspires to associate with others whom he looks up to (identification always goes up) and from whom he can obtain a "psychological lift." This, however, will seldom or never happen unless the teacher arranges for such associations through formed groups. Otherwise, the child who is persistently ignored or undesired is forced to associate only with others whom he does not admire or like, or he is forced into a lone-wolf position. In either case he is left in a social vacuum without a strong incentive for personality improvement; or if not a vacuum, he may be compelled into a psychological maelstrom of conflicting desires which frequently force him into hostile aggressiveness in an irrational effort to bolster his ego against threats to his stability.

What does our present evidence show in regard to the proportion of pupils in elementary and junior high school classes who are seriously lacking in social rewards? This question cannot be given a very definitive answer of general value since there is large variability among classes in the proportion of pupils who are found to be isolated, or nearly so, on any kind of measurement involving either a social preference or a leadership role. This wide variability is found not only among different kinds of school populations, but also between two classes on the same grade-level in the same building. Data reported by Atkinson (1), Bronfenbrenner (10-11), Flotow (18), Moreno (37), and Smith (42), and corresponding unpublished data obtained by the writer in twenty-five classes, show a range from 0 to 40 per cent of pupils who were complete isolates or near-isolates on any one choice-criterion in the populations studied — with the most typical range

[2] See Chapter 1.

being between 20 to 30 percent. Even when the results from several different choice-criteria are combined, there are nearly always a few pupils who are "left out" completely. This is particularly true in newly formed groups or in groups in which few socializing activities have been carried on. In a good many elementary school classes that the writer has studied, more than one third of the pupils have no one within their particular class whom they regard as a close friend, chum, or pal.

The low degree of interpersonal responsiveness that exists in some school groups is illustrated in the case of a homeroom in a junior high school (35). The thirty-five pupils in this room were asked to write their preferences for classmates to go to a show with, study with, have as a guest in their homes, and to share a secret with. Results showed that 34 per cent did not receive a single choice on any one of the above criteria. These pupils had been together for only about three weeks and no effort had been made by the teacher in charge to initiate social contacts among them.

As a result of the sociometric testing in this homeroom, the teacher in charge was impressed with the need of introducing more socializing activities. This she did by organizing the room into subgroups according to rows, each row having a captain. The row groups carried on numerous cooperative activities such as keeping attendance records, holding parties, exchanging Christmas gifts and valentines, and participating in a charity drive. Also, those pupils who were isolates were put in charge of projects that would bring them into favorable contact with other children, such as being responsible for sending cards to all pupils who were sick or absent, or making identification bands for the homeroom to use in connection with a school-wide field day.

Although it is not possible to state in scientific terms just what were the effects of those socializing efforts, since a control group was not available, a readministration of the same sociometric questionnaire at the end of the Fall semester showed that only two children failed to receive any choices. This is 6 per cent compared with 34 per cent on the first testing in October.

A socialization program, however, will often produce an increase of negative interpersonal feelings as well as an extension of positive feelings. To know some people better is to dislike them more. What often happens under a program of intensified socialization is that there is a better distribution of choices throughout a group, resulting in some members' being more highly chosen, but at the same time a few may lose ground and become either unchosen or rejected. This double-edged effect must be kept in mind by teachers who use sociometric testing to measure the effect of any program of socialization. They should expect that when they promote group activities they will almost certainly increase the extent of positive attractions among their pupils, but they must also expect that there will likely be a little increase in negative interpersonal attitudes. If teachers expect these negative results they will not be surprised or disappointed at their appearance. Furthermore, teachers need to view some interpersonal conflicts as a necessary aspect of the process of socialization.

The analysis of the distribution of social acceptance and leadership roles throughout a class can be made not only by determining the number who are "left out," but also by examining the extent to which social rewards are concentrated on a few pupils at the top of the prestige hierarchy. In some classes, about 20 per cent of the pupils monopolize nearly all these social rewards. They are repeatedly elected to different offices, they take prominent roles in all programs, they answer most of the teacher's questions in academic work, and they are either chosen by their classmates or appointed by the teacher to lead games or be chairmen of numerous committees. This kind of an arrangement results in a few pupils' being known as "the leaders." As presented in Chapter 10, the concept of group management opposed to this arrangement is that leadership should be distributed throughout a group. From this standpoint a child assumes a leadership role, in regard to either interpersonal affairs or group activities, when he stimulates or influences others. Obviously the members of a class will vary greatly in their capacities to stimulate others. Nevertheless, this concept of distributed leadership does require that every effort be made to provide ways whereby every child can make contributions to his group situation and thereby obtain some social rewards.

The "social value" that any child has in a school group is never in the child alone but always in the child as viewed within a particular social framework, i.e., the extent to which he is seen as being able to contribute to the realization of group objectives, enjoyment of leisure-time pursuits, or satisfaction of more strictly personal needs. This being true, a teacher may raise the social value of a child by introducing new avenues for self-expression, by having more diversified leisure pursuits, and by increasing opportunities for interpersonal enjoyments. As new social grounds are introduced, many pupils will be perceived as having somewhat different individual personalities than before.

These statements, however, should not imply that a well-established social stratification in a class is likely to be greatly changed by widening the range of participation, or by other types of socialization efforts. Numerous studies have shown that there is a strong tendency for the social structure of school groups to remain fairly constant over several months, and even over several years, in spite of many group activities and individual performances.[3] This stability of social structure shows that children's evaluations of each other grow out of conditions and personal qualities that are not easily changed.

Granted that large changes in the over-all social structure of a well-established school group are not likely to be made, what can a teacher expect to accomplish from his efforts to promote a better distribution of social rewards in his class? Primarily he can expect to reduce some of the differences among pupils who are high, average, and low, so that there are fewer pupils who receive no social rewards at all and there is less concentration of positive feelings and leadership roles on a few individuals. Even if many of the same pupils who were previously low are still relatively low, they are better off as individuals with some recognition than with none. What has happened in such instances is that the bottom of the social structure has been raised, and some new contributions have been added to help enrich the lives of all class members. Furthermore, it is quite likely that the few who formerly monopolized the social rewards are also better off, since it is not to their best interests in the long run to become smug and to

[3] See references by Bonney (8), Bronfenbrenner (10-11), Byrd (12), and Gronlund (22). Also see the comprehensive survey of constancy of sociometric scores presented by Mouton, Blake and Fruchter (38), listed with references at the end of this chapter.

imagine that they are more capable or personally charming than they really are.

Other objectives that a teacher may expect to accomplish from efforts to broaden the distribution of social rewards in a school group include: increasing the number of mutually reciprocated relationships, and increasing the extent of acceptance among pupils belonging to various subgroupings in the class, such as between boys and girls, between ethnic groups, and between pupils in different social class categories. Degree of attainment of each of these objectives can be measured with sociometric testing.

It seems clear from our present research on many kinds of groups, both in and out of schools, that as social rewards are better distributed to provide for increased leadership roles and more satisfying interpersonal contacts, there is an improvement in group morale as evidenced in more harmonious relationships, reduced absenteeism, better attitudes toward official leaders, and improved efficiency records. Furthermore, as these conditions are brought about there is a tendency for people to like each other better and to seek mature types of support from each other — thus indicating that when artificial barriers are removed there is, indeed, a genuine desire of people to affiliate with each other.[4] This affiliation is a requirement for any society that accepts the validity of mental hygiene principles. As Northway puts it: "The basic bond of society may consist in the fact that individuals like each other." (39 — p. 41.)

CLIQUE ORGANIZATION

The degree of social integration or unity found in any group is closely related to its clique organization. A clique may be defined as a social

[4] H. A. Murray in his *Explorations in Personality* (New York: Oxford University Press, 1938), Chapter II, has listed the "desire for affiliation" as one of the most basic of human responses. This desire is also closely related to W. I. Thomas' "desire for response" which he lists as one of the four most basic human wishes in his *The Unadjusted Girl* (Boston: Little, Brown and Co., 1923) pp. 4-39. It is also in accord with Asch's emphasis in his *Social Psychology* (Englewood Cliffs, N. J.: Prentice-Hall, Inc., 1952) on social needs being a primary characteristic of the human organism, and with the central theme of Montagu's *The Direction of Human Development* (New York: Harper and Bros., 1955) p. 404.

unit consisting of a small number of persons, usually between three and eight, all or nearly all of whom are attracted to each other. Every school class that has been together for even a few weeks is characterized in varying degrees by cliques. This comes about because particular individuals are attracted to each other for emotional support, mutual assistance, self-realization, companionship satisfactions, and as an aid in developing feelings of personal power and autonomy in relation to adult society. These small social structures provide the basis for communication within the class membership, including the "grapevine" whereby rumor and gossip about everything in the school are quickly transmitted.

What should be the attitude of teachers and other school officials toward cliques? In general they should regard cliques as both inevitable and desirable. Cliques are inevitable because of the fact of human preferences, causing all persons to be more attracted to certain individuals than to others within any group. However, every experienced teacher knows that a clique organization may work against the best interests of a class and also against the maximum development of many pupils in the class.

Values of cliques

Cliques are desirable because they facilitate strong in-group feelings among their members, provide for mutual support in numerous endeavors, and make possible many more intimate satisfactions than can be obtained through associations with thirty or more classmates on a total-group basis. Furthermore, information of clique organization within a class or other school group can be of real value to teachers, counselors, and administrators in knowing which students are involved in strong "centers of influence" in a class, in a club, or in the entire student-body. With this information, a school official can know which students he must count on to help promote school policies in regard to such matters as cheating, behavior at athletic events, secret societies, and the maintenance of scholastic standards. Such information is especially valuable to school officials in selecting individuals to serve on committees to help deal with the more serious problems of misconduct in school, and in dealing with problems arising from clashes between different national, religious, and ethnic groups.

Students elected to class or student-body offices cannot be depended upon entirely for such purposes, since some students who are strong centers of influence in cliques are not elected to these offices.

Another way in which knowledge of cliques may be useful to a school official is in the evaluation of expressed wishes, complaints, gripes, and suggestions. Those coming from students known to be well integrated in a strong clique must be taken seriously or else there is the risk of eventually having poor morale and nonsupport of school policies, and, in more extreme situations, of having to deal with open antagonism and strikes. Some of the suggestions and criticisms offered by isolates and rejects may be found to be sound and valuable in terms of a group's goals, and they should be objectively evaluated; but the social consequences of ignoring isolates and rejects will be insignificant, except in those cases in which bitterness rises to such a pitch as to produce criminal and destructive behavior. "He speaks for no one but himself" is a derisive statement frequently made in reference to the critical remarks of a person who does not belong to any clique.

It is important from the standpoint of harmonious group functioning that those pupils who are outstanding in some form of prestige status, such as elected officials, athletes, committee chairmen, or "centers of influence" on a social basis, show a high degree of mutual support through reciprocated friendships, expressed admiration for each other, cooperation on class projects, choosing each other for committee members and teammates, and belonging to the same cliques. If observation and sociometric data do not show these conditions to exist, but, instead, reveal evidence of hostilities and of strong rivalries among many of those who occupy prestige positions, then the teacher must expect to find considerable intragroup conflict, sabotaging of the efforts of one group by another, and other indications of poor morale, together with feelings of frustration on the part of many individual members. Serious "dissention at the top" produces divided loyalties among struggling cliques rather than united efforts for larger objectives.

When a teacher finds such adverse conditions as these in his class, the best corrective measure would be to increase the number and variety of leadership roles within the class so that recognition is more widely distributed, and so that most of the leaders are not forced to compete for exactly the same kind of recognition, such as that for academic grades. This suggestion follows a point previously made in this chapter, namely that one of the effective ways to correct personality problems of individuals is to enlarge and enrich the social field in which all these individuals function.

Dealing with undesirable cliques

Cliques in a school setting have undesirable aspects when they become very self-contained or ingrown, or when they work against the objectives of the larger group of which they are a part. The trouble with a self-contained clique is that the members associate only with each other and refuse to initiate or to accept friendly advances from nonmembers. This places arbitrary limits on their own development as well as restricting the social field for others.

How should teachers deal with self-contained and antagonistic cliques? No doubt some would say, "Break them up." Although this policy may occasionally be successful, and may also occasionally be justified in regard to extremely antagonistic cliques, this should not be the established principle of procedure. Instead, every effort should be made toward involving all clique members in cooperative or team endeavors with the hope that these efforts will bring about some reciprocated responsiveness between individuals in different cliques and with others who do not belong to any in-group.

An example of how this principle can be utilized is found in a physical education class in a junior high school. In this class consisting of forty girls, the teacher found a clique of five girls who always acted in unison and who frequently disturbed the others by laughing, horse-play, or refusal to participate in certain games. Since various disciplinary measures, including efforts to separate these five girls, had failed to curb the antagonism and aggressiveness of this clique, the teacher decided to try sociometric grouping. After the entire class had made choices of others whom they would most like to have as teammates for the rest of the semester, the forty girls were divided into four teams on the basis of these choices. Since the five clique girls all chose each other, they were placed on the same team along with five other girls who chose one or more of those in the clique.

Now the clique could act together and could gain recognition within the approved functioning of the class. The clique members accepted the other five girls well in team play, and this served to widen their social relationships.

Since each of the four teams was allowed to choose its own leaders, one of the leaders of the clique was elected to be captain of her team. This provided for additional orientation toward larger group objectives. The teacher reported that the hostile, delaying, and disturbing behavior of these five girls completely disappeared.

Guiding principle

The best guiding principle for a school in regard to cliques is not to fight them as such, but (1) try to enlarge and enrich the social environment within the school so that all pupils can belong to at least one clique, and (2) try to incorporate the interests and activities of cliques into the official functioning of the school, as illustrated above in the physical education class.

INTERSEX ASSOCIATIONS AND ATTITUDES

Since coeducation is almost a universal practice in American public schools, it is evident that our society has rendered a value judgment in favor of coeducation. With this policy established, it is inevitable that there will be some associations between boys and girls in our schools, and herein is the chief point of this discussion: namely, that one of the important factors determining the social-psychological climate of a class is the quantity and quality of associations between the sexes. When these associations are frequent and have a satisfying personal quality, the social climate of the class is enriched in a manner that cannot be provided any other way. This enrichment makes for a higher level of social integration, better group cohesion, and more harmonious activities in both work and play.

Fortunately, the great majority of schools no longer follows the restrictive practices found in some schools a generation ago, such as requiring boys and girls to play on opposite sides of the playground, enter the building through different doors, and sit on opposite sides of the classroom. Educators, schoolboard members, and most parents have apparently come to accept the idea that if positive heterosexual attitudes and behavioral adjustments are to be promoted, boys and girls should be encouraged to have many associations in work and play, and arbitrary restrictions should be reduced to a minimum. Furthermore, this kind of policy seems to be in accord with our emphasis on personality compatibility between the sexes as a foundation for marriage success. Certainly it is evident both from everyday observations and from case reports of maladjusted individuals that one of the most fertile sources of personal unhappiness and bad mental health is failure with the opposite sex.

In school situations the chief objectives should be to provide opportunities whereby boys and girls can participate in cooperative endeavors, share ideas and experiences, and learn to be at ease in each other's company. This does not mean that boys and girls should always be mixed in all school activities, especially in the upper grades and in secondary schools. Obviously there is also a need for boys to associate with and to identify with boys *as boys;* likewise, girls need many same-sex identifications. The major objective should be to help both boys and girls to accept certain kinds of behavior as customarily expected of their sex, but at the same time to help them see that one of the most important expectancies of both sexes is that each group develops favorable attitudes toward and satisfactory adjustments with the other.

Predominance of same-sex identifications

Probably most teachers have observed there is a strong tendency for boys and girls to associate very largely with others of their own sex. Furthermore, they have probably also observed that there are nearly always a few who have practically no favorable or reciprocated relationships with individuals of the opposite sex.

These observations are supported by data from sociometric studies, as shown in reports by Koch (30) and by Challman (13) among nursery-school children, and in reports by Criswell (16), Bronfenbrenner (10-11), Seagoe (41), and Smith (42) on the elementary school level. Criswell, for example, found sex-cleavage to be greater than ethnic cleavage among nearly 1000 pupils in 50 classes from the kindergarten through the eighth grade in Brooklyn, when the criterion was choice of seatmates (16). The majority of white boys preferred to sit with a colored boy than with a white girl.

That same-sex preferences in regard to both friendly feelings and overt associations are still very strong on the high school level is indicated in studies reported by Deutschberger (17), Hoult and Bolin (27), and by Kuhlen and Lee (31). When Deutschberger asked over 300 young people in a teen-age canteen to list their best friends, he found that only 7 per cent of these listings crossed over sex-lines, and Hoult and Bolin found less than 5 per cent of the total friendship choices given by students in a California high school to include opposite-sex individuals.

Kuhlen and Lees' research included pupils on the sixth-, ninth-, and twelfth-grade levels with over 100 pupils of each sex on each of these grade-levels. Their findings showed a gradual increase in intersex choosing from the sixth through the twelfth grade, but nevertheless, even among the twelfth-graders, over 35 per cent of them did not receive a single choice from an opposite-sex individual — even when each one of them made two choices on each of nine choice-criteria involving companionship and cooperative activities.

That Kuhlen and Lees' data do not present an exaggerated picture of the number of our late adolescents who have failed to establish even a minimum degree of personal affinity with an opposite-sex person is shown in a more recent and much more comprehensive study conducted under the auspices of Science Research Associates of Chicago. In one issue of their *Guidance Newsletter* (Sept., 1949) the directors of this organization quote the results of one of their surveys made on approximately 15,000 teen-agers in over 100 high schools.[5] One item dealt with boy-girl relationships. On this point it was discovered that 48 per cent of the boys listed "don't have a girl friend" as one of their problems, while 30 per cent of the girls listed "don't have a boy friend" as one of their problems.

Large variability between classes

One of the findings that stands out from any research done on intersex attitudes and overt associations is that there are large variations

[5] These figures are given in the *Examiner Manual for the S. R. A. Youth Inventory* (Chicago: Science Research Associates, 1950).

between schools and between classes on the same grade-level. Apparently these variations are due to differences in social class values and to other kinds of social factors present in different schools. The fact that large variations in intersex attitudes and overt associations can be found among classes on the same grade-level in the same school building points to the conclusion that practices carried on in these particular classes have much to do with the way boys and girls regard each other, and the degree to which they are willing to engage in cooperative endeavors. The writer has found this kind of variation in schools in the North Texas area. In one investigation, which included seventy elementary school classes, the extent of expression of friendly feelings toward opposite-sex members was six or seven times as great in some classes as in others on the same grade-level in the same building (7).

These findings suggest that the degree to which boys and girls in our school classrooms hold (or are willing and able to express) positive feelings toward each other may be as much related to what goes on in these classrooms as it is to anything in their biological inheritance, the physiology of their glands, or the particular stage of physical maturation. In other words, intersex responsiveness, or the lack of it, should not be regarded as something that is simply *in* the individual and is bound to manifest itself at a certain age-level. Rather, such responsiveness should be seen as a complex *interaction* between what is in the individual and what is in the social field around him. If the social field existing in a classroom is rich in positive stimulation for mutually satisfying associations between the sexes, there will certainly be a more favorable social-psychological climate in this class than when attitudes of intersex indifference, repression, or hostility prevail.

Promoting harmonious intersex relationships

All teachers can help promote positive feelings and cooperative activities between boys and girls by maintaining favorable attitudes toward intersex associations, by not making fun of those who show heterosexual interests, by not pitting boys and girls against each other in any kind of competitive situation, by not comparing boys with girls in regard to conduct or grades, and by not insisting upon arbitrary separation of the sexes in seating arrangements in classrooms, assemblies, and lunchrooms.

In a more positive vein, teachers can provide for boys and girls to work together on committees and in other small groupings for carrying on class work. They can also provide for some heterosexual activities during play periods or physical education classes.[6] This need not be the regular procedure, especially in the upper grades and in the secondary schools, but even on these latter levels the boys and girls can sometimes be brought together during physical education period for learning square dancing or social dancing, or for playing various kinds of games such as shuffleboard and ping-pong.

Jennings describes several school situations in which intersex relationships were greatly improved by changing certain school practices. In one elementary school, the practice of requiring boys and girls to play at opposite ends of the playground was gradually altered, first by arranging for mixed squads of boys and girls in the gym classes, and then by shifting some of these social groupings onto the playground (28 — pp. 51-52). Also, traffic squad patrols were arranged with an equal number of boys and girls on each squad. Another example is given of a high school in which the boys and girls always grouped themselves separately in the cafeteria. This condition was changed by certain faculty members who invited a boy and a girl, each of whom had been highly chosen on previous sociometric tests, to act as host and hostess at each table.

Such barriers as those listed above, and the adult attitudes behind them, are undoubtedly responsible for many of the feelings of social distance which grow up between boys and girls in our culture. These practices and attitudes also probably account to some degree for the scarcity of choosing between the sexes in nearly all sociometric testing, as described above. It is quite likely that some children and young people hold more positive attitudes and desires toward opposite-sex individuals than are measured by sociometric tests. Because they sense cultural pressures against admitting interest in the opposite sex, some of the respondents in sociometric testing no doubt hold back

[6] An article advocating such a program and listing games that can be played by both sexes has been written by L. E. Means, a recreation consultant in California, in the *Education Digest,* 1953, 19:44-46.

their spontaneous feelings and thus fail to show their true cross-sex attitudes. These restrictive social pressures probably also interfere with the expressions of normal heterosexual feelings in overt associations, except in such "socially approved" ways as teasing, horseplay, tussling, jokes, derisive remarks, "wolf call" whistling, and skirt twisting.

The over-all objective of the school in promoting harmonious relationships between boys and girls should be not to try to reduce all personal and social differences between them — but rather to help them bridge heterosexual differences in order that they may enjoy each other *as persons* and thus lay the foundation for making marriage choices.

UNDERSTANDING ATTITUDES AND FEELINGS

A frequent source of disharmony and poor morale in a class is a teacher's lack of understanding of the motivations and interests of pupils and the interpersonal status-structure existing among them. In such a class the pupils can be heard to make such remarks as: "She doesn't understand us," "He doesn't know what makes people tick," "She thinks she knows it all," or "He can't get with us." Such statements indicate a serious lack of overt and covert communications between pupils and teacher. Of course, it may be argued that this is not entirely the teacher's fault since some pupils are particularly difficult to communicate with. Although this may be true, the teacher has a much greater responsibility for understanding the pupils than the pupils have for understanding the teacher. The major determining factors in creating the social climate of a class spring from the attitude and behavior of the teacher. How can this task be well done if the teacher is constantly "misreading the cues"? How can a teacher understand pupils without a high degree of empathy with them? How can there be much harmony or integration in a group when the most important person in it is "out of touch" with the others?

Numerous studies on leadership in both school and out-of-school groups have shown that successful leaders are able to make quite accurate assessments of the beliefs, values, interests, and interpersonal feelings of their group members.[7] In fact, without this capacity how could they act as leaders? An individual who performs in a significant leadership role must to a large degree represent those who are led and be regarded by them as their agent, through whom they hope to attain their aspirations.

Are classroom teachers group leaders? Some are much more so than others, partly because they understand children and youth better, and partly because they are concerned with promoting the total growth of pupils as opposed to simply teaching a body of information or training in a skill. The mental hygiene objective is that all teachers should become group leaders.

Improvement of teacher-pupil understanding

How can teachers better understand the motivations and the interpersonal processes existing in and among their class members? In the first place, some teachers would need to study much more extensively in the areas of psychology, mental hygiene, and educational sociology. Also, many of these teachers would need to try to improve their own personal and social adjustments along the lines considered in Chapter 17 on "Mental Hygiene of Teachers." All teachers could improve their understanding of individual pupils by utilizing the various kinds of measurements and assessments described in Chapter 11. One particularly useful instrument for understanding the interests of individual pupils is entitled "What I Like To Do" and is published by Science Research Associates (57 Grand Avenue, Chicago 10, Illinois). This inventory provides scores for each of the following interest areas: Art, Music, Social Studies, Active Play, Quiet Play, Manual Arts, Home Arts, and Science. Grade-levels include the fourth through the seventh.

Importance of direct contacts

No instruments, however, can take the place of a teacher's direct contact with pupils, such as by holding numerous informal conversations with them, by listening to them talk to each other, by inviting suggestions from them, and by encouraging frank discussions in class, as described in Chapter 13.

[7] See reference at end of chapter by Bogen (5), Brookover (9), Gage and Suci (19), and Chowdhry and Newcomb (14).

Value of self-analysis for empathy

Furthermore, probably all teachers could profit by objectively considering the effects of their classroom behavior on pupils, i.e., making an effort to put themselves in the pupils' place. This would be an exercise in empathy. A teacher would have to ask himself, "Can I see myself and my behavior through the eyes of the pupils?" One who tries this should be sure to consider the extent to which his treatment of particular pupils may create barriers between these pupils and the rest of the class. Teachers' behavior most likely to do this is: putting a pupil in charge of the class when the teacher leaves the room, appointing certain ones who "have been good" to report on others or take down names of those who talk, or holding up one child as an example for others. Some teachers completely misperceive how these behaviors are regarded by the pupils, including those who have apparently been favored. They don't understand how such actions turn pupils against each other and against the teacher for attempting to use some of his pupils for his own ends — namely, to control the class. Every teacher who has some success in trying objectively to see himself will not necessarily want to change himself when differences are found, but at least he will have a more realistic and sincere basis for communicating with his class.

Assessing pupils' interpersonal status

Since the interpersonal relationships and the social status hierarchy existing among the members of a class and other social groups are highly important variables in determining the social climate of these groups, it would seem to be especially important for teachers to be able to assess accurately how their pupils regard each other. If a teacher grossly misperceives the interpersonal structure of his class, he is constantly responding to a social climate that isn't there. Furthermore, he plays up or appeals to the wrong pupils in some of his efforts to influence the class. He picks up erroneous clues in regard to the predominant trends in group attitudes. He can't understand why the class reacts so strongly to his criticisms of certain pupils. He cannot properly assess why it is that the suggestions on work-products of certain pupils are generally ignored, even though they are very good from his point of view; nor can he figure out why the drawings or oral reports of certain pupils are usually acclaimed "the best" even though they obviously are not. Finally, he frequently makes misjudgments as to how the class regards him, because he is constantly picking up clues from pupils who are unimportant in the networks. In some cases this kind of teacher doesn't even think of the class as a group, but only as a collection of individuals; consequently he is oblivious to the interpersonal social influences which are constantly affecting the responses of each class member toward all other members in regard to any kind of behavior.

Accurate judgments of interpersonal status

What do we know about the accuracy of most teachers' judgments in regard to the interpersonal social structure of their classes? A number of studies bearing on this point have been made — all of them utilizing one or more of the kinds of sociometric measurements described in Chapter 11. Since these measurements afford the most direct and objective means of determining the interpersonal relationships and preferences existing in a class, they are ideal for the purpose at hand. All that is necessary is to compare the findings of these measurements with teacher judgments obtained previous to the testing. The usual method is to correlate the sociometric scores with corresponding rankings on the same criteria obtained from the teachers. Our present evidence from such studies, as indicated in reports by Gronlund (23) and by Ausubel, Schiff, and Gasser (2), is very consistent in showing that a few teachers are quite accurate in estimating the actual sociometric ranks of their pupils, as indicated by correlations as high as .70 and .80. A few are grossly inaccurate as shown by the correlations that are of a zero order or slightly negative; while most teachers are moderately successful in predicting how their pupils will come out on a sociometric measurement, as evidenced by the fact that most correlation coefficients fall between .50 and .65.

Since many teachers may make inaccurate assessments of the interpersonal alignments existing among their pupils, the question may be raised as to how teachers can improve the accuracy of these kinds of judgments. In general, the answer is to know children better by utilizing all of the means described in this volume for obtaining increased knowledge of individuals and of group processes. However, additional assistance may be offered by pointing out some common sources of error in judging the relative standing of the members of a group in interpersonal desirability.

1. *Observe pupils in a wide variety of representative situations.* Probably one of the most frequent sources of error in judging the feeling responses existing among pupils is that of basing estimates on observations within only one kind of situation, such as classroom academic work. Teachers who are able to observe children in the hallways, in assemblies, in the lunchroom, and on the playground have a much more adequate basis for their judgments than do those who seldom see their pupils outside of class periods.

2. *Evaluate pupils' behavior objectively — free from "halo effects" and personal projections.* It is well-known that some teachers greatly overestimate the status of a few pupils who possess qualities that these teachers greatly admire (referred to as the "halo effect"), or their judgment is distorted because of unconscious projection of their own personal problems.

Misjudgments arising from the "halo effect" are most likely to be found in connection with that student who is industrious, well-behaved, courteous, neat and clean, and makes good grades and offends no one — but who is socially retiring and inhibited. Such a student may be very compliant with teacher requests and able to talk with adults much better than with his agemates. It is easy to see how such nice, agreeable, adult-centered youngsters are able to make a much more favorable impression on their teachers than upon their classmates, since their behavior patterns are much more highly valued by teachers than by most children and adolescents.

The mechanism of projection, discussed in Chapter 3, is a frequent source of teachers' misjudgments of how pupils evaluate each other. Reference is made to the fact that some teachers have personality problems which cause them to magnify the seriousness of certain kinds of behavior that they observe in children. For example, a teacher who has for years been ashamed of his timidity and lack of personal aggressiveness may find it difficult, if not impossible, to view a shy child objectively. He may imagine him to be much worse off in his social relationships than he actually is. On the other hand, a teacher who has repressed his own hostile aggressiveness is likely to be very sensitive to aggressive behavior in others under his supervision. He is inclined to regard such behavior as being very bad and dangerous; consequently, he frequently rates those who exhibit it lower in acceptability with their classmates than they actually are. At the same time he is likely to overrate the supergood child.

Since projection is largely unconsciously motivated, it is especially difficult to overcome this source of distorted judgment. However, if a teacher is sensitive to this problem, the best way to reduce its seriousness is to obtain data from pupils in regard to their interpersonal feelings, their self-regarding attitudes, and their evaluations of different kinds of conduct. These data, when obtained, must be analyzed *objectively* with the dominant purpose of trying to understand how the pupils feel about themselves and about each other.

3. *Recognize that overt behavior is frequently not an accurate reflection of covert feelings or attitudes.* A teacher may notice which pupils come to and from school together, which ones walk down the halls together, and which ones contact each other in numerous other ways. Although such associations are usually valid indications of mutual attractions, they frequently are not. Psychologists have long recognized that overt behavior may conceal as much as it reveals. A pupil may associate with certain other pupils, not because he likes them or admires them, but because of such factors as good manners, politeness, tolerance, and sympathy; perhaps he has a desire to use others for some selfish purpose, or to use another's property, such as a car.

In addition to these disguises of covert feelings, when one realizes that expressions of apparent hostility such as name-calling, quarreling, and hitting (especially among younger boys) are often a part of a friendship pattern, it is not difficult to see that errors in judgment are likely to be found on the part of teachers who try to determine interpersonal attractions among children from observations of overt behavior alone.

4. *Evaluate the interpersonal desirability of pupils, not on the basis of particular traits, but on the basis of their total personalities.* Although it is true that particular traits may be either so favorable or so unfavorable as to affect greatly the impression one makes on others,

it is nevertheless true that a frequent source of error in judging others is that of placing too much emphasis on certain traits, whether these be highly approved, such as kindness and generosity, or highly disapproved, such as pouting, bossiness, or sarcasm.

A teacher, for example, may note that a child pouts more often than most pupils, and the teacher may therefore conclude, because he knows that pouting is a bad trait, that other children must not like this child. It does not follow, however, that because pouting is a disliked trait a child who pouts is generally disliked, since he may have other compensating assets which far outweigh the negative effects of pouting.

Also, children can be found who are courteous, cooperative, kind, and generous, but who are nevertheless not well liked because of other serious weaknesses or handicaps. A teacher who is overly impressed with the importance of these particular virtues could easily overrate the group status of these children. In other words, every individual is evaluated by others as a desired or undesired associate, not on the basis of particular traits, but on the basis of his *total personality.*

REFERENCES

1. Atkinson, G., "The Sociogram as an Instrument in Social Studies Teaching and Evaluation," *Elementary School Journal,* 50, 1949, 74-85.
2. Ausubel, D. P., H. M. Schiff, and E. B. Gasser, "A Preliminary Study of Development Trends in Sociempathy: Accuracy of Perception of Own and Others' Sociometric Status," *Child Development,* 23, 1952, 111-128.
3. Bassett, R. E., "Cliques in a Student Body of Stable Membership," *Sociometry,* 7, 1944, 290-302.
4. Berkowitz, L., "Group Norms Among Bomber Crews; Patterns of Perceived Crew Attitudes, 'Actual' Crew Attitudes, and Crew Liking Related to Aircrew Effectiveness in Far Eastern Combat," *Sociometry,* 19, 1956, 141-153.
5. Bogen, Isidore, "Pupil-Teacher Rapport and the Teacher's Awareness of Status Structures within the Group," *Journal of Educational Sociology,* 28, 1954-1955, 104-114.
6. Bonner, H., *Group Dynamics,* Ch. III. New York: The Ronald Press, 1959.

7. Bonney, M. E., "Choosing Between the Sexes on a Sociometric Measurement," *The Journal of Social Psychology,* 39, 1954, 99-114.
8. ———, "The Relative Stability of Social, Intellectual, and Academic Status in Grades II to IV and the Inter-Relationships Between These Various Forms of Growth," *Journal of Educational Psychology,* 34, 1943, 88-102.
9. Brookover, W. B., "Person-Person Interaction Between Teachers and Pupils and Teaching Effectiveness," *Journal of Educational Research,* 34, 1940, 272-287.
10. Bronfenbrenner, Urie, "A Constant Frame of Reference for Sociometric Research," *Sociometry,* 6, 1943, 363-396.
11. ———, "A Constant Frame of Reference for Sociometric Research: Part II, Experiment and Inference," *Sociometry,* 7, 1944, 40-75.
12. Byrd, E., "A Study of Validity and Constancy of Choices in a Sociometric Test," *Sociometry,* 14, 1951, 175-181.
13. Challman, R. C., "Preschool Friendships," *Child Study,* 8, 1930, 106-107.
14. Chowdhry, K. and T. M. Newcomb, "The Relative Abilities of Leaders and Non-Leaders to Estimate Opinions of Their Own Groups," *Journal of Abnormal and Social Psychology,* 47, 1952, 51-57.
15. Coch, L. and J. R. P. French, "Overcoming Resistance to Change," *Human Relations,* 1, 1948, 512-532.
16. Criswell, J. H., "A Sociometric Study of Race Cleavage in the Classroom," *Archives of Psychology,* No. 235, 1939.
17. Deutschberger, P., "The Tele-Factor: Horizon and Awareness," *Sociometry,* 10, 1947, 242-249.
18. Flotow, E. A., "Charting Social Relationships of School Children," *Elementary School Journal,* 46, 1946, 498-504.
19. Gage, N. L. and G. Suci, "Social Perception and Teacher-Pupil Relationships," *Journal of Educational Psychology,* 42, 1951, 144-152.
20. Goodacre, D. M., "The Use of a Sociometric Test As a Predictor of Combat Unit Effectiveness," *Sociometry,* 14, 1951, 148-152.
21. ———, "Group Characteristics of Good and Poor Performing Combat Units," *Sociometry,* 16, 1953, 168-178.
22. Gronlund, N., *Sociometry in the Classroom,* Ch. V. New York: Harper and Bros., 1959.
23. ———, "The Accuracy of Teacher's Judgments Concerning the Sociometric Status of Sixth-Grade Pupils," *Sociometry Monographs,* No. 25. New York: Beacon House, 1951.
24. Hare, A. P., E. F. Borgatta, and R. F. Bales (eds.), *Small Groups,* Ch. X. New York: Alfred A. Knopf, 1955.
25. Hemphill, J. K., "Group Dimensions — A Manual for Their Measurements," *Research Monograph,* No. 87. Columbus 10, Ohio: The Ohio State University, Bureau of Business Research, 1956, p. 66.

26. Homans, G. C., "Group Factors in Worker Productivity," reproduced in *Readings in Social Psychology*. New York: Henry Holt and Company, 1947, pp. 448-460.

27. Hoult, T. F. and R. S. Bolin, "Some Factors Involved in High School Friendship Choices," *Sociology and Social Research*, 34, 1949, 273-279.

28. Jennings, H. H. (and others), *Sociometry in Group Relations*. Washington, D.C.: The American Council on Education, 1948.

29. Kahn, R. L. and D. Katz, "Leadership Practices in Relation to Productivity and Morale," ed. D. Cartwright and A. Zander, Ch. XL, *Group Dynamics Research and Theory*. Evanston, Illinois: Row, Peterson and Co., 1953.

30. Koch, H. L., "Popularity in Pre-School Children: Some Related Factors and a Technique for Its Measurement," *Child Development*, 4, 1933, 164-175.

31. Kuhlen, R. G. and B. J. Lee, "Personality Characteristics and Social Acceptability in Adolescence," *Journal of Educational Psychology*, 34, 1943, 321-340.

32. Lewin, K., *Resolving Social Conflicts*. New York: Harper and Brothers Publishers, 1948.

33. Libo, L M., "Measuring Group Cohesiveness," *Research for Group Dynamics*. Ann Arbor: University of Michigan, 1953.

34. Mayo, E., *The Social Problems of an Industrial Civilization*. Boston: Division of Research, Graduate School of Business Administration, Harvard University, 1945.

35. McClelland, F. M. and J. A. Ratliff, "The Use of Sociometry as an Aid in Promoting Social Adjustment in a Ninth Grade Home-Room," *Sociometry*, 10, 1947, 147-153.

36. Medley, D. M. and A. A. Klein, "Measuring Classroom Behavior With a Pupil-Reaction Inventory," *The Elementary School Journal*, 57, 1957, 315-319.

37. Moreno, J. L., *Who Shall Survive* (Rev. Ed.). New York: Beacon House, Inc., 1953, 129-134.

38. Mouton, J. L., R. R. Blake, and B. Fruchter, "The Reliability of Sociometric Measures," *Sociometry*, 18, 1955, 7-48.

39. Northway, M. L., *A Primer of Sociometry*. Toronto: University of Toronto Press, 1953.

40. Roethlisberger, F. and W. J. Dickson, *Management and the Worker*. Cambridge: Harvard University Press, 1939.

41. Segoe, M., "Factors Influencing the Selection of Associates," *Journal of Educational Research*, 27, 1939, 32-40.

42. Smith, G. H., "Sociometric Study of Best-Liked and Least-Liked Children," *Elementary School Journal*, 51, 1950, 77-85.

43. Van Zelst, R. H., "Validation of a Sociometric Regrouping Procedure," *Journal of Abnormal and Social Psychology,* 47, 1952, 299-301.

44. Withall, J., "The Development of a Technique for the Measurement of Social-Emotional Climate in Classrooms," *Journal of Experimental Education,* 17, 1949, 347-361.

QUESTIONS AND EXERCISES

1. Do you recall being in classes, particularly in elementary and secondary school, that were characterized by either a very good or very bad social climate as defined in this chapter? If so, can you identify now some of the factors that you believe produced these social-psychological conditions?
2. Point out some of the differences between a teacher's thinking of his class as a group and thinking of it simply as a collection of individual learners.
3. Stimulate a class discussion on the problems of creating high group-morale and at the same time fostering individualism. How can both of these kinds of mental health values be promoted?
4. Can a class be so managed that every pupil shares in the social rewards available there, and that no one feels he is completely "left out"? Prepare an outline-description of such a class.
5. What relation do you see between the kind of class you have described (Q. 4) and the solution of disciplinary problems in the classroom?
6. How do cliques contribute to mental health values on an individual as well as a group basis? How do they often work against these values in both individuals and groups?
7. Can you cite an instance from your experience of a disruptive clique being turned into a social asset by being integrated into the official functioning of a larger group?
8. Visit a local school for the special purpose of observing the kinds of social arrangements which exist between boys and girls. Take some anecdotal records on the contact that boys and girls make with each other during free time.
9. Cite examples in class of teachers you have had who were characterized by a high degree of rapport with their students.

What did they do to develop this kind of relationship? Compare the social climate in the classes of such teachers with that in the classes of teachers you have known who have had very little rapport with students, and who incorrectly assessed the social processes predominant in a given class.

10. If you are in charge of a group at the present time, utilize the suggestions given in this chapter to try to find out how much you are "in touch" with the wishes, interpersonal responses, and attitudes of your group members.

SELECTED FILMS

Motivating the Class. 19 minutes. Very good in showing how a class can be changed from one of disruption and poor effort into a cooperating group with high motivation for learning.

We Plan Together. 20 minutes. Illustrates how a high school class can help particular pupils to become participating members of the group.

Experimental Studies of Social Climate of Groups. 30 minutes. Portrays the effects of democratic, laissez-faire, and autocratic leadership on boys in a club situation. (This film can be obtained from Iowa State University, Extension Division, Iowa City.)

15

SOCIAL DIFFERENTIATION

ONE OF THE THINGS which is probably most obvious to everyone, even to those of limited capacities, is that some people are "better off" than others. This is evident from the fact that individuals and family units vary greatly in the extent to which they possess attractive clothes, houses, cars, etc., and in the extent to which they are favorably regarded on the basis of reputation and character in their respective communities. Some families obviously have much more standing or status than others. When this status is assessed on the basis of income, family history, educational level, and

AND THE PUBLIC SCHOOLS

community reputation, it is possible roughly to divide American families into social classes. When children come to school, they come not only with the stamp of their parent-child relationships as described in Chapter 2, but also with the stamp of their family's social class. This particular broad-gauge stamp is a kind of social *gestalt,* or ground, against which the abilities and personality traits of each child are evaluated. In some instances pupils are misperceived and grossly misjudged because they bear the stamp of an unfavorable social class.

Certainly our knowledge of social classes has shown that the mental health of individuals is by no means simply an individual matter. Instead it is closely bound up with many social and economic conditions which exert powerful influences upon individuals. For some people nearly all of these influences are of a positive nature and thus provide a very favorable ground for the emergence of mentally healthy individuals; for others these influences are charged with many negative aspects which predispose them to mental health hazards irrespective of their personal assets, friendly dispositions, or abilities.

This being true, it is evident that promoting mental health objectives is not always a matter of changing individuals, as such, but is also a matter of changing a social field to make possible more fair evaluations and greater opportunities for all. In school situations these changes in the social field usually include some changes on the part of the teaching staff and in administrative practices as well as in the attitudes of students.

However, the promotion of greater integration among various social class groupings is not taken care of simply by changing attitudes. When persons of widely differing social classes are thrown into fairly close associations, as frequently happens in our public schools, the development of greater interpersonal compatability is not just a matter of inducing higher status individuals to become more tolerant and fair-minded, but is also a matter of inducing some changes in those of lower status. Wide differences in such things as cleanliness, grooming, manners, physical aggression, sexual responses, and dishonesty (especially stealing), cannot be easily bridged, regardless of friendly aspirations or of desires to be fair and objective.

This chapter presents a brief description of social classes in America, a review of some evidence on relationships among pupils from different social class backgrounds, and suggestions for reducing the social distance between pupils in these various categories. The major objective of these efforts should be to remove those barriers that interfere with the maximum development of all children on all of our social class levels. This is one of the primary tasks of public schools in a democratic society. It would be difficult to find an area in which the goals for mentally healthy individuals and those for a democratic society more completely overlap.

SOCIAL CLASS STRUCTURE IN AMERICA

Sociologists, particularly Warner and Lunt (22), Davis, Gardner and Gardner (6), Davis and Havighurst (7), and Hollingshead (10), have in recent years published their findings in regard to social classes in America. Although it has been common knowledge for a long time that some individuals and some families rank higher than others in social and economic factors, the value of these sociological studies lies in their more accurate and detailed descriptions of the social, economic, and psychological characteristics of the different class levels in our society.

The most usual social class divisions consist of the Upper-upper, Lower-upper, Upper-middle, Lower-middle, Upper-lower, and Lower-lower. The two divisions of the upper class do not comprise more than 2 or 3 per cent of most communities and frequently less than this amount. Those placed in the upper class consist primarily of old-line families that are distinguished for their inherited wealth, social prestige, and large homes or estates.

The upper-middle class consists of 6 to 10 per cent of most of our communities. Those placed in this category are engaged primarily in professional or managerial type of work. They are leaders in civic affairs, and place much emphasis upon education, cleanliness, child rearing, conformity to sex and other group mores, and are strongly opposed to fighting and other forms of overt physical aggression.

The lower-middle class consists of 30 to 40 per cent of our more typical towns and cities. This is where the "common man" or "average man" begins in our social class structure.

The upper-lower class comprises 20 to 30 per cent of most of our communities, the proportion depending upon the range of diversification of business and industrial pursuits present in a particular locality. These are the people who are too busy making a living to be much involved in civic affairs. They are often characterized as "poor but honest" and "hard-working type." They live in the poorer districts and generally have large families.

The lower-lower class makes up 10 to 25 per cent of our more typical communities. These are the people with generally bad reputations in regard to honesty, stealing, cleanliness, fighting, and sex behavior. They do not have regular work habits, they assume no civic responsibilities, and live in the most deteriorated areas.

The principal forms of vertical mobility in this country consist in the use of money, education, occupation, talent, skill, philanthropy, sex, and marriage. It seems likely that "getting an education" is the means most used now to achieve upward mobility in the United States. Although this works on a large scale it does not work with equal facility for all class levels. Instead, our present educational system eliminates in disproportionately large numbers those children who come from the lower social classes. It has been estimated that whereas 80 per cent of the upper and upper-middle class children go to college, only 20 per cent of the lower-middle and 5 per cent of the lower-class children reach this level on the educational ladder.

The measurement of social class levels, especially in studies involving school populations, has frequently been done with a rating scale designated "Index of Status Characteristics Scale," as described in *Social Class in America* by Warner, Meeker, and Eells (24—Ch. 2).

EDUCATIONAL IMPLICATIONS

What contributions and suggestions of significance for mental health in schools arise from our data on social classes? In asking this question the assumption is made that mental hygiene objectives are promoted when children of all social classes have maximum opportunities for achieving self-actualization, social interests, and aspirations for the future, as described particularly by Maslow, Adler, and Allport.[1] This obviously means that arbitrary or discriminatory class barriers which may be found to exist among pupils or between pupils and teachers should be reduced or removed. Certainly the standards for positive mental health are violated if any child is forced through compulsory education laws to come to school and is then consistently forced into a position of inferiority, unfair treatment, or failure. Furthermore, the bad consequences for mental health are not confined simply to the victims but are also reflected through attitudes of smugness, conceit, and prejudice in many of those who occupy superior status.

Advantageous position of middle-class pupils

All findings of studies on social classes in our public schools hang together in showing that middle-class children, and especially those in the upper-middle class, occupy a very advantageous position as compared with lower-class children. This is particularly true in schools in which a wide range of social class levels are represented.

[1] See Chapter 1.

Several studies by Abrahamson (1-2), Hollingshead (10), and Smith (19) dealing with the distribution of teachers' marks and school honors and offices, in relation to the distribution of social class levels among junior and senior high school students, have shown striking and consistent relationships between these two sets of variables. Middle-class pupils are shown to have received far more high grades than would have been expected from their proportional representation in the populations studied, while the lower-class pupils are shown to have received a great many more low grades than would have been expected from their proportional representations. These contrasts are shown to be consistent throughout the social class structure but are found to be especially marked between the upper-middle class and the lower-lower class pupils.

Data reported by Hollingshead (10) and Smith (19) on high school populations reveal that middle-class students take prominent roles in cocurricular activities to a far greater extent than do lower-class students. In Smith's study this was true in 28 out of 31 cocurricular areas investigated. Hollingshead presents additional data (Chapter 8) which show how teachers in Elmstown were biased against lower-class students in assigning grades, giving help outside of class, and enforcing school rules.

Other writers have accused some teachers of holding discriminatory attitudes toward lower-class pupils. On the basis of interview data obtained from teachers, Becker (4) concludes that these children are resented by many teachers. Also Prescott (15) in his *Helping Teachers Understand Children* (p. 378) states that some teachers hold rejecting attitudes toward lower-class pupils and he surmises that these attitudes are frequently due to teachers rejecting their own social class origin, and to their desire to be identified with upper-middle class pupils.

A study reported by Bernice Neugarten (14) among fifth- and sixth-graders shows marked advantages for middle-class pupils in regard to interpersonal desirability and reputations. When the positive and negative feelings of these children toward each other were obtained on a friendship questionnaire, and these findings were related to the social class categories within the population studied, it was clearly apparent that the positive choices were most numerous in the upper-middle class and ran consistently less with each lower category, while the negative choices showed exactly the opposite trend. In other words, the higher a child's social class the more he was likely to be designated as a "best friend," and the lower his class the more he was likely to be listed under the heading "don't want as a friend."

When Neugarten related her data on pupils' reputations to the social class divisions, she found an even more striking superiority for the upper-middle class children. These pupils ranked first on every item referring to a favorable reputation, while the lower-lower class children ranked first on every unfavorable reputation item. The other classes fell consistently into a reputation level corresponding to their class hierarchy.

The author points out that it is highly doubtful that the lower-class children were actually as low on all these items as the pupils' ratings indicated. Instead she sees these reputation ratings as evidence of biased responses determined by class stereotypes. However, regardless of the degree of objective validity of the ratings, it was evident from the results that the lower-class child in the elementary school studied had a reputation of being poorly dressed, not good-looking, unpopular, aggressive, not liking school, bad mannered, not playing fair, and of being dirty. These opinions of him were shared even by members of his own social class. On the other hand, the typical child of the upper-middle status enjoyed a reputation exactly the opposite on all the above points. As Neugarten (14) points out, it is clear that after a few years in school the child of the lower class faces a much more difficult task of school adjustment than does the middle-class child.

Turning to the high school data, Neugarten found that her tenth- and eleventh-graders also showed strong preferences for choosing those in the upper class and also rated them much higher on the items bearing on reputation; but they did not show nearly as much rejection of the lower-class students on either of these measurements as was found among the elementary school children. She concludes that this difference is probably due primarily to the fact that a good many lower-class children had long since left the school system, so that those who remained were not typical representatives of this status level. Instead they were the mobile ones who had succeeded to a considerable extent in adopting some middle-class values and behavior patterns. Whatever the reason, the tendency of the upper-middle students was to ignore, but not to strongly reject, those in the lower classes on both the friendship choices and the reputation ratings.

Other investigations in which interpersonal preference and reputation data have been related to social class hierarchies have shown results very similar to those reported by Neugarten. This is particularly true of studies conducted by Atkinson (3), by Cook (5), and by Morgan (13) in which fairly wide social class differences existed within the school groups studied.

However, the point should be stressed that in all the studies referred to above, and also in a study (21) conducted for a master's thesis in the North Texas area, some interpersonal affiliations among pupils in different social classes are reported. Although most of these cross-overs are between pupils in adjacent classes, such as between upper-lower and lower-middle, there are also a few in most school populations which involve pupils two class-levels apart. From the standpoint of mental hygiene objectives, these evidences of personal acceptance between members of varying social classes in our schools must be regarded as important indications of democratic values, of positive social climate, and of greater group cohesiveness.

Tolerance, understanding for lower-class pupils

The foregoing description relative to the advantageous position of middle-class pupils in our schools leads to the conclusion that if mental hygiene principles are to be increasingly realized in the education of lower-class pupils, many teachers will need to become more tolerant and understanding of these children. This is not to say that teachers should favor lower-class children or should give them "breaks" or advantages that they do not earn or deserve. All that is implied is that teachers should become more acquainted with social class differences existing among their pupils, should try to be fair and objective in evaluating the work and the behavior of lower-class pupils, and should try to understand that some behavior they consider extremely obnoxious is regarded by lower-lower class pupils as completely normal. In discussing this point Hughes stresses the "social distance" that usually exists between middle-class teachers and lower-class children in reference to their respective attitudes toward fighting, use of tabooed language, orderly routine, cleanliness, ambition, and sexual expressions. It does not necessarily follow that to understand is to excuse or to ignore, but it should follow that there is a more sympathetic and objective appraisal of the behavior of lower-class pupils, leading to more effective efforts to deal with the problems presented.

Furthermore, teachers who are sensitive to the backgrounds and feelings of lower-class pupils will avoid procedures that unnecessarily expose their socio-economic handicaps. For example, in the elementary grades where lower-class children are present, a teacher should not ask pupils (in connection with health work) to state before the class what they had for breakfast. Furthermore, she should not have a project in which all pupils are expected to bring a monetary contribution from home, nor one in which all pupils are expected to furnish some kind of fairly expensive clothing or costume. Also it seems especially important in such classes that a teacher not have the pupils choose each other overtly for sides in games or other events, since so many lower-class pupils are among those chosen last and are forced to stick out like "sore thumbs." Furthermore, lower-class children should never be identified as a separate group by referring to them in terms of their place of residence (as the "trailer pupils," or "the pupils from across the tracks") or by managing things in such a way that they sit together at lunch periods or during assembly programs. In arranging reading groups, committees, dramatizations, etc., the teacher should make every effort to avoid having lower-class children concentrated in particular groupings.

The importance of teachers' attitudes toward lower-class pupils is more apparent when it is realized how much the responses of teachers may affect the attitudes of other pupils in the class, particularly in the elementary school. Extra and unwarranted barriers to good mental health are indeed placed in the way of lower-class pupils when the teacher shows by both overt and covert attitudes that he is rejecting them. Furthermore, the teacher's feelings toward these pupils may cause them to develop rejecting attitudes toward themselves.

Curriculum adaptations

It seems likely that in most schools in which lower-class children are present in considerable numbers an objective appraisal of their personal-social needs would lead to some curriculum adaptations.

One type of curriculum content which is especially adapted to the needs of lower-lower class pupils is that dealing with cleanliness and personal appearance. In the lower elementary grades this need is sometimes met by having a "clean-up corner" consisting of an improvised dressing unit, a bottle of cleansing liquid, and a box of tissue paper. The procedure usually followed is to have all the pupils checked periodically in the "clean-up corner" so no one is embarrassed by being singled out. Each child is supposed to have his own comb. A different boy and girl can be elected every week or so to act as host and hostess in helping with the check-ups and in helping to keep the supplies in order. Some elementary schools in lower-class districts are equipped with showers and all pupils are required to take a shower once a week.

On the junior high school level it is sometimes possible for a cleanliness project to be initiated through a club. This was done by a teacher known to the writer who taught in a school drawing heavily from lower-class homes. This teacher suggested to the girls the desirability of their having a club that would meet several days a week during the last period in the day. The girls responded immediately, and after much talking and voting finally decided to call it the "Little Junior Miss." Their discussion of club activities (with some teacher suggestions) led to the adoption of a project in personal attractiveness as one of their principal objectives. They set up rules in regard to keeping fingernails clean, brushing teeth, bathing, and keeping hair groomed and clothes pressed, and voted not to wear bluejeans any more except on school picnics. The carrying out of these rules was left up to each girl.

Some of the special activities that developed from this club included the following: the appearance before the group of a high school cosmetology teacher who talked on the care of the hair and skin, the appearance of a physical education consultant who talked on posture and had the girls demonstrate good and poor postures, a "style show" which was put on by several women from one of the local department stores using some of the girls as models, the showing of the Kotex film *The Story of Menstruation,* a visit by the girls to a high school cosmetology class so that these older girls could show the seventh-grade girls how to roll their hair and manicure their nails, the reading of fashion magazines, and a tea at which occasion the girls demonstrated in both appearance and manners what they had learned in the club.

Evidences of the value of this project were found in comments of other teachers in regard to the girls' improved appearance, less marking on the walls and furniture, the complete disappearance of blue-jeans, the interest of the school principal in continuing this type of work, and the greater ease and frequency with which the girls brought personal matters to their teacher (who was also one of the designated school counselors).

On the high school level it seems likely that units of work in English, homemaking, or social-studies classes dealing with such topics as appearance, etiquette, social forms, and certain social skills, offer one of the most practical ways of promoting better social adjustment on this age-level. There are only a few students in most public high schools who could not profit by this type of curriculum content, but it may be assumed that those from lower-class homes would have greater need for it — especially those who aspire to acceptability by middle-class groups.

In some high schools, semester courses in family living are offered. These include considerations of parent-child relationships, use of money, and a variety of other factors known to be important to marriage happiness. One of the criticisms made of such courses is that they tend to emphasize middle-class family practices and values, with practically no serious or favorable consideration given to lower-class family patterns. In a publication dealing with this topic, Robert J. Havighurst is quoted as saying that the teacher of such courses should not endeavor to teach any one pattern of family-class-behavior as the best, but should instead teach what scientific studies have shown in regard to diet, parent-child relationships, marriage happiness, and democratic principles in living.[2]

In a good many high schools social dancing and square dancing are taught in physical education classes, during noon hours, in clubs, or during special periods designated for this purpose. Here again, it

[2] *Guidance Newsletter,* Chicago: Science Research Associates, Jan., 1951.

is safe to assume that some students from all social classes would profit by such instruction, but it also seems likely that a larger proportion of students from lower-class homes would not have learned to dance through their homes or through other agencies outside of school.

In addition, efforts should be made to include more lower-class pupils in all kinds of cocurricular activities through school-sponsored clubs and intramural sports. This kind of a program will not be very successful unless the pupils are consulted in regard to the kind of activities they desire, and are allowed considerable responsibility in conducting these activities. An additional difficulty is that it is frequently hard to arouse and sustain interest in club programs on the part of lower-lower class children, since group membership is not characteristic of their subculture. However, with an appropriate activity and with leadership by an adult who has prestige in the eyes of lower-lower class pupils, such groups *can* be developed into strong social units. A description of how this type of program was carried out in the Thomas Edison Occupational School in Cleveland is given by Robinson (17). The major purpose of a cocurricular program for all pupils is to promote feelings of belongingness and pride, and to stimulate maximum development of abilities and personal qualities.

Finally, in regard to curriculum adaptations to the needs of lower-class pupils, it seems certain that a good many vocational-type courses in the junior and senior high schools should be offered, along with the college preparatory course of study, in order to meet the needs of those who, due to financial limitations and family attitudes, will not continue their education much beyond the compulsory school age. It seems reasonable to assume that if a lower-class student can take courses that interest him and that he sees he can use, his total adjustment to the school situation will be better than when he is forced to take subjects in which he has little interest and can see no subsequent value to himself. Further considerations of curriculum adaptation to aid pupils in the lower social classes are offered by Stendler (20) and by Hardiman and Robinson (8).

Contacts between students of different social classes

It is well-known that most schools in our larger cities draw primarily from a fairly limited social class range due to the location of schools in residential areas that are characterized by particular socio-economic levels. Unless something is done by a school system to bridge this gap, it is missing a chance to help break down antagonistic feelings and prejudices among our major social classes. When a school system undertakes this kind of project, there are two principles that should be followed if the contacts are to result in more favorable interclass attitudes.

The first of these principles is that only the more capable and personally adequate members of the lower classes should be brought into contact with those in the upper-middle class or higher levels. Since many persons in the upper socio-economic brackets generally think of *all* individuals in the lower brackets as class stereotypes, it follows that one way to eliminate this type of thinking is to bring upper-status pupils into contact with lower-status pupils who do not fit their class stereotype. The second principle referred to above is that the kind of interschool projects arranged for the purpose under consideration should be of a cooperative rather than a competitive nature, and they should be activities in which the lower-class students can make a genuine contribution.

These two principles are illustrated in several projects in Los Angeles County described by Hughes (11). In one of them a group of eighth-graders from a lower-status school put on a Christmas program in collaboration with a similar group from a higher-status school. Other projects consisted of youth forums in which students from schools all over the county participated in discussions on school and community problems. After these forums were completed the students were asked to write some evaluative comments. Two of these comments by students from a higher-status school were: *We never thought before that Negroes were as smart as we are* and *We learned that people you think are queer are just like us.*

Encouragement for capable lower-class pupils

A special way whereby a teacher can aid lower-class pupils is to offer extra encouragement to those who show marked abilities and academic motivations. Even under the unfavorable conditions described in a preceding paragraph a few lower-class pupils have nevertheless made excellent academic records. For example, in Abrahamson's junior high school study previously mentioned, six "A's" and 42 "B's" were given to lower-lower class students (2). It is important not only to improve the social-psychological climate for lower-class pupils in our schools, but also to try to stimulate those who do succeed to continue their education. This continued education would promote their self-realization and would also contribute to society. Our present evidence (Havighurst and Neugarten [9 — p. 226]) indicates that an unusually large proportion of bright students in the lower classes either do not finish high school or stop at the end of high school. Although it is important to encourage all bright students to continue their education, it seems to be more essential for teachers and other school staff members to offer special encouragement to talented lower-class students since they are less likely to receive this kind of stimulation through their homes. In many instances the special help most needed is financial assistance. This can best be taken care of by helping lower-class students obtain remunerative work and by aiding them in securing scholarships to colleges and technical schools.

REFERENCES

1. Abrahamson, Stephen, "Our Status System and Scholastic Rewards," *Journal of Educational Sociology,* 25, 1951-1952, 441-450.
2. ———, "School Rewards and Social Class Status," *Educational Research Bulletin,* 31, 1952, 8-15.
3. Atkinson, G., "The Sociogram As an Instrument in Social Studies; Teaching and Evaluation," *Elementary School Journal,* 50, 1949, 74-85.
4. Becker, H. S., "Social Class Variations in the Teacher-Pupil Relationships," *Journal of Educational Sociology,* 25, 1952, 451-465.
5. Cook, L. A., "An Experimental Sociographic Study of a Stratified 10th Grade Class," *American Sociological Review,* 10, 1945, 250-261.
6. Davis, A., B. Gardner, and M. Gardner, *Deep South.* Chicago: University of Chicago Press, 1941.
7. ——— and R. J. Havighurst, "Social Class and Color Differences in Child-Rearing," *American Sociological Review,* 11, 1946, 698-710.
8. Hardiman, Ruth and John T. Robinson, "Social Roots of Learning," *Educational Leadership,* 7, 1949, 159-164.
9. Havighurst, R. J. and Bernice L. Neugarten, *Society and Education.* Boston: Allyn and Bacon, Inc., 1957.

10. Hollingshead, A. B., *Elmtown's Youth.* New York: John Wiley and Sons, 1949.
11. Hughes, M. M., "When the Middle Meets the End," *Childhood Education*, Vol. 24, 1948, 226-231.
12. Lesser, G. S., "The Relationships between Various Forms of Aggression and Popularity Among Lower Class Children," *Journal of Educational Psychology,* 50, 1959, 20-25.
13. Morgan, H. G., "Social Relationships of Children in a War-Boom Community," *Journal of Educational Research,* 40, 1946, 271-286.
14. Neugarten, Bernice L., "Social Class and Friendship Among School Children," *American Journal of Sociology,* 51, 1946, 305-313.
15. Prescott, D., *Helping Teachers Understand Children.* Washington, D.C.: American Council on Education, 1945.
16. Reeves, J. M. and L. Goldman, "Social Class Perceptions and School Maladjustments," *Personnel and Guidance Journal,* 35, 1957, 414-419.
17. Robinson, J. T., "Students and Faculty Work to Improve Life in School," *Journal of Educational Sociology,* 21, 1947-1948, 517-527.
18. Sewell, W. H. and A. D. Haller, "Social Status and the Personality Adjustment of the Child," *Sociometry,* 19, 1956, 114-125.
19. Smith, H. P., "A Study of the Selective Character of American Secondary Education: Participation in School Activities as Conditioned by Socio-Economic Status and Other Factors," *Journal of Educational Psychology,* 36, 1945, 229-246.
20. Stendler, C. B., "Social Class and the Curriculum," *Educational Leadership,* 7, 1950, 371-75.
21. Tiffin, R. E., "A Study of the Relationships Between Social Class Status and Social Acceptance," Unpublished M.A. thesis, North Texas State College Library, 1951.
22. Warner, W. L. and P. S. Lunt, *The Social Life of a Modern Community.* New Haven: Yale University Press, 1941.
23. ———, M. Meeker, and K. E. Eells, "Social Status in Education," *The Phi Delta Kappan,* XXX, 1948-49, 113-19.
24. ———, M. Meeker, and K. Eells, *Social Class in America.* Chicago: Science Research Associates, Inc., 1949.

QUESTIONS AND EXERCISES

1. Stimulate a class discussion on the changing social class structure in America and how these changes are affecting relationships among pupils in our schools. Consider particularly the rapid development of suburban communities.

2. Do you believe that during your own elementary and secondary education you were conscious of social class differences among the students in your school groups? Why or why not?
3. Make a comprehensive list of all the reasons you can think of why upper-middle pupils do so much better in our schools than do lower-class pupils.
4. Stimulate a class discussion of the question of whether or not our schools should try to emphasize some of the attitudes and behavior adjustments of all of our social classes instead of predominantly those of the middle class.
5. Try to imagine yourself as a lower-class child in one of our predominantly middle-class schools and make a list of the negative mental health responses that you would likely develop.
6. Cite examples of teachers you have known who were either very good or very poor in fostering amicable relationships between pupils of various social classes. What did they do or not do?
7. Find out if there are any projects in your community for promoting better understanding between pupils of varying social class origins, such as the one reported by Hughes in this chapter.
8. Stimulate a class discussion on how the social class origin of a teacher is likely to affect his attitude toward pupils from various social classes.

SELECTED FILMS

Social Class in the United States. 20 minutes. Class presentation of contrasts in the lives of three boys who grew up in the same town but who had different social class origins.

Three Steps to Start. 26 minutes. Deals with some social problems of youth and how parents finally develop a plan of action for meeting needs of young people on "both sides of the track."

16

ETHNIC FACTORS AND

AN ADEQUATE TREATMENT of the problems associated with social integration and social climate in our schools must include some discussion of religious and ethnic groups. In some schools, one or the other of these two factors, particularly the latter, is the source of more conflicts or of intragroup cleavage than any other single condition.

It seems certain that our public schools have been very influential in laying a foundation for greater tolerance among our major religious groups. It also seems very likely that our schools have done this, not pri-

RELIGIOUS FACTORS

marily through any special kind of teaching, but rather by providing a very extensive basis in shared experiences among children of all religious faiths. Against the large common ground created by these experiences, differences in religious beliefs are reduced in importance, insofar as they are barriers to interpersonal affiliations and to acceptance in leadership roles. This has always been one of the objectives of those who have promoted a publicly supported, nonsectarian school system.

Although our public schools cannot teach any particular kind of religious doctrine or faith, they do very generally support and reinforce the moral and ethical values that are taught by all religious groups, and by so doing they help to consolidate bonds of unity among children of diverse religious backgrounds. Certainly our public schools are not the pagan institutions they have sometimes been called simply because they do not teach any religious doctrines or stress religious faith, as such.

Fortunately there are some public schools in which very few children face mental health hazards because of their religious affiliations, but there are others in which both overt and subtle barriers are constantly perpetuated among Protestants, Catholics, and Jews.

Problems of social integration arising in schools that have pupils of mixed ethnic origins and skin colors are probably more acute than those arising from religious differences. There are numerous reasons for this condition, but one of the most obvious is that, unlike religious beliefs that are not visible on the surface, differences in skin color are immediately and clearly evident. For those pupils who have developed negative evaluations of any particular skin color these first contacts initiate interpersonal barriers and feelings of distance.

Students of anthropology, sociology, and related disciplines quite generally agree that the term *race,* with its usual connotation of fixed and static differences between groups of people, is misleading and inaccurate.[1] This is true because no physical traits, such as skin color, hair texture, blood types, head shapes, or stature, have been found which universally and consistently distinguish one so-called racial group from another. Instead there are very gradual differences between extremes of all the above characteristics, rather than sharp dividing lines. Consequently the term *ethnic group* is used in this discussion rather than the term *race.* Funk and Wagnalls' *New Standard Dictionary of the English Language* defines *ethnic* as follows: "Of or pertaining to races or peoples; characteristics of a race, nation, or people; descriptive of or based on national peculiarities." Thus this term avoids the implication that the various groups referred to differ in ways that are highly consistent and fixed.

CERTAIN RELIGIOUS FACTORS

Not many efforts have been made to evaluate the influence of religious beliefs and practices on the adjustments of children to school situations. Probably the chief reasons are that public schools are not directly concerned with religious matters and that scientific evaluation of most religious factors is very difficult to accomplish.

[1] See discussion of this topic in *The Encyclopedia Americana* (Chicago: The Americana Corporation, 1957) Vol. 23, 107-111.

Sunday school attendance

One factor which is sufficiently overt to be given at least partial evaluation is Sunday school attendance. Even with this factor, however, there is very little objective evidence in regard to its relationship with a child's personal-social adjustments with his age-mates in school. The writer has obtained some data of this nature from twelve elementary school classes, and has sponsored a master's thesis by Caves in which similar data were obtained from all six grades of an elementary school (7). In the latter study, both sociometric choices and teacher ratings of pupils' personality traits were utilized. From all these data the major finding was that regularity of attendance at Sunday school bore little or no relationship to any of the measurements used. Certainly no reliable predictions could be made in regard to the kind of impression that a particular child was making on his age-mates, or on his teachers, from knowing the regularity of his Sunday school attendance. Although this evidence is insufficient to warrant a broad conclusion, it is supported by Hartshorne and Mays' studies of dishonesty among school children (14 — p. 411) and by Kvaraceus' study of over 700 delinquents in Passaic, New Jersey (18).

Apparently, at present, teachers and counselors will be on safer grounds if they regard the simple overt fact of regularity of Sunday school attendance as a purely sociological factor in a child's background, rather than assuming that high or low frequency of attendance implies any particular quality-level of interpersonal adjustments. The point should be made, however, that the above studies do not have a direct bearing on the influence of religious faith or devotion upon any aspect of mental health, because such highly personalized characteristics were not included in any of these investigations.

Acceptability and major religious groupings

Do we have any evidence that any one form of religious background is superior to others from the standpoint of turning out the kind of people who are acceptable to their classmates in school? The fact is that we do not. This negative answer is based on unpublished data obtained by the writer in twelve elementary school classes and in a published report on the number of friendship choices received by over 1100 students in North Texas State College (6). In none of these populations did any church grouping (Methodists, Baptists, Catholics, etc.) obtain reliably more choices than would be expected from its proportional representation in the populations studied. This finding is supported by the fact that Reilly and Robinson who, in their study of acceptability among 163 girls in a dormitory at Ohio State University, did not find a reliable difference among Catholic, Jewish and Protestant students.

Until contrary evidence is available, teachers and counselors had best assume that all of our major religious organizations, in spite of their differences in doctrine and practice, are turning out very much the same caliber of people in so far as this caliber is measured by desirability as associates by age-mates in schools.

Associations among pupils of different groupings

There seems to be no doubt that one of the primary requirements for better mutual acceptance of individuals of diverse backgrounds is that they have numerous associations with each other under conditions of at least official equality of status. This condition is generally present for pupils of varying religious faiths in our schools; and although several studies have shown that there is a strong tendency for students on sociometric tests to choose others of their own religious affiliation, there is always some choosing between students of different religious categories. This expression of positive feeling between individuals of different religious backgrounds is important, not only for the personality development of the individuals concerned but also as a necessary social-psychological cement that helps to hold together the numerous cultural groupings in our society.

Some studies, such as one reported by Atkinson on a fourth-grade class in South Bend, Indiana, show Jewish, Catholic, and Protestant children to choose each other on sociometric tests with practically no indication of discrimination along religious lines (4); but other investigations show evidence of interpersonal feelings being definitely affected by religious affiliations, such as a study conducted by Harris and Watson among 82 pupils in the upper grades of a private school in New York City (13). Approximately one-third of these pupils were Jewish while the others were gentiles. When these children were asked to list names of their best friends, the results showed that about three-fourths of the choices of both Jews and gentiles were given to others of their own religious affiliation, leaving approximately one-fourth of the friendship preferences which crossed over religious boundaries.

The value of contacts between individuals of different religious and ethnic groups as a means of promoting interpersonal acceptance between them is emphasized in a study reported by Saenger and Shulman (31). These investigators interviewed 300 mothers of school-age children in four adjoining neighborhoods in the Washington Heights district of Manhattan, in regard to the extent of association and of mutual friendships among the children of the respective neighborhoods. This area was chosen because of the many different religious and ethnic groups residing in it.

According to the statements of the mothers, about two-thirds of the children in each religious category had friends in other religious groups, and most of these friendships were sufficiently intimate to lead to home visits. In spite of the considerable degree of interpersonal acceptance between members of different religious faiths there was at the same time considerable hostility between them. In fact 30 per cent of the 300 mothers stated that their children had been involved in trouble with children in other ethnic or religious groups, and that much of this trouble had been of a quite serious nature. This finding illustrates how the process of adjustment between groups is a matter of personal acceptability between individuals rather than between groups as such. In other words, at the same time that Negroes, Jews, Catholics, and Protestants were fighting certain individuals in each of these groups outside their own, they were forming mutual friendships with other individuals in these same groups. This emphasizes the importance of promoting friendships *between individuals* in diverse groups as a means of integration.

INTERETHNIC ASSOCIATIONS

Probably the personal-social adjustments of pupils of different ethnic origins constitutes a more challenging problem for our schools than does the integration of pupils from different religious backgrounds.

This is especially true since the Supreme Court decision of 1954, which declared in favor of integrated schools.

What evidence do we have that pupils of different ethnic groups in our schools are making satisfactory social adjustments with each other? Although we do not have sufficient research from which we can formulate an objective and comprehensive answer to this question, we do have some pertinent data and we do have some general sociological and psychological knowledge that may be applied to this problem.

Causative factors

It is not within the scope of this book to consider in detail the causes of prejudice. This has been done in numerous writings such as those by Allport (2), by Bettelheim and Lewin (5), and by Doob (10). These writings, which include summaries of many research investigations, make it clear that in reference to causative conditions, antagonistic and nonaccepting attitudes between ethnic groups are multidimensional. Some of these causative factors undoubtedly stem from direct teaching in the home; some are due to more unconscious assimilation of prevailing stereotypes; some are due to distorted perceptions of members of certain ethnic groups because of personality maladjustments within the perceiver; some are based on disagreeable experiences with a few individuals of a particular ethnic category; some grow out of situational factors which cause some people to act in a prejudiced manner at particular times and places because it seems to them to be the approved thing to do; some are based on the fear that a certain ethnic group may become sufficiently powerful to be a serious threat to one's own status and security; and others are rooted in very frustrating life-conditions which arouse in some people the need for a scapegoat to explain their misfortunes so they do not have to look within themselves for the blame.

Prejudice and preference

The difference between prejudice and personal preference should be clearly understood. It is obvious that prejudice refers to prejudging individuals in regard to particular behavior traits simply because of knowing that they belong to a certain category without adequate knowledge or experience for forming a reasonable judgment about them. Personal preference, on the other hand, refers to positive or negative feelings toward certain other persons after adequate opportunity to know them. In other words, it cannot be assumed that anyone who dislikes or who holds antagonistic attitudes toward some members of another ethnic group is necessarily prejudiced against them. He *may* be responding to them on the basis of how he regards their worth to him — in the same way as he responds to members of his own group. Therefore, in the ensuing discussion bearing on interethnic associations in our schools, the point should be kept clearly in mind that what is desired is that each school should work toward the reduction or elimination of all barriers between members of different ethnic groupings which prevent them from making fair and unprejudiced assessments of each other.

The fact that interpersonal preferences exist irrespective of prejudice means that even if all arbitrary and unfair barriers between ethnic groups in a particular school were removed there would still be some pupils of different backgrounds and skin colors holding antagonistic and rejecting attitudes toward each other. Furthermore, when interethnic associations are promoted we should expect to get some increase in positive attitudes and interpersonal acceptance, but at the same time we should also expect to get some increase and some sharpening of both negative attitudes and feelings of rejection.[2] From a mental hygiene point of view, the chief hope would be that the gains outweigh the losses.

Planned program for interethnic problems

Thinking, experience, and research all hang together in emphasizing the need for some form of planned attack on the problems arising from hostile and rejecting attitudes among our ethnic groups. This emphasis is contrary to the "do nothing" policy so frequently found, or the policy of acting only when an emergency or a crisis arises. That constructive and specific efforts in this area can make a difference is indicated by several studies among college students (30). In these populations, including several hundred students, it was found that those who could recall having experienced in their school or religious

[2] This point is discussed in a more general way in Chapter 14.

training some positive influences in favor of minority groups, were less prejudiced than were those students who could not recall such influences from their school or church backgrounds.

Numerous other research studies, investigations, and experience reports — such as those by Allen (1), by Cummings (9), by Hayes and Conklin (15), and by Park (26) including data on the effects of specific kinds of teaching related to prejudice, efforts to resolve emotional problems in certain pupils, discussions of conflict situations, role playing, and interethnic contacts under favorable circumstances — all this research has shown that some progress can be made in building up more harmonious relationships among ethnic groups in school populations when teachers have appropriate attitudes and utilize appropriate methods.

Positive choosing and attitudes among ethnic groups

Data from pupil choices on sociometric measurements provide an important basis for assessing the extent of positive and negative feelings that exist among ethnic groups in our schools. On the whole, what do these studies show?

Holloway studied five classes in the upper elementary grades in a school in Dallas, Texas — each class being composed of both Anglo-American and Latin-American elements (16). He found that in all five classes there was a strong tendency for the pupils of English descent to receive a disproportionately large share of the choices. However, he also found that from the standpoint of the number of pupils who chose *each other* as "best friends" or as "other friends" on the scale that he used, the extent of choosing between Anglo-Americans and Latin-Americans amounted, on an average, to about 30 per cent of the students in each class.

Loomis conducted an investigation dealing with choosing among Anglo-American and Latin-American pupils in two high schools in New Mexico, one at Taos and the other at Las Cruces (19). When these students responded to a questionnaire that asked them to list the names of other students with whom they were pals both in school and out of school, it was discovered that about 20 per cent of the total names listed included individuals of opposite ethnic groupings.

Lundberg and Dickson report a study on the extent of choosing between five ethnic groups (consisting of those classified as non-Jewish white, Jewish, Japanese, Negro, and Chinese) in a high school in Seattle, Washington (20-21). When 1360 students in this school responded to a questionnaire asking them to list the names of other students whom they would select as a school leader, as a work associate, as a friend, and as a date, it was found that slightly over 40 per cent of the non-Jewish whites (who constituted the great majority of the student body) designated one or more members of the minority groups on one or more of the choice-criteria. In addition, all ethnic groups showed some out-group choosing.

Joan Criswell studied cleavage between Negro and non-Negro children in a population of approximately 2000 pupils in three elementary schools in New York City (8). In practically all of the classes included in this study there was some choosing between the Negro and the non-Negro pupils, but there was much variation among classrooms. Although there were several classes in which all white choices (within each sex group) were given to other whites, and although there were others in which the whites gave only two or three choices to Negroes, there were still others in which the extent of the Negro choices received amounted to as much as 20 or 30 per cent of the white choices available, and there were a few in which the white choices favored Negroes in excess of whites.

Other studies, such as those by Raths and Schweickart (28), by Radke and Sutherland (27), and by Taylor (34), have shown wide degrees of positive and negative attitudes existing between majority and minority group members. In the study by Radke and Sutherland among 257 children in a Midwestern town, some hostile and negative reactions toward minority groups (especially Jews and Negroes) were found in approximately one half of the pupils, and, as the authors conclude, there was little evidence of constructive teaching on intergroup relations from school, church, or community.

All these investigations show that even when no particular efforts are made to promote interethnic associations, as seemed to be the case in all of the above populations, there is, nevertheless, evidence of some favorable attitudes and interpersonal acceptance among ethnic groups in our public schools. These findings may be interpreted to mean that in most unselected populations in our culture, such as found in our public schools, there are some individuals (apparently about 20 to 25 per cent) who are sufficiently neutral or unprejudiced that they are willing to engage in some types of associations with at least a few persons of widely differing ethnic characteristics.

This interpretation is supported by findings with adult groups as reported by John Dean and Alex Rosen in their *Manual of Intergroup Relations*.[3] From their numerous contacts with groups of mixed ethnic origins in various kinds of community and social-service organizations, as well as from extensive studies, these authors stress the point that although prejudice in some people is deep-seated — since it is based on introjection of a rigid value system or on unconsciously motivated personality needs — in a good many other people such prejudice is fairly superficial and is, therefore, subject to some change under favorable associations and corrective communication. Furthermore, these latter people are inclined to "go along" with whatever seems to them to be the prevailing attitude toward a particular minority group in a particular situation. This means that if a school staff, together with a few students of prestige, can get a climate of opinion started in favor of interethnic tolerance and acceptance, there will be a considerable number of the less prejudiced students who will adopt this kind of social attitude.

Those who are not strongly biased on any issue are inclined to conform to majority expectancies or to follow persons of prestige. This statement is much more likely to be true when the "less prejudiced individuals" have some good interpersonal relationships with at least some of those who compose the majority group or with those who occupy prestige positions.[4]

Promoting interethnic associations

It seems certain that if a classroom is to be utilized for increasing favorable responses among ethnic groups, the teacher in this room must show by his attitude and conduct that he is genuinely interested in this objective. Obviously there are many ways of showing this kind of interest, and any teacher can develop approaches appropriate to his

[3] Published by The University of Chicago Press, 1955.

[4] Research bearing on this point is reported in studies by Marinho (23) and Newcomb (25) listed at the end of this chapter

situation. However, there are a few suggestions that are of general significance, and these will be briefly stated.

Especially in the early stages of interethnic association, a teacher should avoid all appearances of discrimination. One way to do this is to have all groupings, teams, or seating arrangements made on the basis of some impersonal criterion such as alphabetical order.

Role playing can often be used to help pupils of all ethnic groups to understand better how their verbal expressions and overt behavior affect members of other groups. It seems likely that one of the most effective ways of developing greater empathy in any child for members of a group different from his own is to have him try to think, feel, and act like a member of this other group in some representative interethnic conflict situations.

Teachers should wield their influence to eliminate the use of such terms as "nigger" and "dago," but at the same time should also discourage the use of patronizing, sentimental, or idealized expressions such as "Negroes are wonderful people," "The Jews have such marvelous intellectual ability," or "Negroes have a wonderful ability to dance and sing." People who hold unrealistic attitudes toward minority group members are certain to become disillusioned when they have contacts within these groups, and are likely then to develop negative attitudes.[5]

Likewise teachers should avoid frequent references to any particular ethnic group by name such as "the Negro pupils" or the "Latin-American pupils." Instead, each child should be called by his name. Teachers should help all pupils to respond to children of all ethnic origins, not as members of a particular subgroup, but as *distinct individuals*. This objective will be promoted by the teacher's treating members of minority groups *just like any other pupils* and not in any special way, either favorably or unfavorably; i.e., not too cordially or too coolly.

When an interethnic conflict situation arises, such as "name-calling," it is probably best for the teacher to deal with this incident in the presence of other pupils "on the spot" rather than privately at a later time — otherwise it may appear to all pupils that this kind of behavior is not taboo. Speaking on this point Dean and Rosen say:

[5] Dean and Rosen, *op. cit.*, p. 51.

"An important thing about a favorable intergroup-relations atmosphere is that it is not private. A good atmosphere requires public recognition, and the opportunities that friction incidents provide to reaffirm the prevailing policy and practices should not be missed." (p. 102.)

Teachers should be sensitive to the fact that a few children of minority groups are motivated to overcompensate for the discriminations against them (both real and imagined) by a strong drive to be superior to all other pupils in academic achievements. When such a child is discovered the teacher should not disparage his intellectual aspirations but, rather, should set up some social arrangements whereby he is induced to utilize his knowledge and talents in cooperative efforts with his fellow pupils.

In class discussions, and in talks with individuals, teachers should try to link up tolerance with the "American Creed." This creed has been defined as follows by Ralph Bunche: "Every man in the street, white, black, red, or yellow, knows that this is the 'land of the free,' the 'land of opportunity,' the 'cradle of liberty,' the 'home of democracy,' that the American flag symbolizes the 'equality of all men,' and guarantees to all 'the protection of life, liberty, and property,' freedom of speech, freedom of religion and racial tolerance."[6]

Whatever efforts are made to reduce intolerance and prejudice with American, democratic, and religious ideals, there should be no attempts in the schools to get children to sign a pledge, make a promise, or register a vote in reference to attitudes or actions toward another ethnic group. Instead, dependence should be placed on the gradual development of favorable attitudes on a purely spontaneous and voluntary basis.

Finally, teachers can help build up favorable interethnic attitudes by arranging for their pupils to carry on correspondence and to exchange art and written productions with children in foreign countries. Teachers who are interested in these projects, as well as in student exchanges, can obtain information on addresses of agencies to contact for such purposes by writing to UNESCO.[7]

---

[6] *Ibid.*, pp. 2-3.

[7] Unesco Publication Center, United Nations Building, 801 Third Avenue, New York 22, New York.

PROMOTING INTERETHNIC RELATIONS

The suggestions presented below are of a more general nature than those just given in the preceding section, and they apply to religious as well as to interethnic relations.

1. Try to bring individuals of diverse ethnic origins together in total-school situations, as well as in the classroom, *who are as much alike as possible in all respects except in their ethnic characteristics.* This means that such individuals who are brought together in committees or in any form of interacting group activity (especially when such efforts are first made) should be approximately similar in intellectual level, social class background, and personal behavior codes. Such similarities will help decrease sources of friction and will also help increase the probabilities that all representatives of each ethnic group will be able to make an acceptable contribution to each social situation they are in. Mixing individuals of different religious and ethnic backgrounds who are equal in social and economic status, and in personal abilities, is one of the most effective ways to help break down unfavorable stereotypes which members of one group may hold toward those of another group.

This latter statement is supported by evidence from several studies by Allport (3), MacKenzie (22), and Rosenblith (30). In each of these investigations most of the young adults who were used as subjects stated on questionnaire forms that they held more favorable attitudes toward certain minority-group members, particularly Negroes and Jews, after participating with them in some equal-status contacts, i.e., after associating with minority-group members who were equal to themselves in such important characteristics as intelligence, educational level, abilities appropriate to certain situations, and behavior codes.

It is not likely, however, that favorable results will come about even from these kinds of contacts unless the members of the various ethnic groups who are brought together participate with each other in many kinds of cooperative or mutually shared activities, as opposed to simply being in the same room together or engaging only in individualistic endeavors. This point may be applied to the practices in some schools of always having minority-group members demonstrate native dances, customs, etc., on programs. Although there is a place for this type of intergroup education, it is much more important that all ethnic groups participate together in putting on dances, song festivals, dramatizations, etc., than for the various groups to perform separately.

2. Especially during the first attempts to integrate two or more ethnic groups, *try to utilize only the "less demanding" kinds of social situations.* By "less demanding" is meant those which involve the least degree of interpersonal rapport and intimacy. Probably the kind of group which best meets this criterion is a one-sex work group, followed in turn by a one-sex recreational group (as in baseball, volley ball, basketball, etc.), and this is probably followed in turn by a one-sex gang or clique that engages in work, recreational, and social activities. Next in order, according to the above criterion, is probably a two-sex work group, followed by a two-sex recreational pursuit such as classroom games and physical education activities. Finally, it seems certain that the kind of groups which are "most demanding" are those which are of a distinctly social nature, involve both sexes, are held indoors, involve some form of physical contact (as in dancing), and are restricted in numbers so that each person is noticeable and is expected to be an active participant in whatever goes on.

This listing of groups in order of least or most demanding is based on observation and experience rather than on scientific evidence. It would be very desirable to have some research data bearing on the kinds of group situations which are most promising for interethnic associations within the jurisdiction of schools. Undoubtedly there are local circumstances, and particular social-psychological conditions which would often prove to be more crucial than the general listings given above.

3. *Utilize numerous resources to emphasize the contributions of all religious and ethnic groups to our American civilization.* It seems certain that one of the important factors accounting for the development of positive attitudes among different religious and ethnic groups is the presence of a large "common ground" composed of similar standards, values, and ideals. This "common ground" makes for mutual respect and trust and prepares the way for interpersonal rela-

tionships among some members of these diverse groups. In order to increase the awareness of this cultural identity, teachers need to utilize numerous resources to emphasize the distinct contributions to our American way of life that have been made by our Protestant churches, by our Jews, by our Catholics, and also by all of the various ethnic populations in our country. The principal resources used for this purpose consist of stories, factual accounts, pictures, films, and dramatizations. Many excellent materials are available for this type of work in schools.[8]

4. *Work with community agencies that are trying to increase religious and ethnic tolerance.* It seems evident from case reports that the attitudes which children in school hold toward pupils of different religious and ethnic origins are often close reflections of the attitudes held by their parents and other influential adults. Assuming this to be true, it naturally follows that all school personnel should in every way possible work with any community organization that is trying to reduce religious and ethnic barriers. Sometimes class or school programs consisting of speeches, music, dances, and dramatizations can be arranged, in which community adults of different religious and ethnic backgrounds participate. This kind of mutual collaboration in a school setting on the part of respected adults presumably has some effect in influencing children and high school students to do likewise with their peers who are of different faiths and of different nationalities and skin colors.

5. *Teach all children that a large part of their acceptance and of their success in life depends upon their personal qualities irrespective of religious or ethnic discriminations.* This must be done in order to help the members of minority groups understand that they have a large responsibility in helping to remove the unfair barriers that are placed against them. Each minority-group member who wishes to be better accepted by majority-group members needs to see that he should act in such ways as to disprove the validity of the stereotypes held against him. He must believe that if he consistently acts contrary to the unfavorable picture which others have of him, because of his particular group affiliation, that many who know him will come to regard him in terms of his individual qualities and not

[8] See sources of materials at end of chapter.

simply in terms of a group prejudice. It is especially important, as Zawadzki (36) has well pointed out, that minority-group members be warned against allowing prejudices against them to blind them to obvious defects in their own personal behavior — defects that would almost certainly cause them to be rejected irrespective of the existence of any prejudice.

6. *Set an example of tolerant and accepting attitudes toward pupils of all kinds of religious and ethnic origins.* Obviously none of the foregoing suggestions can be effectively carried out unless classroom teachers have attitudes of genuine tolerance for religious and ethnic differences, and can help by their example to develop a climate of feeling in their classes favorable to allowing every pupil to prove his worth without having to combat the barriers of discriminations.

7. *Set up some procedures and organizations for dealing with interreligious and interethnic conflicts.* In those school situations in which conflicts among religious or ethnic groups are likely to occur, it is most important that some form of social machinery be set up for anticipating such conflicts and for dealing with them when overt hostile acts take place. There is no single type of procedure or organization that is always better than any other, but it is essential that whatever is set up include a heavy representation of elected students from all the various factions likely to be involved in conflicts. This elected group of students, together with a few faculty members, should serve as a clearing center for reports and suggestions coming from classes, from homerooms, or from individuals. When this type of social machinery works effectively it frequently "nips difficulties in the bud" before they get out of hand. Also this "Good Neighbor" organization, or whatever it may be called, can instigate discussions and role-playing episodes in classes, homerooms, and assemblies — as a means of promoting better understanding between majority-minority groups and of dealing with specific problems.

REFERENCES

1. Allen, D. T., "Action Research with Children of Different Nationalities," *Psychological Approaches to Intergroup and International Understanding*, ed. by G. M. Gilbert. Austin, Texas: University of Texas, Hogg Foundation for Mental Hygiene, 1956, pp. 19-23.

2. Allport, G. W., "Prejudice: A Problem in Psychological and Social Causation," *The Journal of Social Issues, Supplement Series,* No. 4, 26, 1950.
3. ———, "Techniques for Reducing Group Prejudice," Ch. XXIV, *Forms and Techniques of Altruistic and Spiritual Growth,* ed. P. A. Sorokin. Boston: Beacon Press, 1954.
4. Atkinson, G., "Sociogram as an Instrument in Social Studies: Teaching and Evaluation," *Elementary School Journal,* 50, 1949, 74-85.
5. Bettelheim, B. and K. Lewin, *Securing Our Children Against Prejudice.* Published by the American Jewish Committee, 386 Fourth Ave., New York, p. 31.
6. Bonney, Merl E., "A Study of Friendship Choices in College in Relation to Church Affiliation, In-Church Preferences, Family Size, and Length of Enrollment in College," *The Journal of Social Psychology,* 29, 1949, 153-166.
7. Caves, J. W., "A Study to Show the Relations of Peer Acceptance and Teacher Ratings with Sunday School Attendance and Church Affiliation," Unpublished M.A. thesis, North Texas State College, Denton, Texas, 1948.
8. Criswell, J. H., "Racial Cleavage in Negro-White Groups," *Sociometry,* 1, 1937-38, 81-89.
9. Cummings, H. H. (ed.), *Improving Human Relations.* Washington, D.C.: National Council for Social Studies of the National Education Association, 1949.
10. Doob, L. W., *Social Psychology,* Ch. XII. New York: Henry Holt Company, 1952.
11. Grossack, M. M., "Attitudes Towards Desegregation of Southern White and Negro Children," *The Journal of Social Psychology,* 46, 1957, 299-306.
12. Hager, D. J., "Social and Psychological Factors in Integration," *The Journal of Educational Sociology,* 31, 1957, 57-63.
13. Harris, A. and G. Watson, "Are Jewish or Gentile Children More Clannish?," *The Journal of Social Psychology,* 24, 1946, 71-76.
14. Hartshorne, H. and M. A. May, *Studies in Deceit,* Character Education Inquiry of Teachers College, Columbia University. New York: The Macmillan Company, 1928.
15. Hayes, Margaret L. and Mary E. Conklin, "Intergroup Attitudes and Experimental Change," *Journal of Experimental Education,* 22-23, 1954-55, 19-36.
16. Holloway, H., "A Sociometric Study of Peer Acceptance Between Mixed Groups of Latin- and Anglo-American School Children," Unpublished M.A. thesis, North Texas State College Library, Denton, Texas, No. 1576, 1960.

17. Kupferer, Harriet J., "An Evaluation of the Integration Potential of a Physical Education Program," *Journal of Educational Sociology,* 28, 1954-55, 89-96.

18. Kvaraceus, W. C., "Delinquent Behavior and Church Attendance," *Sociology and Social Research,* 28, 1943-44, 284-89.

19. Loomis, C. P., "Ethnic Cleavages in the Southwest as Reflected in Two High Schools," *Sociometry,* 6, 1943, 7-26.

20. Lundberg, G. A. and L. Dickson, "Inter-Ethnic Relations in a High School Population," *American Journal of Sociology,* 58, 1952, 1-10.

21. ——— and Lenore Dickson, "Selective Association Among Ethnic Groups in a High School Population," *American Sociological Review,* 17, 1952, 23-35.

22. MacKenzie, B. K., "The Importance of Contact in Determining Attitudes Toward Negroes," *Journal of Abnormal and Social Psychology,* 43, 1948, 417-441.

23. Marinho, Heloisa, "Social Influence in the Formation of Enduring Preferences," *Journal of Abnormal and Social Psychology,* 37, 1942, 448-468.

24. Marrow, A. J., *Living without Hate.* New York: Harper and Brothers, 1951.

25. Newcomb, T. M., *Personality and Social Change.* New York: Henry Holt & Co., Inc., 1943.

26. Park, L., "Prejudice and Unmet Emotional Needs," *Journal of Educational Sociology,* 24, 1951, 407-413.

27. Radke, Marian and J. Sutherland, "Children's Conceptions and Attitudes about Minority and Majority American Groups," *Journal of Educational Psychology,* 40, 1949, 449-468.

28. Raths, L. and E. F. Schweickart, "Social Acceptance within Interracial School Groups," *Educational Research Bulletin,* 25, 1946, 85-90.

29. Reilly, Jean Waid and Francis P. Robinson, "Studies of Popularity in College: I. Can Popularity of Freshmen be Predicted?," *Educational and Psychological Measurement,* 7, 1947, 67-73.

30. Rosenblith, Judy F., "A Replication of 'Some Roots of Prejudice,'" *Journal of Abnormal and Social Psychology,* 44, 1949, 470-489.

31. Saenger, G. and H. M. Shulman, "Some Factors Determining Intercultural Behavior and Attitudes of Members of Different Ethnic Groups in Mixed Neighborhoods," *Journal of Psychology,* 25, 1948, 365-380.

32. Stendler, C. B. and W. E. Martin, *Intergroup Education in Kindergarten-Primary Grades.* New York: The Macmillan Company, 1953.

33. Taba, H., E. H. Brady, and J. T. Robinson, *Inter-Group Education in Public Schools.* Washington, D.C.: American Council on Education, 1952.

34. Taylor, Travis, "Intergroup Relations at Cosmopolitan Junior High," *Journal of Educational Sociology*, 21, 1947-48, 220-225.
35. Tumin, Melvin M., "Imaginary vs. Real Children: Some Southern Views on Desegregation," *School and Society*, 86, 1958, 357-360.
36. Zawadzki, Bohdan, "Limitations of Scapegoat Theory of Prejudice," *Journal of Abnormal and Social Psychology*, 43, 1948, 127-140.

MATERIALS FOR INTERGROUP EDUCATION

1. Grambs, Jean D., *Group Processes in Inter-Group Education.* The National Conference of Christians and Jews, 381 Fourth Ave., New York 16, N. Y., 82.
2. Lesser, S. D., "Annotated Bibliographies on Human Relations," Program Service of the Anti-Defamation League of B'nai B'rith, 212 Fifth Avenue, New York 10.
3. Shapiro, Leo, "Promising Practices in Intergroup Education: An Audio-Visual Guide," *Social Education,* 15, 1951, 379-381.

QUESTIONS AND EXERCISES

1. How does the evidence presented in this chapter on the lack of discrimination among our major religious groups, according to the measurements used, help to reinforce the importance of religious tolerance?
2. Stimulate a class discussion on the significance of the fact that the breaking-down of interethnic barriers seems to be largely a matter of interpersonal acceptance between particular individuals rather than between groups as such.
3. Do you have a clear distinction between prejudice and preference? Cite examples from your own experience with people of different ethnic groupings to illustrate the difference between these two kinds of responses.
4. How do the data, summarized in this chapter, bearing on interethnic acceptance, support the individual-to-individual basis of reducing psychological barriers between people?
5. Report to the class some of the best school practices you have observed, or know about, in regard to promoting harmonious relationships among ethnic groups. What seemed to account for these favorable situations?

6. Ask a school official from a school having widely varying ethnic populations to come to your class and present an account of how he and his staff have dealt with the problems encountered.
7. What responsibilities can school officials help minority-group members to assume as their contribution to successful mixing with majority-group members?
8. How do you evaluate the material presented in this chapter on "less demanding" social situations? Can you think of circumstances under which the sequence given in this account would probably not be valid?
9. Do you know of a school that has some social machinery for dealing with interethnic difficulties before they become serious? If so, make a report to the class on how this plan has operated.

SELECTED FILMS

Picture in Your Mind. 16 minutes. Presents background of growth of prejudice, and emphasizes need to examine one's mind for distorted pictures of ethnic groups.

Americans All. 16 minutes. Portrays racial and religious tensions in our country and shows ways for community action to reduce intolerance.

Race and Ethnic Groups. 15 minutes. Analyzes common notions about differences between ethnic groups.

The High Wall. 32 minutes. Describes outbreak of teen-age gang, and explores the roots of prejudice in the home, in feelings of inadequacy and insecurity.

Bill Brought Them. A story of how children can help a neighborhood to overcome prejudice.

TEACHER ADJUSTMENTS 6

17

MENTAL HEALTH AND THE

THE INFLUENCE of a teacher's personality upon pupils has been a topic of discussion whenever and wherever formal education has been under serious consideration, although the importance attached to this influence on the educative process has varied widely with time and place. The oft-quoted statement about a good education consisting of "Mark Hopkins on one end of the log and a student on the other" expresses belief in the critical importance of interpersonal contacts with a stimulating individual as a necessary basis for intellectual growth. No doubt most of the readers

TEACHER'S PERSONALITY

of this book will testify that their lives have been affected in some significant way by at least a few teachers who were more than simply instructors or purveyors of academic content.

Does it follow, however, that the most effective and inspiring teachers are characterized by good mental health, as this term has been defined in this book? If the positive mental health goals presented in Chapters 6 through 10 are taken as criteria, there is not a reliable answer to this question, since these trait-syndromes as such have not been correlated with measures of teaching effectiveness. As a matter of fact, it has proven to be very difficult to obtain scientific evidence bearing on relationships between the mental health of teachers and their teaching effectiveness, regardless of how this effectiveness is defined. In a recent survey of this problem, Eva Goodenough states that although expert opinion has consistently emphasized the importance of the teacher's personality as a factor in teaching success, "most studies which have measured changes in pupil behavior as a criterion have found little relationship between success and measures of teacher personality" (12). Goodenough believes that the chief explanation for these negative findings lies in the inadequacies of measurements, both of pupil behavior changes and of teacher personality. In a journal article, Barr has pointed out numerous unsolved difficulties in our present efforts to obtain valid measurements of teaching success (4).

Several studies conducted by Harold H. Anderson and his associates bear on the question under consideration, since these studies deal directly with the influence of teacher behavior on pupil behavior (2-3). The focus of these investigations is on the extent to which various degrees of dominative and various degrees of integrative behavior on the part of teachers are reflected in the behavior of pupils. On the whole, the evidence from these studies in elementary school classes is consistent in showing that "behavior is circular," i.e., dominative behavior on the part of a teacher tends to arouse similar behavior among pupils, and likewise, integrative or "working together" type of behavior tends to produce corresponding behavior among pupils. The latter statement is especially true in regard to spontaneous and mutually supporting social interactions. These results persisted over a period of two years with the same teachers.

Another frequently quoted study that has a bearing on the present topic is one reported by Lewin, Lippitt, and White in which the effects of different kinds of leadership on a small group of boys were measured (16). The kinds of leadership were dominative, democratic, and laissez-faire. Under each of these conditions the behavior of the boys was a direct reflection of the kind of leadership exercised. When dominative leadership was deliberately used there were, for example, thirty times as many instances of hostility among the boys as under democratic leadership. Under the laissez-faire type of leadership, or more aptly stated, lack of leadership, there was a marked increase in irresponsible behavior, in comparison with the democratic situation. Although both of these series of studies are clear in showing that the quality of behavior that a teacher shows toward his pupils is very likely to be reflected in their interpersonal behavior, it is important to note that all the above evidence bears only on behavior within a particular setting. We cannot assume that whatever responses are acquired under any particular teacher will be transferred to other situations or will produce permanent changes in pupils' personalities. In his comprehensive survey of group processes, Bonner makes the statement that "There is no dependable evidence in support of the belief that learnings and other behaviors are transferred from one group situation to another." (6 — p. 138.)

In regard to the adverse effects of a very maladjusted teacher on pupils' personalities, it is well to remember that the influence of such a teacher is likely to be superficial and temporary unless there is a considerable degree of rapport and identification between the teacher and the pupils. Since these conditions generally do not exist in regard to a very maladjusted teacher, it seems quite probable that the great majority of pupils simply erect psychological defenses against the influence of such a teacher. They may "brush off" whatever attacks he makes upon them, ridicule him among their classmates, and try to make the best of a bad situation until they can be graduated out of it. In writing on this topic from his extensive investigations of teachers' personality problems, Symonds says that although it is generally believed that teachers with serious emotional problems have adverse effects on pupils, "there is no conclusive evidence that the slightly maladjusted person cannot be a competent teacher," and that some neurotic teachers are nevertheless very successful (25-26). However, Symonds further states that most of the very ineffective teachers whom he has studied were emotionally disturbed, and characteristically projected hostility onto their pupils and their colleagues.

TEACHERS' PROBLEMS

It is well-known that all occupational groups contain some members who are handicapped by various forms of personal and social maladjustments. This is true of the high-level professions such as medicine, law, and the ministry, as well as those of lesser prestige. Shaffer and Shoben quote studies on industrial and business employees in both England and the United States which show that between 20 and 25 per cent of these workers were characterized by psychoneurotic disturbances (22 — pp. 567-568).

Undoubtedly there are many emotional and personality problems that are similar among the members of all occupational categories, since so many of these problems arise from early childhood experiences and parent-child relationships, irrespective of occupational levels. In addition to these fairly common or universal problems, the members of each occupational grouping also experience certain problems characteristic of their grouping, due to the nature of their work and to the special roles expected of them. Only the latter type of problems will be considered in this discussion.

Numerous studies have been made to determine what are the most typical sources of personal and social frustrations within the teaching profession. The lists that have resulted from these various studies have varied according to the samplings utilized and the methods of investigation. The most typical kinds of problems resulting from these investigations will be considered here.

Unconsciously motivated satisfactions

In an article describing personality problems of teachers, based on an intensive analysis of fifty autobiographies of women teachers, Symonds states that many teachers find in teaching satisfactions of needs other than those of financial return or of professional achievement (25). Most of these are unconsciously motivated. Examples of teachers with such needs are found in those who have strong inferiority feelings and who are attracted to teaching because they can work with children who must, of necessity, be inferior to themselves. According to Symonds, most of these same teachers also have strong feelings of deference toward those in positions of authority, and therefore feel secure in being a cog in a large wheel operated by those at the top of the administrative hierarchy. Other teachers, according to Symonds, need to be aggressive and dominant as a compensation for what they have suffered at the hands of others; and they see in teaching socially approved opportunities for expressing aggressive and sadistic trends which would otherwise have to be repressed.

Teachers who have repressed personalities find in teaching a comfortable niche because they are leading the kind of life expected of them in some communities. They are well adapted for filling the role of personifying the virtues that the average citizen professes to believe in but frequently does not incorporate into his own life. In this role the teachers can "be themselves" and at the same time satisfy the need of Mr. Average Citizen to have available some public figures who exemplify the kind of virtues that he believes children and youth should absorb as a foundation for their character development.

In addition to the frequently mentioned point about teaching affording to unmarried women sublimated satisfactions to compensate for lack of heterosexual love and for children of their own, Symonds makes the point that teachers who are characterized by strong repressions are also likely to have guilt feelings as a result of these repressions — because they have feelings of defeat and ineffectiveness as persons. These guilt feelings demand some kind of punishment, which in lieu of any form of external punishment generally eventuates in some form of self-punishment, such as working unnecessarily long hours at tedious tasks, putting up with unfavorable working conditions that could be changed, and leading restricted and self-denying lives.

Symonds states that a teacher can satisfy one or more of the above needs and still be a good teacher, provided a particular need does not become extreme or pathological (25). In fact he insists that teaching should meet some psychological needs in a teacher; otherwise teaching would be extrinsic to the teacher as an individual. However, he feels that it is very important for the professional growth of teachers that they become aware of the kind of personal, and frequently unconscious, satisfactions that they derive from their teaching. Writing on this point he says:

> If teachers are blind to the fact that their work is catering to their own needs, they may not be aware of the extent to which they are prostituting the children for their own satisfactions. Teachers need to be aware of the extent to which their drive for success in their pupils is a reflection of their own desire for achievement; their dominance in the school situation caters to their need for security and helps them manage their feelings of inferiority; their eagerness to follow slavishly courses of study and textbooks is an expression of their own need to submit to authority instead of "cooperating" in the common enterprise of education as they believe they are doing; their aggression and tyranny in the classroom is the release of repressed tendencies which should have had direct outlet in other situations when the original frustrations occurred; their

> tenderness and affectionate feeling for their pupils is a sublimated expression of their own need for love objects; their exemplary moral lives are in reality the stunting and repressing of parts of their nature to which they do not dare give more open expression; and their self-sacrifice, instead of wholly having the unselfish meaning that is apparent, is a way of making up for the inferiority and deficiency they feel so keenly. To the extent that teachers can be helped to become aware of the extent to which teaching is satisfying their own needs, they will become freer, more vital, and more potent educational forces, for they will then dare to be natural. (25.)

From data now available it is not possible to know definitely to what extent teachers, as a group, are characterized by the kinds of problems which Symonds describes. Probably not a large proportion have these kinds of motivations to such an extent as to interfere seriously with their teaching effectiveness. However, we can be certain that some teachers have personality problems of sufficient severity as to require counseling, psychotherapy, or psychiatric treatment. It seems likely, too, that such services made available to teachers might actually result in greater benefits to pupils than if such services are rendered directly to the pupils. This point of view was expressed as far back as 1931 by Frances V. Mason after her study of the personalities and backgrounds of over 700 teachers who had been committed to mental hospitals from the New York City area (18). She said: "While behavior clinics for children are very valuable and necessary at the present time, it will be more worth-while to direct effort toward helping teachers to form wise mental habits themselves, so that they in turn may be guides to the young children in their care and thereby reduce the number of maladjusted teachers and pupils."

Of course, it would be desirable to have various kinds of therapeutic services available to both pupils and teachers, but it would seem to be a mistake to provide such services for pupils and none for teachers. Emphasis on the value of psychological and psychiatric services for the teachers has been expressed by numerous writers on mental health, including Bernard (5 — p. 401) and Shaffer and Shoben (22 — pp. 564-566).

Lack of prestige in the profession

This point has been listed in all discussions dealing with problems of teachers. In assessing its importance several considerations are pertinent. In the first place, a teacher who is convinced of the social value of good teaching, and enjoys his work, need not be much affected by attitudes toward his work held by a good many citizens. Although no one can be immune to public attitudes, a mature person can maintain his self-respect even if a lot of other people do not evaluate his efforts as he does. In the second place, there are nearly always some first-rate citizens and community leaders who have genuine respect and admiration for teachers, especially for those teachers who are competent and who have attractive personalities. This leads to the third consideration; namely, that every teacher should feel obligated to help raise the status of the teaching profession by doing high-level work and by being the kind of person who is contrary to the stereotypes of teachers frequently portrayed in jokes, stories, and motion pictures. Increased prestige is never won by directly clamoring for it, by complaints of not being treated right, by self-pity, and certainly not by simply submitting to a low-level social definition. Instead, increased prestige must be primarily earned; but there is also a place for direct efforts to re-educate people whose attitudes are believed to be based on false or inadequate evidence.

Stoddard is quoted in one report as stating that what the public wants is a teacher who is "inexpensive, maintains discipline, is submissive, and socially dull" (1). There is no way of knowing from present data just how accurate this statement is, but however accurately it reflects a true picture, each teacher can help to prove this picture wrong by his own level of competence and his own personal behavior. Furthermore, he can help re-educate Mr. Average Citizen through P.T.A. meetings, newspaper articles, conversations, etc., to see that the routinized teacher cannot stimulate children to the level of academic and personal growth of which they are capable. The more Mr. Average Citizen disparages teachers and thus helps to make the caricature of teachers a reality, the more he helps to cheat his own children out of their educational birthright.

Occasionally a teacher is found who is determined to break through what he considers to be a too rigid role for teachers; in so doing he adopts behavior patterns that arouse various mixtures of ridicule and contempt. He may wear peculiar clothes, go too long without a haircut, express bizarre opinions, and engage in numerous "odd-ball" antics. Although this is not always true, such behavior is frequently indulged in by individuals who are trying to prove how different they are and obviously want to impress others with their unconformity. Such lack of integrity does nothing for the individual teacher or for the teaching profession.

Fortunately the social role expected of teachers is much less restrictive now than it was a generation ago. Few teachers today are forced to sign contracts specifying where they will live and that they will not smoke, drink, or be found in certain public places, etc. This is especially true in the larger towns and cities. Both Bernard (5 — pp. 399-400) and Rogers (20 — Ch. 16), from their surveys of this topic, state that there are many indications of more liberal attitudes during the past thirty years toward teachers' personal and social behavior. A strong tendency has developed to trust teachers' judgments to behave in a manner befitting their community status. This kind of climate of opinion is certain to help promote greater respect for all teachers. Adequate information is not available to account accurately for this more permissive public attitude, but it seems likely that the factors most responsible are: the higher level of academic training of most teachers, the increase in number of married teachers, and, perhaps most important of all, the greatly increased demand for teachers since World War II, resulting in numerous efforts to obtain and hold teachers.

Tension and fatigue — overwork, overcrowded classes

Obviously the best solution to this problem is to reduce the number of demands made on teachers, especially those of a clerical nature, and to reduce the size of overly large classes. The latter is particularly stressed in a National Education Association Research Bulletin dealing with the judgments of over 4000 teachers concerning the causes of behavior problems in schools (31). The authors of this bulletin state that one of the clearest relationships established in their entire study was between bigness of an educational unit and frequency of behavior problems, whether the "bigness" was of the community, the school, or the class. To emphasize the seriousness of this problem the authors state that approximately one half of the respondents in their study had over 30 pupils in their classes; about one-fourth had 35 or more; and 7 per cent had 40 or more pupils.

Regardless of how many duties or pupils a teacher is required to handle, he can help meet his problems by developing more relaxed and less self-demanding attitudes so that he has greater serenity in regard to dealing with changing situations and emergencies, and less disturbance over minor irregularities. Also, especially in the upper grades, teachers can utilize committees of pupils to take responsibility for many chores such as caring for play equipment, watering plants, checking in books, collecting lunch money, setting up audio-visual aids equipment, running errands, etc. All of these activities have some developmental values for children. Some teachers (but not all) who complain that they are greatly overworked are using the personality mechanism of projection, since they are projecting onto others what is really in themselves. "They demand too much of me" is in some teachers a defense against the realization of the truth that "I demand too much of me." It is well-known that chronic fatigue is much less likely to be due to actual amount of work done than it is to self-imposed tensions arising from unnecessary worries, feelings of insecurity or of hostility, and other maladaptive work adjustments.

Association with immature minds

Teachers who complain a lot about having to associate with immature minds are probably those who do not gain satisfaction from identification with professional objectives, who have very few or no adult friends, and who lack internal resources for self-enjoyment. Obviously, small children or even adolescents cannot adequately meet the personal-social needs of an adult, but the stimulation of pupils toward greater maturity should afford a high degree of satisfaction to any professionally minded person.

Work-satisfactions can never be completely sufficient for a mature person. In addition, he needs the companionship that is afforded through marriage or through close friendships, and preferably through both these sources. Every teacher, like every other adult whether married or unmarried, needs friends with whom to go places, with whom to participate in recreational pursuits, and with whom to share interests, joys, and sorrows. It is particularly important that those who are unmarried have at least one close friend in whom they can confide, since having someone to talk to about personal problems helps in avoiding repression of disturbing emotional content.

Satisfactions from work and from interpersonal relations with peers must also be supplemented by inner sources of satisfaction if a teacher is to avoid feelings of frustration and incompleteness. In discussing this point Jersild makes a distinction between *aloneness* and *loneliness* (13). He says that as people mature they frequently become increasingly aware of their aloneness in the sense of differing from others in tastes, interests, hopes, desires, and sentiments. However, this feeling of greater differentiation from others does not necessarily mean greater loneliness since the mature person is, in a sense, in good company, namely, his own good company; and particularly so "when he is free to draw upon his resources and has the courage to be himself" (p. 67). Writing on this point in regard to his interview studies of teachers, Jersild says:

> Who, then, is the loneliest one? It is the person who is not at home with his own thoughts, the one who is alien to his own feelings, the one who is a stranger to himself — he is the loneliest person of all. And a large proportion of the people who took part in this study seemed to realize this fact: that loneliness denotes not simply a lack in relations with others but also, perhaps primarily, a lack within oneself. They did not ask merely that a friend should come and relieve their solitude or that gay companions should divert them from their loneliness. They asked for help in understanding themselves. (13 — p. 75.)

Inadequate incomes

No discussion of teachers' problems would be complete without mentioning inadequate salaries. Although the majority of teachers have a high degree of security of employment, most of them suffer from being deprived of numerous benefits that money can buy. Teachers who lack sufficient funds to pay doctors' bills and other expenses are in some cases too worried to have good mental health, and in other cases forced to take remunerative employment outside of teaching duties. Although some teachers are apparently able to engage in such supplementary employment and still maintain healthy attitudes, such a situation has obvious handicaps for an individual's personal and professional life.

According to a research bulletin issued in 1958 by the National Education Association, the *median* starting salary per year for teachers with a B.A. degree in cities of over 100,000 population was $4000 (32). The corresponding figure for maximum salary was $6,250. In these same cities the *median* of the minimum salaries for teachers with M.A. degrees was $4200, while the *median* of the maximum salaries was approximately $6700.[1]

The above-mentioned research bulletin also states that the top salaries for teachers with the maximum preparation in training and experience, in cities of 100,000 population or more, varies from a little less than $6000 to a little over $9000 per year, with a median of $7100. As the authors of the Bulletin say: "Although relatively high as salaries for teachers, the foregoing amounts, particularly the maximum salaries for long experience and high levels of preparation, would seem low as ultimate salary expectations to professional workers in fields other than education." (32.)

From the standpoint of mental hygiene objectives it is just as necessary to raise the ceiling of salary expectations as an incentive and reward for the very competent, as it is to raise the minimum salaries above the poverty line. National, state, and local organizations of teachers are working toward these ends.

PERSONAL QUALITIES & TEACHING SUCCESS

In considering the personal qualities of teachers in relation to their teaching success, the first point to make clear is that there is no one pattern of traits which is necessary to successful teaching. Teaching involves complex and varied activities and varies a great deal according to age-level of pupils, particular subject-matter areas, kind of

[1] The national average salary paid to all teachers in all public schools of all sizes in the United States (including Alaska) in 1958 was $4775. Quoted in *The Texas Outlook,* Vol. 43, 1959, p. 3.

results desired by an administration or a community, and the social class level of the pupils. Barr has made the point that teaching effectiveness is not simply *in* the teacher but is always a relationship between what the teacher has to offer and a complex of conditions within the teaching situation.

However, it would indeed be surprising if some kinds of teacher qualities were not found to be more generally appreciated than others. Numerous studies have shown this to be true. One of these, reported by Witty, is representative of many other similar investigations, is based on a large number of pupil responses, and covers grades from the second through the twelfth (30). From an analysis of the 12,000 letters written by children on the topic "The Teacher Who Has Helped Me Most," Witty presents the following kinds of teacher-behavior which were most frequently mentioned in the pupils' letters. A few pupils' comments are also given.

Cooperative, democratic attitude. "She believes everybody can do the work." "She approaches us as if she considers us intelligent." "She doesn't holler at you."

Kindness, patience, consideration. "She is kind, and she doesn't make a monkey out of you before everybody." "She takes a great deal of interest in each child, his triumphs, his failures, his joys, and his sorrows."

Wide interests. "He uses other books than textbooks and he takes us on trips." "Miss X is a rare person, a well-rounded individual, with many facets to her personality."

General appearance, pleasing manner. "She is always dressed neatly and attractively, and she sets an example for us." "She never looks or acts sleepy. There is a vitality about her that transfers to us."

Fairness and impartiality. "She likes every one of us. You can tell it not by what she says but by what she does." "She gives you exactly what you deserve." "She lets us feel we are something worth teaching."

Sense of humor. "We work hard but we have fun, too." "I think Miss X likes to teach; she makes everyone laugh sometime during the day." "She encouraged us to laugh *with* each other, never *at* each other."

Good disposition, consistent behavior. "She is always the same."

"She has a smiling face, a kind manner, and a pleasing voice — she is a human being and not a nagging, driving bunch of nerves." "Miss X is quiet, calm and patient. Though some of her pupils aren't as bright as others, she is always willing to wait and help them."

Interest in pupils' problems. "I shall never forget her because she has helped me over a period of self-consciousness, and my improvement is due to her making me feel at ease."

Flexibility. "When she found she was wrong she said so, and tried something else." "He lets us find out about many things. He helped us but we helped him too. That's why I like science."

Use of recognition and praise. "She made me know I could do the work." "She praised you when you did well." "You just want to do your best for her, because she is so good to all of us."

Unusual proficiency in a subject. "She made me remember certain fine points and gave me a better understanding of it all." Many pupils praised their teachers for "knowing their subject matter and how to present it."

It is doubtful if anyone would question the value of these qualities for teachers; furthermore, all of them except the last, which bears exclusively on teaching, would help promote better interpersonal relationships between people in almost any situation. However, with the exception of acquisition of subject matter, it is very doubtful that those teachers who are most characterized by the above qualities are the ones who set out deliberately to acquire these qualities. Rather, it is more likely that these kinds of attitudes and behavior are the products of well-integrated and mature personalities. This emphasizes the importance of selection of teaching personnel; nevertheless, it is possible for teachers to make progress toward the attainment of more mature personalities. This kind of progress can be stimulated from numerous sources such as reading, personal experiences, college courses, supervisors, and from in-service training programs that are concentrated on the mental health of teachers.

Symonds (together with several co-authors) has written a series of articles in which he describes how teachers solve personal problems, and also how particular courses in mental hygiene have helped teachers in the personal-social area of their lives (23, 24, 28, 29). One of the main points stressed in these articles is that most teachers who are struggling with some kind of an emotional problem need to learn to take responsibility for directing their lives toward more positive satisfactions for *themselves,* as opposed to a rigid adherence to an unbalanced conception of a teacher's role, and in many instances as opposed to the subtle demands of relatives who have come to depend on the unmarried teacher-in-the-family for part of their support. Symonds gives examples of teachers who stated that they finally "took a stand" and "made a decision" to cut home-ties and do things they had always wanted to do, and, as a consequence, were more proud of themselves and more self-confident than they had ever been (24).

In reporting on the value of courses in mental hygiene for teachers, Symonds points out that such efforts may be entirely on an intellectual level and therefore not materially effect emotional adjustments (23). This condition has been borne out by studies using personality testing before and after such courses. However, in certain courses described by Symonds in which the teachers wrote autobiographies both before and after a mental hygiene course, it was possible to show from the follow-up assessment that some of the teachers could think more freely about themselves and could understand better some relationships between their personalities and their adjustments to teaching situations.

Another possible source of personality improvement for teachers is through counseling services by supervisors, principals, or other qualified staff personnel. In an article addressed primarily to supervisors, Symonds (27) stresses the need of supervisors' trying to help young and inexperienced teachers with their personal-social adjustment problems, as opposed to spending all their time on matters of teaching methods. In recent years much more emphasis had been given in training supervisors to acquire the skills and insights necessary to carry out the kind of aid which Symonds stresses.

A MENTAL HEALTH PROGRAM

In some of the larger school-systems in this country, comprehensive mental health programs for teachers have been conducted on an organized basis. A good example of such programs is found in Detroit (19). This program was given initial impetus in 1947 by grants from several foundations. These grants made possible the employment of specialized persons such as psychiatrists, psychologists, and social workers. This comprehensive program will be described here in considerable detail since other systems could utilize most, if not all, of the procedures and materials that have been developed throughout its operation.

The principal assumption of the staff directing the Detroit program was that the best over-all objective for a school is to create a total school environment that is conducive to the growth of mental health in all pupils, and that the most important single thing necessary to create such an environment is the improvement of teachers' understanding of mental health. To approach this latter objective, a series of weekly meetings were held during which lectures and panel discussions were presented by psychiatrists, psychologists, social workers, and educators. Small groupings were utilized for answering teachers' questions. Furthermore, considerable use was made of radio broadcasts, films, tape recordings, field trips, classroom visitations, teacher conferences, and role playing.[2]

After the psychiatrists had visited some classrooms they were most impressed, not with the need of teachers' trying to change deviate pupils, but with the need of teachers' trying to change themselves so that they could better tolerate deviate pupils. In their conferences with teachers the psychiatrists emphasized the importance of trying to understand one's own personality and of accepting oneself, as a requirement for further growth.

Other activities in the Detroit program included the presentation in faculty meetings and parent-teacher meetings of five mental health plays developed by the American Theatre Wing for The National Association for Mental Health. These plays are titled: *Scattered Showers, Fresh Variable Winds, High Pressure Areas, The Ins and Outs,* and *And You Never Know.* Finally, in the Detroit program much use was made of reading materials, particularly as a basis for group discussions, as well as for individual teacher reading. Some of the pamphlets and books found to be of most value were: *Teacher, Listen, the Children Speak* by James L. Hymes, *An Application to*

[2] Some of the films found to be of most value were: *Feelings of Depressions, Feelings of Hostility, Emotional Health,* and *This is Robert.*

Education of the Needs Theory by Louis Raths, *Self-Understanding — A First Step to Understanding Children* by W. C. Menninger, and *Fostering Mental Health in the Schools,* the 1950 Yearbook of the Association for Supervision and Curriculum Development.

Over a period of five years nearly 4000 teachers participated in various aspects of this program on a voluntary basis. What evidence was available on the carry-over value of this endeavor? The evidence consisted of questionnaire returns and various kinds of observational data. Six months after the completion of the above program over 2000 teachers filled out an unsigned questionnaire dealing with values received from this work. The replies showed that the great majority felt their relations with pupils had been improved. A few responses typical of many others were:

> I pay more attention to the quiet child.
> I don't make so many snap judgments.
> It sort of smoothed out some of my tensions.

Observational evidence consisted of reports by principals and other staff personnel indicating that at least some of the teachers who had participated in the mental health program were referring problem children earlier for psychological services, were sending fewer students to the principal's office, were reading more mental health literature, were working more effectively with parents, were more actively concerned with the extension of school and community mental health services, and showed evidence of greater self-respect.

ENJOYMENT OF THE WORK SITUATION

It seems certain that nothing is more important to the mental health of teachers than their enjoyment of their work. By "enjoyment of work" is meant that they find it stimulating on both a personal and a professional basis; they find in it the means for greater self-realization, for feelings of personal significance, and for respected status among their professional colleagues. A sense of joy in work will be found, however, only by those who have a genuine interest in teaching, who have achieved at least a fair degree of mastery of teaching skills and of subject matter, who are confident of their abilities in classroom management, and who have the maturity to realize that if they don't enjoy their work they are themselves the greatest losers. Although it is true that the pupils suffer somewhat under a bored, depressed, or hostile teacher, they will soon be relieved of his company; but the teacher has himself on his hands for the rest of his professional life.

In the case of a teacher who realizes that he is seriously lacking enjoyment from his work, is there anything he can do to try to develop greater work-satisfaction? One general suggestion is to utilize some or all of the methods of personality assessment described in Chapter 11, for the purpose of learning more about the pupils in a particular class. Learning more about the personality adjustments of pupils and more about their positive and negative feelings toward each other enriches a teacher's perception of these pupils so that they are seen as unique individuals, and not just as pupils. Such perceptions can lead to much more stimulating and rewarding reciprocal relationships between pupils and a teacher; as the teacher perceives the pupils primarily as human beings and only secondarily as learners, so in turn the pupils begin to perceive the teacher as primarily a human being and not simply as an instructor. Thus is created a situation that, if properly managed, can be high in interpersonal rapport and rich in human values. When these factors are present it is safe to say that a teacher will not be bored or depressed, and that his hostility, if he has any, will be turned into appreciation and friendship. Certainly there are rewarding human satisfactions to be had in working with children and youth; and in schools, it is the responsibility of the teacher, not the pupils, to create a situation in which such satisfactions can be realized. If the teacher does not do this everyone in the class loses; but it seems likely that the teacher will lose most, since even during the schoolday the pupils are able to enjoy many responses from each other, whereas the teacher has none except possibly when he can get away from his duties. The word "possibly" is used advisedly, since, although specific evidence is lacking, it seems likely that a teacher who is unable to establish mutually satisfying human relationships with his pupils would in many instances be likewise deficient with others on his own age-level. Thus the teacher who creates psychological barriers between himself and his pupils is caught in a trap from which only he can do what is necessary to escape.

The first step necessary to make this escape is the realization on his part that such barriers not only keep his pupils from enjoying their work, but also keep him from enjoying himself.

It seems likely, too, that many teachers who have created serious barriers between themselves and their pupils have done so because of an overidentification with task objectives, i.e., they are so concerned with covering subject matter or with inculcating particular skills that they crush out human values both for themselves and their pupils. Although serious dedication to one's task is highly laudable, this dedication need not be so narrowly conceived as actually to prevent the attainment of some of the most important objectives of a teaching situation. Probably most of the teachers who do this are motivated at least partly by unconsciously recognized needs to dominate others or to keep them at a safe psychological distance, as a means of protecting themselves against threats of personal inadequacy.

Whatever the motivations involved, such teachers need to learn through counseling or otherwise that teaching at its best is not simply a technical but also a human enterprise involving spontaneity, warm responses, enjoyment, and good interpersonal rapport.

One condition necessary for creating this kind of teaching situation is that the teacher not be worried for fear he will make mistakes, such as not knowing the answer to certain questions, not always doing the right thing in disciplinary situations, not always making completely fair evaluations of pupils' work, and not always pleasing a supervisor. Good teaching is a positive and creative achievement and is not simply the absence of mistakes. Anyone who is anxious about making mistakes cannot be spontaneous, cannot adapt himself quickly to changing situations, and cannot enjoy either his work or himself. Teachers, including those just beginning, need to learn that once they have a basic preparation for their work, it is better to launch into a teaching situation with confidence, good humor, and enthusiasm, and make some mistakes, than to enter into the same situation cautiously with a meticulously outlined procedure and make no mistakes. In the first instance, the teacher will be much more likely to establish rapport with his pupils, to respond in appropriate ways to the responses of the pupils, and to create an interactive process as a basis for learning. Furthermore, both teacher and pupils are likely to say they enjoyed that class. Supervisors who inspire fear in teachers and insist upon their following closely a prescribed procedure are helping to prevent high quality teaching and are also helping to thwart mental hygiene objectives in the classroom.

Conscientious and creative teachers will find enjoyment in their work only if what they do is meaningful to them. This means that they must be able to initiate and carry out some of their own ideas. They must feel free to bring in some subject matter that is not in the textbooks and to plan some activities that they believe will be valuable, and that they believe will be enjoyable to themselves and their pupils. Symonds has made the point that teaching should serve the needs of teachers as well as the needs of pupils and the demands of society (25). Too many teachers have been led to believe that if they are properly motivated they will be willing to sacrifice themselves for their pupils and for professional objectives. The introjection of this kind of an ideal leads to compulsive striving, perfectionistic tendencies, and guilt feelings due to wide discrepancies between actual and ideal selves. Although an ideal of professional service is certainly laudable, it should be built on self-realization, not contrary to it. Every teacher should be helped to realize that the most significant thing that he has to offer pupils is himself. When a teacher's self is withered under the influence of a repressive ideal, or under the coercive control of arbitrary restrictions, then he may still purvey knowledge or coach in a skill; but this is only a sham situation, and joy is absent for both teacher and learners.

A teacher who finds some meaningful goals in his work, and who pursues them with seriousness and enthusiasm, will sometimes meet with hostile responses from other staff members. He may be accused of setting too fast a pace, of disturbing the status quo, of being foolish or visionary, or of being a compulsive and rigid character who is more to be pitied than admired. A teacher who meets such hostility must face the question of whether he is to be inner- or outer-directed. If he genuinely believes in what he is doing as an important source of self-realization, both for himself and his pupils, then he should maintain his self-respect and integrity by continuing his course. Obviously, however, he should not play-up his endeavors nor make derogatory remarks about the work of other teachers. If need be, he can confine his associations to other teachers who have attitudes and values similar to his own; and if the situation becomes intolerable, he can move to another school where his talents are better appreciated.

It is important to emphasize, however, that if the kind of teacher just described is to meet the criteria of good mental health, he must have some strong objective interests in his work and he must genuinely enjoy what he is doing. If he meets these conditions he will not exploit pupils by having them do things that are of little value to them but are somehow useful to him, he will not stimulate pupils to become overly attached to him on a personal basis, and he will not play favorites in order to dominate some by kindness and dominate others by indifference and discrimination.

In other words, a mature form of work-enjoyment depends upon mature personality development. A teacher may say that he "loves his work," but this is not sufficient evidence that his teaching promotes the maximum growth of either himself or his pupils. He may be using his pupils and his work situation primarily to meet subjective, neurotic needs within himself, as pointed out in a preceding division of this chapter. What he does under the name of "good human relations" may consist largely of efforts to keep everybody happy on a superficial basis, ineffectual expressions of sympathy for pupils having difficulties, submitting to the whims of pupils regarding assignments and grades, and an overuse of wisecracks and humorous stories. Although a particular teacher may enjoy doing these things, the end result is not greater self-realization for either teacher or pupils. Instead, such results can be attained only when a teacher conceives of good human relations as consisting of reciprocated interactions that are friendly, cooperative, and mutually stimulating toward maximum growth potentials. All the suggestions offered throughout this book bear on the achievement of this objective.

ADMINISTRATIVE POLICIES AND TEACHERS' MENTAL HEALTH

Obviously the mental health of teachers is affected not simply by their personal lives or by their classroom situations, but also by administrative practices and policies. This includes a multitude of things, such as the uses made of standardized tests, the bases for promotion, retirement benefits, and incentives offered for professional growth. However, it is not within the province of this discussion to consider these factors. Instead, attention will be confined to principal-teacher relationships, since it is the principal that teachers most frequently contact.

From the standpoint of mental hygiene objectives it is important that a school principal maintain a considerable degree of personalized associations with his staff members, and especially so with at least a few of them with whom he feels the greatest personal compatibility. He needs to join in numerous informal conversational groups, participate with staff members in community activities and recreational pursuits, and visit in some of their homes — and in all of these associations he must do more listening than talking. Within the school setting these objectives are aided by having at least one faculty room in each building — a room equipped with easy chairs, a coffee pot, and soft drink and candy machines — in which both men and women can retire to chat and to have a few minutes of relaxation. The placing of chairs so that people sitting in them face each other, or the placing of chairs around small tables accommodating only four to six persons, tends to promote interpersonal communication.

These kinds of experiences are necessary, not only as sources of personal satisfactions for the principal and the teachers, but also as a means of providing the principal with a social basis for understanding his co-workers. If he is markedly deficient in being able to maintain such relationships he becomes an isolate in his own group. He is the last one to know what is going on; and since he is out of contact with his teachers, this void in his experiences may cause him, particularly if he has insecure feelings, to build up imaginary threats to his status.

An important asset for a principal, in all of his social as well as work relationships with teachers, is a sense of humor, and the skill to introduce humor at appropriate times and places. Exact data is lacking on just what is the contribution of humor to the establishment of interpersonal rapport in both social and work-type situations, but observation suggests that it does indeed lubricate the wheels of social interaction, and that it is one of the most effective means of pouring oil on troubled waters.

Probably more important than personal-social contacts to good relationships between a principal and his teachers is the establishment of such a high degree of mutual trust between them that the teachers feel free to express their feelings and to state their ideas in faculty meetings, conferences, and committees. Unless teachers can be freed from obvious and subtle threats to conform blindly to administrative edicts, there can be but little honest or effective communication between teachers and their principal. When such conditions exist they create psychological barriers that persistently work contrary to the best mental health of teachers, and no amount of superficial "good human relations" on a social basis can compensate for these barriers.

The importance of teachers' being given a responsible role in helping to determine school policies is emphasized in an N. E. A. research bulletin that summarizes the views of over 4,000 teachers on how schools could better deal with problem-behavior in classrooms (31). One of the findings reported in this bulletin is that those teachers who were in schools that allowed them a responsible voice in determining disciplinary policies had fewer difficulties in managing problem-behavior in their classrooms than did those who lacked such a voice. The authors of this bulletin stress the point that their survey shows the need for teachers, particularly those in large school-systems, to have more authority over pupils in their classes, and also the need of more teacher-administrator consultations on disciplinary policies in the total school setting.

Certainly one of the conditions for mutual trust between an administrator and his teachers is that the administrator allow the teachers considerable leeway to use their own judgment in regard to their personal conduct and their professional work. Serious deviations, when they occur, can be dealt with on an individual basis. This means that there should not be a multitude of rules and regulations to govern teachers' behavior, such as where to live, where not to go when off duty, when not to talk to other teachers in the halls, when to be in their rooms, order of procedure to follow in conducting a class, etc. Also, teachers should feel free to try out some new ways of doing things without threat of being dealt with severely if they make mistakes or if their efforts do not turn out well.

Use of praise

Whether noteworthy achievements are accomplished by individuals or by groups of individuals, the use of praise by the principal has implications for mental hygiene. Although there are certainly times when a particular teacher should be praised in a public meeting or in a written report, the major emphasis in these forms of communication should be centered on noteworthy achievements of committees, departments, teams, or other kinds of units. Interpersonal feuds are sometimes started among teachers when one of them is given more publicity or public praise than others, especially if this happens several times in one semester. Just as the highly publicized football star may be undermined by his teammates who refuse to block for him, so the teacher who is given the publicity spotlight too frequently or too dramatically may become isolated among other teachers. One way to avoid arousing this kind of jealousy is for the principal to praise a teacher privately. It seems likely that this needs to be done much more than it is. Although mature people do not lean heavily on praise from others, it is nevertheless true that an important aspect of mental health among any group of employees is the knowledge that their efforts are appreciated by their official superiors.

It would seem to be of particular importance that the principal give special recognition to those instances in which two or more teachers cooperate in some project such as a classroom unit, an assembly program, or a disciplinary problem. It may be assumed that such recognition would tend to build up a *we feeling*, and would put emphasis on mutual aid as contrasted with individual competition. It seems evident that a school faculty cannot be welded into a strong social unit unless there are a good many more rewards and satisfactions coming from reciprocal aid than from rivalry.

Use of criticism

In the interests of preserving a teacher's self-respect and of protecting his desire and need for status, he should never be criticized by his principal in the presence of other teachers or of pupils. When criticism is given in private the teacher should be asked to explain how certain conditions came about, rather than "bawled out"; and the emphasis should be on how did *we* fail, not simply on how did *you* fail.

Principal as a "trouble shooter"

Many situations that might result in some kind of failure or need for criticism can be avoided if the principal of a school is a good "trouble shooter," in the sense that the is able to discover where tensions, weaknesses, or conflicts are developing and has the necessary skills to reduce their severity or to resolve them completely. If he cannot do this, then little problems grow into big ones. Especially is this likely to be the case when interpersonal difficulties arise between teachers; small feuds are likely to grow into overt conflicts resulting in persistent back-stabbing, transfers to other buildings, or dismissals. One condition necessary before a principal can be effective in *facilitating* the work of his teachers in their respective classrooms or in their relations with each other, is that he not be so burdened with office routine that he has very little time to spend in contact with his teachers.

Preferred work assignments

It is doubtful whether any administrative act is of more value in laying the foundation for successful teacher achievement and harmonious relationships among staff members than that of giving each teacher the grade or subject assignments, the equipment, and co-curricular duties that he most prefers. This means that teachers' wishes, complaints, and suggestions must be given sincere and serious consideration. It means that when a teacher cannot have just what he wants he should be given a thorough explanation. It also means that when changes in customary procedures are made, an explanation of such changes should be communicated to all those affected, in advance of the changes.

Sometimes administrators say that they do "pay attention" to teachers' expressed desires, but as a matter of fact they may exert very little conscientious effort to do anything to solve the problems presented. One of the best indications of good relationships between a teaching staff and a principal is the statement from many of the teachers in regard to the principal: "He really tries hard to get you what you want." He is not likely to have this reputation unless he is "teacher-centered" as contrasted with "office-centered" or "board-of-education-centered." If he is "teacher-centered" he will inevitably be "pupil-centered," since good teaching is one of the surest ways of promoting the total welfare of children.

Committee appointments

One special way whereby a principal can try to give teachers preferred assignments is by making committee appointments of teachers who are congenial with each other. A study by Cooper emphasizes this point (10). He tells of an elementary school teaching staff that was asked to fill out a questionnaire, one item of which was: *If you were to serve on a committee to prepare a bulletin for the school, with which two persons in the school would you prefer to work?* The teachers registered their choices and these preferences were then checked against three appointments of instructional co-ordinators, which had previously been made by the principal of this school. This check-up revealed that the co-ordinator for the upper grades had received a high proportion of the choices, the one for the middle grades received only one choice, while the one for the lower grades received a fair proportion of the preferences.

The most significant aspect of this study was the discovery that progress in committee work on the different levels bore a close relationship to the proportion of choices received on the preference measurement. Definite, written proposals and specific changes in classroom practices had already been achieved in the upper grades under the well-liked co-ordinator; harmonious relationships existed among the lower-grade teachers and some progress had been made; but among the middle-grade teachers under the disliked co-ordinator little progress on the bulletin was evident and trouble was brewing.

The value of personally congenial committee members and chairmen should not be overemphasized. There is also a need to mix up the total faculty occasionally in work assignments and social events in order to give opportunities for new personal associations to arise.

Focus on mental hygiene objectives

More important than any particular administrative act or policy is the over-all attitude of administrators. It seems certain that the mental health of teachers, and their success in realizing mental health objectives with their pupils, is very much affected by whether or not there is an administrative focus on these objectives. If the teachers in a school know that their principal, vice-principal, and superintendent appreciate the value of total personality development of children, there is a favorable climate for doing the kind of things discussed in this book. If, on the other hand, an indifferent or negative attitude in official circles is sensed, then there is certain to be a withering of incentive on the part of many teachers for developing the kinds of sensitivities and skills necessary to accomplish the goals of mental health in our schools. As stated at the beginning of this volume, the attainment of these goals is not based primarily on teachers' introducing a lot of new things into their classrooms, but rather it is based on their developing the insights, procedures, and attitudes necessary for promoting in all children maximum growth toward self-realization, social effectiveness, and concern for others.

REFERENCES

1. Alilunas, L. J., "Needed Research in Teacher Mental Hygiene," *Journal of Educational Research,* 38, 1945, 656.
2. Anderson, H. H. and J. E. Brewer, "Studies of Teachers' Classroom Personalities," II: "Effects of Teacher's Dominative and Integrative Contacts on Children's Classroom Behavior," *Applied Psychology Monograph* No. 8, Stanford, California, Stanford University Press, June, 1946, 128.
3. ———, "Studies in Dominative and Socially Integrative Behavior," *American Journal of Orthopsychiatry,* 15, 1945, 133-139.
4. Barr, S. S., "Problems Associated with the Measurement and Prediction of Teacher Success," *Journal of Educational Research,* 51, 1957-1958, 695-699.
5. Bernard, H. W., *Mental Hygiene for Classroom Teachers.* New York: McGraw-Hill Book Company, Inc., 1952.
6. Bonner, H., *Group Dynamics.* New York: The Ronald Press, 1959.
7. Charles, D. C., "The Stereotype of the Teacher in American Literature," *Educational Forum,* 14, 1950, 299-305.
8. Clark, E. J., "The Relationship Between the Personality Traits of Elementary School Teachers and Their Evaluation of Objectionable Pupil Behavior," *Journal of Educational Research,* 45, 1951, 61-66.
9. ———, "Teacher Reactions Toward Objectionable Pupil Behavior," *Elementary School Journal,* 51, 1951, 446-449.
10. Cooper, D. H., "The Potentialities of Sociometry for School Administration," *Sociometry,* 10, 1947, 111-121.

11. Crowder, F., "Educational Strait Jackets," *Survey Graphic*, 36, 1947, 617-619.

12. Goodenough, Eva, "The Forced Choice Techniques As a Method of Discovering Effective Teacher Personality," *Journal of Educational Research*, 51, 1957, 25-31.

13. Jersild, A. T., "When Teachers Face Themselves," *Teacher's College Bureau of Publications*, Columbia University, 1955.

14. Kline, Frances F., "Satisfactions and Annoyances in Teaching," *Journal of Experimental Education*, 18, 1949, 77-89.

15. Kvaraceus, W. C., "Mental Health Hazards Facing Teachers," *Phi Delta Kappa*, 32, 1951, 349-350.

16. Lewin, K., R. Lippitt, and R. K. White, "Patterns of Aggressive Behavior in Experimentally Created 'Social Climates,'" *Journal of Social Psychology*, 10, 1939, 271-299.

17. Levin, H., "The Influence of Classroom Control on Kindergarten Children's Fantasy Aggression," *The Elementary School Journal*, 55, 1955, 462-466.

18. Mason, F. V., "A Study of Seven Hundred Maladjusted School Teachers," *Mental Hygiene*, 7, 1931, 576-599.

19. Rankin, P. T. and J. M. Dorsey, "The Detroit School Mental-Health Project," *Mental Hygiene*, 37, 1953, 228-248.

20. Rogers, Dorothy, *Mental Hygiene in Elementary Education*. Boston: Houghton Mifflin Company, 1957.

21. Shaffer, L. F., "Experimental Contributions to Mental Hygiene," *Review of Educational Research*, 19, 1949, 379-385.

22. ——— and E. J. Shoben, *The Psychology of Adjustment* (2nd Ed.). Boston: Houghton Mifflin Company, 1956.

23. Symonds, P. M., "Change in Self Attitudes Following a Course in Mental Hygiene," *Journal of Educational Research*, 35, 1942, 321-325.

24. ———, "How Teachers Solve Personal Problems," *Journal of Educational Research*, 38, 1945, 641-652.

25. ———, "Personality Adjustments of Women Teachers," *American Journal of Orthopsychiatry*, 11, 1941, 14-19.

26. ———, "Personality and the Teacher," *Journal of Educational Research*, 40, 1946-47, 652-661.

27. ———, "Supervision as Counseling," *Teachers College Record*, 43, 1941-42, 49-56.

28. ——— and Helen R. Haggerty, "The Therapeutic Value for Teachers of the Course in Mental Hygiene," *Journal of Educational Psychology*, 33, 1942, 561-583.

29. ——— and R. T. Ford, "Welfare of the Teacher," *Review of Educational Research*, 22, 1952, 206-211.

30. Witty, P., "An Analysis of the Personality Traits of the Effective Teacher," *Journal of Educational Research,* 40, 1946-47, 662-671.

31. ———, "Teacher Opinion on Pupil Behavior," *Research Bulletin of the National Education Association,* 1201 Sixteenth St. N.W., Washington, D. C., 34, 1955-56, 107.

32. ———, "1958-59 Salary Survey in Progress," *Research Bulletin of the National Education Association,* 1201 Sixteenth St. N.W., Washington, D. C., 36, 1958, 115-120.

QUESTIONS AND EXERCISES

1. Cite an example from your experience of how a teacher's attitude toward a class has had a marked effect on the way the students regarded this class and also on the quality of their learnings.
2. Stimulate a class discussion on the many variables involved in efforts to measure the effects of personality traits on teaching success.
3. Set up some criteria whereby you could judge whether or not personality maladjustments on the part of a teacher would seriously interfere with his teaching.
4. Give examples of teachers you have known to illustrate what "teaching does to teachers." In the case of teachers who fit the usual teacher-stereotype, do you believe that teaching moulded them the way they are, or that they were largely this kind of person before entering teaching?
5. Discuss the question of how teaching can serve the personality needs of teachers without playing too dominating a role.
6. Consider the implications for school policy of the theory presented in this chapter that the mental health of children is best promoted, not by concentrating on the children, but by concentrating on improvement of the mental health of teachers.
7. Consider relationships between adequate pay and the mental health of teachers. In the cases of our more maladjusted teachers do you think more pay would make any difference? Why or why not?

8. Point out contributions and limitations of a course in mental hygiene for teachers as a source of better personal-social adjustments.
9. Why is it not necessarily true that a teacher who says he "loves his work" is a really good teacher?
10. Study a local school system to see to what extent administrative policies in reference to teachers are promoting or interfering with mental health objectives.

SELECTED FILMS

Teacher Crisis. 17 minutes. Presents a clear and realistic picture of some of the major factors in our teacher shortage.

The Teacher. 17 minutes. Relates the story of a teacher who decides to stay in teaching, and stresses the role of teachers in our society.

Teaching. 10 minutes. Emphasizes the advantages and opportunities of teaching.

INDEX

A

B

C

J

K

L

M